To Rick,
Hope it he l,
your sleep!
Brad

MW00574644

*Bradford S. Gentry*
*Quint Newcomer*
*Shimon C. Anisfeld*
*Michael A. Fotos, III*
*Editor*

# Emerging Markets for Ecosystem Services: A Case Study of the Panama Canal Watershed

*Emerging Markets for Ecosystem Services: A Case Study of the Panama Canal Watershed* has been co-published simultaneously as *Journal of Sustainable Forestry*, Volume 25, Numbers 1/2 and Numbers 3/4 2007.

*Pre-publication REVIEWS, COMMENTARIES, EVALUATIONS . . .*

"The value of this book is that it covers the science, business opportunities as well as social, cultural and political constraints in which markets for ecosystem services are embedded. THIS INTEGRATED VIEW IS ESSENTIAL in order to support decision-makers in the case study region with their effort to design and implement schemes for payments for ecosystem services. . . . A source for all those interested in the issue of markets for ecosystem services either from an academic or practical perspective. The recommendations for developing ecosystem services in Panama are certainly HELPFUL for actors in this region. . . . It is also REMARKABLE that the lecturers together with the students made such an enormous effort to produce a volume, as an output of the course, which is far beyond the output an academic course would normally achieve."

**Dr. Thomas Koellner**
*Leader of Research Group "Ecosystem Services"*
*Institute for Environmental Decisions Natural and Social Science Interface ETH Zurich*

*More pre-publication*
*REVIEWS, COMMENTARIES, EVALUATIONS . . .*

"A STELLAR CONTRIBUTION to the understanding of the potential for the application of market forces by examining in detail a neatly bounded case involving several prominent forms of ecosystem services in an actual, dynamic, large-scale setting. . . . ENORMOUSLY INSTRUCTIVE. . . . Probably the most valuable feature of this book is the consolidation and integration of lessons provided in the two Integrated Assessment segments and especially in Brad Gentry's Conclusion chapter. Here, policy and other actions are developed and advanced that fully consider the realities of circumstances in the Watershed. . . . The emergence of this fine book–with its strong practical spirit–will do much to instruct, but it will do even more to encourage both study and application."

**William B. Ellis, PhD**
*Senior Visiting Fellow*
*Yale School of Forestry*
*and Environmental Studies*
*Former Chairman and CEO*
*Northeast Utilities*

"A MUST for those who are planning to get involved in any aspect of the system of Payment for Environmental Services (PES) at the governmental, local or field level. . . . Should inspire those who are engaged in designing systems for specific services from the global (carbon sequestration, biodiversity) to the more local services (water, aesthetic value of the landscape). . . . Brings critical assessments that can guide in determining realistic goals for any PES system. OF REAL VALUE also to professors and students at the undergraduate and graduate levels in forestry, environmental, and rural development subjects."

**Florencia Montagnini, PhD**
*Professor and Director*
*Program in Tropical Forestry*
*Global Institute of Sustainable Forestry*
*Yale University*
*School of Forestry and Environmental Studies*
*Author of* Environmental Services of Agroforestry Systems

Haworth Food & Agricultural Products Press™
An Imprint of The Haworth Press, Inc.

# Emerging Markets for Ecosystem Services: A Case Study of the Panama Canal Watershed

*Emerging Markets for Ecosystem Services: A Case Study of the Panama Canal Watershed* has been co-published simultaneously as *Journal of Sustainable Forestry*, Volume 25, Numbers 1/2 and Numbers 3/4 2007.

# Monographic Separates from the *Journal of Sustainable Forestry*

For additional information on these and other Haworth Press titles, including descriptions, tables of contents, reviews, and prices, use the QuickSearch catalog at http://www.HaworthPress.com.

*Emerging Markets for Ecosystem Services: A Case Study of the Panama Canal Watershed,* Bradford S. Gentry, Quint Newcomer, Shimon C. Anisfeld, and Michael A. Fotos, III (Vol. 25, No. 1/2 & 3/4, 2007). *A comprehensive examination of various aspects of the emerging markets for watershed services, carbon sequestration, and biodiversity protection in the Panama Canal Watershed.*

*Sustainable Forestry Management and Wood Production in a Global Economy,* Robert L. Deal, Rachel White, and Gary L. Benson (Vol. 24, No. 1 & No. 2/3, 2007). *An examination of sustainable forest management from a global view using diverse examples of important forestry issues.*

*Plantations and Protected Areas in Sustainable Forestry,* William C. Price, Naureen Rana, and V. Alaric Sample (Vol. 21, No. 4, 2005). *This updated collection of papers from the 2001 two-day symposium at Grey Towers National Historic Site sponsored by the Pinchot Institute explores crucial forest management issues in the United States and elsewhere.*

*Sustainable Forestry in Southern Sweden: The SUFOR Research Project,* edited by Kristina Blennow and Mats Niklasson (Vol. 21, No. 2/3, 2005). *"The authors are all very competent and well-known members of their respective disciplines. The text reads well and will be OF INTEREST TO FOREST MANAGERS AND SCIENTISTS ALIKE." (Klaus von Gadow, PhD, Professor of Forest Management, Institute of Forest Assessment and Forest Growth, Georg-August-University Göttingen, Germany)*

*Environmental Services of Agroforestry Systems,* edited by Florencia Montagnini (Vol. 21, No. 1, 2005). "TIMELY AND APPROPRIATE. . . . *All those interested in agroforestry and the ongoing environmental debate will find this book quite useful." (P. K. Ramachandran Nair, DrSc, PhD, Distinguished Professor, Agroforestry & International Forestry Director, Center for Subtropical Agroforestry, University of Florida)*

*Illegal Logging in the Tropics: Strategies for Cutting Crime,* Ramsay M. Ravenel, Ilmi M. E. Granoff, and Carrie Magee (Vol. 19, No. 1/2/3, 2004). *"This book goes far beyond the usual ailing against illegal logging, to explore with utter realism what to do about it." (William Ascher, PhD, Donald C. McKenna Professor of Government and Economics, Claremont McKenna College)*

*Transboundary Protected Areas: The Viability of Regional Conservation Strategies,* edited by Uromi Manage Goodale, Marc J. Stern, Cheryl Margoluis, Ashley G. Lanfer, and Matthew Fladeland (Vol. 17, No. 1/2, 2003). *Top researchers share their expertise on conservation and sustainability in protected regions that extend across national borders.*

*War and Tropical Forests: Conservation in Areas of Armed Conflict,* edited by Steven V. Price (Vol. 16, No. 3/4, 2003). *"AN EXEMPLARY COLLECTION . . . HIGHLY RELEVANT for academic, policy, and activist audiences, and a state-of-the-art account of what environmental governance might mean in areas of armed conflict. . . . The first systematic effort to explore the profound implications for policy and practice of forest conservation operating in the context of war and civil strife. Comparative and interdisciplinary in scope and approach, this book powerfully shows how conservation practice can become militarized, how conservation efforts can become an important part of peacemaking, how local communities must be active in such settings, and how global market and political forces can fuel violently exploitative resource extraction." (Michael Watts, PhD, Director and Chancellor's Professor, Institute of International Studies, University of California, Berkeley)*

*Non-Timber Forest Products: Medicinal Herbs, Fungi, Edible Fruits and Nuts, and Other Natural Products from the Forest,* edited by Marla R. Emery, Rebecca J. McLain (Vol. 13, No. 3/4, 2001). *Focuses on NTFP use, research, and policy concerns in the United States. Discusses historical and contemporary NTFP use, ongoing research on NTFPs, and socio-political considerations for NTFP management.*

*Understanding Community-Based Forest Ecosystem Management*, edited by Gerald J. Gray, Maia J. Enzer, and Jonathan Kusel (Vol. 12, No. 3/4 & Vol. 13, No. 1/2, 2001). *Here is a state-of-the-art reference and information source for scientists, community groups and their leaders, resource managers, and ecosystem management practitioners. Healthy ecosystems and community well-being go hand in hand, and the interdependence between the two is the focal point of community-based ecosystem management. The information you'll find in* **Understanding Community-Based Forest Ecosystem Management** *will be invaluable in your effort to manage and maintain the ecosystems in your community.* **Understanding Community-Based Forest Ecosystem Management** *examines the emergence of community-based ecosystem management (CBEM) in the United States. This comprehensive book blends diverse perspectives, enabling you to draw on the experience and expertise of forest-based practitioners, researchers, and leaders in community-based efforts in the ecosystem management situations that you deal with in your community.*

*Climate Change and Forest Management in the Western Hemisphere*, edited by Mohammed H. I. Dore (Vol. 12, No. 1/2, 2001). *This valuable book examines integrated forest management in the Americas, covering important global issues including global climate change and the conservation of biodiversity. Here you will find case studies from representative forests in North, Central, and South America. The book also explores the role of the Brazilian rainforest in the global carbon cycle and implications for sustainable use of rainforests, as well as the carbon cycle and the valuation of forests for carbon sequestration.*

*Mapping Wildfire Hazards and Risks*, edited by R. Neil Sampson, R. Dwight Atkinson, and Joe W. Lewis (Vol. 11, No. 1/2, 2000). *Based on the October 1996 workshop at Pingree Park in Colorado,* **Mapping Wildfire Hazards and Risks** *is a compilation of the ideas of federal and state agencies, universities, and non-governmental organizations on how to rank and prioritize forested watershed areas that are in need of prescribed fire. This book explains the vital importance of fire for the health and sustainability of a watershed forest and how the past acceptance of fire suspension has consequently led to increased fuel loadings in these landscapes that may lead to more severe future wildfires. Complete with geographic maps, charts, diagrams, and a list of locations where there is the greatest risk of future wildfires,* **Mapping Wildfire Hazards and Risks** *will assist you in deciding how to set priorities for land treatment that might reduce the risk of land damage.*

*Frontiers of Forest Biology: Proceedings of the 1998 Joint Meeting of the North American Forest Biology Workshop and the Western Forest Genetics Association*, edited by Alan K. Mitchell, Pasi Puttonen, Michael Stoehr, and Barbara J. Hawkins (Vol. 10, No. 1/2 & 3/4, 2000). *Based on the 1998 Joint Meeting of the North American Forest Biology Workshop and the Western Forest Genetics Association, Frontiers of Forest Biology addresses changing priorities in forest resource management. You will explore how the emphasis of forest research has shifted from productivity-based goals to goals related to sustainable development of forest resources. This important book contains fascinating research studies, complete with tables and diagrams, on topics such as biodiversity research and the productivity of commercial species that seek criteria and indicators of ecological integrity.*

*"There is clear emphasis on the genetics, genecology, and physiology of trees, particularly temperate trees. . . . These proceedings are also testimony to what does or should distinguish forest biology from other sciences: a focus on intra- and inter-specific interactions between forest organisms and their environment, over scales of both time and place." (Robert D. Guy, PhD, Associate Professor, Department of Forest Sciences, University of British Columbia, Vancouver, Canada)*

*Contested Issues of Ecosystem Management*, edited by Piermaria Corona and Boris Zeide (Vol. 9, No. 1/2, 1999). *Provides park rangers, forestry students and personnel with a unique discussion of the premise, goals, and concepts of ecosystem management. You will discover the need for you to maintain and enhance the quality of the environment on a global scale while meeting the current and future needs of an increasing human population. This unique book includes ways to tackle the fundamental causes of environmental degradation so you will be able to respond to the problem and not merely the symptoms.*

*Protecting Watershed Areas: Case of the Panama Canal*, edited by Mark S. Ashton, Jennifer L. O'Hara, and Robert D. Hauff (Vol. 8, No. 3/4, 1999). *"This book makes a valuable contribution to the literature on conservation and development in the neo-tropics. . . . These writings provide a fresh yet realistic account of the Panama landscape." (Raymond P. Guries, Professor of Forestry, Department of Forestry, University of Wisconsin at Madison, Wisconsin)*

ALL HAWORTH FOOD & AGRICULTURAL
PRODUCTS PRESS BOOKS AND JOURNALS
ARE PRINTED ON CERTIFIED ACID-FREE PAPER

# Emerging Markets for Ecosystem Services: A Case Study of the Panama Canal Watershed

Bradford S. Gentry
Quint Newcomer
Shimon C. Anisfeld
Michael A. Fotos, III
Editors

*Emerging Markets for Ecosystem Services: A Case Study of the Panama Canal Watershed* has been co-published simultaneously as *Journal of Sustainable Forestry*, Volume 25, Numbers 1/2 and Numbers 3/4 2007.

Haworth Food & Agricultural Products Press™
An Imprint of The Haworth Press, Inc.

www.HaworthPress.com

Published by

Haworth Food & Agricultural Products Press™, 10 Alice Street, Binghamton, NY 13904-1580
USA

Haworth Food & Agricultural Products Press™ is an imprint of The Haworth Press, Inc., 10 Alice Street, Binghamton, NY 13904-1580 USA.

*Emerging Markets for Ecosystem Services: A Case Study of the Panama Canal Watershed* has been co-published simultaneously as *Journal of Sustainable Forestry*, Volume 25, Numbers 1/2 and Numbers 3/4 2007.

© 2007 by The Haworth Press, Inc. All rights reserved. No part of this work may be reproduced or utilized in any form or by any means, electronic or mechanical, including photocopying, microfilm and recording, or by any information storage and retrieval system, without permission in writing from the publisher. Printed in the United States of America.

The development, preparation, and publication of this work has been undertaken with great care. However, the publisher, employees, editors, and agents of The Haworth Press and all imprints of The Haworth Press, Inc., including The Haworth Medical Press® and Pharmaceutical Products Press®, are not responsible for any errors contained herein or for consequences that may ensue from use of materials or information contained in this work. With regard to case studies, identities and circumstances of individuals discussed herein have been changed to protect confidentiality. Any resemblance to actual persons, living or dead, is entirely coincidental.

The Haworth Press is committed to the dissemination of ideas and information according to the highest standards of intellectual freedom and the free exchange of ideas. Statements made and opinions expressed in this publication do not necessarily reflect the views of the Publisher, Directors, management, or staff of The Haworth Press, Inc., or an endorsement by them.

Cover photographs by Quint Newcomer

**Library of Congress Cataloging-in-Publication Data**

Emerging markets for ecosystem services : a case study of the Panama Canal Watershed / Bradford S. Gentry . . . [et al.].
    p. cm.
    "Has been co-published simultaneously as Journal of Sustainable Forestry, Volume 25, Numbers 1/2 and Numbers 3/4 2007."
    Includes bibliographical references.
    ISBN 978-1-56022-173-9 (hard cover : alk. paper)
    1. Carbon sequestration–Economic aspects–Panama–Panama Canal Watershed. 2. Watershed management–Economic aspects–Panama–Panama Canal Watershed. 3. Biodiversity conservation–Economic aspects–Panama–Panama Canal Watershed. I. Gentry, Bradford S.
SD387.C37E44 2007
338.4'76399–dc22
                                 2007034610

# The HAWORTH PRESS Inc.
## Abstracting, Indexing & Outward Linking
### PRINT and ELECTRONIC BOOKS & JOURNALS

This section provides you with a list of major indexing & abstracting services and other tools for bibliographic access. That is to say, each service began covering this periodical during the year noted in the right column. Most Websites which are listed below have indicated that they will either post, disseminate, compile, archive, cite or alert their own Website users with research-based content from this work. (This list is as current as the copyright date of this publication.)

Abstracting, Website/Indexing Coverage .......... Year When Coverage Began

- *International Bibliography of Book Reviews on the Humanities and Social Sciences (IBR) (Thomson)*
  *<http://www.saur.de>*.................................. 2006
- *(CAB ABSTRACTS, CABI) <http://www.cabi.org>* .............. *
- ***Academic Search Premier (EBSCO)****
  *<http://search.ebscohost.com>*.......................... 2006
- ***MasterFILE Premier (EBSCO)****
  *<http://search.ebscohost.com>*.......................... 2006
- *Abstract Bulletin of Paper Science & Technology (Elsevier)*
  *<http://www.elsevier.com>*.............................. 1993
- *Abstracts in Anthropology*
  *<http://www.baywood.com/Journals/*
  *PreviewJournals.asp?Id=0001-3455>*..................... 2006
- *Academic Source Premier (EBSCO)*
  *<http://search.ebscohost.com>*.......................... 2007
- *AGBIOS <http://www.agbios.com>* ........................ 2007
- *AgBiotech News & Information (CAB ABSTRACTS, CABI)*
  *<http://www.cabi.org>* ................................. 2006
- *Agricultural Engineering Abstracts (CAB ABSTRACTS, CABI)*
  *<http://www.cabi.org>* ................................. 2006
- *AGRIS/CARIS <http://FAO-Agris-Caris@fao.org>* ........... 1993

(continued)

(continued)

(continued)

(continued)

**\*Exact start date to come.**

## Bibliographic Access

- *Magazines for Libraries (Katz)*

- *MediaFinder <http://www.mediafinder.com/>*

- *Ulrich's Periodicals Directory: The Global Source for Periodicals Information Since 1932 <http://www.bowkerlink.com>*

*Special Bibliographic Notes related to special journal issues (separates) and indexing/abstracting:*

- indexing/abstracting services in this list will also cover material in any "separate" that is co-published simultaneously with Haworth's special thematic journal issue or DocuSerial. Indexing/abstracting usually covers material at the article/chapter level.
- monographic co-editions are intended for either non-subscribers or libraries which intend to purchase a second copy for their circulating collections.
- monographic co-editions are reported to all jobbers/wholesalers/approval plans. The source journal is listed as the "series" to assist the prevention of duplicate purchasing in the same manner utilized for books-in-series.
- to facilitate user/access services all indexing/abstracting services are encouraged to utilize the co-indexing entry note indicated at the bottom of the first page of each article/chapter/contribution.
- this is intended to assist a library user of any reference tool (whether print, electronic, online, or CD-ROM) to locate the monographic version if the library has purchased this version but not a subscription to the source journal.
- individual articles/chapters in any Haworth publication are also available through the Haworth Document Delivery Service (HDDS).

As part of
Haworth's
continuing
commitment
to better serve
our library
patrons,
we are
proud to
be working
with the
following
electronic
services:

## AGGREGATOR SERVICES

EBSCOhost

Ingenta

J-Gate

Minerva

OCLC FirstSearch **FirstSearch**

Oxmill

SwetsWise SwetsWise

## LINK RESOLVER SERVICES

1Cate (Openly Informatics)

ChemPort
(American Chemical Society) **ChemPort·**

CrossRef

Gold Rush (Coalliance)

LinkOut (PubMed)

LINKplus (Atypon)

LinkSolver (Ovid)

LinkSource with A-to-Z (EBSCO)

Resource Linker (Ulrich)

SerialsSolutions (ProQuest) **SerialsSolutions**

SFX (Ex Libris) ⊘S·F·X

Sirsi Resolver (SirsiDynix) ⑤SirsiDynix

Tour (TDnet)

Vlink (Extensity, formerly Geac) ((extensity))

WebBridge (Innovative Interfaces)

# Emerging Markets for Ecosystem Services: A Case Study of the Panama Canal Watershed

## CONTENTS

SECTION 2: WATER

WATER SUPPLY

WATER DEMAND

SECTION 3: BIODIVERSITY

SECTION 4: INTEGRATED ASSESSMENTS

CONCLUSION

# ABOUT THE EDITORS

**Bradford S. Gentry, JD,** is Co-Director of the Center for Business and the Environment at Yale, as well as a Senior Lecturer and Research Scholar at the Yale School of Forestry and Environmental Studies. Trained as a biologist and a lawyer, his work focuses on strengthening the links between private investment and improved environmental performance. He is also of counsel to the international law firm of Baker & McKenzie, an advisor to GE's office of corporate environmental programs, and a member of the advisory boards of Climate Change Capital in London and the Trust for Public Land in Connecticut, as well as the governing board for the Institute for Ecosystem Studies in New York. His teaching includes multi-disciplinary courses on the emerging markets for ecosystem services, as well as legal, financial and managerial strategies for land conservation.

**Quint Newcomer, PhD,** is currently the Director of the University of Georgia's campus in Costa Rica. He earned a Master of International Management from Thunderbird–The Garvin School of International Management, a Master of Environmental Management from Yale University, and PhD from Yale University's School of Forestry & Environmental Studies. His dissertation studies evaluated the Payment for Environmental Services program in Costa Rica as a mechanism to implement the Path of the Tapir Biological Corridor. As a PhD student, Quint worked for two semesters as a teaching fellow with Professor Brad Gentry on the course, Emerging Markets for Ecosystem Services. Prior to attending Yale, Quint worked as Environmental Certification Manager for a forestry and wood products company in Costa Rica, and as Director of the Monteverde Institute.

**Shimon C. Anisfeld, PhD,** is a Senior Lecturer and Research Scientist at Yale School of Forestry & Environmental Studies, where he teaches courses in water resource management, environmental chemistry, and coastal ecology. His interests include river water quality and the improvement of urban water supplies, as well as the use of payments for ecosystem services to help protect drinking water sources and improve the health of aquatic ecosystems. He received an AB in chemistry from Princeton University in 1987 and a PhD in organic chemistry from MIT in 1993.

**Michael A. Fotos, III, PhD,** is a 1978 graduate of Yale College with an MPA from Harvard University and a PhD in Political Science from Indiana University, Bloomington, IN. His research and teaching interests include the politics of environmental policy, political institutions and policy theory, and research methods in the social sciences. At Trinity College, Dr. Fotos recently co-taught an inter-disciplinary seminar for science majors on the environmental and social impacts of a proposed floating LNG transfer facility in Long Island Sound. Dr. Fotos has held senior state government posts overseeing natural resource and economic development agencies. He has also managed land protection programs for a major NGO. He is presently working on a private business model for sustainable land use in suburban and ex-urban communities. Dr. Fotos volunteers as a guest lecturer at the Yale School of Forestry & Environmental Studies and as a director of the Connecticut Farmland Trust.

# Foreword

I sit to write this foreword just two days after the National Referendum for the Canal expansion occurred in Panama. A popular vote was needed by law to decide whether Panama as a country should embark itself in the Canal expansion mega-project that will take 15 years to accomplish.

I have spent a good deal of the past three months reading articles, listening to debates and presentations, and discussing the Canal expansion topic. But it was not until a few days before the National Referendum campaign period that I heard a sensible and logical lecture by the Dean of INCAE, the #1 Business School in Central America, that put in perspective the whole of the discussions I had heard until then.

The gist of his message was, the Canal expansion would not represent the end-all and be-all to better quality of life for Panamanians. Economically speaking, it does represent an increase in revenues for the government, and environmentally and socially the project represents manageable risks. But is that enough? Will this bring development and progress to Panama?

The real benefit at the end of the day will depend on the opportunities generated around the expansion of the Canal operations. Of course, the rest of the lecture was how we Panamanians need to prepare ourselves for this challenge, target our education system to produce professionals in those areas where the demand will be highest, facilitate investment procedures, and I suppose, believe in ourselves and take a chance.

Having just lived through this experience, I find it most propitious that this publication goes to print. It is the opportunities lying in emerging markets, such as the environmental services one, that will allow Panama to overcome its battle with poverty and move from a developing economy to a developed one. Being realistic, there is a long way to go, but I believe this improved Panama will be a reality.

[Haworth co-indexing entry note]: "Foreword." Herrera, Mirei. Co-published simultaneously in *Journal of Sustainable Forestry* (Haworth Food & Agricultural Products Press, an imprint of The Haworth Press, Inc.) Vol. 25, No. 1/2, 2007, pp. xxv-xxvii; and: *Emerging Markets for Ecosystem Services: A Case Study of the Panama Canal Watershed* (ed: Bradford S. Gentry, Quint Newcomer, Shimon C. Anisfeld, and Michael A. Fotos, III) Haworth Food & Agricultural Products Press, an imprint of The Haworth Press, Inc., 2007, pp. xix-xxi. Single or multiple copies of this article are available for a fee from The Haworth Document Delivery Service [1-800-HAWORTH, 9:00 a.m. - 5:00 p.m. (EST). E-mail address: docdelivery@haworthpress.com].

Available online at http://jsf.haworthpress.com
© 2007 by The Haworth Press, Inc. All rights reserved. *xix*

I want to acknowledge the vision of the Emerging Markets course professors, in particular Brad Gentry and Mark Ashton, for considering Panama once again in their applied classes. I also congratulate the participating students; I find the articles produced by the class to be outstanding, practical and very good, especially considering certain limitations to information access, language barriers and physical distance.

In a moment at this nation's history, where the Canal has taken such a prominent position, it is appropriate for this publication to present various positions on making the environment a responsible business. Panama needs more advocates to make conservation goals compatible with socio-economic prosperity, and increase the awareness and the will for such compatibility. This is a common characteristic I found in the Canal expansion proposal and in the articles of this publication. More examples like these are needed to expand to new horizons.

Another particular I would like to praise was the integrated approach utilized by the authors, allowing the final articles to have a view of the forest and not only the individual trees. I was delighted to find included in the articles, specific policy recommendations to enhance market opportunities, as well as technical and socio-economic recommendations.

Policy recommendations always have very local nuances; perhaps it would not be too bold to suggest a forum in the near future to debate the results from these analyses with a local Panamanian audience, in order to disseminate new thinking, and also encourage reflection on these topics among the Panamanian community.

Once again, I congratulate the organizers and the findings from the Emerging Markets course from Spring 2005; I hope this experience has been as rewarding for you as it was for us.

*Mirei Herrera*
*Yale F&ES MES*
*1994*
*Deputy Director*
*Natural Renewable Resources Institute (INRENARE)*
*1994-1997*
*General Administrator*
*National Environmental Authority (ANAM)*
*1998-1999*
*Panama Program Director*
*The Nature Conservancy (TNC)*
*2000-2003*
*Executive Director*
*Central America Leadership Initiative (CALI) Foundation*
*2006*

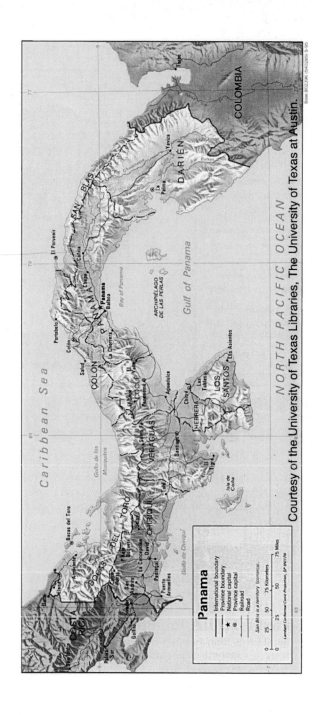

Courtesy of the University of Texas Libraries, The University of Texas at Austin.

*xxi*

# INTRODUCTION

# Emerging Markets for Ecosystem Services: Setting the Context

Shimon Anisfeld

**SUMMARY.** The papers in this volume examine various aspects of the emerging markets for ecosystem services (watershed services, carbon sequestration, and biodiversity protection) in the Panama Canal Watershed. This introductory chapter provides context by: outlining the questions addressed; describing the structure and underlying framework of this volume and the nature of the course that produced it; and briefly

Shimon Anisfeld is Lecturer and Research Scientist in Water Resources and Environmental Chemistry at Yale School of Forestry and Environmental Studies, New Haven, CT 06511 USA (E-mail: Shimon.Anisfeld@yale.edu).

The faculty and students who participated in the Spring 2005 Emerging Markets for Ecosystem Services course are very grateful to all those in Panama who were so generous with their time and open with their thoughts. Mark Wishnie and José Manuel Pérez of PRORENA (a joint project of Yale and STRI) hosted our trip, and, in addition to arranging our itinerary and providing us with access to all their contacts, shared generously their own knowledge and expertise. The guest editors and authors of these papers greatly appreciate the cooperation of ACP and ANAM, and the financial support of The Agora Foundation and the Frank Levinson Donor-Advised Fund at the Peninsula Community Foundation. The Dean's Office of the Yale School of Forestry & Environmental Studies also provided funding for the Panama trip.

[Haworth co-indexing entry note]: "Emerging Markets for Ecosystem Services: Setting the Context." Anisfeld, Shimon. Co-published simultaneously in *Journal of Sustainable Forestry* (Haworth Food & Agricultural Products Press, an imprint of The Haworth Press, Inc.) Vol. 25, No. 1/2, 2007, pp. 1-14; and: *Emerging Markets for Ecosystem Services: A Case Study of the Panama Canal Watershed* (ed: Bradford S. Gentry, Quint Newcomer, Shimon C. Anisfeld, and Michael A. Fotos, III) Haworth Food & Agricultural Products Press, an imprint of The Haworth Press, Inc., 2007, pp. 1-14. Single or multiple copies of this article are available for a fee from The Haworth Document Delivery Service [1-800-HAWORTH, 9:00 a.m. - 5:00 p.m. (EST). E-mail address: docdelivery@haworthpress.com].

Available online at http://jsf.haworthpress.com
© 2007 by The Haworth Press, Inc. All rights reserved.
doi:10.1300/J091v25n01_01

*1*

discussing how the limitations of science affect attempts to market eco-system services. doi:10.1300/J091v25n01_01 *[Article copies available for a fee from The Haworth Document Delivery Service: 1-800-HAWORTH. E-mail address: <docdelivery@haworthpress.com> Website: <http://www.HaworthPress.com> © 2007 by The Haworth Press, Inc. All rights reserved.]*

**KEYWORDS.** Panama Canal Watershed, carbon sequestration, water-shed services, biodiversity services, interdisciplinary instruction, eco-system services markets

## MARKETS FOR ECOSYSTEM SERVICES

There has been growing interest over the last several years in the use of market mechanisms for protecting forest ecosystems (Landell-Mills and Porras, 2002; Pagiola et al., 2002). On one level, the notion is at-tractively simple: if we want to preserve and restore natural landscapes and the associated services that they provide to humans, then we must find ways to pay landowners for the values of those services by provid-ing funding for maintaining those landscapes. For example, should downstream water users be willing to pay upstream land owners for the higher quality of water draining from forested watersheds? Should gov-ernments struggling to reduce their carbon emissions be willing to pay for the sequestration of carbon in growing forests? Should pharmaceuti-cal companies–for whom the genetic and chemical diversity of the bio-sphere provides a potential source of new drugs–be willing to pay for the preservation of that diversity in forests?

In practice, however, many complex questions arise from attempts to implement markets for ecosystem services:

- How do we quantify the value of the services supplied?
- How much of this value can be captured by payments from exist-ing sources of demand for these services?
- Will these payments be enough to compete with other options for the landowner, such as land conversion to agriculture?
- How do we convince the recipients of the services to pay for ser-vices that they have, in many cases, been receiving for free for many years?
- How do we deal with equity issues associated with the fact that some users of these services will be paying for their provision, while others will be free riders benefiting from the same services without payment?

- How can we best structure payments?
- At what scale do these payments work best?
- How do we ensure that the funds are used to protect the desired landscapes and provide the desired services?
- How should land be managed to maximize the ecosystem services provided?
- To what extent can land be managed to provide multiple types of ecosystem services and other products (e.g., timber) at the same time?
- How do we ensure that the benefits of these arrangements are distributed equitably and are used to improve human welfare as well as ecosystem health?

The articles in this volume are designed to contribute to the growing body of literature addressing these questions.

## *CONTEXT AND FRAMEWORK OF OUR ANALYSIS*

This volume emerged from a course held at Yale School of Forestry & Environmental Studies (Yale F&ES) during the Spring term 2005, entitled "Emerging Markets for Ecosystem Services: Developing an Integrated Framework for Analysis." The course was initiated and led by Bradford Gentry, who had been doing work in this field for several years and had taught a related course two years earlier. At an early stage in planning the class, Brad realized that this would be a challenging course to teach, in part because covering this subject requires drawing on three quite different areas: science, business and policy. To complement Brad's legal and policy background, he invited this writer–a natural scientist with expertise in water–to co-teach the course; and invited Mike Fotos–a political theorist at Trinity College–and Mark Ashton–a forest ecologist at Yale F&ES–to participate significantly by lecturing and responding to other presentations. Beyond that, the course was a truly collaborative effort among experts from different disciplines, with significant contributions from David Cromwell (Yale School of Management), William Ellis (F&ES, business), Thomas Koellner (ETZ, science and business), Florencia Montagnini (F&ES, forest science), and Oswald Schmitz (F&ES, biodiversity science). We also benefited greatly from having Quint Newcomer as our teaching assistant. Quint worked with Brad as the teaching assistant for the initial seminar course on emerging markets for ecosystem services, and had spent the previous several years studying participation in the Payment for Environmental

Services program in Costa Rica for his doctoral research (F&ES, social ecology). As such, he was able to provide both a good understanding of social theory and a detailed knowledge of the interactions of people with forests in Latin America.

In selecting the 12 students who would participate in the course (from a group of approximately 25 who applied), we likewise looked for a mix of backgrounds. The selection process yielded an impressive group that brought to the table a variety of different perspectives from previous coursework, research, and work experience.

The course was designed to address the many questions raised above regarding the feasibility of developing markets for ecosystem services. We wanted to think about both the current status of these markets, and what could be done to improve them in the future. Our framework for analysis involved the following steps (not necessarily sequentially):

- Understand the *science* involved in supplying the service. For example, to what extent do reforestation activities lead to improvements in downstream water quality, and how should land be managed to optimize these improvements? We believe that markets are more likely to succeed if they are rooted in the provision of real services that can be measured and quantified by scientists.
- Understand the nature of the possible *business* opportunities. For example, is there demand for improvement in downstream water quality–demand that can be translated into a willingness to pay– and how do the magnitude of those potential payments relate to the costs (including opportunity costs) of reforestation? We believe that markets for ecosystem services will expand only if they make financial sense to the players involved.
- Understand the *social*, *cultural*, and *political* constraints on markets and use them to recommend *policy* tools to improve the prospects for markets for ecosystem services. For example, do upstream land managers have the technical, financial, and organizational capacity, knowledge, and will that are required to bring their "product" to market? Do they have the ability and the legal tools and institutions to act collectively? Can government agencies or NGOs help nurture these markets by helping reduce transaction costs, or by providing information (e.g., on costs and benefits) to land managers, or by participating in joint ventures, or by providing tax breaks for reforestation, or through other tools? We believe that real markets for ecosystem services are very much tied to the specific socio-cultural context of a given country, and that appropriate use of policy

tools can eliminate or minimize many of the financial, socio-cultural, and political constraints on ecosystem services markets.

In order to bring our theoretical discussions of these questions down to earth, we decided to ground our answers in a particular case study, namely, the development of payments for ecosystem services in the Panama Canal Watershed (PCW). The course was thus built around a weeklong trip to Panama (March 6-13, during Yale's spring break), during which the students explored the feasibility of ecosystem services payments in the PCW through site visits, interviews, and discussions with a wide variety of stakeholders and observers (see Table 1). The

TABLE 1. Informants in Panama and Their Affiliated Institutions

- Dimas Arcia, AED
- Diego Camaño, CEASPA
- Todd Capson, STRI
- Luis Castañedo, AED
- Gina Castro, AED
- Norma Cedeño, PRORENA
- Arturo Cerezo, ACP
- Phyllis Coley, University of Utah
- Jose Deago, PRORENA
- Ricardo Delvalle, EcoForest (Panama), S.A.
- John Dixon Francois, Cattle rancher
- Andreas Eke, Futuro Forestal S.A.
- Charlotte Elton, CEASPA
- Mirei Endara de Heras, Fundación Smithsonian
- Laurencio Guardia, formerly with IDAAN
- George Hanily, TNC
- Beatrice Harrick, ANARAP

- Stanley Heckadon-Moreno, STRI
- Beth King, STRI
- Thomas Kursar, University of Utah
- Rosilena Lindo, ANAM
- Rene Lopez, ANAM
- José Manuel Pérez, PRORENA
- Alibel Pizzaro, CEASPA
- Robert Stallard, STRI
- Oscar Vallarino, CICH
- Jean Marc Verjans, EcoForest (Panama), S.A.
- Bridget Warren, ACP
- Klaus Winter, STRI
- Mark Wishnie, PRORENA
- Jessica Young, AED
- Smallholders in Chagres: don Fabriciano, don Teodoro, don Narvay, don Luis, don Beto, don Carlos Ivan

*Institutions noted above:*

ACP: Panama Canal Authority
AED: Academy for Educational Development
ANAM: National Environment Authority (institution of the Panamanian Government)
ANARAP: National Association of Reforesters
CEASPA: Panamanian Center for Studies and Social Action
CICH: Inter-institutional Commission for the Panama Canal Watershed
IDAAN: The National Aqueducts and Sewers Institute
PRORENA: Native Species Reforestation Project
STRI: Smithsonian Tropical Research Institute
TNC: The Nature Conservancy

time in Panama was most enlightening, and the knowledge gained during our visit there forms the core of this volume.

## STRUCTURE OF THIS VOLUME

With the exception of the introduction and conclusion, all the articles in this volume were originally written by students as part of the course requirements. The articles cover three different types of ecosystem services: watershed services, carbon sequestration, and biodiversity protection. They include analyses of both the supply of and the demand for these services, and they include both assessments of current market conditions and recommendations for improving conditions in the future. The original framework for the papers thus had a clean division into 12 different subjects (see Figure 1). As we explored "biodiversity protection" during the first part of the course, however, it became clear to us that this term actually refers to a group of different services, which should be analyzed and marketed separately. The biodiversity group thus chose to divide their four papers up by type of service (bio-prospecting, eco-tourism, certified products, and land acquisition), and to cover both demand/supply and current/future within each of those papers, rather than as separate papers (see table of contents).

The charge to the students was to write an analysis of their subject that would be grounded in the perspective of the land manager in Panama. Thus, for example, the current-market supply-side papers were to focus on whether selling ecosystem services (e.g., carbon sequestration)

FIGURE 1. Original structure for the 12 individual student papers. The biodiversity papers were ultimately broken up by type of biodiversity service, rather than by supply/demand; current/future.

### Assessment of Existing Markets

| Supply | Demand |
|---|---|
| 1. Water<br>2. Carbon<br>3. Biodiversity | 4. Water<br>5. Carbon<br>6. Biodiversity |
| 7. Water<br>8. Carbon<br>9. Biodiversity | 10. Water<br>11. Carbon<br>12. Biodiversity |

### Recommendations for Improved Markets

made sense as a way to manage land in Panama–and, if so, what land management practices would optimize the equation. Similarly, the current-market demand-side papers assessed the degree of existing demand for these services, while the future-market supply-side and demand-side papers covered recommendations for how supply and demand for different ecosystem services could be increased in the future through the use of a variety of policy tools. Full-scale net present value analyses for different options were deemed to be outside the scope of our work, but some sense of costs and benefits was included in the papers.

The land management scenarios that are considered in the articles are those that we observed on the ground in Panama. They include different spatial scales and contrasting types of activities. One typical scenario in Panama is the landowner who is undertaking large-scale reforestation of degraded agricultural lands, with either an exotic timber species (typically teak, *Tectona grandis*) or a mix of native species. Several companies and individuals are currently engaged in this plantation-type activity. To what extent do markets for ecosystem services–as opposed to timber–affect their choices of whether to reforest, whether to use native species, and how to manage the plantation?

A second typical scenario is the smallholder (usually with no land title) who is deciding whether to implement small-scale agroforestry practices, such as tree planting, use of improved pasture grasses, etc. These practices are, of course, often directly beneficial to the smallholders themselves (e.g., allowing greater cattle production per unit area). But to what extent do these practices result in flows of ecosystem services to those *outside* the land being managed (e.g., improved water quality downstream)–and to what extent will those external beneficiaries be willing to provide support to the smallholders?

## SUMMARY OF PAPERS

### Carbon

The first section of this volume deals with the market for carbon sequestration from Panamanian forests. Because of the climate change implications of carbon emissions, this is a global market, but one in which Panama may have a significant role to play, due to the high rates of tree growth (and carbon uptake), and the large amount of land potentially available for reforestation.

This section opens with Jesse Grossman's summary of our current understanding of carbon sequestration in four different land types in Panama: natural forests, exotic plantations (primarily teak), native plantations, and agroforestry systems. He concludes that the plantations and agroforestry systems have great potential to sequester carbon in biomass and soils, although there is still much uncertainty about growth rates and optimal management, especially for native species. Natural forests represent a large carbon pool, but exhibit a much lower rate of carbon sequestration.

Michael Lichtenfeld writes about increasing the ability of land managers to provide carbon sequestration services by focusing on three barriers to selling carbon credits: high transaction and management costs; imperfect information; and a lack of institutional support. He suggests a variety of policy tools that could be used to reduce these barriers.

Sandra Lauterbach analyzes the current status of the rapidly evolving demand for carbon sequestration. She finds that the regulated markets for carbon offsets (driven by the Kyoto Protocol) are large and relatively well-organized, but operate under restrictive rules for defining carbon sequestration. These rules exclude the preservation of natural forests from eligibility, and impose significant technical and monitoring constraints on other types of activities, such as plantations and agroforestry practices. Voluntary markets are much less constrained but are also more fragmented and harder to identify. Both regulated and voluntary markets are much easier to enter for larger projects (e.g., plantations) than for smallholders.

Alexander Hovani and Mike Fotos suggest policy alternatives for increasing demand for land-use-based carbon sequestration. These include improving both the regulated and voluntary markets, increasing the focus on land-use activities, and improving the institutional climate by lowering transaction costs and contractual risks.

*Water*

The second section deals with markets for watershed services, such as water quantity and quality improvement. The scale of these markets is the Panama Canal Watershed, within which several water users would potentially benefit from reforestation and forest preservation activities. The Panama Canal Authority (Autoridad del Canal de Panamá, ACP) is perhaps the most obvious and important water user, since every ship passing through the canal requires spillage of freshwater to the ocean.

Krista Anderson opens this section with a summary of the links between land use and water quantity and quality. She points out that refor-estation is likely to improve water quality, but that its effects on water quantity are more mixed and more uncertain. In contrast to popular perception in Panama, a substantial increase in forest cover is likely to *reduce* annual runoff from the watershed, although there is the possibility that it might *increase* dry season flows, which could be beneficial to water users. More research is necessary to establish whether this would in fact be the case.

Michelle Lichtenfels proposes steps that could be taken to encourage land managers to protect water quantity and quality. She focuses on providing funding to support such efforts, e.g., through an environmental fee paid by ships passing through the Canal, or through a Drinking Water Fund paid for by urban water users. She also points out the importance of strengthening the institutions which are responsible for watershed planning and protection, especially the Comisión Interinstitucional de la Cuenca Hidrográfica (CICH).

On the demand side, Mike Fotos, Fuphan Chou, and Quint Newcomer analyze the various water users within the Panama Canal Watershed, and their willingness to pay for water quantity and quality protection. They identify five major users: ACP; private shippers who use the Canal; hydroelectric producers; CICH, and Instituto de Acueductos y Alcantarillados Nacionales (IDAAN, the urban water utility). They believe that the value of water to these users is substantially higher than current payments, but that scientific uncertainty and institutional factors pose barriers to capturing the full value of watershed protection.

In the final piece in this section, Mike Fotos, Quint Newcomer, and Radha Kuppalli suggest several steps that should be taken in order to increase the demand for watershed protection. The highest priority steps are those that will improve public awareness of the water issue and those that are most likely to obtain political traction, through linkages to key issues for the government of Panama, such as job creation.

## *Biodiversity*

The third section of this volume covers markets for biodiversity, markets which cover a range of scales from local to international, and which take advantage of Panama's location in the Central American biodiversity "hot spot." As discussed above, the structure of this section differs from the preceding ones, in that each article covers a specific type of biodiversity service, and analyzes both supply and demand, and both current and future markets.

This section opens with Patrick Burtis' analysis of bioprospecting–the search for economically valuable genetic material in plants and other organisms, e.g., for the development of new pharmaceuticals. The potential funding from pharmaceutical companies and research agencies to support the hunt for genetic material is a form of payment for the ecosystem service of biodiversity. Pat discusses the strengths and limitations of current approaches to bioprospecting, including an innovative approach currently underway in Panama, and makes suggestions to guide future efforts.

Catherine Schloegel's paper analyzes sustainable tourism (socially and environmentally responsible tourism) as a source of funding to support biodiversity. She addresses questions such as whether nature tourism actually leads to effective conservation of biodiversity, and proposes several steps that could be taken to support the sustainable tourism industry in Panama and link it more closely to biodiversity conservation.

Economic surveys routinely reveal people's willingness to pay for the preservation of natural landscapes that they will never experience, reflecting the "existence value" of biodiverse landscapes in their natural state. Steven Wallander examines the current state of the market for the existence value of Panamanian forests, as reflected in conservation financing provided by non-Panamanian sources (e.g., debt-for-nature swaps). He projects high demand for these ecosystem services, and discusses some of the challenges facing these transactions.

Yuko Miyata examines the market for eco-labeled products, that is, products that are in some way certified as being produced in a manner that protects biodiversity. This market is well-developed internationally for certain products (e.g., certified timber, shade-grown coffee), but is currently virtually non-existent for Panamanian forest products. Yuko suggests ways to overcome the institutional, socio-cultural, and economic barriers to certification.

### Integrated Assessment

In this section, we tie together the results from the individual studies into two integrated papers. The first paper by Steven Wallander and co-authors addresses the current status of markets for ecosystem services in Panama, including an analysis of the possibility for managing land to provide multiple ecosystem services, as well as traditional products (e.g., timber, carbon sequestration, and sustainable tourism from a plantation of native species). Both native plantations and small-scale agroforestry have the potential to be viable as suppliers of ecosystem services.

The second integrated paper by Michelle Lichtenfels and coauthors suggests ways to improve markets for ecosystem services in Panama. The policy, legal, and fiscal tools that emerge from this analysis have the following general goals: (1) increasing conservation of existing forest ecosystems; (2) promoting increased reforestation; (3) strengthening relevant institutional capacity; (4) lowering transaction costs; and (5) building the Panama brand for environmental services.

Finally, the volume closes with Bradford Gentry's conclusion, in which he summarizes the results of our studies and shares his thoughts on the state of ecosystem services markets.

## ON THE LIMITATIONS OF SCIENCE

In reading the articles in this collection, one is struck repeatedly by the interplay between the cautionary attitude of the scientist and the hardnosed demands of the business community. The following thoughts on scientific uncertainty may be helpful in reading this material.

In theory, the steps needed to put a value on the ecosystem services provided by a particular parcel of land are quite simple: identify the type of service provided (e.g., carbon sequestration in a growing forest); quantify the magnitude of the service provided (e.g., kg C sequestered per ha per year); and quantify the value of each unit provided (e.g., the dollar value of a kg of sequestered C). However, both of the quantification steps are, in many situations, fraught with difficulty. Of particular concern is our inability in many cases to accurately estimate how much of a particular service is being provided—or, in some cases, even whether it is being provided at all.

Thus, for example, one would be hard-pressed to find a "bankable" estimate of how much downstream nutrient loads will decrease as a result of reforestation. Such estimates as *do* exist are based on models, are not site-specific, and have large ranges depending on the researcher or model chosen. Even more disheartening is trying to get an estimate of how reforestation will affect dry-season flows: even the direction of change is uncertain, much less the magnitude. How can we expect buyers to buy a service that is unquantified and may not even exist? This is certainly different from our picture of how markets generally work:

when one buys a ton of pork bellies, one expects to get a ton, not some unknown quantity that may be a ton or may be a half a ton or may be none at all.

Thus, at the most basic level, the uncertainty in the science of ecosystem services threatens to undermine the entire foundation of ecosystem markets. There are several approaches for dealing with this uncertainty.

## Managing Risk

Buying ecosystem services is not like buying a ton of pork bellies: there is a much greater risk that the services you have bought will not in fact be provided. Some of that risk has to do with other factors (e.g., political risks), but some of it has to do with the limitations of predictive ecosystem science: the ton of C that we predicted would be sequestered by tree growth may well turn out to be half a ton, if the trees grow more poorly than expected. Thus, according to this approach, the market price must simply reflect the risk that is associated with the scientific uncertainty. However, does this approach work if the service provided will never be–or can never be–accurately quantified? Thus, for example, it is highly unlikely that the changes in downstream water quality associated with reforestation of a particular parcel will ever be quantified. How then can that service be marketed?

## Improving Science

A second approach to scientific uncertainty is to try to minimize it, both through carrying out more basic research (e.g., how do dry season flows change as a result of reforestation?) and through greater investment in monitoring to improve estimates. Several of the articles in this volume contain calls for more research into outstanding questions, and I believe those calls are fully warranted. However, I also believe–as argued above–that certain services will never be adequately assessed or quantified.

## Attending to Perception

Some argue that the actual existence of the services being marketed is irrelevant. The only thing that matters is the perception of the buyers. If buyers believe that the services exist, they will be willing to buy them. In fact, they may even be willing to buy them (e.g., as part of an image campaign) if they don't believe they exist, as long as others (e.g., the public at large) do believe they exist. While this certainly has some validity, I would question the long-term viability of markets that are based on incorrect perceptions.

## Appealing to the Precautionary Principle

In certain situations, it may be wisest to simply acknowledge the limitations of science, and accept that we may never be able to prove that a certain ecosystem service is being provided–much less quantify how much. Instead, we may be better off asking buyers to invest in reforestation or forest protection as a sort of insurance policy. The following statement, while lacking in specifics, is, in a general sense, strongly supported by the scientific evidence: "In the context of the large-scale deforestation of Latin American landscapes, we believe that protection of remaining forests or modest reforestation efforts offer the greatest likelihood of producing healthy, resilient terrestrial and aquatic ecosystems." Do statements like these–frustrating as they are in their generality–provide the best bet for encouraging payments for reforestation? This approach is perhaps strongest for watershed services.

I close this introductory chapter with a word of caution on the contradictions of marketing ecosystem services. For many of us, the desire to preserve and restore forested landscapes originates from a value judgement that these landscapes are important and worth preserving, not from a dispassionate analysis of the carbon sequestration value of a hectare of forest or the flow regulation service provided to downstream water users. It is the entire package–the fully functioning forest ecosystem–that we appreciate, not the individual services that it provides. We are attempting– rightly, I believe–to capture the market value of the individual services in order to provide funds for the restoration of the whole. But in doing so, we must be careful not to limit the value of the forest to the value of the particular service that we are able to capture and monetize. We must see the forest as well as the trees.

At the same time, if we want to be taken seriously in the business community, our larger environmental ethic may be a liability. Can our assessment of the value of forest ecosystem services be taken seriously if we are predisposed towards forest preservation and restoration? I see two solutions to this dilemma. The first is to make sure that our analyses are impeccable and transparent, and are based on realistic and conservative assumptions. The second is to point out that our value judgement of the importance of forests is an informed judgement, one based on solid scientific and social evidence. The fact that not all the values of forests can be captured in current markets does not mean that those values don't exist or aren't important to human welfare.

## REFERENCES

Landell-Mills, N. and I. Porras, 2002. Silver Bullet or Fools' Gold? A Global Review of Markets for Forest Ecosystem Services and Their Impacts on the Poor. International Institute for Environment and Development, London.

Pagiola, S., J. Bishop, and N. Landell-Mills (eds.), 2002. Selling Forest Environmental Services: Market-Based Mechanisms for Conservation and Development. Earthscan, London.

doi:10.1300/J091v25n01_01

# SECTION 1:
# CARBON

# CARBON SUPPLY

# Carbon in Terrestrial Systems: A Review of the Science with Specific Reference to Central American Ecotypes and Locations

Jesse Muir Grossman

**SUMMARY.** This analysis reviews the state of the knowledge regarding carbon sequestration in terrestrial biomass with specific focus on tropical systems in Central America and Panama. Natural forests, exotic plantations, native species plantations, and agroforestry systems are considered in light of their carbon sequestration potential, their initiation and maintenance costs, and their ability to access the emerging regulated and informal carbon markets. All four of these systems show great potential to take up or store carbon and thus contribute to atmospheric reductions of $CO_2$. Research, investment, and institutional support are required to

Jesse Muir Grossman is the CEO and Co-Founder of Soltage, Inc., a solar renewable energy provider headquartered in Jersey City, NJ. Jesse Muir Grossman earned a Master of Environmental Management at the Yale School of Forestry and Environmental Studies, New Haven, CT 06511 USA (E-mail: jgrossman@soltage.com).

[Haworth co-indexing entry note]: "Carbon in Terrestrial Systems: A Review of the Science with Specific Reference to Central American Ecotypes and Locations." Grossman, Jesse Muir. Co-published simultaneously in *Journal of Sustainable Forestry* (Haworth Food & Agricultural Products Press, an imprint of The Haworth Press, Inc.) Vol. 25, No. 1/2, 2007, pp. 17-41; and: *Emerging Markets for Ecosystem Services: A Case Study of the Panama Canal Watershed* (ed: Bradford S. Gentry, Quint Newcomer, Shimon C. Anisfeld, and Michael A. Fotos, III) Haworth Food & Agricultural Products Press, an imprint of The Haworth Press, Inc., 2007, pp. 17-41. Single or multiple copies of this article are available for a fee from The Haworth Document Delivery Service [1-800-HAWORTH, 9:00 a.m. - 5:00 p.m. (EST). E-mail address: docdelivery@haworthpress.com].

Available online at http://jsf.haworthpress.com
© 2007 by The Haworth Press, Inc. All rights reserved.
doi:10.1300/J091v25n01_02

assist in the clear definition and expansion of carbon supply possibilities for market transactions. doi:10.1300/J091v25n01_02 *[Article copies available for a fee from The Haworth Document Delivery Service: 1-800-HAWORTH. E-mail address: <docdelivery@haworthpress.com> Website: <http://www.HaworthPress.com> © 2007 by The Haworth Press, Inc. All rights reserved.]*

**KEYWORDS.** Carbon sequestration, ecosystem services, Panama Canal Watershed

## INTRODUCTION

The relationship between increased atmospheric carbon dioxide ($CO_2$) levels and global climate change has attained a high degree of scientific certainty (UNFCCC, 1997; IPCC, 2001a; Kennedy, 2004; Naughton-Treves, 2004; Osborn and Briffa, 2004). Humans have increased atmospheric carbon dioxide from 280 parts per million (ppm) to 368 ppm over the past two hundred years (IPCC, 2001b). This increase in atmospheric carbon dioxide, due primarily to fossil fuel combustion and land use change, has led to perturbations in the natural global carbon cycle which are expected to result in a global average warming of between 1.5°C and 5.5°C over the next 100 years, dramatic changes in rainfall patterns, a rise in ocean levels, and potential disruption of other processes such as the thermohaline current (Kasting, 1998; IPCC, 2001b).

Efforts to mitigate this global climate change through a reduction of atmospheric $CO_2$ have focused on three broad themes:

- *emissions abatement:* the reduction of $CO_2$ emissions through increased energy efficiency and the use of new energy options, such as solar or wind power, which use little or no carbon;
- *emissions avoidance:* the protection of existing carbon stocks to prevent their release into the atmosphere;
- *carbon sequestration:* the conversion of atmospheric $CO_2$ into a different carbon form that does not contribute to climate change, e.g., through uptake by plants.

There has been a recent conjoining of these efforts to reduce atmospheric carbon which has been loosely modeled after the emissions trading programs put in place to reduce atmospheric emissions of sulfur dioxide. In carbon emissions trading, emitting parties can effectively reduce overall emissions not only through internal processes but also through the external purchase of carbon offset units or 'credits' generated through rec-' ognized carbon sequestration or emissions avoidance activities.

While the emissions trading approach to overall atmospheric $CO_2$ reduction has been regarded as problematic by some groups, regulated and voluntary markets have recently been established that support the exchange of carbon credits from supplier to purchaser. With these markets, opportunities have emerged to generate potentially significant profits from the sale of carbon credits, and projects are rapidly being capitalized that are geared partially or wholly to the supply of carbon credits to these markets. Given the youth of these markets, there is still a great deal of uncertainty regarding final market definition and ultimate volume. Despite this uncertainty, however, there has been rapid development of perceived market niches and a great deal of speculation in both voluntary markets and those defined by the Kyoto Protocol (KP) and the European Union's Emissions Trading Scheme (ETS). For additional discussion of the nature of those markets and the demand for carbon credits, see Lauterbach (this volume).

Under the Kyoto Protocol, protection of existing forests is not an acceptable source of carbon credits, but afforestation and reforestation (A/R) projects are potentially eligible to function as a source of carbon credits under the Clean Development Mechanism (CDM). As of April 2005, there have been three A/R projects proposed to the CDM executive board, the decision making body of the CDM. To date two of those projects have been rejected for methodological reasons and one is under review (see Appendix 1 for more information on CDM projects; UNFCCC, 2005).

This paper focuses on understanding the process of capturing carbon in terrestrial ecosystems to sell as carbon credits on voluntary and regulated markets. The following analysis combines a broad literature review with information gathered during a field excursion to Panama in order to examine the present state of carbon sequestration science and the activities occurring in four land-use types: tropical forests, native species plantations, exotic plantations, and agroforestry systems. General descriptions of land-use activities are complemented with very specific focus on Central American and Panamanian case studies that ground this examination within a specific context. Finally, this analysis focuses not only on the biophysical concerns relative to these land-use types, such as carbon sequestration rates and ultimate carbon pool size, but also touches on some socio-economic considerations included in land-use choices.

## BACKGROUND:
## CARBON UPTAKE IN FORESTS

Through the process of photosynthesis, plants and other photo-synthetic organisms convert carbon dioxide and water into sugars and other organic compounds using solar energy (Kasting, 1998). Some of this organic matter is incorporated into the organism as structural and reproductive tissues, while some of the carbon is re-released into the atmosphere through respiration. Since trees accumulate C in relatively long-lived woody material, they are considered net carbon sinks, i.e., they absorb more carbon through photosynthesis than is respired (Brown, 1997). These natural carbon sequestration processes underpin the logic behind the present efforts to use the growth processes of organisms to reduce the overall concentration of $CO_2$ in the atmosphere.

Rates of carbon uptake are not constant throughout the lifespan of an organism, and are generally much higher in younger plants, when competition for light and other resources necessitates relatively rapid growth. In later stages of life, plants reach an approximate state of dynamic equilibrium with respect to carbon absorption, and new growth of biomass is nearly completely offset by plant die-off and respiration (Phillips et al., 1998). This scenario holds true for stand-level dynamics as well, with young stands, natural or managed, exhibiting very high rates of growth which then slow down as the functional priorities of the collective organisms move away from resource competition and biomass accumulation to long-term goals of reproduction and resource accretion.

Terrestrial forests are considered to be among the most important global carbon pools (Montagnini and Porras, 1998; Brown, 2002b; Grace, 2004). Although it is evident from Table 1 that there are carbon reservoirs that dwarf forests by orders of magnitude, forests are the single most dynamic pool on the planet, and also that which is most susceptible to anthropogenic perturbation. Fully 80 percent of the carbon exchange in terrestrial systems occurs at the interface between the forests and the atmosphere (Montagnini and Nair, 2004). Other carbon reservoirs such as soils, fossil fuels, and the deep ocean are more static reservoirs, with relatively little movement of carbon either in or out of these pools.

Anthropogenic perturbations to natural forests through land conversion, burning, and other development have changed terrestrial forests from a net sink of carbon, which was the case in pre-industrial times, to a carbon source (IPCC, 1996; Kasting, 1998). Tropical forests, where most of the forest carbon is thought to reside, are now classified as a net emitter of 1.6 ± 1.0 Gt of carbon per year (IPCC, 2001b). These

TABLE 1. World's Carbon Reservoirs (adapted from Kasting, 1998 and IPCC, 2001b)

| Reservoir | Size (Gt C) |
|---|---|
| Atmosphere | 750 |
| Tropical Forests | 340 |
| Temperate Forests | 139 |
| Boreal Forests | 57 |
| Tropical Savannahs and Grasslands | 79 |
| Temperate Grasslands and Shrublands | 23 |
| Deserts and Semi-deserts | 10 |
| Tundra | 2 |
| Croplands | 4 |
| Soils | 1,580 |
| Surface Ocean | 1,020 |
| Deep Ocean | 38,100 |
| *Fossil Fuels* | |
| Coal | 4,000 |
| Oil | 500 |
| Natural Gas | 500 |

emissions, combined with the 5.5 ± 0.5 Gt of carbon per year emitted from fossil fuel burning, have overloaded the natural global climate cycle (IPCC, 2001b). The oceans and the land cannot absorb all of this additional carbon, and the global atmosphere records a net addition of approximately 3.2 Gt of carbon annually (see Figure 1) (IPCC, 1996; IPCC, 2001b).

## *METHODS FOR MEASURING CARBON IN TERRESTRIAL ECOSYSTEMS*

Carbon quantification in terrestrial systems begins with an estimation of the biomass of the unit under investigation (e.g., a single tree). The accepted conversion of biomass dry weight to carbon weight in terrestrial vegetation is: *carbon = biomass* × *0.5* (Shepherd and Montagnini, 2001; IPCC, 2003). More specific studies focusing on single species–with attention especially focused on groups such as bamboo, cycads, and other organisms that do not adhere to the 'typical tree' model of growth–have refined this conversion further, with carbon weight ranging from 45 to 50 percent of the organisms' biomass (IPCC, 2003). Carbon

FIGURE 1. Processes in the Global Carbon Cycle (reprint from IPCC, 2001b)

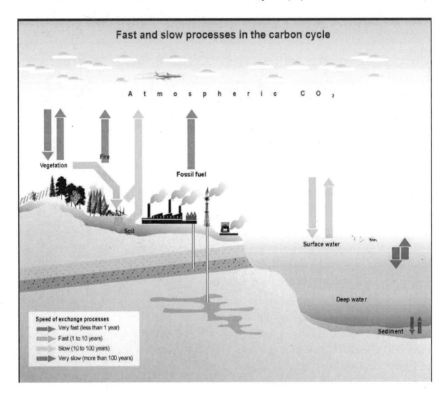

is traded across marketplaces in units of carbon dioxide equivalents ($CO_2e$) or carbon credits (CC). To derive $CO_2e$ from carbon content, the carbon mass is multiplied by 3.664 (the ratio of the masses of $CO_2$ and C; Keogh, 2003). For these and other conversions, see Appendix 4.

Carbon in an ecosystem can be described either in terms of total carbon content (mass per unit area) or in terms of the *rate* of carbon sequestration (mass per unit area per unit time). For example, there may be up to 250 Mg C ha$^{-1}$ in Bornean peat swamps (carbon content; Page et al., 2002), while Central American small-holder agroforestry systems have an average mean annual increment (MAI) of approximately 2.5 Mg C ha$^{-1}$ year$^{-1}$ (carbon sequestration; Watson et al., 2000).

Carbon pools in forests are generally segmented into above ground biomass (AGB); coarse woody debris and litter (dead biotic matter that is no longer attached to a growing individual); and belowground biomass, which includes carbon contained in the roots of plants as well as in the soil (Brown, 1997; Brown, 2002a; IPCC, 2003). Most reporting methods of carbon sequestration and pools encompass only the AGB, since this is the easiest to measure, but there are methods for measuring other pools if they are relevant to decision makers and/or land managers (see IPCC, 2003 'supplementary materials' for examples of allometric equations to estimate the litter and belowground root biomass of forests as well as the soil carbon in different regions of the world).

The biomass of terrestrial vegetation can be determined through destructive sampling in which a species under examination is harvested, dried, and weighed to determine the dry biomass weight. When surveying biomass or carbon on a forest or stand basis, it is important to use a proper sampling design that will answer relevant questions with a high degree of statistical certainty. References from the Intergovernmental Panel on Climate Change (IPCC), the United Nation's Food and Agriculture Organization (FAO), and research institutions such as Winrock International provide good guidance and best practices for sampling biomass and carbon in forest locations across the globe (see Brown, 1997; Brown, 2002b; IPCC, 2003).

In addition, allometric regression equations can be used for many tree species and forest types and provide a high degree of accuracy ($r^2 = 0.92 - 0.98$ for various forest types, and $r^2 = 0.93 - 0.99$ for individual species; IPCC, 2003). As the three examples of allometric equations in Table 2 demonstrate, the dependent variable that is used in these equations is in

TABLE 2. Allometric Equations for Estimating the Above-Ground Biomass of Tropical and Temperate Hardwood Species (IPCC, 2003)

| Equation | Forest Type | $R^2$ | DBH range (cm) |
|---|---|---|---|
| $Y=\exp[-2.289+2.649*\ln(DBH)-0.021*\ln(DBH)^2]$ | Tropical Moist Hardwoods | 0.98 | 5-148 |
| $Y=21.297-6.953*(DBH)+0.740*(DBH)^2$ | Tropical Wet Hardwoods | 0.92 | 4-112 |
| $Y=0.5+[(25000*(DBH)^{2.5}/((DBH^{2.5})+246872)]$ | Temperate US Eastern Hardwoods | 0.99 | 1.3-83.2 |

Y = aboveground biomass, kg (tree)$^{-1}$
DBH = diameter at 130 cm above ground
ln = natural logarithm
exp = "e raised to the power of"

most cases the diameter of the trees at 130 cm above the ground, also called the diameter at breast height (DBH), and in some cases the height (HT) of the tree. These equations have greatly simplified the process of biomass and carbon estimation in forests around the world.

The supplemental papers provided in the IPCC's report on "Good Practice Guidance for Land Use, Land-Use Change and Forestry" (2003) provide an excellent overview of inputs and decisions needed to calculate biomass data from various native and exotic species and ecosystems around the world.

## ANALYSIS OF LAND USE OPTIONS

The remainder of this paper focuses on four land-use activities and their ability to achieve atmospheric carbon reductions through the strategies of carbon sequestration and emissions avoidance. These four land use types–natural forests, native species plantations, exotic species plantations, and agroforestry systems–are analyzed with the best available data to determine rates of sequestration, ultimate carbon pool potential, costs of each land use activity, and potential market accessibility. These four land use types are chosen because they represent a logical suite of management options open to landholders and investors who would be interested in undertaking carbon-based ventures in Panama and similar countries. These options have also been selected to illustrate the complex interactions and tradeoffs in terms of the environmental, social, and economic costs and benefits that each of these land-use options represents.

### Tropical Forests

As illustrated in Table 3, tropical forests harbor more carbon in above ground biomass than any other land use type examined. Though younger forests and plantations sequester carbon at faster rates, the carbon storage values per hectare are much greater in natural forests than in managed or disturbed areas. The size of this pool is in part due to complex long-term, non-linear interactions, through which an extremely efficient level of resource utilization is achieved.

Though there is no dispute on the size of the carbon pools found in natural forests, there has been recent debate over whether mature forests are net carbon sources or sinks. Chave et al. (2003) demonstrate that the Panamanian tropical forests located at Barro Colorado Island contain

TABLE 3. Carbon Storage and Costs for Different Land Use Options

| Land-Use Type and Project Lifespan | Location | Amount of Aboveground Carbon Stored (Mg C/ha)[1] | Data Source | Average Annual Project Cost ($USD/ha) | Market Accessibility |
|---|---|---|---|---|---|
| **Natural Forest** Infinite | Panama | 140.5 ± 10 | (Chave et al., 2003) | 6 | Voluntary |
|  | Cameroon | 270.5 | (Duguma et al., 2001) | 6 | Voluntary |
|  | Brazilian Amazonia | 114-160 | (Brown and Lugo, 1992) | 6 | Voluntary |
| **Teak Plantation** 25 years | Panama | 29 | (Stoffler, 2001) | 260 | Kyoto |
|  | Panama. | 31 | (Block, 1999) | 260 | Kyoto |
| **Native Plantation** 20 years | Costa Rica | 72 | (Montagnini and Porras, 1998) | 260 | Kyoto |
|  | Costa Rica | 117 | (Shepherd and Montagnini, 2001) | 260 | Kyoto |
| **Agroforestry** 20 years | Sub-humid tropics | 21 | (Schoreder, 1994) | 15 | Kyoto |
|  | Humid tropics | 50 | (Schoreder, 1994) | 15 | Kyoto |
|  | Humid tropics | 50 | (Palm et al., 2000) | 15 | Kyoto |
|  | Humid tropics | 70 | (Watson et al., 2000) | 15 | Kyoto |
|  | Panama | 30 | (Hauff, 1999) | 15 | Kyoto |

[1] For natural forests, this is an estimate of the steady-state carbon pool. For plantations and agroforestry, this is an estimate of the carbon pool at the end of the indicated project lifespan, and represents carbon sequestered over the course of the project.
Note: Data sources are for data on carbon storage.

$281 \pm 20$ Mg AGB ha$^{-1}$, and an MAI of 0.20 Mg AGB ha$^{-1}$ yr$^{-1}$ with an error range that includes zero. This implies the possibility that this forest could be either a small net source or sink of carbon to the atmosphere. Phillips et al. (1998) reviewed 50 data sets from neotropical forest sites and observed a small sink in 38 of the sites that averaged 0.71 Mg C ha$^{-1}$ yr$^{-1}$. With such small levels of uptake or release of carbon, it seems safe to therefore say that mature natural forests are very large pools of carbon, yet are unlikely to be positively or negatively contributing significant amounts of atmospheric carbon if left in their natural state.

Disturbance of tropical forests through logging, land conversion, and burning, however, have led to massive emissions of $CO_2$ into the atmosphere that account for up to 20-29 percent of the global greenhouse gas emissions from anthropogenic sources (Mahili and Grace, 2000; Naughton-Treves, 2004). Efforts to preserve tropical forests have met with markedly mixed success. Many of the tropical forests are in developing countries and regions whose primary concerns are related to immediate needs that do not have the luxury of including long-term global climatic stability. Governments are often not able to fund adequate forestry governance projects within their borders, and cross-border cooperation on regional conservation issues is often difficult.

This fact seems to have stimulated the realization that if tropical forests are to survive the present global capitalization, there must be some very immediate and concrete financial incentives that make intact tropical forests more profitable than deforested lands, on regional, national, and local levels. With their vast pools of biomass, there exists a huge potential for natural forests to supply carbon credits on global markets. The capital influx resulting from market connections could, in theory, pay for the protection and monitoring of a forest while at the same time providing the local landowners and communities with sustainable development options. However, existing forest management was not included in the Kyoto Protocol due to concerns in developed countries regarding issues such as additionality and leakage, and the present market available to this huge carbon pool is therefore constrained to the less-defined voluntary markets (UNFCCC, 1997).

Examples of informal market transactions can be found in Panama and Costa Rica, where a US-based NGO, the Nature Conservancy, has brokered deals to ensure the continued protection of the carbon sinks in large natural forest areas. These transactions involved multiple stakeholders, including the respective national governments, institutional lending agencies, and the US Government (Hanily, personal communication,

March 2005). Large transactions of this type with natural forests have been the exception rather than the norm, however, given the varying receptiveness of governments to deals which may raise issues of national sovereignty and the availability of large natural forest blocks without complicated legal designations.

What are the costs of protecting the carbon in natural forests? By definition, these systems have little to no human management, and there are therefore no costs involved in their establishment or maintenance. Costs for protection and monitoring can vary with location and governmental requirements. We estimate the costs of on-the-ground monitoring and protection in Panama to be approximately $5.25 ha$^{-1}$ year$^{-1}$, based on information gathered regarding the monitoring of a 4,000 ha plot of tropical forest abutting a large teak plantation (Verjans, personal communication, March 2005). With an assumption of a five person crew with each individual accruing a daily wage of $25, working 10 days per month, and with a $500 per month cost of food, gas, and other transport for the team, there is a total annual expenditure for this 4000-ha site of $21,000, or $5.25 per hectare.

Monitoring through remote sensing is extremely efficient in terms of resource deployment and financial investment, and it can serve as a stand-alone monitoring method or be used in concert with on-the-ground efforts (Foody et al., 2001). Monitoring costs are relatively simple to calculate, with costs including the annual purchase of satellite imagery, the employment of a skilled remote sensing technician, and a periodic ground-truthing or verification of site conditions. Costs are roughly estimated to be $1,500 for image acquisition and $600 for the employment of a technician (20 hours at $30 per hour) for a total of $2,100. Image ground-truthing in this analysis is estimated to be $500 per annum. An assumption of a similarly sized 4,000 ha plot yields an annual cost of $0.65 per hectare. These data, while calculated specifically for the tropical forest areas, will be applicable to all land-use types in this analysis.

Relevant costs also interesting to examine for natural forests are the option values that would be present if this forest was converted into an alternative land-use. Common land conversion trajectories for forested lands in Panama include a conversion to pastoral land and/or agricultural plantations. Costs and benefits per hectare of these land-use types could be referenced against costs and benefits for natural forests included in this analysis to provide a more complete economic valuation for natural forests.

## Tropical Tree Plantations

Plantations of tree species have been estimated to cover 187 million ha worldwide and are increasing at a rate of 4.5 million ha per year (Montagnini and Nair, 2004). Tropical plantations are generally comprised of a few well-studied species of exotic trees, including trees of the genus *Acacia*, *Eucalyptus*, and *Tectona* that are planted in a pantropical distribution. Information about planting procedures, growth rates, rotation times, and expected harvests are very well established, making these species attractive to landowners and investors. Furthermore, the massive economic growth in nations such as India and China signal a wood market whose future is likely to be one of continued growth and profitability.

Tropical tree plantations are thought to have great potential to absorb carbon from the atmosphere and to store this carbon in the living tissue or through durable goods made out of the trees' physical structure once they are cut (Montagnini and Nair, 2004). Tropical plantations have very fast growth rates relative to more mature forest ($10$-$13$ Mg C ha$^{-1}$ yr$^{-1}$), yet are considered to be a relatively small global sink due to their small physical area on the globe (Montagnini and Porras, 1998). Plantations occupy less than 10 percent of the area that is being deforested, and aggregated tree planting is equivalent to only 0.3 percent of the carbon released by deforestation (Montagnini and Porras, 1998; Beruenig, 1996).

Of the 42,125 ha of plantations established in Panama between 1990 and 2000, over fifty percent were plantations of teak (Stoffler, 2001). Estimates of aboveground carbon pools in a teak plantation after 25 years (the average lifespan of a teak plantation in Panama) are shown in Table 3, and correspond to an average sequestration rate of slightly over 1 Mg C ha$^{-1}$ yr$^{-1}$. This ignores wood removed through the various pruning and thinning cycles (Herrera Duran, 2001; Stoffler, 2001).

Whether or not teak plantations in Panama will be able to participate in emerging carbon markets is an open question at this point. While there are Panamanian organizations, such as EcoForest, that are seeking to trade the carbon their teak trees sequester in regulated markets, there are many hurdles that must be overcome (Verjans, personal communication, March 2005). Two main complications are the additionality and leakage requirements that must be met for activities to be accepted as viable CDM projects. Additionality means that the project must be able to demonstrate how access to carbon markets has resulted in a greater sequestration of carbon than was present in a baseline or 'business as usual' scenario. The concept of leakage is similar to the economic term of 'benefit leakage,' and is introduced to address concerns that the increased sequestration of carbon at one location may result in an increased release of carbon in nearby areas.

The fact that no CDM afforestation/reforestation (A/R) projects have been accepted to date speaks to the difficulty of overcoming these hurdles through existing forestry projects, and these problems may prove difficult to solve for the existing forestry companies. The business model of most forestry entities in Panama today is to provide the best quality wood at the lowest market prices. Carbon sequestration, however, is optimized when a high volume of relatively undifferentiated biomass is grown on a unit of land. This potential conflict in priorities arises from the fact that, at this time, the forestry companies in Panama are not looking to produce biomass on their plantations *per se*, but desire the maximization of biomass that has high value on the timber markets. A shift towards increasing biomass on their sites may negatively impact the revenues accrued from timber sales. It remains to be seen if the combined goals of timber production and carbon sequestration can be harmonized in Panama to an extent that is acceptable as an A/R methodology by the CDM Executive Board.

Tree growth characteristics are highly determined by site-specific climatic and edaphic factors. Teak growth rates can change by over 30 percent based on the environmental conditions in different locations in Panama (Stoffler, 2001). Therefore, when planning any such project, it is very important to consider how local conditions may impact the overall profitability of the project. Furthermore, many mono-specific plantations such as teak are extremely demanding on soil nutrients and water, and probably lead to long-term decreases of site fertility, thus limiting the overall sustainability of many single-species plantations (Montagnini and Porras, 1998).

The costs for teak plantations in Table 3 come from an extensive study by a graduate student at CATIE conducted on a Panamanian teak forest planted on EcoForest land (Herrera Duran, 2001). Herrera Duran (2001) derived an aggregated cost per ha of $6,500 over the 25 year lifespan of the teak rotation, with gross revenue expected to be on the order of $15,000 per hectare at time of final harvest.

## Native Species Plantations

Despite the fact that native plantations are a relatively recent idea in a world-wide plantation market dominated by exotic species, they have attracted a great deal of attention and research in the last decade. The basic concept and business model of a native species plantation is very similar to that of an exotic species plantation, with heavy initial site preparation and planting costs followed by plantation management and maintenance operations that may involve pruning and thinning throughout the rotation, with goals to yield the maximum amount of high quality wood per hectare. Native plantations are considered somewhat risky as a large business venture at present because the global markets for native wood are much less defined than their exotic counterparts, even for wood with similar characteristics. This may be offset, however, by a margin of product differentiation that may be achieved through the positive attributes of native species plantations (e.g., farmers' preferences, benefits for wildlife, range of utility of mixed species, etc.). Further, the environmentally sensitive embrace of native species may give native plantation projects some competitive advantage in the application for CDM projects, which could allow native plantations to access important regulated markets.

The tree species used in native plantations are very site specific. In Central America there are approximately fifty native species that are currently being grown in test plots to determine their growth characteristics and rates, site preferences, and other variables (Montagnini and Porras, 1998; Shepherd and Montagnini, 2001; Piotto et al., 2004; PRORENA, 2004; Montero and Montagnini, 2005). These plantations are still young and most of them have not reached their full rotation age, and therefore recommendations should be regarded as preliminary. With that caveat, however, there are several interesting points that emerge.

Productivity in native species plots is higher with mixes of species than in single native species plots, with MAIs approaching rates of between 10-13 Mg AGB ha$^{-1}$ yr $^{-1}$ (Montagnini and Porras, 1998; Shepherd and Montagnini, 2001). This high growth rate is thought to be partially due to decreased intraspecific competition in mixed stands due to differing solar, nutrient, and rooting depth needs. Mixed native species plots also showed no site fertility declines (Montagnini and Porras, 1998). This can be contrasted to mono-specific plantations of exotic species such as teak, which have often been given the nickname 'green desert' from the plants' rapid growth when planted in dense plantations, resulting in the shading out of competitive vegetation. A forthcoming paper (Montero and Montagnini, 2005) outlines allometric equations that have been developed for ten native species of the Atlantic humid lowlands in Costa Rica; these equations were used to derive the carbon sequestration rates shown in Table 3. These data, however, are from trees that have not all reached maturity, so other equations are needed for more mature plantations of some of these species.

Costs were calculated for this plantation through the use of the numbers for teak plantations. Given that the planting systems are extremely similar, this seems like a conservative assumption in light of the fact that with no site fertility declines there will be no need for intensive fertilization of native plantations, which is a high cost activity in teak plantations. Access to supply carbon credits to the Kyoto markets would likely run up against the same problems of additionality discussed above in the Exotic Plantation section, but given that this would be a native species project with other socio-economic and environmental benefits, this may assist in garnering CDM project status and would certainly allow for broader penetration into the voluntary markets as well.

One company, Futuro Forestal, is presently working to sell carbon bundled with numerous other environmental services in mixed-native plantations. The company has just received some large institutional investments, and this voluntary market momentum could bode well for other native plantation projects in Panama (Eke, personal communication, March 2005).

## *Agroforestry Systems*

Agroforestry systems, as defined by Nair (1989), consist of the deliberate growth of woody perennials on the same unit of land used for agricultural crops and/or animals, with a significant environmental or ecological interaction between the woody and non-woody components of the system. This can be further subdivided into categories including agrisilviculture–where crops and woody plants are grown in complex; silvopasture–which includes animals and trees on the same plot of land; and agrosilvopasture–which combines animal husbandry, agriculture, and woody perennial plant cultivation on one unit of land (Ruark et al., 2003). Agroforestry has been practiced informally for centuries, with farmers or pastoralists planting trees on their land to fix nitrogen, provide shade, to serve as a source for fruit or nuts, or for the additional expected income from timber sales.

Recently, there have been institutional and/or state-driven campaigns with goals of increasing the amount of land in agroforestry practices for reasons of income generation for small landholders, improved productivity and sustainability across landscapes, and revegetation of degraded landscapes. There is also a growing interest in the role of agroforestry in carbon sequestration (Nair, 1989; Montagnini and Nair, 2004). Average carbon storage by agroforestry practices has been estimated to approach 21 and 50 Mg C ha$^{-1}$ in subhumid and humid regions, respectively, for projects with a 20 year lifespan (Schoreder, 1994; Palm et al., 2000).

A review by Hauff (1999) on agroforestry systems in the Panama Canal Watershed notes two projects: Agua Buena, supported by the Institute for Renewable Natural Resources (INRENARE), and Rio Cabuya, supported by the National Association for the Conservation of Nature (ANCON). Tree planting densities in these locations are similar to those used in other tree plantation activities (2.4 m × 2.4 m to 3.7 m × 3.7 m), and were planted with a mixture of agricultural crops alongside tree species including natives such as *Ochroma pyramidale, Bombacopsis quinata, Guazuma ulmifolia*, and *Anacardium occidentalis* along with exotics including *Acacia mangium, Gmelina arborea*, and *Tectona grandis* (Hauff, 1999).

With similar planting densities to those of conventional plantations, the carbon sequestration rates in Table 3 are derived from Hauff (1999), assuming approximately 140 trees per hectare, a harvest after 20 years, and an average DBH of 35cm at harvest. In an agroforestry system dominated by *Bombacopsis quinata*, for example, this would yield 30 Mg C ha$^{-1}$ or nearly 110 tons of carbon (Stoffler, 2001; IPCC, 2003). This corresponds closely with numbers from other regions found in the literature, and seems to demonstrate the feasibility of agroforestry systems to provide carbon to markets at rates similar or above those of plantations (Montagnini and Nair, 2004).

Costs in agroforestry activities are often markedly lower than those in conventional plantations since in agroforestry systems the bulk of the costs are the initial purchase of seedlings, with the majority of the management occurring through the efforts of the owner or through collective community-based mechanisms which are not monetized.

Agroforestry systems seem ideally suited to supply carbon to the regulated markets through CDM projects. The greatest potential for carbon uptake through agroforestry systems has been demonstrated to occur when they are sited on previously degraded lands, which would fit within the reforestation criteria defined under the A/R CDM framework (Watson et al., 2000; UNFCCC, 2005). Though there have been no A/R CDM projects approved to date, under review before the CDM Board is a project design document (PDD) detailing a large scale agroforestry project in Tanzania, East Africa (TIST, 2005). This decision and rulings on CDM methodologies made in this case and over the next few years will determine the near- to mid-term trajectory of afforestation projects with reference to the supply of carbon to the regulated carbon markets.

Aside from regulated markets, agroforestry activities have great potential to supply carbon to the voluntary markets as well. Agroforestry systems are often focused on human-nature interactions, where one plot of land confers multiple benefits on many differing temporal scales. This is often appealing to investors who are looking to pay for 'green' carbon credits, and should be emphasized when crafting a project to supply carbon credits.

Besides carbon sequestration, agroforestry projects can also contribute to emissions avoidance by reducing deforestation pressures on natural forests. As discussed by Ruark et al. (2003), every 1 ha of land converted to agroforestry systems could protect 5 ha of natural forest from deforestation in that communities would rely on their own cultivated sources for wood and crops and would not have to access local forest areas for those needs. With over 2 million hectares of land in tropical regions accessible to agroforestry options (and over 630 million ha worldwide estimated by one report to the IPCC), agroforestry systems have great potential to reduce pressure on native forests and to significantly reduce deforestation (Palm et al., 2000; Watson et al., 2000; Ruark et al., 2003).

## *ADDITIONAL CONSIDERATIONS*

Generation of the estimates in this report has included data from several different literature sources and personal communications covering projects of different scales and in different locations. Each of these studies has their own sources of error. This should be taken into consideration when using values or figures from this report. For example, a Panamanian land manager desiring to reference the growth rates of native tree species from Costa Rican plots located in a humid region would have to decrease the growth rates by up to 50 percent due to drier conditions in certain locations of Panama (Montagnini, personal communication, March 2005). Even within regions of a country, rates of species growth vary due to a number of site- and system-specific characteristics, including genetic make-up, seed sources, climate, soil type, and management regimes (Montagnini and Nair, 2004).

It should also be pointed out that the only carbon pool included in this analysis is the aboveground tree biomass. There are other large reservoirs of carbon found in forest systems, particularly, soil carbon, which, on a global basis, is 1.5 to 3 times the size of the vegetation carbon pool (Brown et al., 1993; Dixon, 1995; Montagnini and Nair, 2004). Soil carbon is not explicitly discussed in this analysis for the simple reason that soil carbon is not presently eligible for trade on any formal or informal carbon markets, and there are no short-term plans for its inclusion in the ETS markets. However, when forests are cut and turned into agricultural uses, carbon is released from the soils. Therefore, soil carbon is an important carbon pool whose emissions should be monitored.

## *CONCLUSIONS*

This analysis has shown that there is the potential for sequestration and storage of carbon within the suite of land-use activities under investigation: natural tropical forests, native species plantations, exotic plantations, and agroforestry systems. Mature forests, while the largest repository of carbon per unit area, have the lowest sequestration rates, while many plantations and agroforestry systems can grow quickly and absorb more carbon from the atmosphere during a given time period.

To facilitate entrance of carbon sequestration projects into expanding carbon markets, more species- and site-specific research is needed to determine growth rates, plantation mixtures, and general auto-ecological principles of promising tree species for use in carbon sequestration projects. Native species show great potential for use in carbon sequestration projects because they are well-adapted to local conditions, are often less detrimental to soils, complement local and indigenous sources of knowledge and culture, and harbor a greater diversity of species on a landscape than exotic trees. Initial projects in Costa Rica have demonstrated the ability of mixed-species native plantations to grow at rates competitive with those of exotic plantations (Montagnini and Porras, 1998).

At this stage, it appears that three of the four land-use activities surveyed are potentially eligible to supply carbon to regulated markets under the Kyoto Protocol: exotic plantations, native species plantations, and agroforestry. While providing potential for degraded lands to be converted into CDM projects, the absence of forest management activities leaves out the largest carbon reservoir examined–that of the natural forests. From a policy perspective, should the CDM board decide to re-examine this omission, one critical point for consideration is how to effectively integrate the perceived financial benefits of regulated market entrance with the protection and maintenance of this globally-important carbon pool.

# REFERENCES

AES-Tietê. 2005. Reforestation Project Using Native Species around AES-Tiete Reservoirs. Retrieved 25 April 2005 from http://cdm.unfccc.int/UserManagement/ FileStorage/FS_252742709.

Beruenig, E.F. 1996. Conservation and Management of Tropical Rainforests: An Integrated Approach to Sustainability. CAB International, Wallingford, Oxon, UK.

Block, N. 1999. The Potential for Carbon Sequestration Projects as a Mechanism for Conserving Forests in the Panama Canal Watershed. *Journal of Agroforestry* 8:53-65.

Brown, S. 1997. Estimating Biomass and Biomass Change of Tropical Forests: A Primer. Food and Agriculture Organization, Rome.

Brown, S. 2002a. Measuring Carbon in Forests: Current Status and Future Challenges. *Environmental Pollution* 116:363-372.

Brown, S. 2002b. Measuring, Monitoring and Verification of Carbon Benefits for Forest-based Projects. *Phil. Trans. R. Soc. Lond.* 360:1669-1683.

Brown, S., L.R. Iverson, A. Prasad, and D. Liu. 1993. Geographical Distributions of Carbon in Biomass and Soils of Tropical Asian Forests. *Geocarto International* 4:45-59.

Brown, S. and A.E. Lugo. 1992. Aboveground Biomass Estimates for Tropical Moist Forests of the Brazilian Amazon. *Interciencia* 17:8-18.

Chave, J., R. Condit, S. Lao, J.P. Caspersen, R. Foster, and S.P. Hubbell. 2003. Spatial and Temporal Variation of Biomass in a Tropical Forest: Results from a Large Census Plot in Panama. *Journal of Ecology* 91:240-252.

Dixon, R.K. 1995. Agroforestry Systems: Sources or Sinks of Greenhouse Gases? *Agroforestry Systems* 31:99-116.

Duguma, B., J. Gockowski, and J. Bakala. 2001. Smallholder Cacao (*Theobroma cacao* Linn.) Cultivation in Agroforestry Systems of West and Central Africa: Challanges and Opportunities. *Agroforestry Systems* 51:177-188.

Foody, G.M., M.E. Cutler, J. McMorrow, D. Pelz, H. Tangki, D.S. Boyd, and I. Douglas. 2001. Mapping the Biomass of Bornean Tropical Rain Forest from Remotely Sensed Data. *Global Ecology & Biogeography* 10:379-387.

Grace, J. 2004. Understanding and Managing the Global Carbon Cycle. *Journal of Ecology* 92:189-202.

Hauff, R.D. 1999. A Case Study Assessment of Agroforestry: The Panama Canal Watershed. *Journal of Agroforestry* 8:39-51.

Herrera Duran, J.L. 2001. Growth Provenance Analysis and Financial Profitability of *Tectona grandis* L.f. in the West Zone of the Panama Canal. Mag. Sc. CATIE, Turrialba, Costa Rica.

Intergovernmental Panel on Climate Change (IPCC). 1996. Climate Change 1995: The Science of Climate Change. Report of the Intergovernmental Panel on Climate Change, Cambridge, England.

Intergovernmental Panel on Climate Change (IPCC). 2001a. Climate Change 2001: The Scientific Basis. Intergovernmental Panel on Climate Change, Wembly, England.

Intergovernmental Panel on Climate Change (IPCC). 2001b. Climate Change 2001: Synthesis Report. Intergovernmental Panel on Climate Change, Wembly, England.

Intergovernmental Panel on Climate Change (IPCC). 2003. Good Practice Guidance for Land Use, Land-Use Change and Forestry. Intergovernmental Panel on Climate Change, Vienna, Austria.

Kasting, J. 1998. The Carbon Cycle, Climate, and the Long-Term Effects of Fossil Fuel Burning. *Consequences* 4:1-12.

Kennedy, D. 2004. Climate Change and Climate Science. *Science* 304:1565.

Keogh, R.M. 2003. Carbon Models and Tables for Teak (*Tectona grandis* Linn f.) in Central America and the Caribbean. Coillte Consult, Wicklow, Ireland.

Kraenzel, M., A. Castillo, T. Moore, C. Potvin. 2003. Carbon Storage of Harvest-age Teak (*Tectona grandis*) Plantations, Panama. *Forest Ecology and Management* 173:213-225.

Lauterbach, S. 2007. An Assessment of Existing Demand for Carbon Sequestration Services. *Journal of Sustainable Forestry* 25(1/2):75-98.

Mahili, Y. and J. Grace. 2000. Tropical Forests and Atmospheric Carbon Dioxide. *Trends in Ecology and Evolution* 15:332-337.

Montagnini, F. and P.K.R. Nair. 2004. Carbon Sequestration: An Underexploited Environmental Benefit of Agroforestry Systems. *Agroforestry Systems* 61:281-295.

Montagnini, F. and C. Porras. 1998. Evaluating the Role of Plantations as Carbon Sinks: An Example of an Integrative Approach from the Humid Tropics. *Environmental Management* 22:459-470.

Montero, M. and F. Montagnini. 2005. Modelos Alométricos para la Estimación de Biomasa de Diez Especies Forestales Nativas en Plantaciones en la Región Atlántica de Costa Rica. *Recursos Naturales y Ambiente* (*Costa Rica*) 45:118-125.

Mountain Pine Ridge Reforestation Project (MPR). 2004. The Mountain Pine Ridge Reforestation Project. Retrieved 25 April 2005 from http://cdm.unfccc.int/User-Management/FileStorage/FS_127917536.

Nair, P.K.R. 1989. Agroforestry Systems in the Tropics. Kluwer, Boston.

Naughton-Treves, L. 2004. Deforestation and Carbon Emissions at Tropical Frontiers: A Case Study from the Peruvian Amazon. *World Development* 32:173-190.

Osborn, T.J. and K.R. Briffa. 2004. The Real Color of Climate Change? *Science* 306:621-622.

Page, S.E., F. Siegert, J.O. Rieley, H.V. Boem, A. Jaya, and S. Simin. 2002. The Amount of Carbon Released from Peat and Forest Fires in Indonesia During 1997. *Nature* 420:61-65.

Palm C. A., M. van Noordwijk, P.L. Woomer, J. Alegre, C. Castilla, D.G. Cordeiro, K. Hairiah, J. Kotto-Same, A. Moukam, R. Njomgang, A. Ricse, and V. Rodrigues. 2000. Carbon Sequestration and Trace Gas Emissions in Slash-and-Burn and Alternative Land-uses in the Humid Tropics. Alternatives to Slash and Burn Climate Change Working Group, ICRAF, Nairobi, Kenya.

Phillips, O., Y. Malhi, N. Higuchi, W.F. Laurence, P.V. Nunez, R.M.Y. Vasquez. 1998. Changes in the Carbon Balance of Tropical Forest: Evidence from Long-term Plots. *Science* 282: 439-442.

Piotto, D., E. Viquez, F. Montagnini, and M. Kanninen. 2004. Pure and Mixed Forest Plantations with Native Species of the Dry Tropics of Costa Rica: A Comparison of Growth and Productivity. *Forest Ecology and Management* 190:359-372.

Proyecto de Reforestación con Especies Nativas (PRORENA). 2004. Ensayo de Selección de Especies–RPO 07 (2003) y PRO 13 (2004). Proyecto de Reforestación con Especies Nativas, Panama.

Ruark, G.A., M.M. Schoeneberger, and P.K.R. Nair. 2003. Roles for Agroforestry in Helping to Achieve Sustainable Forest Management. UNFF Intersessional Experts Meeting on the Role of Planted Forests in Sustainable Forest Management, New Zealand.

Schoreder, P. 1994. Carbon Storage Benefits of Agroforestry Systems. *Agroforestry Systems* 27:89-97.

Shepherd, D. and F. Montagnini. 2001. Above Ground Carbon Sequestration Potential in Mixed and Pure Tree Plantations in the Humid Tropics. *Journal of Tropical Forest Science* 13:450-459.

Stoffler, K.H. 2001. Informe sobre la Asesoría a ANARAP en el Uso de las Plantaciones Forestales. GTZ, Pamana.

The International Small Group & Tree Planting Program (TIST). 2005. Project Design Document. Retrieved 25 April 2005 from http://cdm.unfccc.int/methodologies/ARmethodologies/Projects/pac/methodologies/ARmethodologies/process?OpenRound=3&OpenNM=ARNM0003&cases=B#ARNM0003.

United Nations Framework Convention on Climate Change (UNFCCC). 1997. Kyoto Protocol to the United Nations Framework Convention on Climate Change. UNFCCC, Kyoto.

United Nations Framework Convention on Climate Change (UNFCCC). 2005. Afforestation and Reforestation CDM Project Activities. Retrieved 25 April 2005 from http://cdm.unfccc.int/methodologies/ARmethodologies/Projects/pac/pac_ar.html.

Watson, R.T., I.R. Noble, B. Bolin, N.H. Ravindranath, D.J. Verardo, and D.J. Dokken. 2000. Land Use, Land-Use Change, and Forestry. Intergovernmental Panel on Climate Change (IPCC), Cambridge Univ. Press, New York.

doi:10.1300/J091v25n01_02

## APPENDIX 1. Summary of Proposed Afforestation/Reforestation (A/R) CDM Project Methodologies

To date, there have been three projects proposed as A/R CDM projects. Two have been rejected and one is under review by the CDM executive board.

1. **The Mountain Pine Ridge Reforestation Project (MPR, 2004)**–This project was rejected for general methodological reasons. Project methodology does not make a good case for additionality criteria, and the concept of leakage was poorly addressed.
2. **Reforestation Project Using Native Species Around AES-Tiete Reservoirs (AES-Tietê, 2005)**–This project was rejected for general methodological reasons. No good measurements of baseline, no way to account for leakage, poor sampling design, etc.
3. **The International Small Group & Tree Planting Program (TIST, 2005)**–Project proposed and awaiting comment period and review. Project proposes a decentralized suite of small-scale agroforestry projects that will create an aggregated carbon pool across the East African country of Tanzania.

## APPENDIX 2. List of Central American Species Currently Under Study with Sources and Other Relevant Information

| | Scientific Name | Allometric Equation | Investigator/ Equation Source |
|---|---|---|---|
| 1 | *Acacia mangium* | | Prorena |
| 2 | *Albizia adinocephalla* | | Prorena |
| 3 | *Albizia guachapeli* | | Prorena |
| 4 | *Anacardium excelsum* | | Prorena |
| 5 | *Anacardium occidentale* | | Prorena |
| 6 | *Astronium graveolens* | | Prorena |
| 7 | *Balizia elegans* | $\ln(Y) = -4.820 + 2.959 * \ln(dbh)$ | Montero and Montagnini, 2005* |
| 8 | *Bombacopsis quinata* | $Y = 0.0103 * DBH^{2.993}$ | Hauff, 1999; IPCC, 2003 ($R^2 = 0.97$) |
| 9 | *Byrsonima crasifolia* | | Prorena |
| 10 | *Calophyllum brasiliense* | $\ln(Y) = -2.829 + 2.704 * \ln(dbh)$ | Montero and Montagnini, 2005* |
| 11 | *Calophylum longifolium* | | Prorena |
| 12 | *Calycophyllum candidissimun* | | Prorena |
| 13 | *Carapa guianensis* | | Prorena |
| 14 | *Cedrela odorata* | | Prorena |
| 15 | *Cedrela tonduzii* | | Prorena |
| 16 | *Chrysofilum cainito* | | Prorena |
| 17 | *Colubrina glandulosa* | | Prorena |
| 18 | *Copaifera aromatica* | | Prorena |

| | Scientific Name | Allometric Equation | Investigator/ Equation Source |
|---|---|---|---|
| 19 | *Cordia alliodora* | | Prorena |
| 20 | *Dalbergia retusa* | | Prorena |
| 21 | *Diphysa robinioides* | | Prorena |
| 22 | *Dipterys panamensis* | ln (Y) = −3.011 + 2.947*ln(dbh) | Prorena; Montero and Montagnini, 2005* |
| 23 | *Enterolobium cyclocarpum* | | Prorena |
| 24 | *Erytrina fusca* | | Prorena |
| 25 | *Genipa americana* | ln (Y) = 4.084 + 2.958*ln(dbh) | Montero and Montagnini, 2005* |
| 26 | *Glirisidia sepium* | | Prorena |
| 27 | *Gmelina arborea* | | Prorena |
| 28 | *Guazuma ulmifolia* | | Prorena |
| 29 | *Gustavia superba* | | Prorena |
| 30 | *Hura crepitans* | | Prorena |
| 31 | *Hyeronima alchorneoides* | ln (Y) = −1.696 + 2.224*ln(dbh) | Prorena; Montero and Montagnini, 2005* |
| 32 | *Hymenaea courbaril* | | Prorena |
| 33 | *Inga punctata* | | Prorena |
| 34 | *Jacaranda copaia* | ln (Y) = 4.398 + 2.765*ln(dbh) | Montero and Montagnini, 2005* |
| 35 | *Lacmelia panamensis* | | Prorena |
| 36 | *Luehea seemani* | | Prorena |
| 37 | *Manilkara sapota* | | Prorena |
| 38 | *Ochroma pyramidale* | | Prorena |
| 39 | *Ormosia macrocalys* | | Prorena |
| 40 | *Pachira quinata* | | Prorena |
| 41 | *Peltogyne purpurea* | | Prorena |
| 42 | *Pithecelobium longifolium* | | Prorena |
| 43 | *Platimiscium pinatum* | | Prorena |
| 44 | *Samanea saman* | | Prorena |
| 45 | *Sapindus saponaria* | | Prorena |
| 46 | *Schizolobium parahybum* | | Prorena |
| 47 | *Spondias mombim* | | Prorena |
| 48 | *Sterculia apetala* | | Prorena |
| 49 | *Swietenia macrophylla* | | Prorena |
| 50 | *Tabebuia guayacan* | | Prorena |
| 51 | *Tabebuia rosea* | | Prorena |
| 52 | *Tabebuia* spp. | | Prorena |

## APPENDIX 2 (continued)

| Scientific Name | Allometric Equation | Investigator/ Equation Source |
|---|---|---|
| 53  *Tectona grandis* | $Y = 0.153 * DBH^{2.382}$ | Prorena; IPCC, 2003 $(R^2 = 0.98)$ |
| 54  *Terminalia amazonia* | $\ln (Y) = -2.538 + 2.641 * \ln(dbh)$ | Prorena |
| 55  *Virola koschnyi* | $\ln (Y) = 4.132 + 2.755 * \ln(dbh)$ | Montero and Montagnini, 2005* |
| 56  *Vochysia ferruginea* | $\ln (Y) = -3.252 + 2.492 * \ln(dbh)$ | Montero and Montagnini, 2005* |
| 57  *Vochysia guatemalensis* | $\ln (Y) = -2.815 + 2.428 * \ln(dbh)$ | Montero and Montagnini, 2005* |
| 58  *Xyloipia frutescens* | | Prorena |

* Allometric equations are for total biomass, data is from ten year old trees, data is significant $r^2 = 0.95$-$0.99$. Prorena data is from PRORENA, 2004

## APPENDIX 3. Overview of Institutional, Educational, Private Sector, and Non-Governmental Organization Involvement with Carbon Supply in Panama

### Educational

- Panamanian university students are working with reforestation groups such as the Native Species Reforestation Program (PRORENA) to gain skills and research experience. Though there is no forestry department in Panamanian universities, capacity in forestry and carbon sequestration activities is actively being built on the ground.

### NGO/Private Sector

- The Nature Conservancy (TNC) has brokered two debt-for-nature swaps in Panama to protect aspects of natural forests including carbon sequestered.
- Asociación Centro de Estudios y Acción social Panameño (CEASPA), largely funded by TNC, is presently working on agroforestry projects with small scale landholders in ecologically sensitive areas, providing information and technical assistance.
- PRORENA is a research NGO performing scientific studies on native reforestation options in Panama. PRORENA is generating preliminary data on native species growth in locations across Panama.
- The Smithsonian Tropical Research Institute (STRI) is a US based NGO and is one of the largest research organizations in Panama. STRI is a strong repository of information and technical ability on many subjects including carbon.
- EcoForest is a teak plantation with Panamanian and European funding. They are positioning themselves to sell CERs through a future A/R CDM project.
- Futuro Forestal is an integrated forestry company that sells bundled ecosystem services, including carbon credits, on informal markets. They have recently garnered a large institutional investor, and their actions relative to carbon sales will be interesting to observe.

**Governmental / Institutional**

- The Panama Canal Authority (ACP) has only slight interest in carbon markets.
- Panama's National Environment Authority (ANAM) supports and houses the designated national representative (DNR) for Panama. ANAM views its appropriate role as being very supportive of any carbon project that is proposed.
- The Academy for Educational Development (AED) is working in Canal watershed sites on sustainable development activities, including reforestation. AED recently embarked upon a large joint venture with USAID to these ends.

## APPENDIX 4. Useful Conversion Units Relating to Biomass, Carbon, and $CO_2$ Equivalents

1 tonne (t) = 1 Megagram (Mg) = 1,000 kilogram (kg) = $10^6$ gram (g)

1 Gigatonne (Gt) = $10^9$ t = 1 Petagram (Pg) = $10^{15}$ g

1 g plant biomass = 0.5 g carbon

1 g carbon = 3.664 g $CO_2$ equivalents

# Improving the Supply
# of Carbon Sequestration Services in Panama

## Michael Lichtenfeld

**SUMMARY.** A global market for carbon sequestration services has emerged in recent years, driven both by regulations under the Kyoto Protocol and by private sector self-interests. However, the development of this market has been stymied by several factors, chief among them a tentative and dubious supply side. Land managers have been wary to enter the carbon market for three main reasons: high transaction and management costs, imperfect information, and a lack of institutional support. These factors have dissuaded potential suppliers from entering the market, even in the face of growing demand from governments and corporations looking to buy carbon sequestration services. As a nation with outstanding potential to capitalize on the global demand for carbon sequestration services, the Republic of Panama has much to gain from the maturation of a carbon market. In order to facilitate the growth of this market and stimulate the supply of carbon offset projects in Panama, policy mechanisms could be used by international, national, and local institutions to stimulate supply by providing financial, informational, and technical support to land managers. doi:10.1300/J091v25n01_03

---

Michael Lichtenfeld works in international cleantech private equity. He earned a Master of Environmental Management at the Yale School of Forestry and Environmental Studies and a Master of Business Administration at the Yale School of Management, New Haven, CT 06511 USA (E-mail: skigreen@hotmail.com).

[Haworth co-indexing entry note]: "Improving the Supply of Carbon Sequestration Services in Panama." Lichtenfeld, Michael. Co-published simultaneously in *Journal of Sustainable Forestry* (Haworth Food & Agricultural Products Press, an imprint of The Haworth Press, Inc.) Vol. 25, No. 1/2, 2007, pp. 43-73; and: *Emerging Markets for Ecosystem Services: A Case Study of the Panama Canal Watershed* (ed: Bradford S. Gentry, Quint Newcomer, Shimon C. Anisfeld, and Michael A. Fotos, III) Haworth Food & Agricultural Products Press, an imprint of The Haworth Press, Inc., 2007, pp. 43-73. Single or multiple copies of this article are available for a fee from The Haworth Document Delivery Service [1-800-HAWORTH, 9:00 a.m. - 5:00 p.m. (EST). E-mail address: docdelivery@haworthpress.com].

Available online at http://jsf.haworthpress.com
© 2007 by The Haworth Press, Inc. All rights reserved.
doi:10.1300/J091v25n01_03

*Article copies available for a fee from The Haworth Document Delivery Service: 1-800-HAWORTH. E-mail address: <docdelivery@haworthpress.com> Website: <http://www. HaworthPress.com> © 2007 by The Haworth Press, Inc. All rights reserved.]*

**KEYWORDS.** Carbon sequestration, ecosystem services, Panama Canal Watershed, Kyoto Protocol

## *INTRODUCTION*

The role of forests in abating global climate change is widely recognized and well documented. Through the photosynthetic process, forests remove $CO_2$ from the atmosphere and store it temporarily in biomass (Dixon et al., 1994; Faeth et al., 1994; Richards and Stokes, 2004; Sabine et al., 2004). Carbon sequestration can be achieved through forest management, reforestation, afforestation, and agroforestry activities. As a result, international efforts to abate climate change have recognized the role of forests in generating carbon off set credits and the trade of such credits. The United Nations Framework Convention on Climate Change (UNFCCC), through the Kyoto Protocol, defines targets and strategies for reducing $CO_2$ emissions in industrialized nations, including carbon sequestration in forests as a means of achieving emissions reductions. As a result, a global market for forest-based carbon sequestration services has slowly emerged.

The Republic of Panama has great potential for becoming an important source of carbon sequestration services for this emerging market. Panama contains the largest continuous tropical rainforest in the western hemisphere outside of the Amazon basin (BBC, 2005), and is therefore a prime location for forest management and conservation sequestration projects. Furthermore, large areas of the country have been deforested for agricultural purposes, creating an opportunity for large and small-scale reforestation, afforestation, and agro-forestry projects. With the ratification of the Kyoto Protocol by Russia in October 2004, and with the first commitment period of 2008-2012 quickly approaching, the global demand for carbon sequestration projects continues to rise. In fact, several industrialized nations have signed Memoranda of Understanding (MOUs) with Panama in anticipation of buying carbon credits.

However, the supply of carbon sequestration services thus far–in Panama and worldwide–has remained modest, as land managers have been reluctant to enter the market. Three major factors currently inhibit the growth of a global carbon market and act as deterrents to future suppliers: (1) the 'Kyoto market' is difficult to enter, due to complicated regulations, restrictive stipulations, and uncertainties regarding post-2012 policies (Bettelheim and D'Origny, 2002); (2) the costs associated with supplying carbon sequestration services remains high enough to deter many potential suppliers, particularly those with small land holdings and limited access to capital (Pagiola et al., 2002); and (3) potential suppliers lack sufficient information about the science and business of carbon sequestration.

These factors have had the combined effect of dissuading potential suppliers in Panama (and elsewhere) from participating in reforestation, afforestation, agro-forestry, and conservation projects. If Panamanian land managers are to enter the emerging market for carbon services, these key issues must be addressed.

Institutions at the international, national, and local levels have an important role to play in addressing these issues by developing and implementing policy mechanisms that encourage potential suppliers to enter the market. These institutions operate at different scales, under different socio-political conditions, and can offer support to land managers in different ways. This chapter reviews the comparative advantages and limitations of each of these institutions, and the areas in which their skills are needed to support carbon credit suppliers. A suite of policy alternatives are considered, with the goals of addressing the challenges facing land managers in Panama and fostering the development of international markets for carbon sequestration services.

## INSTITUTIONS AND POLICY MECHANISMS

Institutions play a fundamental role in the development of environmental markets (Pagiola et al., 2002; Bettelheim and D'Origny, 2002; Landell-Mills and Porras, 2002). Social and political frameworks, organizational relationships, and legal or economic mechanisms create the social environment in which markets emerge. The strengths or weaknesses of these institutions can directly foster or hinder the growth of such markets (Ferraro, 2000; Gunningham and Young, 1997; Gunningham and Grabosky, 1998; Panatoyou, 1993). They are particularly important for their role in capacity building, information sharing, and providing financial or technical assistance to potential suppliers of carbon sequestration services. Institutions can be generally categorized into those that operate at the international level, those nested within the national administration, and those that are non-governmental. They can be further divided into subcategories (see Table 1).

These institutions affect suppliers who may likewise be categorized in terms of scale, project type, and ownership. Suppliers can be managers of small or large properties; these properties may be owned by local or international entities; and their projects may aim to sequester carbon through forest management, reforestation, afforestation, or agroforestry (Figure 1).

Institutions play an important role in fostering the supply of carbon sequestration projects. This role is not limited solely to bringing down costs to suppliers, although this is essential. Encouraging land managers

TABLE 1. Institutions Associated with Carbon Markets in Panama. These institutions have leadership roles to play in fostering the supply of carbon services.

| International | Panamanian National Government | National and Local Organizations |
|---|---|---|
| Regulatory Frameworks | National Legal Framework | Academic Institutions |
| Multilateral Funding Institutions | Finance Ministry | Trust Funds and Private Banks |
| International NGOs | Environment Authority | Religious Organizations |
| International Investors | Other Government Agencies | Research and Advocacy Organizations |

FIGURE 1. Typology of Landowners and Forest Management Regimes for Carbon Sequestration Projects. Three general categories of landowners can choose to sequester carbon using multiple combinations of four forest management regimes.

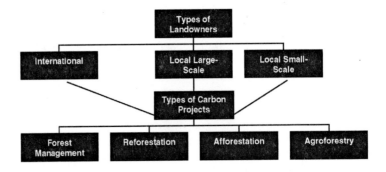

to enter the market also depends on institutional support for regulation, capacity building, and informational or technical assistance. Institutions can serve as both proximate drivers and primary implementers of policy mechanisms that can be crafted specifically to address these needs.

Policies considered in this analysis can be divided into three categories: informational policies, regulatory policies, and financial partnerships (see Table 2).

*Informational policies* are often implemented to require the disclosure of information regarding environmental impacts or other issues from producer to government agencies and consumers. For suppliers of carbon sequestration services, this may mean disclosing information regarding species composition, length of timber rotation, financial profile, and other management characteristics to government agencies engaged in joint ventures or to institutions serving as certification or

TABLE 2. Policy Mechanisms for Stimulating Carbon Projects. Policy mechanisms for affecting supply of carbon projects in Panama can be divided into three general categories. Many instruments and combinations of instruments are available for implementation under each of these categories. Simple examples of each policy type, as they relate to carbon sequestration supply, are offered below.

| | Informational | Regulatory | Public-Private |
|---|---|---|---|
| Policy Mechanisms for Fostering Supply | *Disclosure Requirements*<br>Supplier must give periodic information or evidence of carbon project | *Command and Control*<br>Suppliers must adhere to specified practices, laws, stipulations | *Grants*<br>Suppliers that meet certain criteria or requirements are eligible for grants |
| | *Mandated Research by Government Agency*<br>Supplier or organization mandated by government to focus research on specific issues such as best management practices or risk management | *Tradable Permit Schemes*<br>Suppliers are allowed to trade excess sequestration credits to other suppliers unable to meet demand or looking to hedge risk by buying extra credits<br><br>*Economic Incentives and Disincentives*<br>Suppliers meeting certain requirements receive tax breaks on specified expenses | *Loans*<br>Government provides low-interest loans that do not require heavy collateral or land title to suppliers meeting specified criteria<br><br>*Joint Ventures and Shared Investments*<br>Government guarantees purchase of carbon credits or provides land, security, or legal support for private ventures |

brokering houses. However, other policies may be developed to enhance the flow of information from institutions to suppliers (Buttazzoni, 2003). The kinds of information relevant here are methodologies for measuring carbon stocks, best-management practices, and consumer demands or market trends.

*Regulatory policies* are those imposed by government agencies with the goal of affecting market parameters. These can take the form of command and control legislation, cap-and-trade schemes, and tax or other economic instruments. Each of these types of policy can or have been used to foster and manipulate the emerging carbon market at different scales and with different outcomes. Their appropriate application will be an influential measure in encouraging suppliers to participate in the market (Yohannes and Angeletti, 2003).

*Public-private partnerships* can be one of the most effective ways of supporting sequestration projects. These partnerships can be passive or active. Passive financial partnerships generally direct capital from government agencies to private entities in the form of grants, loans, equity, or insurance. Active partnerships are those in which capital and other resources are contributed by private entities to a venture, with government providing public lands, supportive regulatory policies, or legal protection and enforcement (Gomes-Casseres and Reamer, 2003).

The general policy mechanisms described above offer a variety of tools that can be mixed and matched for optimal management of an environmental problem or emerging market influenced to address the environmental problem. Which policies are appropriate will be determined and implemented by institutions at international, national, and local levels. Such institutions have already played a significant role in shaping Panama's current involvement in the emerging market for carbon sequestration services. However, with land managers still reluctant to enter the market, it is clear that these institutions can improve their effectiveness in stimulating supply. By addressing internal weaknesses and wielding policy instruments, institutions at all levels can foster the development of a global carbon market.

## INTERNATIONAL INSTITUTIONS

### United Nations Regulatory Framework

Driven by growing concern over global climate change, the Kyoto Protocol to the United Nations Framework Convention on Climate Change

(UNFCCC) catalyzed an international carbon market by creating a broad regulatory agenda for reducing greenhouse gas emissions and setting targets for industrial nations to reduce carbon dioxide emissions to an average of 5.2 percent below 1990 levels (CFA, 2005). These targets are to be met by participating nations by the first commitment period of 2008-2012. The Protocol's Clean Development Mechanism (CDM) program allows industrialized nations to achieve a portion of their targeted emissions reductions by purchasing certified emission reduction credits (CERs) from developing nations (see Lauterbach, this volume). In this way, Kyoto Protocol has paved the way for a global, regulatory-driven market for carbon sequestration services.

However, several aspects of the Protocol have prevented it from stimulating maximum participation from land managers. Among these is the complex nature of the regulatory framework. In order for projects to be validated under Kyoto regulations and available for sale to industrialized nations party to the Protocol, a series of bureaucratic steps must be taken. These include application to the designated national representative (DNR), development of a project design document (PDD), application to the CDM Executive Board, and issuance of certified emission reduction (CER) credits. For small-scale land managers, the process can be overly time- and resource-consuming.

The Kyoto Protocol sets strict limitations upon potential sequestration projects, restricting both the kinds of projects allowed and the extent to which they may used to achieve national emission reduction targets. The types of projects allowed under Article 12 of the Protocol, which established the Clean Development Mechanism (CDM), have been restricted to afforestation and reforestation ventures. Under Kyoto, 'afforestation' is defined as the establishment of forests on land that has had no forest on it for at least 50 years, while 'reforestation' refers to the establishment of forests on land that was once forested but was then denuded prior to 1990 (IPCC, 2001). Disallowed under the CDM provisions of the Protocol are forest conservation or management projects, through which natural standing forests are protected from conversion to other land uses and/or managed for optimal sequestration rates with the express purpose of off-setting carbon emissions (IPCC, 2001). Furthermore, projects must demonstrate 'additionality,' defined as the active reduction (or sequestration) of emissions beyond the business-as-usual scenario. Projects must prove that they will not lead to 'leakage,' defined as a situation in which the benefits of a carbon sequestration project are offset by an inadvertently spurred activity, such as deforestation elsewhere or the intensification of energy consumption (Bettelheim and D'Origny, 2002).

While the ultimate goal of the Kyoto Protocol is to reduce greenhouse gas emissions and abate climate change, debate continues over what strategies are most appropriate to meet this goal. The issues mentioned above typify this debate. On one hand, forest management is strongly advocated by those who see such projects as achieving two goals simultaneously– the conservation of natural forest and the sequestration of greenhouse gases (or, more accurately, the preservation of carbon pools). Proponents of forest management point to the fact that standing forests contain significant quantities of sequestered carbon and that their conversion to other land uses would, in effect, emit stored carbon and contribute to climate change.

Others, however, see the Kyoto Protocol as a vehicle for progressive emission reductions (as opposed to preservation of 'pools'), and are more interested in increasing the amount of forests through reforestation and afforestation projects. The fact that the CDM Executive Board has not yet approved a standardized methodology for sequestration projects and has not yet determined a replicable method for assessing the additionality or leakage potential of such projects indicates that these issues remain a point of contention. In the meantime, the stipulations regarding additionality and leakage have had the effect of limiting growth in the carbon market by disallowing the participation of many potential suppliers who do not meet the Kyoto criteria (Aukland et al., 2003; Bettelheim and D'Origny, 2002).

In addition to limitations on the types of projects eligible under the Protocol, restrictions have been established on the extent to which industrial nations may count CDM forest sequestration projects towards meeting their national goals by 2012, limiting such projects to 1 percent of a nation's portfolio. This is partly due to the sentiment among many Parties to the Convention that the Kyoto Protocol should ultimately serve as a stimulus for renewable energy and cleaner technologies, not for growing trees. Considering, however, that the Protocol remains the primary driver behind the international trade of carbon sequestration credits, it seems counterproductive to critics that the Protocol contains a stipulation so severely restricting demand for sequestration projects and subsequently limiting the incentive for suppliers to enter the market.

Another weakness of the international regulatory framework established under Kyoto is the uncertainty regarding methodologies for measuring carbon. The CDM Executive Board has responsibility for approving or rejecting potential carbon sequestration projects. Yet, it has not approved a standard methodology for land managers to use when undertaking afforestation or reforestation projects. Critical components· to any commodity market are the definition of the product and the ability to ensure delivery of the product or service contracted (Panayatou, 1993; Pagiola et al., 2002; Cromwell, personal communication 8 February 2005). Thus, confusion regarding which methodologies to use and which will be approved in the future undermines suppliers'ability to confidently define the commodity.

Perhaps the most serious weakness of the Kyoto Protocol is the uncertainty of its fate. With the first commitment period of 2008-2012 fast approaching, many potential suppliers are hesitant to enter the market in anticipation of significant changes to the regulatory framework after 2012. Uncertainty regarding a post-2012 Kyoto Protocol is of particular concern to forest-based sequestration projects, because the long growing cycles required to optimize carbon sequestration services mean that projects engaged today are especially vulnerable to regulatory changes in the future. One factor of special interest to suppliers in Panama and other forest-rich nations is the issue of forest management. As mentioned, conservation and forest stewardship are not yet eligible under the CDM, but their inclusion in a post-2012 regulatory framework would create a major incentive for conservation among a significant group of land managers: those on already-forested properties.

Naturally, land managers are wary of entering a regulated market that may change its rules drastically—or even cease to exist altogether—in the near future. In Panama, some reforestation companies currently in operation, such as Eco-Forest, have built their projects with the long-term intention to enter the carbon market, but have not yet done so for fear of sweeping changes to (or the complete abandonment of) the Kyoto Protocol after 2012 (Delvalle, personal communication, 10 March 2005). The Koto Protocol has created the regulatory platform upon which an international trade in certified emission reduction credits has emerged. In doing so, it has pioneered a promising strategy for abating climate change. However, the current regulatory framework has simultaneously restricted the growth of a carbon market by enacting strict and complex stipulations while leaving many key issues unresolved. The Protocol would likely be strengthened by:

- Approving a robust and standardized carbon measurement methodology for CDM projects;
- Simplifying the certification process for issuance of CERs;

- Specifying conditions under which forest management and conservation-based projects would qualify for the CDM market; and
- Making significant strides toward determining a course of action for post-2012 climate change abatement and international emissions trading that clearly defines what kinds of sequestration projects will be allowed under future regulations.

The Conference of Parties to the Kyoto Protocol and the CDM Executive Board are two institutions that have critical influence over the development of a carbon market. If they expect to foster a robust forest-based, carbon trading program that will continue beyond the present treaty period, they might begin by addressing some of the flaws in the regulatory framework. Land managers in Panama and other developing nations are especially in need of changes to Kyoto, because many are currently ineligible for certification, are unable or unwilling to complete the application process, or are hesitant to enter a market with an uncertain future.

### Multilateral Funding Organizations

Multilateral funding organizations are capable of providing much needed capital for the development of carbon sequestration projects in Panama. Institutions such as the World Bank and the Global Environment Facility (GEF), currently play an important role in financing sequestration projects worldwide. For example, both institutions have established funds specifically for providing assistance to carbon service suppliers (see Table 3). The World Bank has developed the BioCarbon Fund, a public-private partnership fund of $100 million that targets projects suited for both Kyoto and voluntary segments of the market (World Bank, 2004). Likewise, GEF is currently developing a $200 million carbon fund focusing on projects that incorporate elements of biodiversity and conservation (GEF, 1999; GEF, 2005).

Both of these funds, however, remain modest compared to other institutional investments, both in terms of numbers of projects financed and levels of funding per project (Table 3). Furthermore, to date, neither the World Bank nor GEF have committed funding for carbon offset projects in Panama despite this country's outstanding potential for hosting successful projects as evidenced by its standing forests, easy access to degraded lands suitable for reforestation, and its favorable business climate. Moreover, Panama hosts a number of institutions capable of providing significant financial and technical support to suppliers although

TABLE 3. International Financing Organizations and Carbon Projects Funded. Multilateral banks, bilateral aid organizations, and multilateral funding institutions have offered only modest support for carbon sequestration projects worldwide. These institutions have taken steps to engage the emerging carbon market, but are capable of providing significantly more support than they have been. It may be in their interest to do so because carbon projects can help meet institutional objectives such as economic development, poverty alleviation, and environmental improvement.

| Institution | Level of Funding | Country | Date |
| --- | --- | --- | --- |
| GEF | $2.5 million | Benin | Jan 1992 |
| GEF | $0.75 million | Iran | Jan 2001 |
| GEF | $0.99 million | China | Nov 2002 |
| GEF | $1.5 million | Sudan | Dec 1992 |
| World Bank | $1.8 million | Ecuador | Feb 2005 |
| World Bank | $1.4 million | Honduras | Feb 2005 |
| World Bank | $0.54 million | Argentina | Dec 2004 |
| World Bank | $1.2 million | Peru | Dec 2004 |

this potential has so far been largely untapped due to the lack of progress in KP implementation noted above.

The US Agency for International Development (USAID), which is actively involved in Panama on a variety of levels, has publicly declared its interest in carbon sequestration projects, but has not yet engaged in any (USAID, 2005). The organization is currently researching methodologies for quantifying sequestration services of ecosystems in Latin America, and continues to assert that its biodiversity protection projects are by default sequestering carbon (USAID, 2005). The institution has not yet explicitly expressed plans to finance carbon sequestration projects anywhere. The World Bank, GEF, and USAID are taking part in the evolution of a global carbon market, but might consider playing a greater role in financing such market evolution in Panama.

International funding institutions can significantly foster the supply of carbon credits by infusing capital into sequestration projects that demonstrate appropriate need and present sound business models. While grants are an ideal source of funding for struggling suppliers because they do not require reimbursement or financial collateral on the part of the recipient, low-interest loans are also an important mechanism to finance carbon projects. Multilateral financing agencies are the primary institutions capable of taking on the risk and low return-on-investment expectations common to sequestration ventures. By supporting integrated business models that address the provision of multiple ecosystem goods and services, multilateral agencies might foster increased returns. National governments are often unable or unwilling to give loans to such ventures when they themselves are struggling with national debt. Multinational corporations and other private international investors, on the other hand, might have sufficient free capital to work with, but often have very high demands for returns on the investment and may not wish to take on the kind of risk inherent in sequestration projects. Therefore, international banks are primary candidates for supporting such projects. Furthermore, as carbon projects may be vulnerable to exogenous factors such as fire, climate change, and trespassers (Moura-Costa and Stuart, 1998), multilateral banks might consider providing insurance at reasonable costs to suppliers.

In addition to providing grants and loans, international finance institutions would indirectly support the carbon market by funding policy reform that addresses the needs of land managers. In 2002, the Inter-American Development Bank (IDB) helped to address such needs when it loaned Panama $27 million to implement a strengthened land title policy. By addressing the issue of ownership and property rights, IDB directed its financial resources in an area that will greatly facilitate access to credit and equity capital for rural land holders (IDB, 2002). Furthermore, IDB has expressed a commitment to abating climate change in Latin America and is working to develop a course of action (IDB, 2005).

International finance institutions have a vital role to play in fostering the supply of carbon projects in Panama and around the world. Such institutions might consider developing clear guidelines, both for internal review and for potential recipients, which could include such components as:

1. *The type of projects that are eligible* (creating a balanced reforestation and conservation portfolio);
2. *Specified side-benefits that support institutional goals* (e.g., poverty alleviation and employment in rural areas, watershed protection, etc.);
3. *The mix and composition of species planted* (i.e., emphasizing mixed native species plantations); and
4. *The relative need of potential recipients* (e.g., focusing aid on projects most in need of assistance).

Once such a guideline is put in place, the IFC, GEF, USAID, and others might also consider how to increase their overall spending on carbon sequestration projects given the demonstrated links of these projects with other broad institutional goals (as set forth in point 2, above). These kinds of policies would likely be effective in supporting Panamanian land managers in their attempt to enter the emerging market.

## *International NGOs*

Globally-active non-governmental organizations have played an important role in the development of carbon markets. In 2000, Washington, DC based Forest Trends became Secretariat to the Katoomba Group, an international consortium of business, policy, and environmental organizations that convenes annually to develop innovative approaches to fostering markets for environmental services. The Katoomba Group manages a website (www.ecosystemmarketplace.com) devoted to sharing information on ecosystem services, including carbon sequestration, and emphasizes market analysis and consumer education.

Likewise, organizations such as the World Resources Institute (WRI) and the International Institute for Environment and Development (IIED) provide much needed information on the science and economics of climate change abatement. These institutions support suppliers of carbon services in their decision making process by making available reports and publications on related technical and financial issues. The extent that publications from any of these institutions are available and accessible (in layman's terms) to land managers, large and small, is an important issue. How these institutions and their publications affect international or national policy depends largely on factors such as widespread public interest, timing, political expediency, and the degree to which the topic is perceived as a crisis, especially by the mass media. In the case of climate change, it appears that publications from these organizations that are issued in the coming years will have the potential to make an important impact on policy decisions.

In Panama, some of the responsibility for addressing these concerns would need to be shouldered by organizations like the Academy for Educational Development (AED) and the Smithsonian Tropical Research Institute (STRI), which have a comparative advantage in education and information sharing. AED is currently engaged in research on a system of payments for environmental services in Chagres National Park and watershed management models for areas throughout Panama. The institution works with government agencies, NGOs and local communities to develop effective strategies for sustainable development (Castaneda, personal communication, 8 March 2005). STRI, meanwhile, is one of the world's leading authorities on tropical forest ecology, and is actively engaged in both on-going field research and information dissemination. STRI's library and information resources are available to the Panamanian public, and the Institute runs three, year-round public education programs for all ages (King, personal communication, 7 March 2005).

Finally, The Nature Conservancy (TNC) and other international environmental NGOs have brokered some of the world's first carbon sequestration investments. TNC is active in Panama, but has not yet explored the potential for sequestration projects there. This is due in part to the uncertainties regarding post-2012 regulations and in part due to a perceived lack of sufficient demand (Hanily, personal communication, 8 March 2005). However, the fact that TNC has brokered carbon sequestration deals in other parts of Latin America indicates that this institution has the capacity to play an important role in facilitating transactions in Panama.

In general, international NGOs have played a critical role in the development of a global carbon market. Addressing the issues outlined above would certainly help the markets to mature.

## *A Voluntary Market*

The UNFCCC and the Kyoto Protocol can be considered the stimulus behind international carbon credit trading. However, a voluntary market is also growing, driven by companies and individuals seeking to offset their emissions for a variety of reasons, including internal standards, public relations, and the anticipation of future regulations. This segment of the developing carbon market has no formal certification process or system of standards. All four project types (see Table 2) are tradable in the voluntary market, expanding opportunities for land managers who are otherwise unable to meet Kyoto's CDM stipulations. As mentioned, the World Bank and Global Environmental Facility have developed funds to finance both voluntary and regulated carbon market transactions. By doing so, these institutions are fostering a powerful market segment while gaining institutional experience in brokering and financing such deals. This will likely stimulate greater levels of financing with greater investor confidence. International institutions–particularly multilateral banks and NGOs–that direct more financial and technical support to carbon projects serving the voluntary market will stimulate more trade in carbon credits and help to more rapidly abate climate change.

## NATIONAL INSTITUTIONS

Although international organizations continue to play an increasing role in the carbon market, Panamanian land managers have experienced a general lack of institutional support at the national level. The Panamanian government has recognized the potential for carbon sequestration projects, but assistance to land managers hoping to enter the market has been limited and inconsistent. In spite of this, a few government agencies stand out as actively working towards the development of a carbon market.

Panama's National Environment Authority (ANAM), created in 1998, has taken noteworthy measures to encourage land managers to enter the carbon market. In addition to collaborating with other organizations to provide suppliers with information and capacity building, ANAM has expedited the process of applying for certification from the CDM Executive Board by approving proposed projects (i.e., submitting a "letter of no objection" to the CDM Executive Board) quickly and with little bureaucracy (Gutierrez Espeleta, personal communication, 8 March 2005). ANAM has also provided some marketing assistance to suppliers by advertising proposed projects at international summits and UN conventions. Finally, ANAM is responsible for arranging the existing Memoranda of Understanding (MOUs) with Canada, Spain, Italy and Holland. These MOUs serve as commitments to purchase carbon sequestration credits, and offer a guarantee of demand to potential suppliers.

ANAM continues to play an important role in fostering the participation of land managers in the carbon market, but improvement in certain areas could further assist project development and implementation. For example, this agency has not paid much attention to the non-regulated voluntary market that is emerging, and has not offered suppliers assistance in entering this segment of the market (Gutierrez Espeleta, personal communication, 8 March 2005). Because the US and other countries not party to the Kyoto Protocol remain significant sources of emissions and therefore have great potential demand for voluntarily offsetting corporate or personal emissions, recognizing and working towards the voluntary market may be important. Furthermore, ANAM has not yet taken any major steps to help pool small-scale carbon sequestration projects that have little chance of attracting international carbon buyers individually.

The Ministry of Agricultural Development (MIDA) and the Ministry of Economics and Finance (MEF) also have important contributions to make to the development of carbon services supply. Both of these agencies have been involved in the creation of forestry and reforestation laws in the past, both are capable of providing protection of ownership and resources, and both have the potential to implement economic mechanisms such as tax and loan policies. Yet, these agencies have been relatively inactive with regard to reforestation and carbon markets in recent years. For example, MEF and MIDA have both participated in small-scale rural development projects, but neither agency has engaged in any carbon sequestration projects. In fact, some policies implemented by these agencies may inhibit the growth of carbon services supply in Panama. For example, Law 25 provides heavy subsidization to the cattle ranching industry, and has resulted in the deforestation and subsequent degradation of over 2 million hectares nationwide (Castaneda, personal communication, 8 March 2005; Pérez, personal communications, 7-11 March 2005).

While institutional support for carbon projects appears limited in Panama, the government has, in fact, already demonstrated its capacity to implement economic incentives and other policy mechanisms with the purpose of stimulating forestry projects in the past. Though developed without the goal of carbon sequestration, Law 24 of 1992 illustrates the Panamanian government's willingness to introduce economic incentives as a means of changing market parameters to lower costs to suppliers (in this case, suppliers of timber). The legislation was aimed at reducing costs to land managers engaged in reforestation projects, and thus acted as a stimulus to affect private behavior.

Law 24 included articles that established income tax shelters, property tax exemptions, insurance, and low interest loan programs for reforestation projects (Panamadera, 2003). For example, the legislation allowed all direct investments in reforestation activities to be 100 percent deductible from income tax, while exempting payment of property taxes for land owners who reforest at least 50 percent of their land. Furthermore, Law 24 mandated the creation of 'Preferential Forest Loans' that would be offered by national public and private lending institutions at an interest rate four percentage points below local market average. The institutions making these loans were then able to deduct interest revenues from income taxes owed.

In addition to addressing the issue of high costs facing low-income suppliers, Law 24 also provided institutional and legal support, while fostering the sharing of information. For example, the law encouraged research into reforestation by allowing income tax deductions of investments or donations to specified research organizations. Meanwhile, the government pledged to secure property rights and ensure protection from squatters for landowners engaged in reforestation projects. Law 24 also contained articles aimed at fostering technology transfer from national and international entities to reforestation project managers (Panamadera, 2003).

However, Law 24 became vulnerable to abuses by large-scale plantations owned by wealthy investors, and ultimately failed. At the extreme, large-scale plantation owners took advantage of tax exemptions and other benefits, clearing primary forests to establish non-native (teak) monoculture plantations (Jackson, 2005). One major problem with the law was that it offered large income-tax breaks, which were of little value to low-income and small-scale land managers since deductions are proportional to revenues. Thus, large-scale reforestation projects with high revenues benefited significantly from the Law, while small-scale low income projects (that are most in need of financial support) received relatively little support (Jackson, 2005). The efficacy of the preferential loan program, aimed at low-income and small-scale projects, may have been inhibited by high transaction costs, the requirement of land title (often non-existent in rural Panama at the time), and the high-risk collateral requirements (e.g., the risk of foreclosure on their property in the event of default).

The misapplication of this Law resulted in the recent annulment of many key articles, including those related to tax deductions and exemptions. Although Law 24 was not initially intended to cultivate supply of carbon (it was adopted before the Kyoto Protocol was created), it potentially had direct implications for carbon sequestration projects in Panama. Understanding the pitfalls and loopholes of Law 24 will be critical should Panama decide to craft a new reforestation law aimed at fostering carbon sequestration projects.

In recent years, government efforts to stimulate reforestation and other sequestration projects have been weak. Government agencies have been divided on the issue of environmental services, and this fragmentation has led to a general lack of cooperation among agencies (Harrick, personal communication, 9 March 2005). If reforestation and carbon sequestration are priorities in Panama, there is a need for greater communication and vision between MIDA, MEF, and ANAM, in particular, and between these agencies and other institutions at the national and international level (Pérez, personal communications, 7-11 March 2005).

In terms of Panama's national goals and priorities, reforestation and carbon sequestration projects offer an opportunity for economic development, poverty alleviation, foreign capital investment, rural employment, the improvement of environmental quality, and good international public relations (consider the front-page article in The Economist regarding Panama's outstanding opportunities for ecosystem markets). Governmental institutions in Panama might consider the following strategies to foster the supply of carbon sequestration services.

## Implement Regulatory and Economic Mechanisms

The Panamanian Legislative Assembly might revisit and modify the goals and strategies of Law 24 to address weakness, vulnerabilities, and perverse incentives in the original legislation. Any new law must differ from the original in many ways. First, tax breaks for reforestation on lands deforested prior to a specified date (perhaps 1992, when the original Law 24 was enacted) could help to avoid creating a new incentive for deforestation. Second, tax breaks might be tiered, with special incentives for plantations with native species to avoid the expansion of monoculture, non-native plantations.

Additionally, policies might include incentives for lending to carbon projects (e.g., tax breaks for funding institutions) and information and capacity building programs (e.g., tax breaks for research organizations that work on carbon issues). However, experience from Law 24 shows that specific measures are needed to ensure that these benefits are directed towards small-scale and low-income projects, and do not get co-opted by large-scale, wealthy landowners. Finally, regulatory mechanisms that assist in land titling and strengthen support of property rights and ownership protection are essential to enable suppliers to enter the global carbon market.

## Engage in Public-Private Partnerships

In addition to regulatory and economic mechanisms, there are opportunities for government authorities in Panama to enter into public-private partnerships and joint ventures with local suppliers of carbon services. Through active public investments, these agencies might offer direct grants, low-interest loans, low-cost-of-capital equity, and cheap insurance packages. Business-friendly regulatory frameworks, ownership and property rights security, and, in some cases, offering public lands for private management, are all examples of how the Panamanian government might stimulate the supply of carbon projects through passive investment. These types of public-private partnerships have the potential to be used as effective tools to lower costs to suppliers and encourage land managers in Panama to enter the carbon market.

## *Attracting International Financial Assistance*

The policy alternatives outlined above cannot be funded by Panamanian authorities alone. The nation is debt-ridden, and President Torrijos has been committed to increasing taxes as a means of generating public revenue (Jackson, 2005). Offering tax breaks at this point may not be financially or politically feasible in Panama. It is therefore essential that MEF, MIDA and ANAM, among other institutions, reach out to multilateral funding organizations (such as the World Bank, GEF, USAID, and IDB) and to private investors who can fund the tax breaks and other fiscal reforms necessary to stimulate the supply of carbon services in Panama.

## *Addressing Inter-Agency Relationships*

Governmental institutions in Panama have historically been fragmented and uncooperative in their approach to environmental issues (Harrick, personal communication, 9 March 2005; Pérez, personal communications, 7-11 March 2005). Lack of communication, lack of coordination among governmental institutions, and lack of leadership have all inhibited the development of policies that encourage carbon sequestration projects. Yet, reforestation, afforestation, agroforestry, and forest management are activities that can serve the individual interests of many institutions, including ANAM, MIDA, and MEF, by enhancing environmental quality, improving agricultural performance, and generating income for rural communities. Providing financial and institutional support to land managers who wish to enter the carbon market would also serve their own political interests. The development of integrated, forest-related policies will require greater communication and cooperation among Panamanian authorities.

## *LOCAL AND NATIONAL NGOS*

Local and national non-governmental institutions have, in many ways, taken a leading role in fostering the supply of carbon sequestration projects in Panama. They have been especially active in research and information sharing on the science and social aspects of reforestation and carbon sequestration. The Native Species Reforestation Project (PRORENA), for example, is one such institution conducting research on best-management practices for raising native tree species. They are divided into three main departments: a nursery in which the science of cultivating native seedlings is conducted; a field research department that leads on-the-ground investigation into socio-economic and silviculture issues; and a business research section focused on the financials of reforestation project development. These foci get right to the heart of the challenges facing potential suppliers of carbon services.

Likewise, the Panamanian Center for Research and Social Action (CEASPA) has focused on agroforestry systems in rural areas as a strategy for improving social conditions as well as the environment. CEASPA leads workshops and collaborates directly with small-scale farmers and cattle ranchers to develop better management practices, including reforestation, on their properties. This organization is capacity building at the grassroots level while gaining deeper knowledge of the cultural and social elements of such projects (Elton, personal communication, 7 March 2005). CEASPA's mission includes the development of public policy and the lobbying of governmental regulations that foster sustainable development for rural communities (Elton, personal communication, 7 March 2005).

The National Association of Panamanian Reforesters (ANARAP) is a consortium of public and private parties dedicated to fostering reforestation projects nationwide. The organization has been a leading force in discussions at the governmental and non-governmental level on how to cultivate the supply of carbon sequestration capacity and the regeneration of forests in Panama. With close ties to the Ministry of Agricultural Development, ANARAP has been closely involved in public policy development, fighting to reform Law 24 without abandoning it, and providing government agencies, including the Ministry of Economics and Finance, with information on the effects of policy on environmental and socioeconomic indicators (Harrick, personal communication, 9 March 2005).

ANARAP has worked to stimulate the supply of carbon services in Panama by actively researching regulatory (economic) policy options and advertising opportunities for carbon projects in Panama to international audiences. During international summits, for example, ANARAP disseminates information about on-going projects in Panama and reaches out to international businesses for guidance on financing such projects (Harrick, personal communication, 9 March 2005).

Furthermore, ANARAP has been working to establish another institution called the Climate Investment Partnership (CIP), dedicated to funding carbon sequestration projects, monitoring them, and marketing to private investors. CIP would focus on reforesting the 2 million ha of degraded lands in Panama believed to be the result of cattle ranching (Harrick, personal communication, 9 March 2005; Pérez, personal communications, 7-11 March 2005). CIP would establish a trust fund managed by a board of directors, and would seek insurance from government institutions.

Local NGOs are actively engaged in the development of carbon services supply in Panama. However, to date none of these institutions have successfully launched a sequestration project. The collapse of an organization called the Foundation for Environmental Services (FUPASA) demonstrates how vulnerable local NGOs can be to changing political conditions and a lack of regulatory or fiscal support. Because NGOs play such an important role in developing environmental markets, the list of recommendations proposed here is extensive. Local NGOs might strengthen their efficacy in stimulating the supply of carbon services in Panama by engaging in the following activities.

### Research and Information Sharing

NGOs in Panama have an outstanding comparative advantage in conducting research on the science, business, and cultural elements of carbon sequestration. Although existing institutions have already demonstrated their capacity in this area, more emphasis could be placed on: (1) addressing specific information needs of suppliers, and (2) disseminating relevant information to local communities and government agencies. Information most needed by land managers includes: methods for measuring carbon stocks, CDM regulations and the approval process, best management strategies for sequestration, and consumer demands or market trends. Likewise, government agencies need timely and appropriate information on cultural and social aspects of sequestration, and the environmental and social impacts of existing government policies to form effective regulatory and economic policies.

### Collaboration with International and Religious Institutions

Some Panamanian NGOs have entered into partnerships with international organizations. CEASPA, for example, collaborates with The Nature Conservancy to conduct work in Chagres National Park. Yale

University has collaborated with the Smithsonian Tropical Research Institute to develop and implement PRORENA. However, more collaboration is necessary among other institutions, both laterally (between national NGOs) and vertically (between local and international NGOs). This is particularly important for locating funds for carbon projects, for sharing information, and for lobbying government policy.

In addition, environmental NGOs in Panama might explore collaborations with religious institutions. With a strong religious community throughout the country, both land managers and government agencies are likely to pay close attention to endorsements by Christian organizations. Religious organizations in Panama are concerned about rural development issues, poverty alleviation, and the stewardship of God's creations, including the environment. Enlisting religious organizations into the effort to develop carbon sequestration projects in rural areas may therefore come naturally, and offer a strong and effective alliance.

### Providing an Intermediary Role

One of the major impediments to getting carbon projects off the ground is the lack of an intermediary body that can perform certain functions such as project bundling, monitoring, advertising, and brokering. Ancillary service providers for carbon projects have sprung up around the world (Pagiola et al., 2002), but local NGOs may be in the best position to take on this role due to their knowledge of local environments, politics, and economic frameworks, as well as their existing relationships with local communities and institutions. Panama currently lacks a consortium of local NGOs which could form such an intermediary body, lowering costs to suppliers by pooling small projects together and taking on costly responsibilities.

### Certification of Carbon Credits

As discussed, the voluntary market for carbon credits is small but emerging. In addition to taking on the responsibility of pooling carbon projects, monitoring them, and brokering deals, an intermediary consortium of NGO representatives might also certify carbon credits for a voluntary market, based on specific criteria (Figure 2). Different levels of certification might be granted, based on species (e.g., native vs. exotic), project type (e.g., agroforestry vs. conservation), ownership (e.g., local vs. international), and secondary benefits (e.g., biodiversity protection vs. rural development).

FIGURE 2. Possible Criteria for Certification of Non-Kyoto Compliant Carbon Credits. Projects could be categorized and certified based on management. characteristics, as seen below. This figure reveals the potential for 180 different projects, however certification would likely focus on a small fraction of project types deemed most appropriate for widespread implementation.

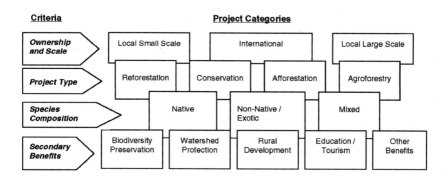

Such a certification system would achieve three main goals. First, it would differentiate products and allow for the introduction of price premiums on certain project types. This could raise the market value of carbon, providing a greater sense of scientifically-backed and independently-verified products. Second, certification might attract funding from international NGOs or multilateral banks. For example, USAID is very interested in watershed protection, and might consider lending or granting funds to carbon projects certified to deliver this secondary benefit. Finally, certification would simultaneously increase supply and demand by providing confidence to both land managers and consumers about the quality, quantity, and definition of the product delivered.

## RECOMMENDED POLICY ALTERNATIVES

Panama has great potential for becoming a leading supplier of carbon sequestration services for the global market. With extensive areas of both primary forest and degraded landscapes, the opportunities for reforestation, afforestation, agroforestry, and forest management sequestration projects are plentiful. Furthermore, institutions at various scales in and around Panama are actively involved in cultivating the supply of carbon services. These include international regulatory frameworks, multilateral banks, national authorities, and local and international NGOs. Finally, demand for carbon credits is rising quickly worldwide, and Panama is currently sitting on Memoranda of Understanding with four countries ready to initiate trade. The potential for meeting this demand by increasing the supply of carbon services in Panama is enormous.

In order to reach this potential, policy mechanisms must be developed and implemented. These policy tools should address three major issues: the costs of sequestering carbon, the availability of information to land managers regarding science and business, and the complexities and uncertainties of the Kyoto regulatory framework. General categorizations of institutions, policy mechanisms, and supplier types have already been discussed (Tables 1-3). After considering the current state of affairs related to relevant institutions, land managers, and sequestration projects, the most feasible options for supporting carbon service suppliers in Panama are consolidated into the five points presented below. These alternatives are assessed on the following bases: cost-effectiveness, political feasibility, delivery of results, and potential for creating long-term changes. When assessing each of these policy options, it is important to remember the three major issues facing suppliers in Panama today: (1) high transaction costs; (2) imperfect information; and (3) lack of institutional support.

### Policy Options for UNFCCC and the CDM Executive Board

- Determine a standardized carbon measurement methodology for CDM projects.
- Simplify the certification process for the issuance of CERs.
- Allow forest management and conservation-based projects to participate in the regulated market.
- Set an agenda for post-2012 climate change abatement and international emissions trading.

The above recommendations get to the heart of one major issue facing suppliers today: institutional support. Ultimately, these policy options aim to: (1) simplify the process of project development and approval; (2) allow the participation of a wider array of potential suppliers; and (3) provide a sense of confidence and security to a currently apprehensive and tentative supply side. These options would require funding for

Conference of the Parties summits and administrative tasks, however such costs should not be prohibitively expensive.

In terms of political feasibility, changes to the regulatory framework set forth in the KP are certainly possible, but are also a sensitive issue that may demand exhaustive negations and bureaucracy. Reaching agreements among various parties with different interests will be challenging, but not infeasible.

Changes to the international regulatory framework administered by the UNFCCC and CDM Executive Board would likely help to increase supply of carbon sequestration services worldwide, and would also likely have long-term positive effects on the global carbon market.

## *Policy Options for Multilateral Funding Institutions*

- Increase levels of direct funding for carbon sequestration projects in general, and, specifically, for Panamanian projects.
- Focus financial support in impoverished and rural areas.
- Provide insurance and risk financing services for carbon sequestration projects.
- Develop a set of criteria by which proposed sequestration projects could be assessed so that such projects can be confidently supported.

Multilateral funding organizations have a critical role to play in addressing two of the supplier's three main concerns: high costs and institutional support. Clearly, such organizations are capable of subsidizing costs to suppliers through soft loans, grants, equity, and other means of financial support. Simultaneously, international financial institutions can foster political and regulatory support for carbon suppliers by financing policy reform and subsidizing legal frameworks at the national level (as IDB did when it financed land tenure reform in Panama).

Developing or strengthening policies to provide funding for carbon sequestration policies is entirely feasible. Carbon service projects in Panama should be attractive to these institutions because of the country's natural potential for large-scale reforestation and forest protection/management ventures. Panama's stable government, growing economy, and business-friendly legal environment should give confidence to international funding organizations.

These alternatives would require significant financing, but they are policy-oriented in nature. Allocating funds to carbon projects is mostly a matter of budgeting and priority shifting among public agencies. These policy changes would likely have direct and tangible results on recipient projects, and have the potential of affecting change throughout the global market by increasing the supply of carbon services.

## Policy Options for International NGOs

- Increase research into carbon sequestration projects and the emerging market for tradable credits.
- Direct publications and information to national governments, local NGOs, and land managers in the developing world.
- Increase active involvement in carbon projects in Panama, e.g., The Nature Conservancy-Panama and Conservation International-Mesoamerica.

International NGOs have a comparative advantage in addressing one major issue in particular that currently impedes the growth of the carbon market: lack of information. International NGOs are veritable warehouses of information, are on the cutting edge of technology, science, and business, and are well-suited to publish and disseminate this information to potential suppliers worldwide.

The cost of the recommendations may be high, particularly for nonprofit organizations; expanding research and effectively disseminating the results require significant capital. However, the political feasibility is high, and as the market continues to grow, it may be in these institutions' interests to lead the wave of scientific advance with regard to carbon measurement, forestry management, and carbon investment and trade.

## Policy Options for Panamanian National Authorities

- Enact new laws providing appropriate economic incentives for reforestation, in general, and, in particular, carbon sequestration (e.g., tax breaks for suppliers and funding institutions).
- Engage in public-private partnerships and joint ventures with carbon sequestration suppliers to provide capital and other non-monetary support (e.g., land, secure property rights, and access to information).
- Attract international funding for policy programs and capacity building.

- Strengthen political will to develop a carbon market and improve interagency relations (e.g., communication and cooperation) to· develop a carbon market, based on shared interests in national economic development, alleviating poverty, improving environmental quality, and attracting foreign investment.

As the leaders of a unique and well-positioned nation, Panamanian elected and appointed officials have a critical role to play in addressing all three of the suppliers' concerns: high costs, lack of information, and institutional support. The government of Panama has a national interest in providing for a domestic supply of carbon sequestration services to meet the growing global demand and it has the opportunity and capacity to do so by approving and implementing appropriate regulatory, informational, and financial policies.

However, such policies will be costly to implement. While it is clear that the fiscal instruments described above can be critically important tools for fostering carbon projects, Panama is not in a financial position to offer tax breaks, subsidize information dissemination, or invest in carbon projects. Thus, these policy mechanisms might be funded with external money, i.e., soft loans and grants from multilateral banks, bilateral aid organizations, or multilateral grant making institutions (e.g., World Bank, USAID, and GEF, respectively). Such funding can also be secured through private international institutions, donors, investors, and multinational corporations. It would be helpful for Panamanian government agencies to work towards attracting aid and investments from international institutions, public and private for this purpose.

The political feasibility of these policy mechanisms is unclear. Many of these issues are very politically sensitive, and the partnerships needed to address these issues may be difficult to forge. However, it is clear that greater political will and cooperation are needed among government agencies in Panama to develop carbon projects that effectively address (or at the very least are in concert with) other national goals and objectives.

Developing the aforementioned policies would likely have direct impacts (in the short and long term) on land managers and carbon services suppliers. This is because bringing down costs, providing information, and offering institutional support to rural and low-income populations while fostering conservation and reforestation can help Panama to achieve other national goals such as poverty alleviation, economic development, rural employment, and the improvement of environmental quality.

## Policy Options for Local and National NGOs

- Concentrate on information dissemination to land managers and government agencies.
- Collaborate with international NGOs and local religious organizations to harness support for carbon projects.
- Take on an intermediary role in pooling small-scale projects, facilitating CDM approval process, marketing projects in the international arena, and monitoring projects.
- Develop a certification process aimed at increasing the supply of carbon credits for trade on the voluntary market.
- Create a national institution, composed of NGO representatives, that takes on the intermediary role and certifies projects for the voluntary market.

Local NGOs are often the heroes of environmental movements and political reforms. These institutions have outstanding capacity to gather and disseminate information to suppliers, especially in rural areas. These organizations can also provide technical and institutional support. If best management practices, business administration skills, and other informational support systems are adopted, suppliers may in fact see their costs go down due to greater efficiency. Should local NGOs partner to pool small projects together or to develop a well-marketed certification process, costs may also fall for suppliers because pooling will offer greater opportunities for market access (in the former case), while certification may stratify products and enable premiums, raising the value of the product (in the latter case).

Realistically, these alternatives are likely to be very costly. Significant capital would be required to realize the last three options in particular. Furthermore, some of these strategies might be politically sensitive, particularly the development of a certification process, due to scientific uncertainties and conflicts of interests among NGOs party to the certifying institute.

The capacity for innovation among local NGOs to develop and implement creative strategies for improving market demand for carbon sequestration services should not be underestimated. The work that has already been done in Panama attests to this.

## CONCLUSION

Panama has great potential to become a leading supplier of carbon sequestration services worldwide. To meet this potential, policy instruments that use regulatory frameworks, economic incentives, information flows, and capacity building strategies might be crafted and implemented to stimulate the supply of carbon services in Panama. Such policy instruments would likely be developed and wielded by institutions at various scales to affect land managers' decisions about entering the carbon market. Potential carbon credit suppliers–large and small, local and international–are currently hesitant to enter a market with such an uncertain future, high costs, and a high degree of complexity at the science, business, and legal levels. Global, national, and local institutions have pivotal roles to play in addressing these issues and fostering the supply of carbon services in Panama.

## REFERENCES

Aukland, L., P. Moura-Costa, and S. Brown. 2003. A Conceptual Framework and Its Application for Addressing Leakage: The Case of Avoided Deforestation. *Climate Policy* 3:123-136.

Bettelheim, E.C. and G. D'Origny. 2002. Carbon Sinks and Emission Trading under the Kyoto Protocol: A Legal Analysis. *Philosophical Transactions of the Royal Society of London* A360:1827-1851.

British Broadcasting Corporation (BBC). 2005. Country Profiles: Panama. Retrieved 28 June 2005 from http://news.bbc.co.uk/1/hi/world/americas/country_profiles/1229332.stm.

Buttazzoni, M. 2003. Creating the Information Infrastructure for Ecosystem Services. In: B. Gentry (ed.). 2005. Emerging Markets for Ecosystem Services: Draft Framework for Analysis (January 9). Yale School of Forestry and Environmental Studies, New Haven, CT.

Conservation Finance Alliance (CFA). 2005. Carbon-offset Projects. The Conservation Finance Guide. Retrieved 20 May 2005 from http://guide.conservationfinance.org/chapter/index.cfm?IndexID=22.

Dixon, R.K., P.E. Schroeder, and J. Winjun (eds). 1994. Assessment of Promising Forest Management Practices and Technologies for Enhancing the Conservation and Sequestration of Atmospheric Carbon and Their Costs at the Site Level. Report of the US Environmental Protection Agency No. EPA/600/3-91/067. Environmental Research Laboratory, Corvallis, Oregon.

Faeth, P., C. Cort, and R. Lvemash. 1994. Evaluating the Carbon Sequestration Benefits of Forestry Projects in Developing Countries. World Resources Institute, Washington, DC.

Ferraro, P. 2000. Constructing Markets for Ecosystem Services: Limitations of Development Intervention and a Role for Conservation Performance Payments. Paper presented at the 8th International Association for the Study of Common Property Conference, Indiana University, Bloomington, IN,

Global Environment Facility (GEF). 1999. Elements for a GEF Operational Program on Carbon Sequestration. GEF/C 13/14.

Global Environment Facility (GEF). 2005. Additional Information to Support the GEF Strategy to Enhance Engagement with the Private Sector. GEF Council. November.

Gomes-Casseres, L. and J. Reamer. 2003. Public-Private Partnerships in Ecosystem Markets. In: B. Gentry (ed.). 2005. Emerging Markets for Ecosystem Services: Draft Framework for Analysis (January 9). Yale School of Forestry and Environmental Studies, New Haven, CT.

Gunningham, N. and M. Young. 1997. Mixing Instruments and Institutional Arrangements for Optimal Biodiversity Conservation. Pp. 141-165 in Organisation for Economic Cooperation and Development (OECD). 1997. *Investing in Biological Diversity: the Cairns Conference.* OECD Proceedings, Paris.

Gunningham, N. and P. Grabosky. 1998. Smart Regulation: Designing Environmental Regulation. Oxford University Press, UK.

Inter-American Development Bank (IDB). 2002. IDB Approves $27 Million Loan for Land Titling in Panama. Retrieved 28 June 2005 from http://www.iadb.org/NEWS/Display/PRView.cfm?PR_Num=229/02&Language=english.

Inter-American Development Bank (IDB). 2005. Responding to Climate Change in Latin America and the Caribbean. Retrieved 28 June 2005 from http://www.iadb.org/NEWS/Display/WSView.cfm?WS_Num=ws02305&Language=English.

Intergovernmental Panel on Climate Change (IPCC). 2001. Summary for Policymakers, Climate Change 2001: Impacts, Adaptation, and Vulnerability. Report of Working Group II, IPCC, Geneva.

Jackson, E. 2005. Torrijos Gets His Tax Increase. Panama News Online 11(6) (Feb 6-19). Retrieved 28 June 2005 from http://www.thepanamanews.com/pn/v_11/issue_03/business_01.html.

Landell-Mills, N. and I.T. Porras. 2002. Silver Bullet or Fool's Gold? A Global Review of Markets for Forest and Environmental Services and Their Impact on the Poor. IIED/Earthscan, London.

Lauterbach, S. 2007. An Assessment of Existing Demand for Carbon Sequestration Services. *Journal of Sustainable Forestry* 25(1/2):75-98.

Moura-Costa, P. and M.D. Stuart. 1998. Forestry-based Greenhouse Gas Mitigation: A Short Story of Market Evolution. *Commonwealth Forestry Review* 77:191-202.

Pagiola, S., J. Bishop, and N. Landell-Mills. 2002. Selling Forest Environmental Services: Market-based Mechanisms for Conservation and Development. Earthscan, London.

Panamadera, S.A. 2003. Panama's Law 24. Retrieved 28 June 2005 from http://www.panamadera.com/law_24.htm.

Panayotou, T. 1993. Green Markets: The Economics of Sustainable Development. International Center for Economic Growth, San Francisco.

Richards K.R. and C. Stokes. 2004. A Review of Forest Carbon Sequestration Cost Studies: A Dozen Years of Research. *Climatic Change* 68:1-48.

Sabine, C.L., M. Heimann, P. Artaxo, D.C.E. Bakker, C.T.A. Chen, C.B. Field, N. Gruber, C. Le Quere, R.G. Prinn, J.E. Richey, P. Romero Lankao, J.A. Sathaye, and R. Valentini. 2004. Current Status and Past Trends of the Global Carbon Cycle. Pp. 17-44 in: C.B. Field and M.R. Raupauch (eds.). 2004. The Global Carbon Cycle. Integrating Humans, Climate and the Natural World. Island Press, Washington, DC.

United States Agency for International Development (USAID). 2005. Sustainable Land Use and Forestry. Retrieved 28 June 2005 from http://www.usaid.gov/our_work/environment/climate/policies_prog/carbon_overview.html.

World Bank. 2004. Carbon Finance at the World Bank. Retrieved 3/28/05 from http://www.prototypecarbonfund.org.

Yohannes, D. and I. Angeletti. 2003. Using Policy Tools to Promote the Market for Ecosystem Services. In: B. Gentry (ed.). 2005. Emerging Markets for Ecosystem Services: Draft Framework for Analysis (January 9). Yale School of Forestry and Environmental Studies, New Haven, CT.

doi:10.1300/J091v25n01_03

# CARBON DEMAND

# An Assessment of Existing Demand for Carbon Sequestration Services

Sandra Lauterbach

**SUMMARY.** The market for carbon sequestration services is developing rapidly. The objective of this paper is to analyze existing market demand for carbon credits and review existing institutions supporting demand generation. Existing carbon demand is driven primarily by regulated, and to a lesser extent, non-regulated or voluntary markets. While regulated carbon markets are potentially large and driven by the Kyoto Protocol, the challenge for a forestry-based carbon project in Panama is its ability to meet CDM regulated constraints. The challenge in non-regulated carbon markets is identifying potential consumers in an extremely fragmented market. While there is significant demand for carbon credits, meeting demand for carbon credits in the regulated and voluntary markets from forestry-based carbon sequestration projects will remain a challenge. Landowners may have options to pursue these

Sandra Lauterbach graduated from the Yale School of Forestry and Environmental Studies, New Haven, CT 06511 USA, with a Master of Environmental Management. Ms. Lauterbach is currently the Vice-President of The Climate Investment Network for Carbon Sequestration and Biomass Energy (CINCS) (E-mail: Sandra.Lauterbach@ aya.yale.edu).

[Haworth co-indexing entry note]: "An Assessment of Existing Demand for Carbon Sequestration Services." Lauterbach, Sandra. Co-published simultaneously in *Journal of Sustainable Forestry* (Haworth Food & Agricultural Products Press, an imprint of The Haworth Press, Inc.) Vol. 25, No. 1/2, 2007, pp. 75-98; and: *Emerging Markets for Ecosystem Services: A Case Study of the Panama Canal Watershed* (ed: Bradford S. Gentry, Quint Newcomer, Shimon C. Anisfeld, and Michael A. Fotos, III) Haworth Food & Agricultural Products Press, an imprint of The Haworth Press, Inc., 2007, pp. 75-98. Single or multiple copies of this article are available for a fee from The Haworth Document Delivery Service [1-800-HAWORTH, 9:00 a.m. - 5:00 p.m. (EST). E-mail address: docdelivery@haworthpress.com].

Available online at http://jsf.haworthpress.com
© 2007 by The Haworth Press, Inc. All rights reserved.
doi:10.1300/J091v25n01_04

markets; however, reforestation and afforestation project profitability and viability will be dependent on how carbon markets evolve. Current political and institutional infrastructures in Panama do not concentrate on building international demand for forestry-based carbon credits. As a result, there may be immediate opportunities for Panama to develop institutions and policies for growing carbon market demand, while supporting carbon credit supply. doi:10.1300/J091v25n01_04 *[Article copies available for a fee from The Haworth Document Delivery Service: 1-800-HAWORTH. E-mail address: <docdelivery@haworthpress.com> Website: <http://www.HaworthPress.com> © 2007 by The Haworth Press, Inc. All rights reserved.]*

**KEYWORDS.** Carbon sequestration, Panama Canal Watershed, ecosystem services

## INTRODUCTION

As a result of the increasing prominence of the role of greenhouse gas (GHG) emissions in climate change, governments and industry are beginning to reduce GHG emissions using regulatory and voluntary initiatives (World Bank, 2004). Emissions reductions are being achieved not only by pollution control technologies and efficiencies, but also through market trading and purchasing of carbon offsets. Carbon sequestration projects provide offsets for emissions reductions and range from underground storage to forest-based carbon sequestration projects. This paper will analyze the potential for forestry-based carbon sequestration projects in Panama based on existing carbon market demand. Reviewing market segments, carbon products, pricing, competitors, international and local infrastructures and risks will provide a basis for understanding the financial feasibility of forestry-based carbon projects in the current environment.

## ANALYSIS FRAMEWORK AND METHODOLOGY

Analyzing existing demand for carbon sequestration services in Panama requires a systematic approach to assessing demand drivers. Table 1 illustrates a summary view of the areas of inquiry, the analytical process steps and the questions and data required to assess existing demand. Based on this analysis, several landowner options can be identified and the feasibility of these options can be evaluated. The remainder of this paper will focus on analyzing each area of inquiry.

TABLE 1. Analytical Process for Assessing Existing Carbon Sequestration Service Demand

| Area of Inquiry | Process Steps | Questions | Data Required |
|---|---|---|---|
| Market Overview: Market Segments, Drivers, Market Size | Identify potential consumers and market drivers | Segment and analyze consumers<br>What are the characteristics of these buyers?<br>What are the market trends? | Size market segments<br>Consumer segments, segment description, overall market size, market segments size, trends, number of trades, growth, etc. |
| Products and Pricing | Identify potential products (based on consumer needs)<br>Review current product pricing | What are potential products that can be sold based on consumer needs and supply? | Description of product types, constraints, product pricing |
| Competitors | Identify potential competitors | Are there similar products/services? How do these products work?<br>Who else is providing these services? What is their performance? | Description of competitive projects |
| Transactions | Analyze transaction/distribution channels (e.g., intermediaries, bilateral exchanges) | How can these products be distributed? What are the exchanges that take place? | Description of distribution/trade types, description of intermediaries |
| Infrastructure | Identify existing supporting infrastructure (e.g., government, NGO, policies, regulations) | What are the existing infrastructure and policies that can support products? | Description of existing policies on international, national, local levels that support market for these products |
| Land Owner Options: Feasibility and Risk | Analyze financial feasibility: potential revenue and costs of providing these services | Are these options financially feasible? What are the risks associated with these options? How might risks be mitigated? | Costs of transaction, pricing, volume, timing of demand |
| Conclusions and Recommendations | What options are most attractive? | Prioritize and screen options: screening based on markets, risks, financial feasibility<br>Make recommendations to land owners | N/A |

## MARKET ANALYSIS

### *Market Segments*

There is no single market for carbon sequestration services as the market is complex and changing rapidly. At a basic level, consumers of carbon sequestration services are entities that need or want to purchase carbon credits to offset greenhouse gas emissions. Buyers include industry, governments, non-governmental organizations (NGOs), and individuals. There are a number of ways in which analysts have segmented the carbon demand market. This analysis will focus on the segmentation between regulated and non-regulated markets, as this is most relevant to forestry-based carbon projects in Panama. Regulated markets are supported by existing or proposed governmental requirements, while non-regulated markets are those that rely less (or not at all) on government involvement or regulation.

While this analysis focuses on segmentation based on regulations, it is also worth noting the segmentation between high-volume trading and project-based markets. High-volume trading has high liquidity and involves many actors. Project-based trading involves a limited number of actors, following a more bilateral approach. Prior to Kyoto ratification, project-based trading was dominant. However, the ratification of Kyoto and the entry into force of the EU Emissions Trading System (ETS) has helped high-volume trading to grow. (The uniformity of the emission allowances issued by governments as part of the EU ETS also facilitates more high-volume trading than is seen by the credits generated across a range of different projects in different locations.) Despite this, in the short-term, high-volume trading markets are not viable for forestry carbon projects in Panama, as many of these high-volume platforms do not trade forestry or Clean Development Mechanism (CDM) credits. For example, the EU ETS includes a linking directive that allows for CDM projects to be traded, but does not currently support forestry-based carbon credits projects. It has been argued that the EU has disregarded forestry credits based on the scientific uncertainty and increased risks of these projects (Burge, 2005). It is important to note that there are many critics of the EU ETS' policies against forestry-based credits. As many impoverished countries have limited resources, forestry-based projects are seen as one of the few viable ways for these countries to participate in the carbon market (Burge, 2005). The European Carbon Exchange (ECX) predicts that it will be 2008 before CDM credits are traded (ECX, 2005). While these restrictions may change, in the short-term, high-volume trading markets are likely not to be viable for forestry-based carbon projects in Panama. The focus, then, is on project-based trading in regulated and non-regulated markets.

*Regulated Markets.* The Kyoto Protocol is the most prominent regulation driving carbon credit demand. As a market driver, Kyoto is well documented. However, because it is the most influential market driver, it is important to review briefly Kyoto's relevance to potential projects in Panama, and consider how regulation is evolving. The Kyoto Protocol was signed in 1997. Following Russia's ratification in October 2004, its requirements entered into force on February 16, 2005. As of June 2005, 150 nations or other entities have ratified the Protocol, with 38 industrialized countries agreeing to reduce GHG emissions. The US and Australia have notably not ratified Kyoto and have no near-term plans to do so. The Kyoto Protocol requires industrialized countries that have ratified it to reduce emissions by an average of 5.2 percent below 1990 levels. Each country has targets for the initial commitment period, from 2008 to 2012. Moreover, each country is responsible for determining how best to achieve its emissions reductions commitments–either by reducing emissions within its own borders or by purchasing emission reductions from other countries.

Market-mechanisms exist under Kyoto to facilitate greenhouse gas (GHG) trading. Trading mechanisms have been successful in reducing other uniformly distributed pollutants, such as sulfur dioxide ($SO_2$) in the US market (Saxton, 1997). The adoption of trading under the Kyoto Protocol is intended to enable cost-effective GHG reductions, allowing lower cost offsets to be purchased by emitters (Conservation Finance, 2005). Among the market mechanisms are Joint Implementation (JI) and the Clean Development Mechanism (CDM) authorized under Articles 6 and 12 of the Kyoto Protocol, respectively. JI allows Annex B (or industrialized) countries to reduce GHGs by purchasing Emission Reductions Units (ERUs) generated from projects located in other Annex B countries. The CDM allows emitters to purchase offsets from projects in non-Annex B countries by purchasing Certified Emissions Reductions (CERs) (Conservation Finance, 2005).

Panama is a non-Annex B country, and any carbon sequestration project would be considered under the CDM. CDM projects have two purposes: (1) to help industrialized countries meet emissions reductions targets cost effectively, and (2) to help developing countries better achieve sustainable development (GreenStream Network, 2004). In the context of Panama, CDM projects would need not only to ensure the reduction of GHGs, but also to address local sustainable development issues. This will be discussed in more detail below.

While approved CDM methodologies (a list of CDM Executive Board approved methodologies can be found at: http://cdm.unfccc.int/methodologies/PAmethodologies/approved.html) include projects for incineration of hydrofluorocarbon waste streams, landfill gas capture, biomass energy generation and renewable energy electricity production, the methodologies that are most relevant for this analysis are those for LULUCF (land use, land use change and forestry) projects (UNFCCC, 2005b). All CDM methodologies require approval by the CDM Executive Board (CDM EB), the group responsible for managing the CDM process and approving projects under the United Nations Framework Convention on Climate Change (UNFCCC) (UNFCCC, 2005d). The first CDM methodologies were approved in 2003. However, while several LULUCF projects are being proposed and reviewed, as of January 2006 only one LULUCF project had been approved, while nine had been rejected and eight were under consideration (UNFCCC, 2005a).

Contributing to the delay in generating carbon credits from LULUCF projects has been significant controversy over whether the CDM should include LULUCF projects at all. Reviewing these arguments briefly is helpful in understanding constraints placed on the CDM CER market. Arguments against forestry projects under Kyoto include: transience–the fact that sequestration may be temporary and uncontrollable over time; uncertainty–the difficulties in accurately estimating the carbon storage; biodiversity–the concern that some land use options, such as monoculture plantations, may sequester carbon, but may not contribute to increased biodiversity; and finally, land rights–concern that people reliant on forests may be displaced (Climate Action Network, 2005). Despite these arguments against forestry credits, afforestation and reforestation projects are allowable CDM options under Kyoto. These will be discussed in more detail below.

Who are the consumers in the regulated market? Prior to the Kyoto Protocol coming into force, the largest carbon credit consumers were private Japanese companies, which accounted for 41 percent of the 2003 to 2004 volume (World Bank, 2004). For the same time period, the Netherlands was the second largest buyer. The Carbon Finance Group of the World Bank, including the BioCarbon Fund (BCF), Prototype Carbon Fund, and Community Development Fund, was the third largest buyer. These consumers represented approximately 88 percent of the market from 2003 to 2004 (World Bank, 2004). In terms of CDM consumers overall, the largest buyers at this time were private consumers (accounting for 57 percent of the market) versus public (24 percent of the market) or private-public partnerships (18 percent of the market) consumers (World Bank, 2004).

Looking specifically at the potential demand from the three largest consumers, it is evident that while Japan is one of the biggest carbon buyers, one of the challenges for carbon projects in Panama will be Japan's focus on Asia. Japan's focus on CERs generated in other Asian countries can provide advantages in proximity and experience in the area (Dhakal, 2001). Given that China and India are expected to be major sources of CDM credits, there is an understanding that Japan is likely to buy credits primarily from these countries for efficiency and other reasons (Dhakal, 2001).

The World Bank BioCarbon Fund has the goal of investing in LULUCF projects. However, the BCF has already selected participants for its current round of funding. As of December 2004, the BCF was no longer accepting additional projects (BCF, 2004a). Therefore, there will be challenges in having new carbon projects from Panama accepted by the BCF in the short-term.

The Netherlands potentially could be an attractive buyer. In 2001, Panama signed an MOU with the Netherlands, which aims at transferring 20million $tCO_2e$ by 2012 (Netherlands Government, 2001). This commitment is project dependent, and the Dutch government has signed additional commitments with other Central and South American countries including Uruguay, Costa Rica and Colombia. Overall the Dutch government has been a large carbon credits purchaser, with US$250 million targeted for carbon investment (Collins, 2003). The Dutch government provides funds to purchase CERs through its Certified Emissions Reduction Unit Procurement Tender (CERUPT) (FIELD, 2005). This mechanism allowed the Dutch government to fund several energy projects in Panama (Reyes, 2005). However, in early 2005 the Dutch government announced a reduction in its CER purchases (GTZ, 2005). Analysts predict this may negatively impact CER demand (GTZ, 2005). Therefore, while there is substantial opportunity to sell carbon credits to the Netherlands, the challenge will be to understand how this buyer is planning to move forward with its CER purchases.

Another opportunity for generating demand under Kyoto in Panama lies within the Memoranda of Understanding (MOUs) signed with other countries. To date, Panama has also signed MOUs with Canada, Italy and Spain (Reyes, 2005). While the MOUs differ, by signing these agreements, Panama may be able leverage these relationships and build demand for carbon credits sourced from within its borders.

Kyoto is the primary driver in the regulated carbon market. However given that the US is the largest total emitter of carbon and the largest per capita emitter, a brief review of US regulated demand is necessary. Not ratifying Kyoto has stalled efforts to manage climate change at the US federal level. The McCain-Lieberman Climate Stewardship Act aims to reduce national emissions and establish a market for emissions by capping emissions at 2000 levels by 2010. While this act was previously defeated, it was reintroduced in March 2005 (Griscom, 2005). The program would allow emitters to purchase offsets from carbon sequestration projects, which could account for up to 15 percent of an emitter's target (NRDC, 2005). However given uncertainty regarding US climate change policy, US federal regulations will likely play a minimal role in driving demand for carbon sequestration projects in Panama in the near-term.

In terms of US states, while more states are passing regulations regarding climate change, many states do not currently include forestry-based projects as an option (Shinkle, 2005). One exception is Oregon, which has capped emissions from new facilities. Through the Climate Trust, a non-profit organization, Oregon allows new emitters to purchase carbon credits that can include forest-based carbon sequestration projects (WRI, 2003; Climate Trust, 2005). One project is based in Ecuador, indicating that a project in Panama may be viable. In addition, in December 2005, seven northeast US states passed a Regional Greenhouse Gas Initiative (RGGI) that included the potential for offset allowances from forestry projects; however, initially these offsets are limited to projects in the United States. As such, it appears that existing US state demand for forestry-based credits generated in developing countries is relatively minimal.

*Non-Regulated/Voluntary Markets.* Non-regulated markets are ones in which greenhouse gas emitters seek to reduce emissions for reasons other than meeting regulatory requirements. These markets may also be called voluntary, as participation is not mandated. Emissions reductions in the voluntary market are called verified emissions reductions (VERs). There are several reasons that an emitter may undertake voluntary reductions. Prior to 2005, the primary reason consumers purchased credits was to prepare for Kyoto. Consumers currently purchase VERs to: improve company reputation; demonstrate corporate responsibility and social commitment; obtain favorable reactions from the press, shareholders and customers; and gain knowledge of carbon markets and experience in trading (GreenStream Network, 2004). Growth in this market is largely driven by the voluntary commitments made by a few key companies, such as Entergy and Dupont (Zaborowsky and Reamer, 2004).

Voluntary consumers can be corporations, NGOs, universities and even individuals (World Bank, 2004). In terms of corporate voluntary emissions reductions commitments, few are legally binding. Chicago Climate Exchange (CCX), a voluntary exchange where members agree to reduce emissions, is one exception to this rule (Zaborowsky and Reamer, 2004). Yet, while CCX allows some forestry-based carbon sequestration projects, it currently does not include many non-US forestry projects (CCX, 2005a). This may limit its potential as a trading platform for credits from a project in Panama.

As the voluntary market follows several different models, to understand consumers it is helpful to look at several specific cases. For example, the Pew Center's Business Environmental Leadership Council (BELC) is a group of companies that have agreed to voluntary reductions. Examples include ABB, Alcoa, Intel, Lockheed Martin, and American Electric Power. Trading is allowed for companies to meet targets; however, most companies are meeting targets by improving the efficiency of their energy use, rather than by buying credits (Pew Center, 2005). Models like this would limit demand for carbon credits, if carbon credits were even considered an option at all. The World Wildlife Fund's Climate Savers Initiative is similar to the Pew Program. Climate Savers works with companies such as IBM, Nike and Polaroid that agree to voluntary reductions, which can be offset with the purchase of renewable energy credits or through implementation of energy efficiency programs (WWF, 2005). To date, this program has not been expanded to include carbon sequestration land use credits.

Another market limitation may be organizations that are focused on US-based carbon credits. One example is Pacific Forest Trust. Through the Forest Forever Fund, Pacific Forest Trust sells carbon credits to energy companies, such as Green Mountain Energy, from private forestland in the Pacific Northwest. While this model may be expanded in the future, currently the US focus would limit demand for carbon credits from Panama.

An additional example is Climate Care, a UK based company, which sells offsets to non-regulated emitters. Climate Care calculates emissions for organizations, companies or individuals and then sells carbon offsets. Revenues are used to fund energy efficiency, renewable energy and forestry projects (Climate Care, 2005).

As the voluntary market is very fragmented, with many different types of consumers and models, one difficulty is identifying potential target consumers. Market fragmentation will result in increased marketing dollars spent to identify and attract these consumers.

## Market Size

Greenhouse gas credits are traded in a uniform commodity specified as a ton of carbon dioxide equivalent or $tCO_2e$. All greenhouse gas reductions or removals are translated into this standard measurement for the purposes of trading. Given uncertainty regarding estimates of the overall carbon market size, it is difficult to estimate CDM market size within the overall carbon market and the forestry-based CDM segment within the CDM market. One estimate suggested that the carbon market was approximately 12million $tCO_2e$ in 2001, 27million tCO2e in 2002 and 70million $tCO_2e$ 2003, representing substantial growth over three years (Vayrynen, 2004). Estimates from the World Bank suggested that the CDM market was approximately 82 million $tCO_2e$ from 2003-2004, representing even larger growth. From 2003 to 2004, it was estimated that LULUCF projects were 4 percent of the total emissions reductions market (World Bank, 2004). Assuming that LULUCF projects could maintain approximately 4 percent of the carbon market, a fair, albeit rough, estimate may place the market size for all LULUCF projects at 6 million $tCO_2e$ per year. The market size for carbon LULUCF projects will be heavily dependent on project approvals which will be discussed in detail below.

In terms of carbon market growth, total estimates of the potential market vary. Some projections estimate that the carbon market could be in the low tens of billions of dollars by 2012, while other estimates predict the market could be as high as $100 billion or even $1 trillion (Conservation Finance, 2005). Predictions forecast that CDM CERs will be approximately 250 million $tCO_2e$, with a range of 50 million $tCO_2e$ to 500 million $tCO_2e$ in 2010 (Haites, 2004). There is minimal information on the growth of LULUCF CER market. However, because LULUCF carbon credits can only account 1 percent of base year commitment under the Marrakesh Accords, there is currently a limit on the potential growth of the regulated market (UNFCCC, 2005g). A more immediate driver of how quickly the LULUCF CER market will grow will be the timing of CDM methodology approval.

The non-regulated, VER market is predicted to be much smaller than the regulated markets. The market is fragmented with light volumes (Evolution Markets, 2004). One source estimated a mere 200 VER trades from 1993 to 2003 (Collins, 2003). While actual volume may be higher (as many trades are unreported), it is evident that the VER market will be smaller than the regulated market (Collins, 2003). Future market growth may be hindered by an increased focus on regulated markets. One source predicts a drop in market volume for VERs after 2008 and the implementation of Kyoto (Zaborowsky and Reamer, 2004).

### Forest-Based Carbon Sequestration Products and Pricing

*Product.* The product in the regulated carbon market is the carbon credit. A carbon credit is equal to 1 $tCO_2$ equivalent ($tCO_2e$), where 1 $tCO_2e$ equals 0.272 tons of carbon (International Carbon Bank Exchange, 2005). Other GHGs have different conversion rates based on their global warming potential (GWP). Relevant to a project in Panama under Kyoto, forestry-based carbon credits in developing countries are eligible as CERs (Certified Emission Reductions). One CER equals one carbon credit.

In terms of carbon accounting, several concepts are important to assess potential carbon projects in Panama. Currently only afforestation and reforestation credits are accepted under CDM. The definition of afforestation under Kyoto is conversion of land that has not been forested for 50 years, while reforestation is conversion of non-forested land to forested land (Natural Resources Canada, 2004). Reforested land must have been established since January 1, 1990 on land that was previously deforested. Forest management or deferred deforestation projects are not currently included under CDM. To participate in the Kyoto market, a carbon sequestration project in Panama must adhere to afforestation and reforestation definitions and cannot include managed forests projects.

Article 12 of the Kyoto Protocol requires that a project must be "real, measurable and additional" (Figueres, 2002:24). Kyoto provides constraints to ensure these goals are met. The constraints include additionality, permanence, leakage and monitoring and verification. Additionality requires that projects demonstrate that carbon offsets are "additional to any that would otherwise occur" and "additional to any that would occur in the absence of the certified project activity" (Conservation Finance, 2005:1). Additionality requires setting a project baseline, which is established based on approved methodologies (Figueres, 2002). It is important to note that baseline setting has been controversial and has followed several different methodologies. The UNFCCC defines assumptions required for additionality in terms of financial additionality and rates of return for CER-generating projects, as well as emissions reductions (UNFCCC, 2005i). (The UNFCCC website provides a draft additionality tool for afforestation and reforestation to determine if a project is additional at http://cdm.unfccc.int/Panels/ar/ARWG04_Annex1_AR_Additionality_Tool.pdf.)

The goal of permanence is to ensure the long-term viability of the carbon credits. Given that there are inherent risks of carbon sequestration, such as if forests are damaged or cut, specific carbon credits have been designed to address these risks (BCF, 2004b). Developed under COP9, temporary certified emissions reductions (tCERs) are one option that expire after five years, but can be renewed if agreed upon (BCF, 2004b). Long-term CERs, or lCERs, extend this option to 20 to 30 years (BCF, 2004b). tCERs and lCERs need to be monitored every five years with the intention of transitioning these to permanent CERs by year 60 (BCF, 2004b).

Leakage is another important concept. Leakage requires that projects demonstrate that they do not shift the carbon burden to other sites. For example, if a reforestation effort requires fertilizer or if it forces land use activity to deforest in another area, this must be accounted for in the project methodology. Finally, monitoring and verification require that projects have plans to measure carbon credits for the duration of the project (Conservation Finance, 2005).

VERs are more difficult to define than CERs. While some may be Kyoto compliant, many differ from a typical CER and the market lacks uniformity. VER quality can vary by project; therefore, there is a perceived higher risk associated with these products potentially impacting pricing (Zaborowsky and Reamer, 2004). VER variability can be driven by the project type as well as the baseline and validation methodologies (Zaborowsky and Reamer, 2004). The tradeoff that may exist is that Kyoto driven markets have substantial carbon credit constraints, while the flexibility and lack of uniformity in VERs may make navigating this market more difficult.

*Price.* Carbon credit prices drive project revenue and are measured in tons of $CO_2e$. There is significant lack of clarity regarding project-based carbon credit pricing based on lack of information, supply uncertainty, demand uncertainty, lack of a heterogeneous asset, delivery risk, timing and contract duration (WRI, 2003). The World Bank estimates the cost of reducing one ton of carbon to be between $15 and $100 (World Bank, 2004). While in terms of averted costs, emitters may buy carbon credits up to this amount; current CDM carbon prices are well below this.

Prices vary by transaction, market segment and quality of the credit. 2003 Pre-compliance prices per metric ton of $CO_2e$ ranged from \$2 to \$6.50 (Vayrynen, 2004). CDM prices per ton are predicted to be lower than other carbon credits in a range of \$2.50 and 4.00 (World Bank, 2004; Haites, 2004). Given market uncertainty, predicting prices for CDM forestry-based projects is difficult; therefore, this analysis uses an estimate of between \$2.50 and \$4.00. To contrast, the EU ETS carbon credits began trading at US\$10.40/t$CO_2e$ in January 2005. As of August 2005, the price for a ton of carbon dioxide equivalent was EU23.30 or US\$28.48.

The prices of VERs in non-regulated markets vary significantly because carbon buyers are not obligated to make purchases. While there may be higher prices for specific VERs, estimated prices of VERs are generally lower than CERs (World Bank, 2004). While some analysts have predicted a price of between \$.50 and \$2.50 per ton of $CO_2$ in the voluntary markets, as of June 2005, the CCX Carbon Financial Instrument (CFI) was trading for \$1.30 (Zaborowsky and Reamer, 2004; CCX, 2005b). The CFI is equivalent to 100 metric tons of $CO_2$. Therefore, while carbon products in a regulated market may have greater market constraints, carbon prices are lower in non-regulated markets.

### Competitor Carbon Project

Geographically, sellers of JI and CDM products have been primarily in Asia (51 percent), Latin America (27 percent), OECD countries (10 percent), and transitioning economies and Africa (12 percent) (World Bank, 2004). China is host to the only approved A/R CDM methodology to date. As of January 2006, there are eight additional CDM forestry methodologies under consideration. These include afforestation and reforestation projects in Brazil, Belize, Albania, Mexico and Moldova (UNFCCC, 2005c).

Energy CDM projects in Panama have progressed and three Panamanian energy projects have been registered as of January 2006. Clearly, while existing institutional structures under Kyoto may support CDM energy projects in Panama, the focus has not been on potential CDM forestry projects. One study referenced six potential CDM forestry projects in Panama (see Table 2), including four reforestation projects, one agroforestry project and one cultivated forestry project (Sempris, 2002). Interviews in Panama have demonstrated interest from private companies such as EcoForest and Futuro Forestal to sell carbon credits (Eke, personal communication 10 March 2005; Verjans, personal

TABLE 2. Panamanian Forestry-Based CDM Projects (Sempris, 2002)

| Project Location | Promoter | Project Type | Surface (ha) | Status |
|---|---|---|---|---|
| Chucunaque River | Dobboyala Foundation | Reforestation | 6,000 | Project Idea |
| Cerro Patacón | Mayor of Panama City | Reforestation | 15 | Project Idea |
| Chiriquí | AES Panama | Reforestation | 1,250 | Project Idea |
| El Cope National Park | San Felix | Agroforestry | N/A | Project Idea |
| Bayano | AES Panama | Reforestation | 200 | Project Idea |
| Asore | Veraquas Reforester's Association | Cultivated Hardwoods | 1,000 | Project Idea |

communication, 10 March 2005). However, these projects all remain in the idea phase. Only one project has moved beyond idea to design, having received a "Letter of No Objection" from the National Environment Authority (ANAM) (Salena, personal communication, 8 March 2005). This project is a proposal by Prime Forestry, a Panamanian subsidiary of a Swiss company, for several teak plantations in Panama to sell carbon credits (Prime Forestry, 2005). As is evident, there is some interest toward establishing CDM forestry projects, but this remains at a very nascent stage.

### Transaction Processes and Costs

Analyzing the transaction process and costs provides an assessment of whether market demand can be met efficiently. As established, there is demand for carbon credits; however, project feasibility is dependent on how efficiently credits reach the market. Project costs can be divided into initial investment and ongoing forestry costs, and initial and ongoing transaction costs. Initial forestry investment and ongoing forestry maintenance costs are assessed by Grossman (this volume) in his review of existing carbon supply. Initial transaction costs and ongoing transaction costs refer to costs associated with obtaining approvals in the regulated market, as well as design, monitoring and validation costs for regulated and non-regulated markets.

How is a CDM CER sold as a carbon credit? For the most part, the CDM approval process defines the transaction process in the regulated market. While different sources define the process steps slightly differently, the major process steps involved in obtaining approval include developing a project idea note (PIN) and project design document

(PDD), obtaining host government approval, evaluating and registering the project, implementing the project, as well as conducting ongoing monitoring, reporting and verification of a project (500PPM, 2004). Credits are required to be approved by the CDM EB. The time required for project approval can vary depending on the project type, novelty, size, and complexity (World Bank, 2005). A voluntary project would follow similar steps, but some steps such as project registration are not required (500PPM, 2004).

The project size impacts transaction costs. Small-scale projects, sequestering less than 8 kilotonnes of $CO_2e$ per year, can go through simplified CDM EB approval under rules approved at COP10. The fixed transaction costs for simplified projects are estimated to be between $8,000 and $80,000 versus $100,000 to $1.1 million for larger projects (Haites, 2004). Interviews in Panama indicated that the costs of developing a project to meet regulatory requirements were estimated to be from $200,000 to $500,000 (Verjans, personal communication, 10 March 2005).

Table 3 demonstrates costs estimates by process step for regulated and non-regulated market projects. This analysis demonstrates that there are significant differences in transaction costs. Regulated markets have substantially higher initial costs than non-regulated markets. This analysis does not account for higher marketing costs in non-regulated markets associated with identifying carbon credit buyers, as data in the non-regulated market is limited. However, even including marketing costs in the non-regulated market, it is likely that the transaction costs in regulated market will be significantly higher. Ongoing transaction costs in both the regulated and non-regulated markets are similar.

In addition, while there is evidence that there is a market for smaller projects, some sources suggest that projects producing too small quantities will not be competitive because fixed costs are too high (Haites, 2004). If transactions costs are too high for small projects, aggregation of supply to share fixed costs may be an option.

## *Infrastructure and Policy*

At an international level, Kyoto regulatory policy and infrastructure drives demand. The primary drivers behind CDM demand include the CDM Executive Board (CDM EB), Conference of Parties (COP), and the Designated Operational Entities (DOEs) (Mansour and Elewa, 2004). As discussed above, the CDM EB is tasked with the CDM methodology approval process. The CDM EB is also responsible for ensuring that the

TABLE 3. Transaction Costs by Process Step for Regulated and Non-Regulated Markets (adapted from 500PPM, 2004)

| Process Step | Regulated Market–Low Estimate ($000) | Regulated Market–High Estimate ($000) | Non-Regulated Market–Low Estimate ($000) | Non-Regulated Market–High Estimate ($000) |
|---|---|---|---|---|
| Project Design Document | 9 | 52 | 3 | 4 |
| Government Approval | 6 | 19 | 0 | 1 |
| Project Evaluation | 9 | 39 | 3 | 4 |
| Project Registration | 6 | 39 | 0 | 0 |
| Implementation and Monitoring | 4 | 19 | 4 | 6 |
| Reporting and Verification | 5 | 19 | 0[1] | 0 |
| Certification and Credit Issuance | 0 | 0 | 0 | 0 |
| Total Initial Investment | 39 | 187 | 12[2] | 13 |
| Per Year Costs | 5 | 19 | 4 | 6 |

Assumptions:

- 1 Euro = $1.3US
- Non-regulated annual costs include monitoring. Regulated annual costs include reporting and verification

[1] While some sources suggest that the costs of reporting and verification will be non-existent for the non-regulated market, it is likely that some verification activities will be required to ensure that reductions are being met.

[2] Transaction costs for non-regulated markets would also need to include costs associated with marketing carbon credits to attract voluntary buyers. Given limited data in the non-regulated market, such costs are difficult to estimate.

process is efficient and transparent (UNFCCC, 2005d). Despite this goal, there exists a perception that the CDM EB and is underfunded for its mission and potentially bureaucratic (IETA, 2004; Mansour and Elewa, 2004).

The COP defines the nature and scope of CDM mechanisms and publishes guidance and procedures for the CDM EB (UNFCCC, 2005e). The DOEs support credit demand by registering projects, validating emissions reductions and certifying projects where necessary (Mansour and Elewa, 2004). DOEs include companies such as SGS and Det Norske Veritas. In addition, the CDM Methodology Panel supports demand by reviewing methodologies for reductions and establishing baseline processes (UNFCCC, 2005h). These organizations function to support supply and demand in the regulated market.

In the non-regulated markets, there are no large international institutions overseeing projects or the issuance of credits. In terms of infrastructure, the non-regulated market has several NGOs, such as Climate Trust, that may act as aggregators; however, no one organization or institution drives demand in this area. Key roles as market makers are also played by brokers such as Natsource and Evolution Markets.

Within Panama, current policies and institutions to support demand for forest-based carbon credits are minimal. As is evidenced in Table 4, the majority of the demand generation is at the international level. ANAM plays a potentially important role in driving demand as the Designated National Authority (DNA). As the DNA, ANAM is responsible for managing host country project oversight, approving project participation and ensuring that projects help increase sustainable development (UNFCCC, 2005f). ANAM has also signed MOUs with several countries (as described above), and provided preliminary approval for one forestry-based carbon project (Salena, personal communication, 8 March 2005).

While these efforts are important, existing institutions could be more effective at driving demand for forestry-based projects and potentially play a greater role in sustainable development activities. As outlined in the CDM goals, sustainable development is an essential component of CDM projects. Based on interviews, it appears that there is some focus, albeit minimal, on the sustainable development aspect of forestry-projects from NGOs (Pizarro, personal communication, 8 March 2005). It has been argued that the relative lack of approved CDM methodologies for forestry projects and exclusion of LULUCF projects in the EU ETS greatly limits the potential for these projects to contribute to sustainable development and poverty alleviation. A number of researchers have linked the ability to sell carbon credits from reforestation efforts with the potential to reduce poverty (Burge, 2005). However, market limitations will need to be addressed before these projects can contribute to sustainable development. Center for Panama Social Studies and Action (CEASPA), a Panamanian non-governmental organization, is aggregating groups of small landholders to implement better agro-forestry practices; however, the organization's focus is not on aggregation for the purposes of supporting carbon credit demand. Table 4 summarizes the international and Panamanian institutions and the current role they play in supporting demand and supply. It is clear that there may be an opportunity for more Panamanian governmental and institutional

TABLE 4. Institutions and Carbon Roles and Activities

| Institutions / Carbon Roles & Activities | Supply Activities | | Demand Activities | | | | | | | | |
|---|---|---|---|---|---|---|---|---|---|---|---|
| | Scientific Research | Scientific Translation | Project Financing | Project Assessment | Project Development | Landowner Aggregation | Contracting/Legal | Marketing | Monitoring/Verifying | Regulatory Support | Sustainable Dev't. Support |
| **Academic Institutions** | | | | | | | | | | | |
| STRI | ▓ | | | | | | | | | | |
| Panamanian Universities | | | | | | | | | | | |
| **NGOs** | | | | | | | | | | | |
| PRORENA | ▓ | | | | | | | | | | |
| FUPASA (incative) | | | | | | | | | | | |
| CEASPA | | | | | | ▓ | | | | | ▓ |
| ANARAP | | | | | | | | | | | |
| Panamanian Regulatory Agencies (e.g., ANAM) | | | | | | | | | | ▓ | |
| **International Regulatory Agencies** | | | | | | | | | | | |
| CDMEB | | | | | | | | | | ▓ | |
| CDM Meth Panel | | | | | | | | | | | |
| Private Sector (e.g., Banking & Finance) | | | | | ▓ | | | | | | |
| **Landowners** | | | | | | | | | | | |
| Private Landowners | | ▓ | | | ▓ | | | | | | |
| Gvt. Landowners | | | | | | | | | ▓ | | |
| Consultants (e.g., SGS) | | | | | | | | | | | |

Note: Grey indicates areas where institutions are active

involvement in supporting demand and supply for LULUCF carbon credits. This would need to be balanced against other country priorities. ·

In terms of policies, to date carbon policy development has primarily been at the international level. Policy tools in Panama to support demand growth are minimal. Moreover, tax incentives to support reforestation projects, specifically Law 24, have been cut back (Herrick, personal communication, 10 March 2005). While it is unclear what impact this may have on carbon credits, it may likely impact overall forestry market investment (Herrick, personal communication, 10 March 2005). Moving forward, one option is to review potential policies to further support carbon credit demand generation (see Lichtenfeld, this volume; Hovani and Fotos, this volume).

## *Landowner Options: Feasibility and Risks*

A summary of market segments and identification of potential opportunities and risks within these markets provides the basis for an assessment of landowner options in Panama.

Based on Table 5 below, regulated markets provide a significant opportunity for forestry-based carbon projects in Panama; however, challenges exist with the relative lack of CDM approved methodologies

TABLE 5. Opportunities and Challenges in Regulated and Unregulated Carbon Markets

| Market | Opportunities | Challenges |
| --- | --- | --- |
| Regulated Market | • Large potential market<br>• Potentially higher prices for carbon<br>• Potentially willing buyers driven by regulation– regulatory infrastructure driving demand | • Only one approved CDM A/R methodology as of January 2006<br>• Time consuming and expensive process<br>• Need to manage additionality, leakage, permanence questions |
| Non-Regulated Market | • May have less restrictions than regulated markets and provide more flexibility<br>• Does not require approval<br>• Transaction costs to bring credits to market are lower than in regulated markets | • Prices for carbon credits may be lower if product cannot be differentiated<br>• Requires additional marketing $ spent to find buyers<br>• Potentially a smaller overall market |

for LULUCF projects. The time-consuming methodology approval process may impede efforts to develop carbon projects. While non-regulated markets may provide opportunities, this market is incredibly fragmented. Prices are also potentially lower in the non-regulated market. In addition, identifying voluntary buyers can increase marketing costs. One overall challenge is that Panama lacks existing infrastructure and policies to help generate demand. To date, demand generation has been driven almost entirely by international institutions.

In addition to understanding opportunities and challenges for these projects, it is important to understand the viability of these projects based on profitability. Assessing options for landowners in Panama requires reviewing land uses in Panama. Based on interviews, the most likely land use scenarios for forestry-based projects to meet regulated and non-regulated demand would be small and large landholders in natural forests, teak plantations, natural plantations and agroforestry. Using broad assumptions about revenue and costs, several carbon projects can potentially be profitable. Large landowners are likely to be more profitable than smaller landowners as higher fixed transaction costs can be allocated over higher revenues from larger land areas. Aggregation of supply of credits from small landholders may be an opportunity to decrease costs and achieve economies of scale. Understanding the breakeven number of hectares within each land use option could demonstrate the minimum project size required. For teak and natural forest plantations and agroforestry, analysis of carbon credit revenue and costs would need to include additional revenue streams from forestry and agricultural activities. If operations included other revenue streams, e.g., timber sales in teak and natural plantations or agroforestry, carbon sales could provide incremental profit that could offset investment costs. Profitability of these projects would also need to be weighed against opportunity costs of other land uses. Finally, these projects would need to prove that they would not be profitable in the absence of carbon financing to adhere to addditionality constraints.

## *RECOMMENDATIONS AND CONCLUSIONS*

The global carbon sequestration services market is large, evolving rapidly and driven by regulated and non-regulated demand. Opportunities and challenges exist in the regulated and non-regulated markets. While the regulated market is large, there are no approved CDM methodologies and substantial obstacles to meeting constraints based on additionality, leakage and permanence. Transaction costs may also be a barrier to market entry for smaller landowners. While non-regulated markets are smaller, fragmented and potentially have lower prices, these markets may be more flexible. Currently, there is little infrastructure in Panama to build demand for forestry carbon credits. Thus, while there is existing demand for carbon credits, one challenge will be to determine how forestry-based projects in Panama can viably and profitably tap into this emerging carbon demand.

## REFERENCES

500PPM GMbh. 2004. "Voluntary Funds–A Means of Lowering Transaction Costs." Presentation in Hamburg Germany, June 8, 2004. Retrieved June 2005 from www.goldcdm.net/fileadmin/goldcdm/downloads/papers/040608thomas.ppt.

BioCarbon Fund (BCF). 2004a. "The BioCarbon Fund Will No Longer Be Reviewing PINs Effective Immediately."Retrieved March 2005 from http://carbonfinance.org/ biocarbon/router.cfm?Page=News.

BioCarbon Fund (BCF). 2004b. "Managing Permanence in the BioCarbon Fund." BioCF Technical Note No. 1. Retrieved March 2005 from http://carbonfinance.org/ docs/PermanenceRiskMan.doc.

Burge, R. 2005. "Africa, Europe, and carbon: a proposal." OpenDemocracy.net. Retrieved August 2005 from http://opendemocracy.net/globalization-G8/africa_ climate_2635.jsp

Chicago Climate Exchange (CCX). 2005a. "Emissions Offsets." Retrieved March 2005 from http://www.chicageclimatex.com/about/program.html.

Chicago Climate Exchange (CCX). 2005b. "CCX Carbon Financial Instruments Market Data." Retrieved June 2005 from http://www.chicagoclimatex.com/trading/ pricelimits.html.

Climate Action Network. 2005. "The Unspeakable in Pursuit of the Unmeasurable." Retrieved March 2005 from http://www.climatenetwork.org/eco/cops/cop6/ 2.1100.pursuit.html.

Climate Care. 2005. "Restoring Rainforests." Retrieved March 2005 from http:// www.climatecare.org/projects/view.cfm?content_id=82B8A28E-F552-437A-A6E1A7E00E7BA234.

Climate Trust. 2005. "Oregon Power Plant Offset Program." Retrieved March 2005 from http://www.climatetrust.org/programs_powerplant.php.

Collins, M. 2003. "Evolution of the Carbon Market, CDM and Project Financing." UNIDO Workshop Presentation, May 19-20, 2003. Johannesburg.

Conservation Finance. 2005. "Carbon Offset Projects." Retrieved March 2005 from http://guide.conservationfinance.org/chapter/index.cfm?Page=1.

Dhakal, S. 2001. "CDM Market: Size, Barriers and Prospects." Institute for Global Environmental Strategies, Japan.

European Climate Exchange (ECX). 2005. "Questions and Answers." Retrieved March 2005 from http://www.europeanclimateexchange.com/index_flash.php.

Evolution Markets. 2004. "US GHG Markets Fact Sheet." Evolution Markets. Retrieved March 2005 from http://www.evomarkets.com/ghg/assets/US_Fact_sheet%20_Jan04.pdf.

Figueres, C. 2002. "Establishing National Authorities for the CDM: A Guide for Developing Countries." International Institute for Sustainable Development (IISD) and Center for Sustainable Development in the Americas (CDSA), Winnipeg, Manitoba.

Financial Information Engine on Land Degradation (FIELD). 2005. "CERUPT–Certified Emissions Reduction Unit Tender." Retrieved March 2005 from http://www.gm-unccd.org/FIELD/Private/Eco/FR_CER.htm.

Gesellschaft für Technische Zusammenarbeit (GTZ). 2005. "CDM Highlights 21." *Newsletter February 2005*. Retrieved March 2005 from http://www2.gtz.de/climate/download/cdm-highlights/CDM_Highlights-02-05.pdf.

Green Stream Network. 2004. Energy and Environment Partnership with Central America. Central American Carbon Finance Guide. Green Stream Network, BUN-CA. First edition, September.

Griscom Little, A. 2005. "Operation Squander: As Kyoto Goes Live, US Green Groups Offer Tepid Response." *Grist.com*. Retrieved March 2005 from http://www.grist.org/news/muck/2005/02/16/little-kyoto/.

Grossman, J.M. 2007. Carbon in Terrestrial Systems: A Review of the Science with Specific Reference to Central American Ecotypes and Locations. *Journal of Sustainable Forestry* 25(1/2):17-41.

Haites, E. 2004. "Estimating the Market Potential for the Clean Development Mechanism: Review of Models and Lessons Learned." Prepared for the World Bank Carbon Finance Business, PCF Plus Report 19. Washington, DC.

Hovani, A. and M. Fotos. 2007. Policy Alternatives to Increase the Demand for Forest-Based Carbon Sequestration. *Journal of Sustainable Forestry* 25(1/2):99-117.

International Carbon Bank Exchange. 2005. "How Much is A Carbon Credit Worth?" Retrieved March 2005 from http://www.icbe.com/emissions/faqsoncarbon.asp.

International Emissions Trading Association (IETA). 2004. "COP10–Three Years after Marrakech: Lessons Learned in the Clean Development Mechanism." *IETA Position Paper*. Toronto, Canada.

Lichtenfeld, M. 2007. Improving the Supply of Carbon Sequestration Services in Panama. *Journal of Sustainable Forestry* 25(1/2):43-73.

Mansour, B. and M. Elewa. 2004. "Overview of CDM Guidelines on UNEP CDM Guidebook / E7 Guide." Presentation at the CD4CDM Second National Workshop, January 12-13, 2004, Cairo.

National Resources Defense Council (NRDC). 2005. "Questions and Answers about the Climate Stewardship Act." Retrieved March 2005 from http://www.nrdc.org/globalWarming/csa/qcsa.asp.

Natural Resources Canada. 2004. "Forest Carbon Accounting Definitions." Retrieved March 2005 from http://carbon.cfs.nrcan.gc.ca/definitions_e.html.

Netherlands Government. 2001. "Memorandum of Understanding on the Co-operation in the Field of the Clean Development Mechanism (CDM) under Article 12 of the Kyoto Protocol between the Netherlands and the Republic of Panama." Retrieved

March 2005 from http://www2.vrom.nl/docs/internationaal/MOU-%20Panama% 20version%2026.11.pdf.

Pew Center. 2005. "Business for Environmental Leadership Council: BELC." Retrieved March 2005 from http://www.pewclimate.org/companies_leading_the_ way_belc/.

Prime Forestry. 2005. "The Prime Forestry Group Launches Its First CDM Project in Panama." *Press Release.* Retrieved June 2005 from http://www.primeforestry.com/ downloads/PRESSPANAMA.pdf.

Reyes, E. 2005. "Panama: Ready for CDM / Carbon Market Investments." Presentation for the ESTAP Annex I Technical Conference April 4-7, 2005. Taiwan. Retrieved June 2005 from http://www.etsap.org/worsh_4_2005/31.pdf.

Saxton, J. 1997. "Tradable Emissions." Joint Economic Committee, United States Congress. Washington, DC.

Sempris, E. 2002. "Initial CDM Project Portfolio for the Republic of Panama." USAID, Panama City, Panama.

Shinkle, K. 2005. "EU Trades Pollution As Kyoto Pact Begins." *Investor's Business Daily* February 17.

United Nations Framework Convention on Climate Change (UNFCCC). 2005a. "Approved A/R Methodologies." Retrieved April 2005 from http://cdm.unfccc.int/ methodologies/ ARmethodologies/approved_ar.html.

United Nations Framework Convention on Climate Change (UNFCCC). 2005b. "A/R Methodology Progress Table." Retrieved April 2005 from http://cdm.unfccc.int/ Projects/pac/methodologies/ARmethodologies/process?OpenRound=1&OpenNM= ARNM0001&cases=B#ARNM0001.

United Nations Framework Convention on Climate Change (UNFCCC). 2005c. "CDM Executive Board." Retrieved April 2005 from http://cdm.unfccc.int/EB.

United Nations Framework Convention on Climate Change (UNFCCC). 2005d. "COP–COP/MOP." Retrieved April 2005 from http://cdm.unfccc.int/Reference/ COPMOP.

United Nations Framework Convention on Climate Change (UNFCCC). 2005e. "Designated National Authority (DNA)." Retrieved 5 April 2005 from http://cdm.unfccc.int/ DNA.

United Nations Framework Convention on Climate Change (UNFCCC). 2005f. "Terms of Reference for the Methodologies Panel." Retrieved April 2005 from http://cdm. unfccc.int/EB/Meetings/013/eb13repan1.pdf.

United Nations Framework Convention on Climate Change (UNFCCC). 2005g. "Tool for demonstration and assessment of additionality." Retrieved June 2005 from http://cdm.unfccc.int/EB/Meetings/016/eb16repan1.pdf.

United Nations Framework Convention on Climate Change (UNFCCC). 2005h. "Land Use, Land Use Change and Forestry (LULUCF)." Retrieved August 2005 from http://unfccc.int/methods_and_science/lulucf/items/3063.php

United Nations Framework Convention on Climate Change (UNFCCC). 2005i. "Approved Baseline and Monitoring Methodologies." Retrieved August 2005 from http://cdm.unfccc.int/methodologies/PAmethodologies/approved.html.

University of New South Wales. 2004. "Carbon Accounting Under Kyoto." Retrieved March 2005 from http://www.forest.nsw.gov.au/env_services/carbon/accounting/ Default.asp.

Vayrynen, J. 2004. "State and Trends of the Carbon Market." Presentation for the Prototype Carbon Fund. Helsinki, Finland.
World Bank. 2004. "State and Trends of the Carbon Market 2004." International Emissions Trading Association (IETA), Washington, DC.
World Bank. 2005. "Carbon Finance at the World Bank: Project Cycle." Retrieved
March 2005 from http://carbonfinance.org/router.cfm?Page=ProjCycle.
World Resources Institute (WRI). 2003. "Tapping into Carbon Markets." World Re-
sources Institute, March 13, 2003, Presentation at the Sustainable Resources Sum-
mit, Washington, DC.
World Wildlife Fund (WWF). 2005. "Climate Savers." Retrieved March 2005 from
http://worldwildlife.org/climate/projects/climateSavers.cfm.
Zaborowsky, P. and J. Reamer. 2004. "Reality Check for the US G.H.G. Markets."
*Evolution Markets Executive Brief.* New York. Retrieved March 2005 from http://
www.evomarkets.com/assets/evobriefs/nw_1083009636.pdf.

doi:10.1300/J091v25n01_04

# Policy Alternatives to Increase the Demand for Forest-Based Carbon Sequestration

Alexander Hovani
Mike Fotos

**SUMMARY.** National, regional, and international actors can use a range of different policies to increase the demand for forest-based carbon sequestration. Demand for these services has the potential to significantly impact the decisions of landowners, land managers, and private investors by increasing the incentives for creation or maintenance of forest ecosystems. The Kyoto process is at the center of discussions regarding the market for carbon services although it is not the only relevant source of demand. The authors recommend an approach to climate change regulation that requires actions beyond the current scope and term of the Kyoto Protocol. The four areas addressed in this paper are: (1) increasing regulation-based demand for carbon reductions by improved implementation and increasing coverage, (2) increasing voluntary demand for carbon reductions, (3) increasing the percentage of carbon

Alexander Hovani earned a Master of Forestry at the Yale School of Forestry and Environmental Studies and a Master of Business Administration at the Yale School of Management, New Haven, CT 06511 USA (E-mail: lexhovani@gmail.com).

Mike Fotos is Visiting Assistant Professor of Public Policy at Trinity College, Hartford, CT 06106 USA. He was a guest lecturer for the course Emerging Markets for Ecosystem Services in the Spring of 2005 at the Yale School of Forestry and Environmental Studies, New Haven, CT 06511 USA.

[Haworth co-indexing entry note]: "Policy Alternatives to Increase the Demand for Forest-Based Carbon Sequestration." Hovani, Alexander, and Mike Fotos. Co-published simultaneously in *Journal of Sustainable Forestry* (Haworth Food & Agricultural Products Press, an imprint of The Haworth Press, Inc.) Vol. 25, No. 1/2, 2007, pp. 99-117; and: *Emerging Markets for Ecosystem Services: A Case Study of the Panama Canal Watershed* (ed: Bradford S. Gentry, Quint Newcomer, Shimon C. Anisfeld, and Michael A. Fotos, III) Haworth Food & Agricultural Products Press, an imprint of The Haworth Press, Inc., 2007, pp. 99-117. Single or multiple copies of this article are available for a fee from The Haworth Document Delivery Service [1-800-HAWORTH, 9:00 a.m. - 5:00 p.m. (EST). E-mail address: docdelivery@haworthpress.com].

Available online at http://jsf.haworthpress.com
© 2007 by The Haworth Press, Inc. All rights reserved.
doi:10.1300/J091v25n01_05

99

reduction that derives from land use, land use change, and forestry, and (4) ways to stimulate demand for forest-based carbon sequestration generally by reducing transaction costs and contractual risks and in a particular country by recommending policy changes in Panama. doi: 10.1300/J091v25n01_05 *[Article copies available for a fee from The Haworth Document Delivery Service: 1-800-HAWORTH. E-mail address: <docdelivery@ haworthpress.com> Website: <http://www.HaworthPress. com> © 2007 by The Haworth Press, Inc. All rights reserved.]*

**KEYWORDS.** Contractual markets for carbon services, carbon reductions, Kyoto Protocol, Panama Canal Watershed, carbon sequestration demand

## HIERARCHY OF CARBON DEMAND

Companies and countries buy carbon emissions reductions after making a series of choices. Even regulated entities that must adhere to carbon emission limits must decide to comply through the purchase of certified emissions reductions (CERs) from forest-based sequestration. When a particular supplier is considering demand for their product, there are additional considerations that may influence demand for those particular project-based CERs. The following diagram, Figure 1, shows some of these decisions.

To increase the demand for forest-based sequestration in a particular place, the keys are to: (a) guarantee that forest-based emissions reductions are allowed under regulatory schemes, (b) decrease the risk of selecting forest-based sequestration as opposed to other alternatives for Kyoto Protocol regulated entities, (c) increase the regulatory requirements–more regulated entities with tighter restrictions, (d) increase the interest in carbon sequestration among non-regulated entities (both companies and individuals), and (e) demonstrate that the particular place of interest is at least equivalent to if not better than alternatives as a place to buy carbon sequestration credits.

## THE BUYER'S PERSPECTIVE

Carbon buyers want predictability and simplicity, but find it almost nowhere in the fledgling carbon markets. In terms of Kyoto, developing a CDM project is extremely complicated, and many of the most important

FIGURE 1. Decision-making and Forest-based Carbon Demand. The gray boxes show the endpoints of interest to Panamanian landowners. Bold lines show decision pathways that policies to increase demand for supply of forest-based carbon sequestration should focus on.

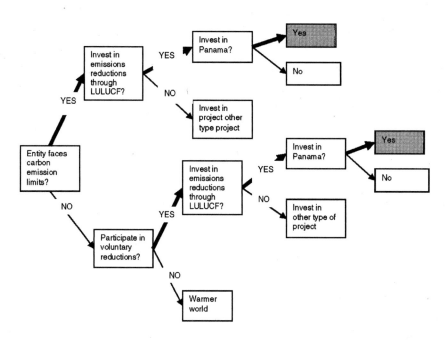

rules have not been clarified by regulatory bodies. Even sophisticated suppliers hire many experts in the process of quantifying carbon stocks and flows to create a baseline, registering, monitoring, verifying, and finally brokering the sale of carbon credits (Conservation Finance Alliance, 2003). This process is extremely expensive for the supplier of services, who in addition must account for the opportunity cost of the land (Kant, 2004). Buyers of carbon sequestration services are confronted with the risk of supplier default which may ensue from the problems enumerated above.

Drawing the line between supply and demand with reference to carbon credits is difficult because many projects are implemented by companies in order to create their own CERs, and therefore the supplier and buyer are the same. Vertical integration is a strategy available to buyers who face a high risk of supplier default and thus many potential transactions are either unobserved (because they are internal to the buyer) or they never happen because the transaction costs (necessary to efficiently allocate risks) are so high that socially-efficient arms-length transactions do not happen. In addition, the obstacles and uncertainties that suppliers face increase the riskiness of credits that buyers are seeking and decrease their level of demand. Therefore, a more predictable, transparent landscape for project developers is extremely important to increasing demand for carbon services (Haites and Seres, 2004). However important to demand, policies affecting suppliers' ability to successfully navigate the CDM process and succeed in their reforestation are addressed in the analysis for increasing the supply of carbon services (Lichtenfeld, this volume). On the other hand, policies, perhaps in the form of officially-sanctioned buyers' cooperatives, can enable buyers of carbon services to pool their contractual risks and thus reduce the risk of participation in the contractual market.

The perceived probability of success of reforestation ventures in general and, in this case, in a particular country will impact buyers' willingness to consider credits from these sources. In many countries, plantation forestry is an underdeveloped and poorly understood sector, particularly with respect to using native species. Social and political instability are other factors that can jeopardize a plantation, which must exist for 40 years or more to generate mature trees for timber harvest. Weather related events, such as hurricanes or fires, represent another category of risk that buyers must consider (World Bank, 2003).

Companies such as Natsource, Evolution Markets, and Ecosecurities run profitable businesses based on providing information and services in the face of vast uncertainty and large information gaps. These companies offer to help manage the risks buyers face. Some of these risks are difficult to reduce, such as country risk and risk of lower than expected forest growth. Others, such as regulatory risks in the host country and in the Kyoto process, are much more clearly avoidable or reducible. Risk factors include counter-party risk, carbon regulatory risk (host-country, Kyoto process), country investment risk, technology performance risk (reforestation techniques–native species), and carbon performance risk (variability, ownership, permanence) (NatSource, 2005). As noted above, pooling could be particularly helpful in ameliorating these risk factors.

### Risk and Prices

Carbon transactions are not standardized, making it difficult to compare prices. There are many factors that determine the price paid for carbon projects (Lecocq, 2004). These include (Lecocq, 2004):

- Sponsor creditworthiness
- Project viability
- Confidence in ongoing carbon asset management
- Contract structure and upfront payments
- Liabilities the seller is willing to undertake if project fails
- Cost of validation and potential certification
- Host country support
- Additional environmental and social benefits

All of these factors have an impact on the demand for forest-based carbon projects, and represent opportunities for policies that help change either the underlying riskiness or the perceived riskiness of carbon projects.

## POLICY OPPORTUNITIES

### Overview

Reducing the riskiness or perceived riskiness of the sequestration and carbon sale process will increase demand for the service. Each of the areas of risk represents an important opportunity for policy shifts that will make projects more appealing to buyers of carbon and thus increase demand.

### Categories of Policy Tools for Increasing Demand for Carbon

*Improved Implementation of Existing Regulatory Framework.* As per comments above, make the CDM certification process more forest-friendly, and allow or encourage pooling of project risks.

*Direct Regulation of Carbon.* The existing carbon emission regulatory frameworks are the starting point, but in addition to those that exist, many policy changes are necessary to form a complete response to the climate challenge and create incentives for landowners. The most pressing areas are (Bonnie et al., 2002):

- Bringing more countries into regulatory frameworks;
- Reducing emission allowances;
- Increasing the role of sequestration in Kyoto and other frameworks; and
- Dealing seriously with protection of existing carbon pools.

A wide range of regulations could address these objectives, some of which are described below.

*Information Tools.* Information architecture is a requirement for any type of program on carbon sequestration, required or voluntary, and represents an important opportunity for simplifying the carbon markets and making them more predictable, both of which will have major impacts on investor willingness. Methodologies for creating baselines of carbon, measuring changes from different land uses, and calculating the fate of carbon once sequestered are thorny and complicated, and provide an opportunity for significant pooling of resources. Information gaps are a significant obstacle to Kyoto compliance, and also undermine confidence in the accuracy of voluntary programs. Information gathering is one of the main costs to developers of carbon projects under Kyoto. Uncertainty regarding methods and lack of supporting data are major hindrances.

Better access to information can increase demand for forest-based carbon sequestration in both regulated markets and voluntary transactions. For example, the simple existence of enforced public reporting of carbon emissions could spark action on the part of industry to reduce or offset emissions.

*Shared Investments.* Passive public investments are another way to reduce the variability and riskiness of carbon sequestration projects, and thus increase buyer demand. Active joint ventures are another option. Examples might include the government leasing state-owned land to companies that would manage it for ecosystem services; providing loans to forest managers; giving grants and providing technical support through extension services for switching to better land uses; or creating equity funds to invest in management for ecosystem services (Gentry, 2005). These options would not only increase the flow of capital and lower the hurdles for private investment; they would also add confidence for potential buyers of carbon credits. Almost all of the characteristics of risk described above would be improved by judicious government investment. Given debt levels that exist in Panama, these investments would have to be carefully analyzed for cost-effectiveness and may be more acceptable if used as a replacement of existing government expenditures rather than additional investment.

*Marketing.* The benefit of marketing mainly pertains to the competition between suppliers of carbon services. A particular country or supplier within a country would likely improve the attractiveness of their services through publicizing them, bundling them with other opportunities, and finding better ways to deliver those services. Panama is a good example of this opportunity. In addition to gaining a preferred supplier status with several countries, there is opportunity for Panama to capitalize on the fact that so many financial institutions and shipping-related companies operate in Panama to gain their business as carbon buyers. The many tourists that visit Panama each year are a possible pool of carbon investors that Panama could reach out to with a strategic marketing campaign.

*Facilitate Transactions.* The Costa Rican Government created the National Forestry Financing Fund (FONAFIFO) to act as an intermediary between forest landowners and potential buyers of ecosystem services, including carbon sequestration (Pagiola et al., 2002). By pooling the carbon credits offered by many forest managers and serving as a "retail-to-wholesale" broker, an organization such as FONAFIFO reduces the marketing related costs of land managers desiring to sell services, and also reduces the contractual risk for buyers.

## *Framework for Policy Analysis*

It is not possible in the scope of this paper to create a well supported scorecard rating each policy option according to the most important criteria, however the following considerations (see Table 1) were considered qualitatively in assessing the appropriateness of different options. The terminology is used below to evaluate the policies.

## *RECOMMENDATIONS*

### *Developing Country Governments*

Carbon sequestration projects are an exciting opportunity for countries to generate foreign investment, but they also represent significant challenges. There are many things that countries are doing and can try to do in the future to attract carbon investors to invest in projects in their country (see Table 2).

For governments, the range of policies that could support carbon demand is broad. Some policies are relatively simple to implement, and others are more complicated. It is therefore critical to evaluate the effectiveness of the government in general before deciding on a policy or set of policies to advocate. Some of the main issues are the quality of public administration, property rights and rule-based governance, quality of budgetary management, and efficiency of resource mobilization (Gentry,

TABLE 1. Framework for Policy Analysis

| | |
|---|---|
| **Feasibility** | |
| Cost effectiveness | Is there money available for implementation, and is the policy a good use of the money? |
| Demand on institution | Does the institution (or government) planning the policy have the capacity to implement it effectively? |
| **Context** | |
| Political viability | Given the constraints that different institutions work within, how likely is the measure to be approved and supported? |
| Cultural compatibility | Are there cultural obstacles that will either hinder or prevent the policy from succeeding? |
| **Effectiveness** | |
| Environmental | How likely are the environmental impacts of a particular policy, either direct or indirect? |
| Equity | How equitable and fair is the distribution of benefits of the policy across society? |
| **Catalytic Effect** | |
| Adaptability | Is the policy one that could potentially be replicated in other areas? Are there potential synergies? |
| Capacity building | Will the policy result in capacity development with benefits beyond the intended environmental outcomes? |
| Innovation | Is the policy innovative in a way that might catalyze further development and environmental benefit? |

2005). Other socio-political considerations include structural policies, goods and factor markets, economic management, and policies for social inclusion (Gentry, 2005).

## *Panama*

Panama has several advantages over other countries in terms of supporting carbon investment, but faces many of the same obstacles facing other countries. The government continues to benefit from the long history of scientific research that resulted from the U.S. presence and the Smithsonian Tropical Research Institute. It is in the dollar zone which stabilizes monetary policy and makes the country more attractive to investors. Panama occupies a prominent position among the nations of Latin America and attracts many foreign businesses because of the Panama Canal. On the other hand, like other nations in the region, its governmental institutions are weak, including, for instance, the National

TABLE 2. Policy Alternatives for Improving Demand for Carbon-Related Ecosystem Services

| Type of Tool | Actor | Action | Description | Examples for Panama | Key Characteristics |
|---|---|---|---|---|---|
| Information | Developing country government | National carbon inventory framework | Standardize models, assumptions, methodologies; Centralize information; Include training for parties interested in participating. | USAID project | Difficult to implement well. Important to consider equity issues. Simplifies process. |
| Information | Developing country government | Standardization of contracts | Create norms for carbon contract to help reduce uncertainty and transaction costs. This is something that would only work as a complement for other aspects of a carbon program (inventory, pooling). A centralized insurance mechanism could help this standardization. | | Simplifies process |
| Information | Industrialized country government | Technical assistance | Many countries that can host CDM projects lack the ability to support project development; aid agencies can help. | USAID working on carbon inventory projects. | Opportunity for equity improvements |
| Information | Multilaterals | Capacity building | Participating in carbon markets requires sophistication not available in many lesser-developed countries (LDCs). | | Capacity building; Adaptable |
| Information | Kyoto bodies | Continue role as interpreter | The Intergovernmental Panel on Climate Change (IPCC) has been very effective at creating easy to use documents and materials on Kyoto procedures. It must continue to do this and collaborate with other entities to improve dissemination. | | Simplifies process |

## TABLE 2 (continued)

| Type of Tool | Actor | Action | Description | Examples for Panama | Key Characteristics |
|---|---|---|---|---|---|
| Investment | Developing country government | Aggregating projects and selling credits from a fund to reduce risks | Country-level (moderate diversification); Together with other countries in region; Together with other countries around globe (highest diversification). | | Requires high level of technical expertise. Potentially best accomplished through partnership. |
| Investment | Multilaterals | Modeling effective funds | Though the Prototype Carbon Fund has been in existence for many years, its role is still vital. The newer Community Development Carbon Fund and BioCarbon Fund are even more needed. | | Environmentally effective; Capacity building benefits |
| Investment | Multilaterals | Equity investment | This is a way to recoup some investment and model opportunities for private-sector financing of projects. The risk of an equity investment is coming down and may be practicable soon. | | Politically feasible; Cost effective |
| Investment | Multilaterals | Grants | Particularly for capacity development of institutions at the national level and for NGOs to work with small-holder community-based projects. | | Capacity building |
| Marketing | Developing country government | Memoranda of Understanding (MOUs) | Countries that can host CDM projects can sign Memoranda of Understanding with Annex I countries that agree to buy carbon credits preferentially from that supplying country. This relationship can add incentives for project developers to work in the country. | MOUs with Italy, Holland, Canada, Spain | Easy to do, but meaningless unless projects are available. Also, MOUs not binding, so connections are not guaranteed. |

| Type of Tool | Actor | Action | Description | Examples for Panama | Key Characteristics |
|---|---|---|---|---|---|
| Marketing | Developing country government | Marketing based on interest in country | Partnering with marketing firms; To retail market via tourism connections | Canal users– CNC; Other companies operating in Panama; Cruise ship customers to plant a tree– offsetting vacation; | Cost effective ; Low demand on institutions; Politically feasible; Way to focus on small-scale landowners |
| Marketing | Industrialized country government | Memoranda of Understanding (MOUs) | Countries that can host CDM projects can sign MOUs with Annex I countries that agree to buy carbon credits preferentially from that supplying country. This relationship can add incentives for project developers to work in the country. | MOUs with Italy, Holland, Canada, Spain | Easy to do, but meaningless unless projects are available. Also, MOUs not binding so connections are not guaranteed. |
| Regulatory | Industrialized and rapidly growing country governments | Regional programs | The U.S., Australia, India, and China are the notable abstentions from Kyoto and must begin addressing their emissions in other ways, potentially through regional programs. These programs should include options for sequestration and forest conservation in the tropics. | | Will most likely be more flexible than Kyoto and possibly simpler to comply with leading to more land use projects completed. |
| Regulatory | Industrialized country government | Voluntary reporting | A requirement, similar to the Emergency Planning and Community Right to Know (EPCRA) program in the U.S. could create incentives for voluntary action by companies forced to report emissions. | | Relatively low cost, though the benefits are unpredictable. |

## TABLE 2 (continued)

| Type of Tool | Actor | Action | Description | Examples for Panama | Key Characteristics |
|---|---|---|---|---|---|
| Regulatory | Industrialized country government | Debt-for-nature (carbon) | Carbon infrastructure could be built into debt-for-nature swaps. This could focus on conservation of carbon pools (as has been the case) and in addition sequestration knowledge and inventories. This would be akin to an investment in future conservation since it might improve the chances for more investment. | Chagres debt-for-nature | Mechanisms are already in place; Capacity building; Adaptable to other places |
| Regulatory | Multilaterals | Conservation of carbon pools | The Kyoto Protocol does not address the conservation of existing carbon pools and yet their protection is of supreme importance and could benefit from market-based mechanisms. Multilaterals could take the lead in developing ways to combine this with existing carbon infrastructure. | | Cost effective |
| Regulatory | Kyoto bodies | Raise the land use, land use change, and forestry (LULUCF) limit | Currently LULUCF projects can only account for 1% of a country's emissions allowance. This undervalues the potential importance of sequestration and also the impact that the projects can have on developing countries. The limit should be raised substantially and re-stated as a floor rather than a ceiling under KP and successor agreements. | | |

| Type of Tool | Actor | Action | Description | Examples for Panama | Key Characteristics |
|---|---|---|---|---|---|
| Regulatory | Kyoto bodiest | Incorporate carbon pool conservation | Carbon emissions from conversion of forest to farmland and other uses continue to be one of the leading sources of emissions. Protection of existing forest carbon pools must be incorporated directly into carbon regulatory frameworks. The Conference of the Parties needs to reconsider the status of pools in Kyoto or find another way to approach the issue. | | |
| Regulatory | Kyoto bodies | Make decisions beyond first commitment period | Uncertainty beyond the first commitment period seriously hinders demand for carbon services. Reconciling future commitments and the ways that temporary (tCERs) and long-term (lCERs) certified emissions reductions will fit in will be critical to maintaining and increasing demand. | | |
| Regulatory | Kyoto bodies | Methodology approval | The absence of an approved methodology for LULUCF credits is a major impediment to progress and creation of demand. The search for perfection may become the worst enemy of progress. | | |
| Regulatory | Kyoto bodies | Methodology approval | The absence of an approved methodology for LULUCF credits is a major impediment to progress and creation of demand. The search for perfection may become the worst enemy of progress. | | |

Environmental Authority (ANAM). Moreover, Panama relies on foreign sources for technical and scientific support for many projects due to its own under-developed scientific and research capacity.

Thus, Panama's success in carbon markets will depend on its ability to partner with development agencies and industrialized countries on technical, legal, and economic issues related to carbon services. The prospect for successful partnerships rests in part on the government's ability to leverage the interest that exists in the Panama Canal among Canal users and donor governments, especially including the U.S. and the Kyoto signatories.

Currently, ANAM's role is limited to a small amount of marketing of products at various stages of implementation, providing basic assistance about the Clean Development Mechanism (CDM) process, and providing easy approval of projects (ANAM, 2004). Panama has at times provided fiscal incentives for reforestation. Such incentive policies have the potential to increase the supply of carbon sequestration services. However, many of the reforestation projects that benefited from earlier tax incentives have not been successful due to poor site maintenance, leading to an erosion of confidence in reforestation in Panama among landowners, investors, and government officials (Eke, A., personal communication, March 2005).

With a relatively small investment, the country could do an effective job of marketing its carbon sequestration services to companies that operate in Panama and to tourists visiting the country. The country already has a 'brand' and could build on that to differentiate its carbon offerings in global commodity markets. A number of websites focus on offsetting emissions from travel (Climate Care, 2005; Sustainable Travel International, 2005), but cruise ship passengers and others who visit the Canal would be more likely to want to participate in something directly relevant to their trip.

### Industrialized Countries

Governments of industrialized countries can take important actions to increase the demand for forest-based carbon sequestration, including enacting forest-friendly regulatory measures, provision of information tools, and promotion of investment opportunities. They can act both within their own countries, in terms of requiring or incentivizing companies to offset emissions, or in collaboration with developing countries to help them manage their carbon investments (see Table 2).

## Multilateral Institutions

The World Bank, the Global Environment Facility (GEF), and the United Nations Development Program (UNDP) have been some of the most important actors in the development of carbon markets. The World Bank is one of the three biggest buyers each year of carbon credits (see Lauterbach, this volume), and operates a Prototype Carbon Fund, Community Development Carbon Fund (which focuses on small landowners and works with intermediaries), and the BioCarbon Fund (focused specifically on carbon sequestration through land use, land use changes, and forestry (LULUCF)). In addition, the World Bank provides capacity building support to host-countries through its Carbon Finance-Assist program and through the World Bank Institute. The GEF provides money for projects that have transboundary implications, funding the incremental cost of those projects. UNDP provides technical assistance at the local level on a wide range of environmental fronts, including carbon market participation (UNDP, 2003) (see Table 2).

Providing money for projects, modeling efficient markets, and building capacity in host countries are the most important roles for multilateral institutions. They will all either create direct demand or stimulate significant demand in others (Kiss et al., 2002).

## Kyoto Bodies

The Kyoto process is at the center of carbon services discussions, and yet it has been painfully slow with respect to afforestation and reforestation (A/R). Not a single A/R methodology has been approved by the CDM Executive Board and the uncertainty that this brings strongly discourages demand for land-based carbon projects (Conference of the Parties to UNFCCC, 2003).

Currently, the CDM limits the carbon sequestration projects during the first commitment period to 1% of a developed country's base year emissions. It also only considers reforestation and afforestation, not forest management (Conservation Finance Alliance, 2003). The limits relating to the quantity levels of land use projects, types of activities allowable, and approved methodologies (where the effective limit is zero) are among the most important factors under Kyoto that can be favorably influenced by policy changes (see Lichtenfeld, this volume).

The uncertainty attending the next commitment period after 2012 is another obstacle to demand that is likely to grow in importance as time goes by. The sooner Kyoto signatories and key non-signatory nations such as the U.S., Australia, China, and India decide what will follow the KP, the better it will be for carbon markets. Conversely, the longer the delay, the greater the uncertainty facing buyers and sellers and thus the more severe the restriction will be on the demand for carbon services.

We conclude with several recommendations concerning what comes after the expiration of the Kyoto Protocol in 2012. The successor agreement should include: (1) bringing the U.S., Australia, and the developing countries with the fastest growing rates of greenhouse gas emissions into existing or future treaty agreements; (2) reducing the carbon intensity of the world's economy through a variety of means, including the protection of existing carbon pools–i.e., saving the world's remaining primary forests; (3) the ratcheting down of emissions allowances to increase the trading value of emission credits; and (4) the assurance that forest-based sequestration occupies a favored place in the trading market and other regulatory frameworks dealing with greenhouse gases.

We recognize that politics and the unintended consequences of treaty implementation are not trivial matters when it comes to achieving the objectives outlined above. Moreover, it is beyond the scope of this paper to prescribe lobbying campaigns for major international agreements such as what will succeed Kyoto. We simply note that energy policy is a matter of vital strategic interest to two major military powers, China and the U.S., who remain outside the Protocol. India and Australia are two nations with their own strategic considerations regarding China, and the logic of strategic rivalry frequently overwhelms other values in such situations. Thus, advocates for action on climate change should be prepared to consider accepting regulatory frameworks that may depart from conventional approaches to pollution abatement.

As noted above and elsewhere in this volume (see Lauterbach, this volume), the design and implementation of the Kyoto Protocol make it difficult to create and market LULUCF carbon credits. We recommend three elements for inclusion in greenhouse gas regulatory conventions that will help alleviate this problem. First, regulatory frameworks should recognize emission avoidance as a primary strategy for ameliorating threats to the global climate and that a central strategy for emission avoidance is the conservation of existing forests. For example, land use change (e.g., the clearing and burning of forests) may account for one-third of $CO_2$ emissions in developing countries and over 60 percent of such emissions in the least developed countries (Baumert and Pershing, 2004). Market-based (i.e., "voluntary") financial support for the conservation of primary forests in particular strikes us as a policy element that can command consensus support among environmental NGOs, G-8 negotiators, and forest owner/managers.

Our second recommended element is that future agreements establish a market-share "floor" rather than "ceiling" for LULUCF-based carbon sequestration credits. Doing so simply recognizes the causal influence of risk-aversion in bureaucratic decision-making. For example, the Kyoto Protocol requires its CDM Executive Board to comply with a cap on LULUCF credits–an outcome of zero such credits guarantees compliance with its implementation mandate. Whereas, approval of an LULUCF methodology or project may initiate a cycle of project approval that leads to an outcome where forest-based sequestration amounts exceed treaty limits. Hence, it comes as no surprise to us that this body has not yet seen clear to approve a methodology, not to mention any projects, for qualifying forest-based carbon sequestration. On the other hand, placing a floor under forest-based carbon sequestration would reverse the bureaucratic incentives and, presumably, lead to the timely approval of both methodology and projects.

Our third and final recommended element is that regulatory frameworks and international donor agencies include legal, financial, and logistical support for the pooling of LULUCF project risks. Given an appropriate regulatory framework, existing financial and insurance markets may be sufficient when it comes to project-related risks such as pests, weather, or fire. On the other hand, country and political risks may be better addressed through international treaty and aid relationships.

## CONCLUSION

Many countries and industries are searching for carbon credits to satisfy their regulatory commitments, and forest-based sequestration is a cost-effective option. The actual investment in these projects has been low, however, due to the complexity of the process and the risks to buyers and sellers that accrue from its many undetermined details. For demand to increase there must be a comprehensible process and a reliable supply of projects available. Increasing the supply of credits and the security of that supply from developing countries will require a concerted effort by developing countries, industrialized countries, multilateral institutions, and the Kyoto bodies.

Many things can be done to increase the demand for forest-based carbon services–improving the performance of existing regulatory frameworks especially as they relate to approving the use of forests for carbon sequestration and the reduction of transaction risks and costs; bringing other countries under the purview of international carbon regulations; reversing present limits on land-use offsets by making them floors rather than ceilings; and providing effective legal and financial protection of forest carbon sinks. Given the assumption that forests constitute a crucial component of an effective response to climate change, these measures are important. Moreover, they will be attended by the needed benefits of additional foreign and domestic investment in sustainable forest management, not just in Panama but in many other countries where forests are at risk.

# REFERENCES

Autoridad Nacional del Ambiente (ANAM). 2004. Contributing to Mitigate Global Warming: CDM's potential in Panama. Brochure.

Baumert, K. and J. Pershing. 2004. Climate Data: Insights and Observations. Paper prepared for The Pew Center on Global Climate Change. December.

Bonnie, R., M. Carey, and A. Petsonk. 2002. Protecting terrestrial ecosystems and the climate through a global carbon market. *Phil. Trans. R. Soc. Lond.* 360:1853-1873.

Climate Care. 2005. Air Travel Calculator. Retrieved 3/31/05 from http://www.co2.org/airtravelcalc/airtravelcalc.cfm.

Conference of the Parties to UNFCCC. 2003. Report of the Conference of the Parties on its Ninth Session, 1-12 December 2003. Milan, Italy.

Conservation Finance Alliance. 2003. Carbon-offset projects. The Conservation Finance Guide. Retrieved 3/31/05 from http://guide.conservationfinance.org/chapter/index.cfm?IndexID=22.

Gentry, B. (ed.). 2005. Emerging Markets for Ecosystem Services: Draft Framework for Analysis. Yale School of Forestry and Environmental Studies, New Haven, CT.

Haites, E. and S. Seres. 2004. Estimating the Market Potential for the Clean Development Mechanism: Review of Models and Lessons Learned. The World Bank, International Energy Agency (IEA), International Emissions Trading Association (IETA).

Kant, P. 2004. The Real Costs of Carbon Sink Projects in Tropical Ecosystems of India: an Analysis of Their Profitability. ITTO PD 39/98 Rev. 2 (M), International Workshop on Environmental Economics of Tropical Forest and Green Policy, March 2-5, 2004. Beijing, China.

Kiss, A., G. Castro, and K. Newcombe. 2002. The role of multilateral institutions. *Phil. Trans. R. Soc. Lond* 360:1641-1652.

Lauterbach, S. 2007. An Assessment of Existing Demand for Carbon Sequestration Services. *Journal of Sustainable Forestry* 25(1/2):75-98.

Lecocq, F. 2004. State and trends of the carbon market: 2004. Development Economics Research Group, The World Bank.

Lichtenfeld, M. 2007. Improving the Supply of Carbon Sequestration Services in Panama. *Journal of Sustainable Forestry* 25(1/2):43-73.

NatSource. 2005. Fact Sheet on the Greenhouse Gas Credit Aggregation Pool. Retrieved April 6th 2005 from http://www.natsource.com/markets.

Pagiola, S., J. Bishop, and N. Landell-Mills (eds). 2002. Selling Forest Environmental Services: Market-based Mechanisms for Conservation and Development. Earthscan Publications, Ltd., London.

Sustainable Travel International. 2005. My Climate Carbon Offsets. Retrieved 4/1/05 from http://www.sustainabletravelinternational.org/documents/op_carbonoffsets.html.

World Bank. 2003. Mobilizing Private Capital: Guarantees and Contingent/Risk Finance. World Bank, Paris Office (Workshop presentation, November 19-20).

doi:10.1300/J091v25n01_05

# SECTION 2:
# WATER

# WATER SUPPLY

# Existing Supply of Watershed Services in the Panama Canal Watershed

Krista Anderson

**SUMMARY.** Markets for ecosystem services are gaining the interest of both entrepreneurs and environmentalists as a way to further environmental protection and conservation goals while turning a profit for investors and land managers. The Panama Canal Watershed is currently struggling with the effects of land use change on its water quality and quantity. This paper examines two types of land management in the Panama Canal Watershed (large-scale reforestation with native species and smallholders' agroforestry projects) to analyze the supply side of a possible market for watershed services. Forest cover provides the following watershed services: (1) regulates water flow by controlling flooding and peak flows, and possibly increasing dry season flows; and (2) improves water quality by increasing dissolved oxygen levels and reducing erosion,

Krista Anderson earned a Master of Environmental Management at the Yale School of Forestry and Environmental Studies, New Haven, CT 06511 USA. She is an Analyst with the U.S. Government Accountability Office in Boston, MA (E-mail: anderson_kb@yahoo.com).

[Haworth co-indexing entry note]: "Existing Supply of Watershed Services in the Panama Canal Watershed." Anderson, Krista. Co-published simultaneously in *Journal of Sustainable Forestry* (Haworth Food & Agricultural Products Press, an imprint of The Haworth Press, Inc.) Vol. 25, No. 1/2, 2007, pp. 121-145; and: *Emerging Markets for Ecosystem Services: A Case Study of the Panama Canal Watershed* (ed: Bradford S. Gentry, Quint Newcomer, Shimon C. Anisfeld, and Michael A. Fotos, III) Haworth Food & Agricultural Products Press, an imprint of The Haworth Press, Inc., 2007, pp. 121-145. Single or multiple copies of this article are available for a fee from The Haworth Document Delivery Service [1-800-HAWORTH, 9:00 a.m. - 5:00 p.m. (EST). E-mail address: docdelivery@haworthpress.com].

Available online at http://jsf.haworthpress.com
© 2007 by The Haworth Press, Inc. All rights reserved.
doi:10.1300/J091v25n01_06

sedimentation, pathogens, eutrophication, and chemical contaminant loading. Based on the research presented in this paper, large-scale reforestation may not be desirable in the Panama Canal Watershed unless decreased water yield is an acceptable outcome or improved dry season flows can be shown. Consequently, this paper concludes that efforts to develop markets for watershed services in the Panama Canal Watershed should focus on smallholders and water quality improvement, at least until scientists agree that increasing forest cover increases dry season water yield. doi:10.1300/J091v25n01_06 *[Article copies available for a fee from The Haworth Document Delivery Service: 1-800-HAWORTH. E-mail address: <docdelivery@haworthpress.com> Website: <http://www.HaworthPress.com> © 2007 by The Haworth Press, Inc. All rights reserved.]*

**KEYWORDS.** Watershed services, ecosystem services, hydrological services, Panama Canal Watershed

## BASIC DEFINITIONS AND QUESTIONS

### Introduction

This article analyzes the watershed services supplied by two types of land management within the Panama Canal Watershed (PCW): (a) large-scale native-species reforestation efforts; and (b) agroforestry activities of smallholders in Chagres National Park. I present an overview of potential watershed services; identify and prioritize watershed services that can currently be supplied in the PCW; suggest land management practices to provide or improve supply; and discuss estimates of some supply costs and benefits. The goal is to approach these issues from the perspective of land managers and smallholders in Panama. I emphasize the Chagres smallholders for three reasons: (1) large-scale reforestation may be less desirable because it could significantly reduce water yield in the PCW; (2) the park surrounds the headwaters of the Chagres River, which is critical to the PCW; and (3) smallholders' activities in Chagres are socially and politically controversial due to the area's protected status. Information presented in this article was obtained through library research, as well as a research trip to Panama during 6-13 March 2005.

### What Types of Land Management Options Are Available?

A variety of land management options are available to landowners and smallholders, including agriculture; livestock pasture; agroforestry (including silvipasture); forest plantations (including native or intro-duced species, as well as mixed species or monoculture); natural forest preservation, regeneration, and reforestation; and timber harvesting from agroforestry, plantations, and natural forests. These land uses can result in divergent economic and ecological consequences at local to global scales. The next sections introduce the possible watershed ser-vices supplied by increasing or maintaining forest cover in general, then evaluate the watershed services supplied in the Panama Canal Watershed (PCW) by native species reforestation and agroforestry.

## What Watershed Services Are Possible?

Land can be managed to provide an array of watershed services that benefit downstream users. Forest cover potentially benefits both water quantity (i.e., flow regulation) and water quality.

### Total Water Yield Regulation

The general public and policymakers often assume that increasing forest cover will increase water yield in a basin. However, numerous scientists have refuted this assumption and shown that the opposite is generally true: increased forest cover reduces runoff and *lowers* annual flows (Bruijnzeel, 2004 and 1990; Hsia and Koh, 1983; Lal, 1983; Bosch and Hewlett, 1982; Hibbert, 1967). The increase in total water yield associated with deforestation (or the decrease in yield associated with reforestation) is primarily a function of the higher evapotranspi-ration rates of trees compared to lower vegetation. This applies to both dry and humid conditions, although there are exceptions, such as cloud forests, where cloud-water deposition onto tree leaf surfaces may ex-ceed water loss and increase the total water available to streams. How-ever, it is difficult to measure the amount of water stripped from the clouds, and even more difficult to determine its contribution to stream flows (Bruijnzeel, 2001).

### Dry Season Water Yield Regulation

Forest cover can affect the magnitude and timing of dry season flows. In some circumstances, the increased groundwater recharge in a for-ested basin (due to greater infiltration capacity in forest soils) is be-lieved to act as a "sponge," gradually releasing water over time and increasing flows during the dry season. Ultimately, though, competing site-specific processes control the flow regime. The science in this case is much more ambiguous than for annual flows, and reforestation may or may not significantly affect dry season flows in a given location. The condition of soils and the effects of trees on soil characteristics are probably more important for dry season flows than the simple presence or absence of forest vegetation. Bruijnzeel (2004:185) explains that "although reforestation and soil conservation measures are capable of reducing the enhanced peak flows and stormflows associated with soil degradation, no well-documented case exists where this has also produced a corresponding increase in low flows . . . The 'low flow problem' is identified as the single most important watershed issue requiring further research." For a discussion of the current state of research, refer to Bruijnzeel (2001; 2004).

*Flood Control*

Riparian forests help reduce flooding by attenuating flood waters along river channels. Other forests may also help to reduce the extent of flooding by increasing infiltration and reducing the volume of water flowing as direct runoff from storm events. Landell-Mills and Porras (2002), however, note that the relationship between forest cover and flood control may depend on the size of the watershed, with a relationship existing only in catchments of less than 50,000 ha. In larger catchments, flooding is controlled more by extreme precipitation events that saturate soils over large areas, even in forested catchments.

*Water Quality Improvement:*
*Erosion Control and Reduced Sedimentation*

Forest cover plays an important role in controlling erosion, which can contribute to degradation of water quality as sediment loads increase in highly eroded landscapes. Excessive levels of sediment in water can reduce the storage capacity of reservoirs as they gradually fill in with transported soil. High sediment levels also damage hydroelectric turbines, degrade aquatic habitat, increase the filtration required for drinking water, and transport disease-causing pathogens in the water supply.
Bruijnzeel (1990) presents a useful comparison of surface erosion rates under a range of land use scenarios in tropical forest and tree crop systems. Some of the types of erosion that could be affected by forest cover include sheet, surface, streambank, splash-induced, and gully erosion, as well as landslides. In general, natural mixed forests reduce

erosion transport by reducing surface runoff and increasing infiltration. By lowering peak flows, reductions in surface runoff decrease streambank erosion and improve channel stability in streams. Forests also increase slope stability, and thus reduce erosion, because the tree roots bind the soil together and reduce the soil water pressure. On steep slopes, landslides are more likely to be the dominant type of erosion problem and are highly influenced by the intensity and duration of rainfall events (Bruijnzeel, 1990). However, important differences exist between shallow landslides (<3 m) and deeper landslides (>3 m). Although maintaining or increasing forest cover on steep slopes may alleviate the extent of shallow landslides, forest cover is not likely to prevent deeper landslides. Landslides are also more likely to result from modifications caused by road construction. Forsyth (1996), on the other hand, reports that forested landscapes may increase gully erosion because the roots and trunks can preferentially direct water flows.

Overall, topography, climate (particularly precipitation), soil conditions, forest canopy, understory vegetation, and the organic litter layer are the most important bio-physical features influencing erosion. The type of tree species in the canopy also plays an important role by modifying the drop sizes of precipitation that can result in splash-induced erosion. Larger leaves, such as those of *Tectona grandis* (teak), can generate larger drops that subsequently enhance erosion (Calder, 2001). However, Bruijnzeel (1990) and others (Wiersum, 1985; Dalal et al., 1961) argue that the role of forests in developing and maintaining litter cover and understory vegetation is more important to erosion control than the ability of forest canopies to break down raindrops.

Anthropogenic landscape modification is also critical to erosion. Roads and traffic, for instance, can facilitate landslides, gully formation, and sediment mobilization. If a forested area is harvested for timber, the use of some types of logging equipment and poor logging techniques may increase the degree of soil compaction and thus increase surface runoff. Livestock grazing can have a similar effect on soil compaction and runoff and can remove the understory vegetation that binds soils.

In summary, while many factors affect erosion rates, "undisturbed forested watersheds generally yield the lowest amount of sediment of any vegetative cover or land use condition" (Brooks et al., 1997:224).

## Water Quality Improvement: Reduced Pathogen Levels

During precipitation events, forest cover reduces surface runoff and increases the residence time of water in the soil, thus improving stream water quality. Payment et al. (2003:65) note that "rainfall events are one of the most important causes of degradation in source water quality affecting surface waters and ground waters. Rainfall drives the movement of pathogens into and through water bodies and can move soil, resuspend sediments, cause overflow of combined and poorly maintained sewers, degrade groundwater through infiltration and so on." Lower sediment loads in drinking water help reduce the levels of pathogens transported with the sediments. Although turbidity "is not associated specifically with faecal material . . . increases in turbidity are often accompanied with increases in pathogen numbers" (Payment et al., 2003:68).

Bradley (1977) notes that changes in water quality can be linked to between 20 and 30 infective diseases, which he groups into viral, bacterial, protozoal, and helminthic diseases. Some of these diseases are water-borne, such as typhoid, cholera, and hepatitis. Other common diseases, such as diabetes, myocarditis, Guillian-Barré syndrome, gastric cancer, and reactive arthritis, have also "been associated with, or are suspected to be caused by, infection with viral or bacterial pathogens excreted by humans or animals" (Medema et al., 2003:13; Hunter et al., 2003:90). Emerging pathogens also threaten water supplies, requiring "constant vigilance in terms of what may pose a "new threat" (Medema et al., 2003:14). For examples of emerging pathogens, see Hunter et al. (2003:90).

Pathogenic organisms and viruses can be readily transmitted through water by fecal contamination (Medema et al., 2003; Evison and James, 1977). Tropical streams are especially susceptible to difficulties in assimilating waste discharges. In particular, the seasonal rainfall patterns in the tropics cause high ratios of maximum to minimum discharge and extended periods of low flows. These conditions reduce the assimilation capacity by reducing the dilution of waste loads, especially in flat areas with little turbulence to oxygenate the water through surface diffusion (Pescod, 1977).

Common in heavily polluted water supplies, pathogenic viruses, bacteria, protozoa, and metazoans must be removed by water treatment processes. Although pathogen levels can be addressed by drinking water treatment processes, the chemicals used as disinfectants can create potentially harmful disinfection byproducts (DBPs) by reacting with other compounds in the water supply. These DBPs (including total trihalomethanes, haloacetic acides, bromate, and chlorite) may increase the risk of cancer and nervous system problems (USEPA, 2005). Thus, by helping to reduce pathogen levels in the water supply, increasing forest cover also helps to reduce the degree of disinfection required and the secondary harmful effects of DBPs.

*Water Quality Improvement:*
*Reduced Eutrophication and Chemical Contaminant Loading*

Streams draining forested landscapes are also likely to have lower nutrient and chemical loads than streams in agricultural or developed watersheds. Excess nutrients may be taken up by vegetation, particularly along riparian buffer strips. Some types of vegetation are effective in bioremediation of chemical contaminants, which are also filtered by the soil as the water infiltrates the ground surface before being discharged to surface waters. Nutrient loss from soils is also controlled by the reduced erosion associated with forest cover. Excessive supplies of nutrients such as nitrogen and phosphorus result in overproduction of aquatic biomass, known as eutrophication (Chapin et al., 2002). Eutrophication can also lead to production of organic sediments from decaying aquatic biomass. Human and animal wastes and high levels of runoff from agricultural lands are common sources of these nutrients. Forest cover both reduces runoff and increases nutrient uptake, thereby helping to reduce eutrophication and the subsequent production of organic sediments.

*Water Quality Improvement:*
*Increased Dissolved Oxygen Concentrations*

Eutrophication and excessive amounts of decaying organic matter can lead to lower dissolved oxygen (DO) levels. Forest cover regulates DO levels by reducing runoff of nutrients and organic wastes. Aquatic life typically requires a DO level of at least 3 milligrams per liter (mg/l). In addition, Pescod (1977) identifies DO as one of the most important water quality parameters for hydropower plants and industrial water users, since low DO and associated sulfide production can lead to corrosion (Pickford, 1977).

*Watershed Services Provided by Wetlands*

Wetlands also provide a variety of watershed services, including regulation of stream flow and groundwater recharge, flood control, and erosion protection at shorelines and stream banks. Physical and biochemical processes that occur as water passes through wetlands improve water quality by reducing nutrients, sediment, and contaminants.

Wetlands also provide unique habitat for a diverse array of species. Coughanowr (1998) provides an overview of tropical wetland types and functions.

## CURRENT SUPPLY OF WATERSHED SERVICES IN THE PANAMA CANAL WATERSHED

### Types of Land Management

This paper considers two types of land management in the PCW. The first is hypothetical large-scale reforestation with mixed native species or a combination of native and introduced species. The analysis undertaken here does *not* apply to monoculture plantations of exotic trees such as teak. There has been growing interest in native species reforestation in the PCW, including an active commercial venture (Futuro Forestal) and a research program (the Smithsonian Tropical Research Institute's Native Species Reforestation Project, PRORENA).

The other land management scenario evaluated is small-scale agroforestry (including silvipasture) in Chagres National Park. With topographical grades of 25 to 60 percent, the smallholders' lands typically range in area from a few ha for subsistence farmers to 40 ha for medium size ranchers. Soil permeability is generally moderate [1.5 to 12.5 centimeters per hour (Intercarib, S.A., 1996a)]. The soil is considered suitable for pasture and forests and insufficiently arable for agriculture (Intercarib, S.A., 1996b). Some smallholders in this area are currently implementing agroforestry and silvipasture techniques such as planting live fences, planting lines for soil conservation, planting riparian vegetation strips, improving pasture grasses and cattle management, mixing trees with crops, and planting trees on steep slopes. The following section prioritizes the watershed services that can be supplied by potential large-scale reforestation projects and by the activities of smallholders in Chagres National Park.

### Prioritizing Watershed Services

#### Total Water Yield Regulation

In a study commissioned by the World Bank, Calder et al. (ND) demonstrated that reforestation in the PCW would *decrease* total water yield. Their approach used a Hydrological Land Use Change model with local land use and land cover data to evaluate the effects of reforestation on total flows for the Panama Canal. Modeling results demonstrated that reforestation would reduce total flows to the Panama Canal by as much as 10 percent. Based on this model and the general scientific consensus presented earlier, reforestation in Panama would not provide increased annual yield as a watershed service.

## *Dry Season Water Yield Regulation*

A 1997/98 study of the Agua Salud subwatershed, located in the central part of the PCW, examined differences in flow between two experimental microwatersheds, No. 2 and No. 3 (Heckadon-Moreno et al., 1999). The 127 ha of No. 2 are forested, while only 89.6 of 160 ha are forested in No. 3. The two catchments have similar topography, geology, soils, and drainage areas. The study found that during the rainy season, surface flow in the partially deforested catchment was 62 millimeters greater than in the forested catchment. In the dry season, however, flow in the forested catchment was almost twice that measured in the partially deforested catchment. Although these results appear promising in terms of demonstrating increased dry season water yield from forested landscapes, Aylward (2002:6) cautions that it "remains a significant jump to extrapolate from an effect found over a 9 month period in two 100 ha watersheds to the remainder of the large sub-basins in the PCW. Further . . . 1997/98 was a very unusual hydrologic year, this due to the El Niño event of that period and the subsequent drought conditions in Central America."

Ibáñez et al. (2002) conducted another watershed monitoring experiment in the PCW by comparing runoff and seasonal flows in forested and deforested catchment areas in Soberania National Park. Their results indicated that 26 percent of precipitation in the deforested catchment flowed directly into the river, but only 14 percent flowed directly into surface water in the forested catchment. In other words, more water infiltrated the soil and was available for later release. Ibáñez et al. (2002) found that stream flow in the forested catchment was lower in the wet season and higher in the dry season in comparison to the deforested catchment. They attribute this result to the increased soil compaction (and decreased permeability) within the deforested catchment.

Dry season flows are perhaps the most critical issue affecting the Panama Canal. However, although Ibáñez et al. (2002) and Heckadon-Moreno et al. (1999) suggest that forest cover positively influenced seasonal flow patterns in small catchments, the relationship between land use and dry season flows is not yet clearly established. For example, Calder et al.'s modeling results (ND) did not demonstrate significant changes in dry season flows in response to land use change. An additional factor to consider is that reforesting degraded landscapes may not produce the same benefits to dry season flow as preserving forested areas, since it may take decades after reforestation before soils recover their infiltration and water storage capacities. Thus, while forest cover may indeed improve dry season flows in some circumstances, it will take more research and a definitive scientific consensus before reforestation efforts in the PCW can convincingly claim to provide this service. It is possible, however, that the Autoridad del Canal de Panamá (ACP) and others interested in increased dry season flows may be willing to support reforestation even if the benefits are not proven.

## Erosion Control and Reduced Sedimentation

According to Lal (1983:222), "soils in the humid tropics, with a few exceptions, are structurally unstable. They slake readily under the impact of raindrops. Quick desiccation following an intense storm causes a surface crust to develop that drastically reduces the infiltration rate." These effects are even greater for soils devoid of vegetation, partly due to the lower soil organic matter content. Lal further explains that the Universal Soil Loss Equation for these soils defines their erodibility as generally low to medium; thus, the high risk of erosion in the tropics is more influenced by rainfall intensity than soil characteristics, although both factors are critical.

*Saccharum spontaneum* (Gramineae), an invasive species of wild sugarcane, also contributes to erosion and sediment production in the PCW. This grass rapidly forms uncontrollable monocultures on degraded soils (Hammond, 1999). During the dry season, *S. spontaneum* frequently burns to the ground, leaving behind soil that is even further degraded. The bare soil that remains is then highly erodible during the heavy rains of the wet season. This species is extremely difficult to remove, but higher growth forms like trees and shrubs can successfully provide enough shade to retard, and eventually eliminate, its growth. Thus, reforestation can further reduce erosion and sediment production by restricting the growth of *S. spontaneum*.

Chagres National Park is located in the Chagres catchment of the Lake Alajuela subwatershed, which is characterized by steep slopes and narrow valleys. During the period from 1970 to 1996, the Chagres River produced the greatest discharge of the six major rivers in the PCW, with

961 million m³/year (see Table 1). The Chagres also produced the greatest sediment yield of these six rivers between 1987 and 1996 (97,629 tons/year), but it is only the fourth largest producer of sediment per unit of watershed area (see Table 1). The land in Chagres National Park is 99 percent forested; based on Chagres' low sediment yield relative to the other major rivers, the forest cover appears to supply lower sediment levels as a watershed service.

Erosion and sedimentation have historically been concerns for the PCW, although Stallard notes that "the data and reports for the Panama Canal Basin suggest that investigators are of two minds about the importance of deforestation" (Stallard, 1999:5). Between 1970 and 1985, Lake Alajuela lost an estimated 5 percent of its capacity due to sedimentation (Heckadon-Moreno, 1993). Alvarado (1985) estimated that the loss would approach 26 percent by 2035. However, according to Ibáñez et al. (2002), sediment volume in the watershed's six major rivers has not increased since the onset of detailed data collection (1981 and 1987), and the volume may even have decreased. Although Ibáñez et al. (2002:88, 90) ". . . do not reject the role that deforestation might play in causing increased erosion . . .," they note that ". . . there is no evidence yet, from 16 yr of records, that deforestation is leading to increased erosion in the watershed or sedimentation in the reservoirs." They attribute variation in erosion primarily to variability in precipitation (both total rainfall and the number of landslide-provoking storms). In contrast, Heckadon-Moreno et al. (1999) and Stallard (1999) note that while the

TABLE 1. Overview of Panama Canal Subwatersheds (Heckadon-Moreno et al., 1999; PMCC, 1997)

| Subwatershed | Watershed Area (ha) | Discharge (million m³/year) | Sediment Yield (tons/yr) | Sediment Yield (tons/km²-year) |
|---|---|---|---|---|
| Boqueron | 41,400 | 253 | 48,658 | 879 |
| Chagres | 13,500 | 961 | 97,629 | 255 |
| Ciri Grande | 11,700 | 300 | 35,823 | 115 |
| Gatún | 17,400 | 212 | 35,606 | 293 |
| Pequení | 18,600 | 437 | 56,838 | 664 |
| Trinidad | 9,100 | 212 | 19,434 | 92 |

*Note:* In other tropical regions with forested watersheds and similar geology, natural sediment production is in the range of 100 to 600 tons/km²-year.

rainfall patterns have not changed, sediment levels have been decreasing since 1980. They attribute this change to establishment of protected forest areas at the headwaters of the rivers, increased surface area of regenerating *rastrojo* (stubble), and forest regeneration following decreased deforestation. They attribute the deeper erosion to landslides during long periods of intense rain. Loewenberg (1999) also notes that, according to Panama Canal Commission representatives, much of the sediment that is dredged from the Canal originates from debris slides along the Canal's steep slopes.

Despite the lack of definitive evidence that deforestation increases sediment in the PCW, the existing forest cover may help maintain the relatively stable levels of sedimentation observed. In addition, the ACP is currently implementing reforestation projects to control erosion along the Canal's steep slopes. The ACP has reforested at least 70 ha and believes that the associated understory vegetation has been particularly important in reducing erosion (A. Cerezo, personal communication, 7 March 2005). Although ACP struggles with erosion in at least some locations, dry season flows appear to be more critical in the PCW than sedimentation. However, the relationship between erosion/ sediment production and land use is more established than the relationship between land use and dry season flows. As a result, land managers in Panama should focus on erosion control and sediment reduction, at least until the controls on dry season flows are better understood for the PCW, at which time land managers may be able to improve flows with greater certainty.

## Water Quality Improvement

According to the ACP, industrial contaminants, pesticides, and fertilizers are not currently problems for the water quality at the Miraflores treatment plant (B. Warren, personal communication, 11 March 2005). The most significant water quality issue in the PCW is turbidity from soil erosion. Algal blooms are sometimes problematic as well and are likely related to the significant increase in concentrations of phosphates and nitrates in the PCW between 1975 and 1998 (Heckadon-Moreno et al., 1999). Eutrophication is most problematic in the middle of the Chagres River above Gamboa, near the intake for the Miraflores water treatment plant, and at the mouths of the Paja, Baila Monos, and Caño Quebrado at Lake Gatun (Heckadon-Moreno et al., 1999).

Currently, there is no sewage treatment in the PCW. The Instituto de Acueductos y Alcantarillados Nacionales (IDAAN) is responsible for sewage collection and wastewater treatment. Most of the urban population is serviced by IDAAN's sewage collection, and most of the rural population uses poorly managed individual septic tanks or latrines (P. Castro, personal communication, 28 March 2005). Due to the lack of sewage treatment, pathogens (bacteria, viruses, and parasites) and organic matter are serious problems in the PCW. The IDAAN, which provides drinking water only to communities of at least 1,500 people, identifies the following as the principal water-related illnesses: those caused by bacteria (typhoid and paratyphoid fever, dysentery, cholera, and acute gastroenteritis and diarrhea); those caused by viruses (hepatitis A and B, poliomelitis, and acute gastroenteritis and diarrhea); and those caused by other pathogenic organisms (amoebic dysentery and gastroenteritis) (IDAAN, 2005).

Given these conditions in the PCW, there is clearly potential for forests to improve or at least maintain the future water quality as the population and development continue to increase. Land managers may be able to supply water quality improvement by reducing pathogens, nutrient loads, organic sediment production, and surface runoff, as well as increasing dissolved oxygen concentrations. Agroforestry/silvipasture and reforestation are likely to differ in their ability to improve water quality, depending on the location and extent of such projects.

### *Prioritizing Areas for Reforestation*

Prioritizing areas for future large-scale reforestation projects as well as small-scale agroforestry projects must incorporate numerous factors to determine which locations can best supply the watershed services desired by potential buyers in a future market. These factors include watershed area and location, topography and geology (particularly the type of soil substrate and infiltration rates), precipitation, current land uses, proximity to water treatment plant intakes, current extent and type of vegetative cover, discharge, current contamination levels, current and future population pressure, and current and future degrees of industrialization and urbanization. Selection of locations for supplying watershed services also requires understanding the nature of demand for these services, as well as identifying potential buyers. Thus, this paper does not attempt to make generalized recommendations for priority areas. However, Table 1, above, summarizes the area, discharge, and sediment yield of six major subwatersheds. Although there are many other subwatersheds in the PCW, the rivers for which these six subwatersheds are named represent 60% of the surface drainage in the PCW, and together they contribute 2,375 million m³/yr. Table 2, below, lists locations in the PCW where levels of pathogens, DO, nitrates, nitrites, ammonia, and phosphates are problematic.

## Managing Land to Provide Watershed Services

This section briefly discusses how land in Panama can be better managed to decrease erosion and sedimentation as well as improve water quality (see Storey (2002) and Williams (1994) for additional detail and practical guidance on implementing various types of soil and water conservation techniques). First, since plant species differ in both their water requirements and their potential for erosion control, large-scale reforestation projects in particular must consider both of these factors (Brooks et al., 1997). Unfortunately, little is currently known about either of these factors, or even basic silvics, for most native species. PRORENA is working hard to fill this data gap. Design of reforestation projects

TABLE 2. Locations of Water Quality Problems in the Panama Canal Watershed (Heckadon-Moreno et al., 1999; PMCC, 1997)

| Water Quality Parameter | Problematic Tributaries | Comments |
|---|---|---|
| Pathogens | Chilibre<br>Chilibrillo<br>Gatún | These three rivers have had pathogen levels 4 to 5 times the international standards. They also have the highest populations and significant ranching and farming. |
| Dissolved Oxygen | *Wet season:*<br>Chilibre, Chilibrillo, Palenque, and Gatún<br><br>*Dry season:*<br>El Tinajones, Los Hules, Caño Quebrado, Chilibre and its tributaries (Ñajú, Las Conchas, Lato), Gatuncillo, and Limón | A dissolved oxygen level of at least 3 mg/l is critical for aquatic life. In the dry season, the highest DO levels shown exceed 7.2 mg/l in the rivers listed. The lowest DO levels in the dry season are <5 mg/l. In the wet season, the lowest DO levels were all >4.8 mg/l. |
| Nitrates, Nitrites, Ammonia | Gatuncillo, Obispo, Chilibre, Quebrada Ancha, Palenque II, Salamanca, Cabuya, Chilibrillo, Palenque Nueva Providencia, Cacao, and Baila Monos | The highest levels of these nutrients are in urban, agricultural, and ranching areas. |
| Phosphates | Chilibre, Chilibrillo near Paraíso, Chagres at the Transisthmus bridge, Ancha, Gatuncillo, Lato, and Obispo | |

should also pay careful attention to developing a mixture of canopy and understory. Ensuring an adequate litter layer is particularly important–removal of a forest's litter layer can increase surface erosion by a factor of 50 to 100 times the initial loss, which is generally less than 0.1 kilogram/$m^2$ for an undisturbed tropical forest (Critchley and Bruijnzeel, 1996).

Land managers may implement agroforestry or silvipasture systems. Examples of these include the following, listed with possible techniques in parentheses: tree plots (woodlots, taungya, and managed woody fallows); perennial crops (perennial intercrops and homegardens); annual crops (trees in lines, alley-cropping, windbreaks, contour barrier hedges, and trees on terraces); pastures (live fences, trees in pastures, and fodder banks); and interstices (fruit, shade, and wood trees) (Current et al., 1995). In addition to planting trees and shrubs, rotational grazing, deferred grazing, and planting of improved pasture grasses can further help silvipasture systems to provide watershed services. The USEPA (2002) describes a range of other agricultural best management practices. If irrigation is used, land managers should adopt appropriate methods for preventing irrigation-induced erosion. Conservation tillage methods, designed to leave crop residues on the soil surface, include no-till, mulch-till, and ridge-till systems. Conservation tillage can minimize the splash effect of rainfall, reduce surface runoff, and increase infiltration. Terrace cultivation is another possible mechanism for decreasing runoff and soil loss. Bench terracing, although labor-intensive to construct, can reduce erosion by up to 90 to 95 percent (Critchley and Bruijnzeel, 1996).

Whether undertaking large-scale reforestation or agroforestry/silvipasture efforts, land managers should pay particular attention to reducing soil loss from steep slopes with shallow and/or impermeable soils and reduced vegetation. In steep agricultural areas lacking soil conservation measures, surface erosion can reach 20 to 50 kg/$m^2$ during heavy rainfall (Bruijnzeel, 1990). To improve water quality, land managers should carefully manage those areas closest to stream channels. Preventing cattle from accessing riparian areas is one way to reduce the water-borne transport of pathogens and organic matter from animal wastes. Land managers should plant residual vegetation strips (conservation buffers) in clearcut areas and align these perpendicular to the slope to control erosion by providing barriers to downslope flow of water and soil particles (Brooks et al., 1997). This may not be effective in steep terrains, however, due to the prevalence of channelized surface erosion. Even in mountainous areas, though, land managers should maintain such vegetated strips along riparian buffer zones. Land managers should also preserve existing wetlands and consider restoring degraded or filled wetlands.

If timber is to be harvested, best management practices should be followed. For example, ground-based machinery should be used carefully, and skyline logging could be used on steep slopes. Roads and trails should be carefully located and managed to improve erosion control. Bruijnzeel and Critchley (1994) provide guidance on improving logging practices and note that these measures can reduce sediment loads by 50 to 75 percent.

## Costs of Supply and Benefits to Land Managers

Land managers must determine whether it is economically desirable to manage their land to supply watershed services. To do so, they need to understand the demand–both existing and potential–for such services. Fotos, Chou, and Newcomer (this volume) discuss the existing demand for watershed services in the PCW; Fotos, Newcomer, and Kuppalli (this volume) explore alternative policy approaches for stimulating demand for such services.

It is outside the scope of this paper to determine the hypothetical magnitude of payments that potential buyers might be willing to make for watershed services in the PCW. However, based on the effects on water storage reservoirs and navigation, Intercarib S.A. and Nathan Associates (1996c) estimated a present value of $9/ha for the benefits of erosion control through reforestation in the PCW. Examples from Costa Rica also provide some idea of the possible magnitude of payments for watershed services. As part of Costa Rica's payment for environmental services (PSA) program, hydroelectric power (HEP) producers are paying $10/ha/year to landowners with land titles and $30 ha/year to landowners lacking titles (Pagiola, 2002). Those landowners with title to their land also receive $32/ha/year from Costa Rica's National Fund for Forest Financing (FONAFIFO), which provides payments for the environmental services (not just watershed services) provided by forest protection. For reforestation, FONAFIFO pays a total of $538/ha over a period of 5 years. Another study in Costa Rica estimated the benefits of reforestation to HEP producers and determined a range of $6/ha/year to $50/ha/year (Pagiola, 2002). This study reported an average of $20/ha/year and noted that benefits vary with factors such as watershed size.

The following sections attempt to provide basic information on the possible magnitude of supply costs, as well as to identify some of the likely benefits to suppliers. These benefits would accrue independently of any payments received for ecosystem services; as a result, some land management options may be cost-effective even in the absence of additional payments for providing ecosystem services.

## Smallholders Engaged in Agroforestry

Many smallholders residing in Chagres National Park practice subsistence agriculture and are unlikely to be otherwise employed. Income is generally minimal–a typical monthly income might be in the range of $60, earned from the sale of surplus crops in local markets. Capital resources are uncommon, so smallholders' current costs are primarily the opportunity costs of their labor. Laborers in this area might be paid approximately $6/day for work on neighboring farms. For the agroforestry projects currently being promoted in Chagres by the non-governmental organization Centro de Estudios y Acción Social Panameño (CEASPA), nails and wire for fencing represent the main capital costs. CEASPA provides these to project participants, and the smallholders typically collect the seeds and/or seedlings for planting themselves (Pizarro, personal communication, 9 March 2005). Other capital costs might include plastic piping for transporting water from nearby supplies. One farmer in Chagres estimated that the labor costs for reforesting his land were at least $2,000/ha (Fabriciano, personal communication, 9 March 2005). Similarly, small-scale ranchers in Chagres have costs dominated by the opportunity costs of labor. Some ranchers are converting their pastures to silvipasture, planting riparian buffer strips, and improving their pasture grasses. Some collect the seeds themselves, while others obtain theirs from an agricultural warehouse.

Possible benefits to Chagres smallholders from agroforestry and silvipasture include the following: valuable timber or other wood products; fuelwood for personal use or sale at local markets; improved soil fertility due to increased organic matter, less nutrient depletion, and possibly increased nitrogen-fixation; and valuable shade-grown crops such as pepper, ginger, or coffee. Ranchers could also benefit from the ability to raise more (and better nourished) cattle per ha when improving pastures with more nutritious grasses and trees that provide shade for the animals. For example, one rancher in Chagres hoped to increase his cattle to 6 per ha; for comparison, the national average number of cattle per ha is 0.83 on farms less than 50 ha (Academy for Educational Development, 2004). During the 9 March 2005 field visit, one rancher estimated that an investment by CEASPA of $600 would allow him to produce up to four times as many cattle (Dixon Francois, personal communication, 9 March 2005).

A study of over 50,000 farms constituting 21 agroforestry projects (projects in this study used the following tree species most frequently: *Eucalyptus camaldulensis, Gliricidia* spp., and *Leucaema leucocephala*) in eight countries of Central America found net present values (NPVs) (Current et al, (1995) used a discount rate of 20 percent) of "more than $500 per hectare in over half of the taungya and one of the managed fallows systems" (Current et al., 1995:9). Taungya is the agroforestry practice of maintaining trees while inter-cropping annual crops between them. In Panama, however, where the farm sizes ranged from 5 to 25 ha, low prices for wood products resulted in "consistently lower NPVs and internal rates of return (IRRs)" (Current et al., 1995:9). The authors of the study also noted, however, that opportunity costs for capital are significantly lower in Panama compared to the other countries in the study, so agroforestry practices should not be ruled out as undesirable. The study also determined that the payback periods for all but one of the agroforestry systems were between one and six years. In a comparison of the agroforestry systems' returns to those of an alternative farming practice, Current et al. (1995) found that 40 percent of the cases had returns at least 25 percent higher than the alternative, and over one-half had returns at least 10 percent higher than the alternative system.

Gomez (1995) performed an economic analysis of the Agroforestry Project for Community Development (IRENARE/CARE) project in Panama. Analysis of taungya and woodlot projects on farms of 3 to 6 ha (with *Acacia mangium, Eucalyptus camaldulensis,* and *Pinus caribea*) revealed IRRs of 15.5 to 25 percent and payback periods of 5 to 10 years. Gomez (1995) found that the alternative corn production would yield higher returns than all of the agroforestry systems analyzed. However, he also noted that "although the returns to investment were lower than corn production, the woodlot and taungya systems generated good rates of return that were considerably higher than the opportunity cost of capital in Panama . . . In addition, the systems provided a means for farmers to produce the tree products they need on their farms" (Gomez, 1995:153). The average investment for these agroforestry projects ranged from $16 to $46/ha and 6.5 to 23 work-days/year.

*Potential Large-Scale Reforestation Projects*

This paper does not attempt to determine the future costs of hypothetical large-scale reforestation projects. However, the costs of projects implemented under PRORENA provide an estimate for comparison. For a reforestation project in Soberania National Park, PRORENA is planting approximately 70 native species, with plantings targeted to the crests of hills as well as flat areas, at a density of 1,100 trees per ha and spacing of 3 m by 3 m. In the first year, costs were approximately $1,000 to $1,200/ha, including site preparation, planting, monitoring, and maintenance, but excluding seedlings (J.M. Pérez, personal communication, 7 March 2005). The cost of seedlings would add another $0.30 per seedling for each of the 1,100 seedlings per ha. Costs for the second year were estimated at $600 to $800/ha, while costs for the third year decreased to $300 to $400/ha. Reforestation costs were primarily for labor–for example, five full-time workers were required in the first year to reforest 7 ha. It is important to note that the costs would probably be substantially less for a reforestation project without a research component. Costs are also likely to vary depending on the intended use of the trees. If timber harvesting is planned, improved harvesting practices would improve supply of watershed services. Although best management practices for timber harvesting may increase costs, Bruijnzeel and Critchley (1994:43) argue that "improved logging practices are not necessarily more expensive than conventional operations."

Under some circumstances, as with agroforestry, large-scale reforestation may be financially viable without additional payments for the ecosystem services provided. In particular, some (but certainly not all) of the native trees are valuable timber species. However, it is difficult to evaluate the economics of native species plantations due to the lack of available information on the species' growth rates. When native species is already profitable, payments for ecosystem services would then serve as additional incentives for managing land in an environmentally sensitive manner.

## DISCUSSION OF SUPPLY CONSIDERATIONS

Analysis of the watershed services provided by reforestation and agroforestry/silvipasture must acknowledge the associated decrease in total water yield as an additional, and perhaps critical, cost of these activities. Demand for water is already high in the PCW, and large-scale reforestation would further restrict the available annual supply of water. However, based on the incorrect assumption that forests increase annual water yield, the Government of Panama proposed to reforest 104,000 ha of agricultural and pasture lands within the PCW. The reforestation program, designed to increase annual and dry season flows and positively affect water quality, became the basis for Law 21, passed in 1997. One study estimated that the economic effects of complete conversion to forest cover in the PCW would amount to a $470 million loss in Panama if dry season water yield does not increase with reforestation (Aylward, 2002). This loss would result from water shortages that would cause loss of revenues from shipping transits; in addition, the global shipping industry would incur costs of $3 billion by using alternative shipping routes (Aylward, 2002). The methods and results of this study have been controversial, and, furthermore, these costs represent the extreme scenario of full reconversion. Nonetheless, they illustrate the potential scale of losses that could result from complete reforestation of the PCW if dry season flows do not increase. Thus, while the sediment and water quality effects of reforestation are likely to be positive, decision-makers need to consider the potential negative effects on water quantity. If reforestation does not increase dry season water yields, improving the agroforestry practices of smallholders in the PCW may be preferable to implementing large-scale reforestation projects that would exacerbate existing competition for water. In sufficient numbers, however, even small, individual agroforestry projects can collectively resemble large-scale reforestation; therefore, attempts to promote widespread agroforestry practices should also consider the possible effects on water supplies.

Two important factors potentially limit the ability of smallholders to supply watershed services in the PCW. First, small farmers or ranchers should be coordinated to supply watershed services, but these potential suppliers have not traditionally engaged in community organizing and collaboration (C. Elton, personal communication, 11 March 2005). Some level of cooperation is necessary to allocate payments for services among the smallholders, as well as to ensure that the smallholders are providing the services sought. Second, some of the land management options for providing watershed services require initial capital for agroforestry and silvipasture projects. According to Aylward (2002), 75 percent of the producers in the PCW, most of which hold less than 10 ha, do not have formal title to their land. Although many smallholders have possession rights, in protected areas like Chagres National Park, settlement is discouraged and formal land title is not an option. Smallholders certainly can participate in future markets for watershed services; however, the lack of formal, recognized rights to their land reduces their incentives to invest in the land and reduces their access to credit for such investments.

Assuming smallholders can overcome these obstacles, watershed services can be supplied at a range of scales. These include regional (within the PCW as a whole), subregional (within subwatersheds), and local (among neighboring parcels of land). The types of services that can be supplied and the beneficiaries of these services vary at different scales. For example, sedimentation might be reduced in a particular subwatershed, with the nearest water filtration plant as the subregional beneficiary. On the other hand, managing a single parcel of land to reduce fertilizer and pesticide use might benefit primarily the water supply of a farmer immediately downstream. Local markets may be particularly desirable for smallholders in Chagres National Park. For example, one smallholder might compensate an upstream neighbor, perhaps in the form of donated labor, to reforest the area around the headwaters of the spring that serves as his water supply. Chagres smallholders indicated to the authors during a March 2005 research trip to Panama that planting trees increases the water available to them in their local springs. Thus, there is potential for informal, local transactions to improve water quality and flow regulation through small-scale reforestation efforts.

A final consideration in evaluating the current supply of watershed services in the PCW is the issue of encouraging settlement in protected areas. Successfully managing land to provide watershed services may increase suppliers' standard of living, both through increased productivity and receipt of payments from consumers of watershed services. In protected areas like Chagres National Park, these benefits to smallholders may encourage permanent settlement and promote migration into the park. If population growth occurs in the park, environmental gains achieved by better land management could be overwhelmed by increased population pressures. Furthermore, if silvipasture allows ranchers to increase their numbers of cattle per ha, ranchers may offset the improvements by overly increasing their production.

## CONCLUSIONS

Managing land to provide watershed services from forest cover can reduce peak flows; attenuate flooding; control surface erosion and shallow mass movement; reduce organic and inorganic sedimentation, and thus reduce turbidity in water supplies; decrease pathogens and other contaminants in water supplies; reduce nutrient loading and eutrophication; and increase dissolved oxygen levels. Forests may improve dry season flows; however, they do not increase total water yield. In the PCW, large-scale reforestation and small-scale agroforestry/silvipasture can provide these services at varying degrees. Based on the research presented in this paper, large-scale reforestation may not be desirable in the PCW unless decreased water yield is an acceptable outcome or improved dry season flows can be shown. At present, then, efforts to develop markets for watershed services should focus on smallholders and erosion control, sediment reduction, and water quality improvement. Economic analyses of agroforestry in Panama and elsewhere in Central America suggest that these types of land management can be economically viable. Finally, this paper elucidates the need for greater research in Panama (and other tropical countries) on the ability of forests to increase dry season flows.

## REFERENCES

Academy for Educational Development (AED). 2004. Caracterización de la Actividad Ganadera en las Subcuencas de los Hules-Tinajones y Caño Quebrado. Retrieved 1 April 2005 from http://www.aedpanama.org/ aed/multimedia/documentos/17.pdf.

Alvarado, L.A. 1985. Sedimentation in Madden Reservoir. Meteorological and Hydrological Branch, Engineering Division, Panama Canal Commission, Balboa Heights, Panama.

Aylward, B. 2002. Strategic Framework. Report to the World Bank. Falls Church, Virginia.

Bosch, J.M. and J.D. Hewlett. 1982. A Review of Catchment Experiments to Determine the Effect of Vegetation Changes on Water Yield and Evapotranspiration. *Journal of Hydrology* 55:3-23.

Bradley, D.J. 1977. Health Aspects of Water Supplies in Tropical Countries. Pp. 3-17 in: R. Feachem, M. McGarry, and D. Mara (eds.). 1977. Water, Wastes and Health in Hot Climates. John Wiley & Sons, London.

Brooks, K.N., P.F. Folliott, H.M. Gregersen, and L.F. DeBano. 1997. Hydrology and the Management of Watersheds. Iowa State Press, Iowa.

Bruijnzeel, L.A. 1990. Hydrology of Moist Tropical Forest and Effects of Conversion: A State of Knowledge Review. UNESCO, Paris, and Vrije Universiteit, Amsterdam, The Netherlands.

Bruijnzeel, L.A. 2001. Hydrology of Tropical Montane Cloud Forests: A Reassessment. *Land Use and Water Resources Research* 1:1.1-1.18.

Bruijnzeel, L.A. 2004. Hydrological Functions of Tropical Forests: Not Seeing the Soil for the Trees? *Agriculture, Ecosystems and Environment* 104:185-228.

Bruijnzeel, L.A. and W.R.S. Critchley. 1994. Environmental Impacts of Logging Moist Tropical Forests. IHP Humid Tropics Programme Series No. 7.

Calder, I.R. No Date. Forest Valuation and Water: The Need to Reconcile Public and Science Perceptions. Understanding and Capturing the Multiple Values of Tropical Forests. Tropenbos International, Wageningen, The Netherlands.

Calder, I.R. 2001. Canopy Processes: Implications for Transpiration, Interception and Splash Induced Erosion, Ultimately for Forest Management and Water Resources. *Plant Ecology* 153(1-2):203-214.

Calder, I.R., D. Young, and J. Sheffield. No Date. Application of the HYLUC Model to Investigate the Direction and Magnitude of the Hydrological Impacts Resulting from a Proposed Afforestation Programme on the Panama Canal Watershed. Draft Paper presented to the Technical Support Team for the Panama Canal Watershed Interinstitutional Commission (CICH).

Chapin, F.S. III, P.A. Matson, and H.A. Mooney. 2002. Principles of Terrestrial Ecosystem Ecology. Springer-Verlag New York Inc., New York.

Critchley, W.R.S. and L.A. Bruijnzeel. 1996. Environmental Impacts of Converting Moist Tropical Forest to Agricultural Plantations. IHP Humid Tropics Programme Series No. 10.

Coughanowr, C. 1998. Wetlands of the Humid Tropics. IHP Humid Tropics Programme Series No. 12.

Current, D., E. Lutz, and S.J. Scherr. 1995. Adoption of Agroforestry. Pp. 1-27 in: D. Current, E. Lutz, and S.J. Scherr (eds.). 1995. Costs, Benefits, and Farmer Adoption of Agroforestry: Project Experience in Central America and the Caribbean. World Bank Environment Paper No. 14. The World Bank, Washington, DC.

Dalal, B.G., W. Ullah, and B. Singh. 1961. Fires in Relation to Watershed Management. Pp. 236-241 in: Proceedings of the Xth Silvicultural Conference, Dehradun, India.

Evison, L.M. and A. James. 1977. Microbiological Criteria for Tropical Water Quality. Pp. 30-51 in: R. Feachem, M. McGarry, and D. Mara (eds.). 1977. Water, Wastes and Health in Hot Climates. John Wiley & Sons, London.

Forsyth, T. 1996. Science, Myth, and Knowledge: Testing Himalayan Environmental Degradation in Thailand. *Geoforum* 27(3):375-392.

Fotos, M., F. Chou, and Q. Newcomer. 2007. Assessment of Existing Demand for Watershed Services in the Panama Canal Watershed. *Journal of Sustainable Forestry* 25(1/2):175-193.

Fotos, M., Q. Newcomer, and R. Kuppalli. 2007. Policy Alternatives to Improve Demand for Water-Related Ecosystem Services in the Panama Canal Watershed. *Journal of Sustainable Forestry* 25(1/2):195-216.

Gomez, M. 1995. Economic and Institutional Analysis of Agroforestry Products in Panama. Pp. 146-162 in: D. Current, E. Lutz, and S.J. Scherr (eds.). 1995. Costs, Benefits, and Farmer Adoption of Agroforestry: Project Experience in Central America and the Caribbean. World Bank Environment Paper No. 14. The World Bank, Washington, DC.

Hammond, B.W. 1999. *Saccharum spontaneum* (Gramineae) in Panama: The Physiology and Ecology of Invasion. Pp. 23-38 in: M.S. Ashton, J.L. O'Hara, and R.D. Hauff (eds.). 1999. Protecting Watershed Areas: Case of the Panama Canal. The Haworth Press, Inc., New York.

Heckadon-Moreno, S. 1993. The Impact of Development on the Panama Canal Environment. *Journal of Inter-American Studies and World Affairs* 35(3):129-149.

Heckadon-Moreno, S., R. Ibáñez, and R. Condit (eds.). 1999. La Cuenca del Canal: Deforestación, Contaminación y Urbanización. Proyecto de Monitoreo de la Cuenca del Canal de Panama (PMCC). Sumario Ejecutivo del Informe Final. Smithsonian Tropical Research Institute, Balboa, Panama.

Hibbert, A.R. 1967. Forest Treatment Effects on Water Yield. Pp. 527-543 in: W.E. Sopper and H.W. Lull (eds.). 1967. International Symposium on Forest Hydrology. Pennsylvania, September 1965. Pergamon, Oxford.

Hsia, Y.J. and C.C. Koh. 1983. Water Yield Resulting from Clearcutting a Small Hardwood Basin in Central Taiwan. Pp. 215-220 in: R. Keller (ed.). 1983. Hydrology of Humid Tropical Regions: Aspects of Tropical Cyclones, Hydrological Effects of Agriculture and Forestry Practice. Proceedings of a symposium held during the XVIIIth General Assembly of the International Union of Geodesy and Geophysics at Hamburg, Federal Republic of Germany, 15-27 August 1983. International Association of Hydrological Sciences, Washington, DC.

Hunter, P.R., P. Payment, N. Ashbolt, and J. Bartram. 2003. Assessment of Risk. Pp. 79-109 in: A. Dufour, M. Snozzi, W. Koster, J. Bartram, E. Ronchi, and L. Fewtrell (eds.). 2003. Assessing Microbial Safety of Drinking Water: Improving Approaches and Methods. Published on behalf of the World Health Organization and the Organisation for Economic Co-Operation and Development by IWA Publishing, London.

Ibáñez, R., R. Condit, G. Angehr, S. Aguilar, T. Garcia, R. Martínez, A. Sanjur, R. Stallard, S.J. Wright, A.S. Rand, and S. Heckadon-Moreno. 2002. An Ecosystem Report on the Panama Canal: Monitoring the Status of the Forest Communities and the Watershed. *Environmental Monitoring and Assessment* 80:65-95.

Intercarib, S.A. 1996a. Plan Regional para el Desarrollo de la Región Interoceánica: Mapa 1, Categorias de Permeabilidad de los Suelos. Prepared by Intercarib, S.A., Nathan Associates Inc. for the Autoridad de la Región Interoceánica (ARI) de la República de Panamá.

Intercarib, S.A. 1996b. Plan Regional para el Desarrollo de la Región Interoceánica: Mapa 3, Capacidad Agrológica de los Suelos. Prepared by Intercarib, S.A., Nathan Associates Inc. for the Autoridad de la Región Interoceánica (ARI) de la República de Panamá.

Intercarib S. A. and Nathan Associates. 1996c. Manejo Ambiental, Aspectos Institucionales, Económicos y Financieros: Volumen 2 de 2, Estudios Sectoriales. Panamá: Intercarib S.A. and Nathan Associates, Inc.

Instituto de Acueductos y Alcantarillados Nacionales (IDAAN). 2005. La Contaminación del Agua. Retrieved 4 April 2005 from http://www.idaan.gob.pa/contaminacion.htm.

Lal, R. 1983. Soil Erosion in the Humid Tropics with Particular Reference to Agricultural Land Development and Soil Management. Pp. 221-239 in: R. Keller (ed.). 1983. Hydrology of Humid Tropical Regions: Aspects of Tropical Cyclones, Hydrological Effects of Agriculture and Forestry Practice. Proceedings of a symposium held during the XVIIIth General Assembly of the International Union of Geodesy and Geophysics at Hamburg, Federal Republic of Germany, 15-27 August 1983. International Association of Hydrological Sciences, Washington, DC.

Landell-Mills, N. and I. Porras. 2002. Silver Bullet or Fools' Gold? A Global Review of Markets for Forest and Environmental Services and Their Impacts on the Poor. IIED/Earthscan, London.

Loewenberg, M. 1999. Sedimentation in the Panama Canal Watershed. Pp. 81-91 in: M.S. Ashton, J.L. O'Hara, and R.D. Hauff (eds.). 1999. Protecting Watershed Areas: Case of the Panama Canal. The Haworth Press, Inc., New York.

Medema, G.J., P. Payment, A. Dufour, W. Robertson, M. Waite, P. Hunter, R. Kirby and Y. Andersson. 2003. Safe Drinking Water: An Ongoing Challenge. Pp. 11-45 in: A. Dufour, M. Snozzi, W. Koster, J. Bartram, E. Ronchi, and L. Fewtrell (eds.). 2003. Assessing Microbial Safety of Drinking Water: Improving Approaches and Methods. Published on behalf of the World Health Organization and the Organisation for Economic Co-Operation and Development by IWA Publishing, London.

Pagiola, S. 2002. Paying for Water Services in Central America: Learning from Costa Rica. Pp. 37-61 in: S. Pagiola, J. Bishop, and N. Landell-Mills (eds.). 2002. Selling Forest Environmental Services: Market-Based Mechanisms for Conservation and Development. Earthscan, London.

Payment, P., M. Waite, and A. Dufour. 2003. Introducing Parameters for the Assessment of Drinking Water Quality. Pp. 47-77 in: A. Dufour, M. Snozzi, W. Koster, J. Bartram, E. Ronchi, and L. Fewtrell (eds.). 2003. Assessing Microbial Safety of Drinking Water: Improving Approaches and Methods. Published on behalf of the World Health Organization and the Organisation for Economic Co-Operation and Development by IWA Publishing, London.

Pescod, M.B. 1977. Surface Water Quality Criteria for Tropical Developing Countries. Pp. 52-72 in: R. Feachem, M. McGarry, and D. Mara (eds.). 1977. Water, Wastes and Health in Hot Climates. John Wiley & Sons, London.

Pickford, J. 1977. Water Treatment in Developing Countries. Pp. 162-191 in: R. Feachem, M. McGarry, and D. Mara (eds.). 1977. Water, Wastes and Health in Hot Climates. John Wiley & Sons, London.

PMCC. 1997. Panama Canal Watershed Ecological Monitoring: Annual Technical Report. Retrieved 22 February 2005 from http://www.anam.gob.pa/portadanew/ROCCAPAWEB/English/Main/Background/BackFrame/BackFrame.htm.

Stallard, R.F. 1999. Erosion and the Effects of Deforestation in the Panama Canal Basin. In: Panama Canal Watershed Monitoring Project (ed.). Report of the Panama Canal Watershed Monitoring Project, Chapter II.8, 8 volumes, 21 CD-ROMs.

Storey, P.J. 2002. The Conservation and Improvement of Sloping Land: A Manual of Soil and Water Conservation and Soil Improvement on Sloping Land. Volume I: Practical Understanding. Science Publishers, Inc., Enfield, NH.

United States Environmental Protection Agency (USEPA). 2002. Agricultural Management Practices for Water Quality Protection. Retrieved 20 February 2005 from http://ww_Hlt96687139wBM_1_.epa.gov/watertrain/agmodule/.

United States Environmental Protection Agency. 2005. List of Drinking Water Contaminants & MCLs. Retrieved 1 April 2005 from http://www.epa.gov/safewater/mcl.html.

Wiersum, K.F. 1985. Effects of Various Vegetation Layers in an *Acacia auriculiformis* Forest Plantation on Surface Erosion in Java, Indonesia. Pp. 79-89 in: S. El-Swaify, W.C. Moldenhauer, and A. Lo (eds.). 1985. Soil Erosion and Conservation. Soil Conservation Society of America, Ankeny, Iowa.

Williams, G.G. 1994. Soil and Water Conservation for Small Farm Development in the Tropics. Peace Corps, Information Collection and Exchange, Washington, DC.

doi:10.1300/J091v25n01_06

# Policy Alternatives for Improving Markets for Water Quality and Quantity in the Panama Canal Watershed

Michelle Lichtenfels

**SUMMARY.** Markets for ecosystem services are receiving ever-increasing attention from the global environmental community as a mechanism to conserve and protect environmental resources. Formal markets for the selling and buying of ecosystem services emerge as institutions and regulatory frameworks are developed and legitimized. For a small country with relatively abundant natural resources, such as Panama, ecosystem service markets have significant potential to provide landowners with a sustainable stream of income while facilitating national environmental protection goals. This paper takes one ecosystem service in Panama–water supply–and assesses a host of policy alternatives to improve markets for water in Panama. The analysis suggests that secured long-term financing mechanisms and strengthened institutional roles are important elements

Michelle Lichtenfels works for Portland Energy Conservation, Inc. (PECI), Portland, OR 97201 USA, where she administers energy efficiency programs for large California utilities. She recently worked as the Forest Carbon Policy Analyst at Environment Northeast, New Haven, CT 06510 USA, where she focused on energy and climate change policy solutions. Michelle Lichtenfels received her Master of Forestry from the Yale School of Forestry and Environmental Studies, New Haven, CT 06511 USA (E-mail: mlichtenfels@ gmail.com).

[Haworth co-indexing entry note]: "Policy Alternatives for Improving Markets for Water Quality and Quantity in the Panama Canal Watershed." Lichtenfels, Michelle. Co-published simultaneously in *Journal of Sustainable Forestry* (Haworth Food & Agricultural Products Press, an imprint of The Haworth Press, Inc.) Vol. 25, No. 1/2, 2007, pp. 147-174; and: *Emerging Markets for Ecosystem Services: A Case Study of the Panama Canal Watershed* (ed: Bradford S. Gentry, Quint Newcomer, Shimon C. Anisfeld, and Michael A. Fotos, III) Haworth Food & Agricultural Products Press, an imprint of The Haworth Press, Inc., 2007, pp. 147-174. Single or multiple copies of this article are available for a fee from The Haworth Document Delivery Service [1-800-HAWORTH, 9:00 a.m. - 5:00 p.m. (EST). E-mail address: docdelivery@haworthpress.com].

Available online at http://jsf.haworthpress.com
© 2007 by The Haworth Press, Inc. All rights reserved.
doi:10.1300/J091v25n01_07

in shaping stakeholder behavior and advancing water markets in Panama. doi:10.1300/J091v25n01_07 *[Article copies available for a fee from The Haworth Document Delivery Service: 1-800-HAWORTH. E-mail address: <docdelivery @haworthpress.com> Website: <http://www.HaworthPress.com> © 2007 by The Haworth Press, Inc. All rights reserved.]*

**KEYWORDS.** Hydrological services, ecosystem services markets, Panama Canal Watershed, watershed management policy

## INTRODUCTION

The Watershed of the Panama Canal comprises approximately 5 percent of the land base of Panama and is the center of commerce and industry in the country. Managed by the Panama Canal Authority (ACP), the Canal provides direct employment to over 9,000 people and boasted a gross income in 2003 of approximately US$863.6 million (ACP, 2003). The government of Panama has capitalized well on the Canal's significant natural resource base, resulting in a return of innumerable social and economic benefits to the country. However, shifting global perceptions of environmental sustainability and Panama's increasingly complex resource management picture invite a deeper analysis of governance and policy mechanisms within the country. In light of imminent decisions to be made about Canal expansion, now is an opportune time to examine policy instruments that may ensure a sustainably-managed resource well into the future for the people of Panama.

## BASIC DEFINITIONS AND QUESTIONS BEING ADDRESSED

This paper takes a look at policy instruments that could be enacted to increase the provision of water-related ecosystem services–including the aspects of quantity and quality–in the Panama Canal Watershed. The need to assess ecosystem services is not unique to Panama or to watersheds, thus the analytical process described in this paper employs a framework that can be applied across temporal and spatial scales, and to other services such as carbon sequestration. In any analysis of this sort, case history and traditional and non-traditional policy tools should be closely scrutinized for their effectiveness and potential relevance with respect to the analysis at hand. Where case studies are not addressed specifically in this analysis, the policy instruments employed in the cases have been described in general terms.

The markets for provision of water and water-related services in the Panama Canal Watershed (PCW) are inextricably linked to demand for such goods and services. For an analysis of existing demand and policy alternatives to stimulate demand for hydrological goods and services, see the two Fotos et al. papers in this volume. Those topics are not discussed further in this analysis. Additionally, Anderson's analysis of existing supply of water-related goods and services in the PCW (this volume) sets the stage for this analysis of how supply might be improved.

From a broad perspective, the goal of this analytical framework is to provide an assessment of how various applied, emerging, and hypothetical policy instruments are or might be used in the water market. The intention is to provide landowners and decision makers alike with a sturdy toolbox from which they may develop their own unique and (often) necessarily creative or resourceful site-specific assemblage of policies. A framework with breadth is as important as the changes each policy effects in the market, especially because watersheds and the services they provide are so locally unique that virtually no two outcomes for valuing these services across scales are liable to look alike.

Analysis of the socio-political and biophysical characteristics of a country provides an important base from which to assess various policy tools. The analytic requirements for an assessment of improvement of water supply policies are encapsulated in three broad categories: (1) public and private institutional analysis; (2) social and cultural context; and (3) a biophysical analysis of water supply.

## *Institutional Analyses*

The structure of institutions and their policies, partners, and representatives have a very important role in shaping the existing and potential markets for ecosystem services. For this reason, the analysis of institutions is a key component of this paper's framework. The World Bank (2005) identifies four areas for country policy and institutional assessments: (1) public sector management and institutions; (2) structural policies; (3) economic management; and (4) policies for social inclusion/equity. The indicators set forth in this type of assessment in turn affect such elements as enforcement, evaluation, monitoring, and biophysical changes across the landscape. Methods for assessing these areas and indicators attempt to capture quantitative data about policy tools within scorecards and matrices such as those developed by Gentry (2005). However, decisions regarding what policy tools to pursue are ultimately subjective.

Table 1 summarizes a selection of country indicators, and a sampling of Panama-specific questions these indicators generate. The Political Risk Services' 2004 Panama Country Forecast provides an excellent source of data for many of these ratings and is a useful reference outside the scope of this paper.

TABLE 1. Ratings and Indicators for Country Assessments (adapted from World Bank, 2005)

| Rating | Indicators | Panama-Specific Questions |
|---|---|---|
| **Economic Management** | 1. Management of inflation and macroeconomic imbalances<br>2. Fiscal policy<br>3. Management of public debt (external and domestic)<br>4. Management and sustainability of the development program | • How does public debt affect policy?<br>• How is the government constrained in imposing higher fees/taxes?<br>• In what ways will plans for Canal expansion impact the economy? |
| **Structural Policies** | 5. Trade policy and foreign exchange regime<br>6. Financial stability<br>7. Financial sector depth, efficiency, and resource mobilization<br>8. Competitive environment for the private sector<br>9. Goods and factor markets<br>10. Policies and institutions for environmental sustainability | • How does the stability of the legislature, presidency, and court system affect private investment in the country?<br>• What is the tolerance for risk among institutions?<br>• How sensitive is corporate behavior to changes in the market?<br>• What kind of watershed conservation practices are promoted by current policies, and at what scale? |
| **Policies for Social Inclusion/ Equity** | 11. Gender<br>12. Equity of public resource use<br>13. Building human resources<br>14. Social protection and labor<br>15. Monitoring and analysis of poverty outcomes and impacts | • What is the gender composition in the Panama workforce?<br>• Why is unemployment so high?<br>• How mobile is the labor force?<br>• What are the social and policy implications of the presence of small landholders in the national parks? |
| **Public Sector Management and Institutions** | 16. Property rights and rule-based governance<br>17. Quality of budgetary and financial management<br>18. Efficiency of revenue mobilization<br>19. Quality of public administration<br>20. Transparency, accountability and corruption in the public sector | • How well established are property rights? For disputes, upon who rests the burden of proof?<br>• How accessible is the GOP to the public and NGOs?<br>• What is the extent of and what forms of corruption are most common?<br>• Are there customary water rights and laws? |

## Social and Cultural Context

The social and cultural context of a region is composed of a variety of people, organizations, and institutions with "potentially different interests, information, roles, analytic and political challenges, and perspectives" (Clark et al., 2000:11). A rigorous social analysis asks such important questions as (Yale University F&ES, 2005a):

- Who are the participants?
- What are their perspectives?
- What are their principal values?
- What are their situations?
- What are their strategies (for affecting policy)?
- How might decisions impact them?
- What policies might they support?

Questions for assessing social context in Panama include:

- What social factors drive land use patterns?
- What is the power structure of various sectors?
- What informal institutions operate in Panama?
- What are the different scales at which the Watershed is effectively managed (basin, sub-basin, sub-watershed, small catchments, etc.) and what are the social causes of these arrangements?
- What are the perceived water supply issues by various groups?

## Biophysical Analysis

A biophysical analysis is an important element in policy development, especially in natural resource rich areas such as the PCW that are highly dependent on these resources for economic livelihood. Land use management decisions are often dispersed and fragmented across a number of private landowners, municipalities, provinces, federal government institutions, and other stakeholders. With so many potential managers and decision-makers, a variety of water supply goods and services can exist for any specific parcel of land.

Information necessary for a biophysical analysis of water supply of the PCW (both quantity and quality) includes:

- Trends in land use and water use;
- Impact of Canal expansion on water demand;
- Rates and importance of deforestation and other land use impacts;

- Variation and impact of dry season flows in the PCW;
- Scale at which the Watershed is most impacted; and
- Current and expected levels of pollutants.

For an analysis of these and other questions regarding the existing water supply, see Anderson (this volume).

## METHODOLOGY

### Data Collection

Research for this analysis was completed, in large part, over the course of March 6-12, 2005 while in Panama, and with great assistance by the Smithsonian Tropical Research Institute in Panama City. During the course of the week, informal interviews were conducted with research organizations; former government ministry officials; representatives from other public institutions, forest industry, and non-governmental organizations; small landholders; and other public and private actors in Panama. These interviews provided insight into the actions and perceptions of these same individuals and institutions, and the social and biophysical context of the country. Follow-up discussion with other students in the class provided additional information, feedback, and ideas to fuel this analysis.

### Data Analysis

Once data on institutions, social aspects, and biophysical aspects of Panama was collected, the aim was then to: (1) identify institutions involved in the supply of water goods and services; (2) identify existing policy tools for supply of water goods and services; (3) assess institutional challenges to providing these goods and services; and (4) use this information to examine potential policy tools for altering the supply of water to the Watershed.

A sample of potential policy tools is found in Appendix 2. This general matrix provides a good starting point for thinking about potential alternatives that could be considered by a variety of institutions.

### Testing Potential Policy Tools

Quantitatively testing the potential of policy tools identified in analysis step 4 was necessary to help distinguish the relative potential of each tool. For this analysis, effective policy tools are those that meet broad goals, including the ability to deliver results, balance costs and burdens, effect change, and take into account political and social feasibility (Yale University F&ES, 2005a; Yale University F&ES, 2005b; Gentry, 2005). The assessment framework uses a scale from 1 to 10 to assess real potential for each tool, with 1 indicating the lowest potential, 5 indicating unknown, and 10 ranking as high potential. Table 2, below, suggests a set of criteria with which to assess potential policy tools.

## DATA ANALYSIS SUMMARY

Because a more detailed analysis of existing water supply is covered in a separate chapter (Anderson, this volume), this analysis is primarily focused on summarizing policies related to water supply and exploring potential policy alternatives in more depth.

TABLE 2. Framework for Assessment of Potential Policy Tools (adapted from Gentry, 2005)

**Deliver Results**

| | |
|---|---|
| Meeting goals | Does tool reduce the cost of supplying ecosystem services or increase the supply of ecosystem services? |
| Environmental effectiveness | Is this an effective way to achieve environmental protection of a given ecosystem? |
| Equity and justice | Who is benefiting from policy? Who is paying? Are benefits distributed equally amongst different actors? What might be the consequences on local communities and low income people? |

**Costs and Burdens**

| | |
|---|---|
| Cost effectiveness and fairness | What is the cost to institutions and individuals? |
| Appropriate level of demand on government | What is the cost to government, and is this expense justified? |

**Change**

| | |
|---|---|
| Adaptability/workability | Can the tool be easily modified to adapt to change in context and trends? |
| Capacity building / innovation | Does the policy tool foster research and development? Does the policy tool encourage sharing of acquired knowledge? |

**Political and Social Structure**

| | |
|---|---|
| Political acceptance | How does the institutional and social analysis inform the ability of institutions to implement the policy tool? |
| Social acceptance | |

*Water Quantity.* The capacity of reforestation to increase the quantity of water within the Canal Watershed has been a subject of research and speculation over the past few decades. The potential to use reforestation as a tool for mitigating erosion, sedimentation, and pollution conflicts at times (Calder, 2001; Calder et al., 2000; Kinner et al., 1999; Stallard, 1999). In addition, while virtually every interviewee had a different speculative understanding of the impact of reforestation on water quantity and quality, no individual debated the virtues of reforestation efforts.

Interviews with smallholders in the Chagres National Park indicate that reforestation, water conservation projects, and capacity building efforts by groups such as Centro de Estudios y Acción Social Panameño (CEASPA) are important aspects of increasing productivity of their silvopastoral systems. For example, reforesting pasture land helps provide shade for cattle, improving their health, and PVC pipe networks allow farmers to direct water away from streams for agriculture and watering cattle, as opposed to impacting streams directly.

From an institutional standpoint, social research has yielded important information on public perception of water supply issues and effectiveness of public institutions to cope with burdens of water supply in Panama. According to multiple sources, approximately 42 percent of potable water processed by the Institute for National Water Supply and Sewerage Systems (IDAAN) is "lost" to water stealing and infrastructure disrepair leakages (Guardia, personal communication, 11 March 2005). Meanwhile, countless interviewees and general water use observed in Panama back the dominant paradigm that water is a "gift from God" (Endara, personal communication, 7 March 2005). Panamanians appear unwilling to pay for water, have a general disregard for basic water conservation efforts, and have a zero to low tolerance of water tariff increases (Guardia, personal communication, 11 March 2005). It is also important to note that access to potable water, equity, and ability to pay for basic water services are already of concern within Panama.

Additionally, high unemployment rates seem to lead to social unrest, and previous experience has shown that Panamanians are highly sensitive to service rate increases, for example, with utility charge increases and city bus fares (PRS Group, 2004). Political pressure from the public in combination with government agencies' budget deficits and dispersed authority over water amongst multiple agencies and the ACP stymies change in public as well as public/private institutions. One unfortunate result of this urban water supply complex is that IDAAN and ACP are pressured to build more water treatment plants to supply an ever-increasing level of water to urban areas and the Canal.

*Water Quality.* In the PCW, land use is comprised of a matrix of forests, agriculture, pasture, and urban uses. Although the rate of deforestation in the PCW has decreased over the last few years, agricultural and pastoral practices retain potential to exacerbate water quality problems. Increasing urbanization contributes to concerns about non-point and point-source pollution. Yet, as discussed above, smallholder efforts in Chagres National Park have contributed at least small positive impacts, improving riparian habitat (and presumably water quality) through the reduction of cattle pathogens directly into streams.

With regard to erosion and sedimentation, evidence from the hydrological modeling studies by Calder et al. (2000) points out that sedimentation in the PCW is more likely linked to intense rain events than deforestation. However, again, recent research by Stallard (1999) conflicts in part with this assumption as it attempts to find causal relationships between land use, surface ground cover, and deep erosion events.

Finally, increasing urbanization and the expansion of agriculture in the PCW have raised the level of concern over point and non-point source pollution containing oil residues, human and agricultural wastes, and agricultural by-products and nutrients. According to a former official of IDAAN, the primary concerns over water quality are turbidity and pathogens, with pathogens ranking particularly high in rural areas (Guardia, personal communication, 11 March 2005).

IDAAN is legally responsible for sewage systems and wastewater treatment in Panama; however, our research includes reports of inadequate or non-existent treatment of wastewater, and no system for collecting fees for wastewater (Castro, personal communication, 28 March 2005).

*Other Concerns.* Research shows that most of the producers in the Watershed have small or medium landholdings, and that a notable number of these producers also engage in subsistence activities as supplementary income (MIDA, 2002). However, it appears that Panama does not have a strong history of aggregating small landholders effectively. Small landholders generally do not form partnerships or cooperatives for engaging in dialogue of and sharing of information and new management practices to improve their silvopastoral practices. One community group suggested that if funding for their activities dried up in the next round of NGO/foundation funding allocations, small landholders would likely disaggregate once more, removing the ability of individual ranchers and farmers to share information and learn from each other towards greater productivity (Pizarro, personal communication, 8 March 2005). From discussions with various groups in Panama, it appears that the role of NGOs may be indispensable to funding and implementing projects in sub-watersheds, especially at small scales of management.

Other social concerns relate to the power structure of government institutions within the Watershed. ACP has almost complete autonomy from the central government, and has by far the greatest and most sustainable income generation. At the other end of the spectrum, other government institutions often operate at annual losses ranging in the millions of dollars. The case of IDAAN is notable. The agency lacks authority to regulate water sources or levy penalties for water contamination, and has difficulties collecting fees from customers (see Fotos, Chou and Newcomer, this volume).

Finally, research conducted within Panama shows a dispersed and ultimately ineffectual authority for physically protecting drinking water sources, providing water to urban areas, and enforcement of water quality standards. At this time, urban watershed management receives little official attention due to a lack of resources and cooperation amongst institutions. The statutorily-empowered partnership for coordinating environmental activities in the PCW, the Comisión Interinstitucional de la Cuenca Hidrográfica (CICH), does not include IDAAN among its members (Fotos, Chou and Newcomer, this volume). If water quantity and quality are of concern within the PCW, all stakeholders must be aligned and empowered to effect land management activities in the Watershed.

## RECOMMENDATIONS

Improved water supply may be effected through policy tools in a number of ways that are centered on improved partnerships between public agencies, non-profit organizations, and land managers. Additional strengthening of public agencies is necessary for a stable business environment and to develop an efficient mechanism for coping with urban water supply issues. Alternative policy options presented here are thought to be reasonable given the institutional and social context of Panama.

1. CICH already functions in part as a stakeholder group within the PCW, but not all stakeholders are included. The inclusion of additional groups, such as IDAAN, local NGOs (e.g., ANCON, CEASPA), and industry groups (e.g., ANARAP), might give CICH more legitimacy and more institutional memory to deal with Watershed concerns. Especially given the facts that CICH administers large funding sources and has a statutory mission to

facilitate integrated watershed management, it is uniquely positioned to address not only rural concerns, but urban concerns as well.

2. CICH might launch and foster development of volunteer regional land-use associations to collect user fees, similar to what has been done in the Cuaca Valley of Central Colombia (Echavarria, 2002). Volunteer fees might then help fund development projects throughout region, reduce reliance on outside (potentially unsustainable) funding, and an association might help engage landowners and smallholders in information sharing across effective scales of learning. Additionally, regional associations also have the capacity to develop institutional memory amongst regional users and smallholders in ways that have been underdeveloped in the past.

IDAAN is a key player in urban water supply issues. Although IDAAN is formally a part of the Ministry of Health, its role in creating and enforcing policy is not fully legitimized by the central government, ACP, or other major actors in the Watershed. Especially with prospective Canal expansion plans, water supply in the PCW will remain a priority. Potential policy decisions identified include:

3. Whether and, if so, how to shift internal resources toward improved fee collection and enforcement activities.
4. Whether and, if so, how to convert block water tariffs for residential water use to a uniform pricing with rebates (UPR) design to promote water conservation and efficiency as suggested by Whittington and Boland (Whittington and Boland, 2000). Water customers will need to clearly see proper economic incentives and price signals if the agency hopes to effect changes in behavior and improve economic efficiency.
5. ACP might create an environmental assessment fee per ship that creates an environmental fund for water-related projects. ACP is the one Panamanian institution with the most control and authority over its mission and resources. ACP has the potential to leverage Canal expansion plans in ways that call on existing partnerships to help pay for ecosystem services. This could be done in a number of ways:

   (a) Leverage existing MOUs;
   (b) As a contingency of Canal expansion lending, multilateral banks could require that ACP administer an environmental assessment fee per ship; and

(c) Channel fees in part towards a Drinking Water Fund and small NGOs working in sub-basins of the PCW, thereby creating a sustainable source of project funding.

6. ACP might develop a Drinking Water Fund that provides incentives for source drinking water protection through payments to existing watershed districts and/or to proposed regional land-use associations. Payment mechanisms exist through a portion of the proposed environmental assessment fee, as well as through channeling water treatment cost savings to the fund.

7. A coalition of academic and private groups that includes the Smithsonian Tropical Research Institute (STRI), the Native Species Reforestation Program (PRORENA), and ANARAP and others in the forest industry might align and form a common agenda to lobby the legislature to rewrite Law 24 to provide tax incentives for reforestation using a sanctioned list of native species. A reworking of Law 24 would help to promote reforestation throughout Panama, and the utilization of native species will further multiple ecosystem goals with respect to biodiversity, carbon sequestration, and water.

A matrix of institutions, existing policy tools, some of their constraints and challenges, and potential policy tools is included as Appendix 3.

In applying the policy assessment framework to the potential policy tools described earlier, the most likely potential tools are (1), (5), and (6) (see Table 3). However, these tools cannot be said to deserve priority consideration. While this assessment is relatively subjective, it does provide some context for relative potential of each policy tool. It is interesting to note that this ranking suggests a greater role of ACP and CICH in advancing water supply markets.

## CONCLUSION

This paper is an initial attempt to take a closer look at policy instruments for the provision of ecosystem services relating to water quantity and quality, using the Panama Canal Watershed as a test case. For a more in-depth analysis of the range of potential policy instruments and markets for the provision of ecosystem services, a closer look is needed at the body of other analyses performed parallel to this analysis and included in this volume. Resource management decisions are not blind to

TABLE 3. Assessment of Potential Policy Alternatives (adapted from Gentry, 2005)

| | Deliver Results | | | Costs and Burdens | | Change | | Political and Social Structure | | Overall Potential |
|---|---|---|---|---|---|---|---|---|---|---|
| | Meets Goals | Environmental Effectiveness | Equity | Cost Effectiveness | Appropriate Demand on Government | Adaptability Workability | Capacity Building / Innovation | Political Acceptance | Social Acceptance | |
| 1. Expand CICH to include ANAM, IDAAN, NGOs, and large-scale forest owners | 8 | 8 | 9 | 8 | 8 | 10 | 10 | 7 | 7 | 75 |
| 2. CICH launch and foster development of volunteer regional land-use associations to collect user fees | 8 | 7 | 6 | 5 | 10 | 10 | 10 | 8 | 5 | 69 |
| 3. IDAAN shift internal resources to fee collection and enforcement activities | 10 | 8 | 4 | 8 | 10 | 4 | 8 | 7 | 4 | 63 |
| 4. IDAAN convert block water tariffs for residential water use to a uniform pricing with rebates (UPR) design | 5 | 8 | 5 | 8 | 10 | 5 | 5 | 5 | 4 | 55 |
| 5. ACP create an environmental assessment fee per ship that creates an environmental fund for water-related projects | 9 | 9 | 9 | 9 | 10 | 9 | 7 | 8 | 9 | 79 |
| 6. ACP develop a "Drinking Water Fund" to promote source drinking water protection through payments to watershed districts and/or proposed regional land-use associations | 9 | 6 | 9 | 7 | 10 | 10 | 10 | 8 | 10 | 79 |
| 7. Coalition of academic and private groups lobby the legislature to rewrite Law 24, providing reforestation tax incentives using specified native species | 7 | 9 | 9 | 9 | 5 | 7 | 8 | 4 | 9 | 67 |

the compromises necessitated by other resource use allocations; therefore, data, analytical assumptions, common policies and potential conflicts amongst policy alternatives should be further analyzed in order to develop an effective, comprehensive national policy package related to ecosystem services provided by the Panama Canal Watershed.

# REFERENCES

Anderson, K. 2007. Existing Supply of Watershed Services in the Panama Canal Watershed. *Journal of Sustainable Forestry* 25(1/2):121-145.

Autoridad del Canal de Panama (ACP). 2003. Annual Report. Retrieved 25 February 2005 from http://www.pancanal.com/eng/general/reporte-anual/index.html.

Calder, I., D. Young, and J. Sheffield. 2000. Application of the HYLUC model to investigate the direction and magnitude of the hydrological impacts resulting from a proposed afforestation programme on the Panama Canal Watershed (DRAFT). Retrieved 22 July 2005 from http://www.cluwrr.ncl.ac.uk/projects/tadpole/panamahyluc.pdf.

Calder, I. 2001. Forest valuation and water- the need to reconcile. Pp 49-62 in: P. Verweij (ed.). 2001. Understanding and capturing the multiples values of tropical forest. Proceedings of the International Seminar on Valuation and Innovative Financing Mechanisms in support of Conservation and sustainable management of tropical forest. Retrieved 22 July 2005 from http://www.tropenbos.org/files/Verweij/011Calder.pdf.

Clark, T.W., D. Casey, and A. Halverson (eds.). 2000. Developing Sustainable Management Policy for the National Elk Refuge, Wyoming. Yale School of Forestry and Environmental Studies Bulletin Series, Number 104. Retrieved 5 April 2005 from http://www.yale.edu/forestry/publications/fespubfiles/bulletin/104.html.

Echavarría, M. 2002. Water user associations in the Cuaca Valley, Colombia: A voluntary mechanism to promote upstream-downstream cooperation in the protection of rural watersheds. Land-Water Linkages in Rural Watersheds Case Study Series. FAO, Rome, Italy. Retrieved 5 April 2005 at http://www.fao.org/ag/agl/watershed/watershed/papers/papercas/paperen/colombia.pdf.

Fotos, M., F. Chou, and Q. Newcomer. 2007. Assessment of Existing Demand for Watershed Services in the Panama Canal Watershed. *Journal of Sustainable Forestry* 25(1/2):175-193.

Fotos, M., Q. Newcomer, and R. Kuppalli. 2007. Policy Alternatives to Improve Demand for Water-Related Ecosystem Services in the Panama Canal Watershed. *Journal of Sustainable Forestry* 25(1/2):195-216.

Gentry, B. (ed.). 2005. Emerging Markets for Ecosystem Services: draft framework for analysis (Working Draft, 9 January). Yale University School of Forestry and Environmental Studies, New Haven, CT.

Kinner, D.A. and R.F. Stallard. 1999. The hydrologic model TOPMODEL. Chapter II.9 in: Panama Canal Watershed Monitoring Project Staff (eds.). Report of the Panama Canal Watershed Monitoring Project. 8 volumes, 21 CD-ROMs.

National MIDA Support Technical Team (MIDA). 2002. National Document of the Strategy and Concept for the Formulation of an Investment Program. Ministerio de. Desarrollo Agropecuario, Government of the Republic of Panama.

Newcomer, Q. 2004. Emerging Markets for Ecosystem Services. *Business Costa Rica* 12(4): 22-24.

Political Risk Services (PRS Group). 2004. Panama Country Forecast. PRS Group, Inc. December 1.

Stallard, R.F. 1999. Erosion and the effects of deforestation in the Panama Canal Basin. Chapter II.8 in: Panama Canal Watershed Monitoring Project Staff (eds.). Report of the Panama Canal Watershed Monitoring Project. 8 volumes, 21 CD-ROMs.

Whittington, D. and J. Boland. 2000. Water Tariff Design in Developing Countries: Disadvantages of Increasing Block Tariffs (IBTs) and Advantages of Uniform Price with Rebate (UPR) Designs. Draft paper. The World Bank.

World Bank. 2005. Country Policy and Institutional Assessment 2003. Assessment Questionnaire. Retrieved 25 February 2005 from http://siteresources.worldbank. org/IDA/Resources/CPIA2003.pdf.

Yale University School of Forestry and Environmental Studies, F&ES 763b. 2005a. "What does the policy literature tell us about efforts to enhance markets for ecosystem services?" Session 6 of Emerging Markets for Ecosystem Services, 15 February 2005. Yale University, New Haven, CT. Adapted from T. Clark. 2002. *The Policy Process: A practical guide for natural resource practitioners.* Yale University Press, New Haven, CT.

Yale University School of Forestry and Environmental Studies, F&ES 763b. 2005b. "How to integrate the science, business, and policy assessments for particular sites in particular countries?" Session 7 of Emerging Markets for Ecosystem Services, 22 February 2005. Yale University, New Haven, CT.

doi:10.1300/J091v25n01_07

APPENDIX 1. Potential Water Supply Goods and Services and Their Suppliers, Managers, and Consumers in the Context of Panama (adapted from Gentry, 2005; and Newcomer, 2004)

| Ecosystem / Land Use | Goods | Services | Suppliers | Managers | Consumers |
|---|---|---|---|---|---|
| **Agriculture and Pasture Lands** | • Food crops<br>• Fiber crops<br>• Genetic resources | • Improve/maintain water quality<br>• Improve/maintain water quantity<br>• Erosion and sedimentation control<br>• Cycle nutrients | • Ranchers<br>• Production farmers<br>• Part-time farmers<br>• Subsistence farmers<br>• National parks | • Agriculture and Livestock Ministry (MIDA)<br>• National Environment Authority (ANAM)<br>• ACP<br>• CICH | • Panamanian urban cities<br>• International markets<br>• Transportation and shipping companies |
| **Forest** | • Timber (natural and plantation)<br>• Habitat for riparian and wetland species<br>• Fuelwood<br>• Drinking and irrigation water<br>• NTFPs<br>• Genetic resources | • Erosion and sedimentation control<br>• Improve water quality<br>• Regulate water flow and timing<br>• Water filtration<br>• Cycle nutrients | • Production farmers<br>• Part-time farmers<br>• Subsistence farmers<br>• Forest industry<br>• National parks and other public landowners<br>• ACP | • Reforestation organizations (PRORENA)<br>• Forest industry (Ecoforest, Futuro Forestal, ANARAP, etc.)<br>• National parks and other publicly managed land<br>• ACP<br>• CICH<br>• NGOs (TNC, CEASPA, etc.) | • Panamanian urban cities<br>• International markets<br>• Transportation and shipping companies<br>• Hydroelectric companies (La Fortuna, Bayano, La Estrella-Los Valles)<br>• State electric utility (IRHE) |

| | Goods | Services | Users | Managers / Agencies | Markets |
|---|---|---|---|---|---|
| **Coastal** | • Fish, shellfish, and other food products<br>• Habitat for riparian and wetland species | • Moderate storm impacts<br>• Dilute and treat wastes<br>• Provide harbors and transportation routes | • Fishing industry<br>• ACP | • Fishing industry<br>• ACP | • Panamanian urban cities<br>• International markets<br>• Transportation and shipping companies<br>• Tourist markets |
| **Freshwater and Riverine** | • Drinking and irrigation water<br>• Fish<br>• Habitat for riparian and wetland species | • Store water<br>• Buffer water flow<br>• Dilute and carry wastes<br>• Cycle nutrients<br>• Provide transportation corridors | • Production farmers<br>• Part-time farmers<br>• Subsistence farmers<br>• Forest industry<br>• National parks and other public landowners<br>• ACP | • Institute for National Water Supply and Sewerage Systems (IDAAN)<br>• ACP<br>• ENTRE<br>• Ministry of Health | • Panamanian urban cities<br>• International markets<br>• Transportation and shipping companies<br>• Hydroelectric companies<br>• State electric utility (IRHE)<br>• IDAAN<br>• ACP |

APPENDIX 2. Potential Policy Tools (adapted from Kuppalli, personal communication, March 2005; F&ES, 2005b; Gentry, 2005)

| Policy Type | Sub-Type | Description | Conditions / Considerations |
|---|---|---|---|
| **Information** | Government required information disclosure | • Government requires entity to disclose information regarding its environmental impact | • Public understanding of information<br>• Information symmetry/access<br>• Government institutional capacity for information management<br>• Private burden to report to government |
| | Non-state market driven (NSMD) | • Includes labeling/certifications, reporting, and ranking | • Relies on 3rd party verification<br>• Often desirable to have more than one scheme<br>• Appropriate stringency of criteria |
| **Affecting Market Frameworks** | Liability rules | • Government regulation makes entity liable for environmental damage and must provide remuneration for damages | • Cost of potential liability must be higher than damage<br>• Requires enforcement<br>• Causal link should be strong<br>• Damage must be quantifiable |

| Policy Type | Sub-Type | Strengths | Weaknesses | Example |
|---|---|---|---|---|
| **Information** | Government required information disclosure | • Fill gaps in knowledge<br>• Process of collecting info can itself change behavior<br>• Allow flexibility in designing response<br>• Encourage participation/support<br>• Politically easier to adopt than many standards | • No control over response<br>• Only change behavior if "care"<br>• No certainty of any substantive impact<br>• Not free | • Require drinking water supply companies to disclose information about origin of water and efforts to protect water supply |
| | Non-state market driven (NSMD) | • See above | • See above | • Eco-labeling based on life-cycle assessment |
| **Affecting Market Frameworks** | Liability rules | • Remedy for harm done<br>• May deter others from causing harm<br>• Can fill gaps in regulatory requirements | • Requires harm to have been done<br>• Transaction costs can be high<br>• Legal effect limited to parties<br>• Court judgments vary in substance<br>• Who has access to the courts? | • Require land developers to ensure watershed protection<br>• Require drinking water supply companies to meet water quality standards |

APPENDIX 2 (continued)

| Policy Type | Sub-Type | Description | Conditions / Considerations |
|---|---|---|---|
| **Affecting Market Frameworks (cont'd)** | Command and control | • Government requires and enforces environmental standards<br>• Government can impose management or technology standards to achieve requirements | • Institutional capacity and enforcement<br>• Liability for non-compliance<br>• Government can allow compensation in place of compliance |
| | Taxes and emissions charges | • Government imposes emissions charge on every unit of pollution generated or on each unit of production leading to pollution<br>• Government imposes tax for usage of ecosystem service | • Charge must provide economic incentive<br>• Pollution charge commensurate to environmental damage<br>• Revenue should be directed appropriately |

| Policy Type | Sub-Type | Strengths | Weaknesses | Example |
|---|---|---|---|---|
| **Affecting Market Frameworks (cont'd)** | Command and control | • Generalized control<br>• Forward looking/ precautionary<br>• Formal processes to adopt<br>• Specify desired outcomes<br>• Can be powerful against some targets | • Can be difficult to adopt/impose<br>• Require enforcement<br>• Have gaps in coverage<br>• Can lead to inefficient allocations of control | • Require water utility to maintain certain level of forest conservation and reforestation in order to achieve water quality standards |
| | Taxes and emissions charges | • Direct cost internalization<br>• Allow market to allocate costs of control<br>• Provide broad incentives to improve and fund investments in public goods | • Political acceptability varies widely<br>*Uncertainty about:*<br>• Amount to be charged<br>• Impact on quantity/ performance<br>• Use of revenues<br>• Effects of tax burden (equity, competitiveness)<br>• Administrative costs | • Require water polluters to pay tax per unit of pollution<br>• Require shipping companies to pay user fee for canal passage |

*167*

| Policy Type | Sub-Type | Description | Conditions / Considerations |
|---|---|---|---|
| **Affecting Market Frameworks (cont'd)** | Property rights | • Government assigns property rights over right to pollute; rights may be tradable | • Detailed regulatory framework<br>• Substantial government involvement in market start-up<br>• Establish the trading scheme by creating demand<br>• Defining standards and rights<br>• Enforcement and monitoring<br>• Entity must manage registry |
| **Shared Investments / Public-Private Partnerships** | Passive public investment | • Includes debt, equity, grants, insurance/guarantees<br>• Government contributes public funds to increase demand for ecosystem services | • Where will secured funds come from?<br>• Could involve debt-for-nature swap deals with private financial institutions |
| | Government subsidies | • Government provides tax breaks for desirable activities | • How to secure long-term financing?<br>• How to ensure incentives are not perverse and/or taken advantage of by landowners/companies? |
| | Joint ventures | • Governments actively participates in payments/ markets for ecosystem services by partnering with non-profit and for-profit entities | • Government of Panama and Panama Canal Authority control vast tracks of land within Canal Watershed that could be used in joint venture activities |

| Policy Type | Sub-Type | Strengths | Weaknesses | Example |
|---|---|---|---|---|
| **Affecting Market Frameworks (cont'd)** | Property rights | *Tradable rights:*<br>• Encourages investment<br>• Promotes innovation and lowest cost solutions<br>• Does have preconditions<br>• Working regulatory structures<br>• Efficient/effective market for trades | *Tradable rights:*<br>• Politically acceptable?<br>• Environmentally effective?<br>• Administratively possible?<br>• Fair?<br>• Should we "commodify" the environment? | • Allow for trading of water quality credit trading within assigned watersheds |
| **Shared Investments / Public-Private Partnerships** | Passive public investment | • Direct payments for ecosystem services<br>• Provide broad incentives for experimentation in improving performance<br>• Need functioning, willing governments | • Politically acceptable?<br>• Varying outcomes/ responses<br>• Administrative costs<br>• Unintended consequences of subsidies<br>• Government turnover | • Buy forest ecosystem services (or related products) from sellers in the market |
| | Government subsidies | • Provides direct income streams and benefits to landowners<br>• Well-crafted policy can target low-income landowners and address multiple policy goals | • History showed benefits from Law 24 provided perverse incentives that favored wealthy landowners | • Provide tax breaks to hydropower companies and farmers to pay for upstream forestland management |

APPENDIX 2 (continued)

| Policy Type | Sub-Type | Strengths | Weaknesses | Example |
|---|---|---|---|---|
| **Shared Investments/ Public-Private Partnerships (cont'd)** | Joint ventures | • Leverages existing government resources with external funding sources<br>• Projects administered by private entities | • Requires administrative oversight<br>• Clear market opportunities and institutional infrastructure do not currently exist in Panama | • Enter into JV with deforested land owner to start reforestation operations<br>• Provide non-profit entity with land to be reforested and included in international ecosystem markets (e.g., carbon) |

APPENDIX 3. Existing and Potential Policy Tools in the Panama Canal Watershed

### Government

| Institution | Existing Policy Tools | Institutional and Social Constraints and Challenges | Potential Policy Tools | Type of Policy |
|---|---|---|---|---|
| National Environment Authority (ANAM) | • Regulates protected areas, air, water, land, EIS, etc. | • Staff turnovers ever 5 years reduce effectiveness<br>• Role of ANAM unclear in watershed decision-making | | |
| Agriculture and Livestock Ministry (MIDA) | • Sustainable development programs | • Do not appear to have a strong role in policy or projects | | |
| Panama Canal Watershed Interinstitutional Commission (CICH) | • Research & project implementation group | • Limited in involvement by some government groups and industry<br>• Balance use of bottom-up approaches and top-down approaches | • Expand CICH to include ANAM, IDAAN, ANARAP, and large-scale forest owners<br>• Develop volunteer regional land-use associations to impose user fees<br>• Administer ACP environmental assessment tax | • Public-private partnerships<br>• Volunteer markets |
| Institute for National Water Supply and Sewerage Systems (IDAAN) | • Filter water<br>• Supply drinking water to Panama | • No authority over water source<br>• Politically challenging to change water fee structure<br>• Few resources to combat water stealing and degraded infrastructure | • Lobby for a position on CICH<br>• Shift resources to fee collection<br>• Long-term: Convert block water tariffs for residential water use to UPR design to promote conservation & efficiency | • Public-private partnerships<br>• Command and control regulations |

APPENDIX 3 (continued)

| Institution | Existing Policy Tools | Institutional and Social Constraints and Challenges | Potential Policy Tools | Type of Policy |
|---|---|---|---|---|
| **Public/Private** | | | | |
| Panama Canal Authority (ACP) | • Law 19 gives ACP authority over PCW, authority to issue permits for water activities | • Haven't worked collaboratively with IDAAN in the past | • Create an environmental assessment fee per ship that creates an environmental fund for water-related projects, leverage existing MOUs as necessary<br>• Provide incentives for source drinking water protection through payments to watershed districts | • Taxes<br>• Subsidies |
| **Academic/Research** | | | | |
| Smithsonian Tropical Research Institute (STRI), Native Species Reforestation Program (PRORENA) | • World-class research institution and facilities<br>• Reforestation tools | • Ostensible desire to maintain politically neutral | • Lobby legislature to rewrite Law 24 to provide incentives for reforestation using sanctioned list of native species | • Public-non-profit partnerships<br>• Encourage use of subsidies |
| **Private** | | | | |
| National Association of Panamanian Reforesters (ANARAP) | • Nation-wide reforestation association | • No large industrial landowner members<br>• Reforestation sector "inefficient"<br>• Legislative process left them out in the past<br>• Weakening of Law 24 weakens incentives to reforest | • Become a larger political player by bringing in new industrial forest landowners<br>• Lobby legislature to rewrite Law 24 to provide incentives for reforestation using sanctioned list of native species | • Encourage government subsidies |

172

| | | | |
|---|---|---|---|
| Small Landowners | • Utilize tools provided by NGOs | • Relatively weak ability to aggregate without influence of NGO | • Public-private partnerships<br>• Encourage government subsidies |
| Forest Industry (e.g., Ecoforest, Futuro Forestal) | • Forest certification<br>• Investment in converting pasture into forest land | • Focuses on economic efficiency and private investment may preclude involvement in public sector | • Join ANARAP or strengthen forest industry lobby in Panama<br>• Lobby legislature to rewrite Law 24 to provide incentives for reforestation using sanctioned list of native species |

*NGO/International/Other*

| | | | |
|---|---|---|---|
| Small NGOs (e.g., Centro de Estudios y Acción Social Panameño—CEASPA) | • Facilitate site specific agro- and silvopastoral projects via funding through TNC, etc. | • Short term projects (2 years) and funding | • Build long-term partnerships with public/private institutions (ACP and CICH) to increase access to long-term funding (environmental assessment tax) | • Public-non-profit partnerships |
| The Nature Conservancy (TNC) | • Channel DFN funding to provide incentives for smallholder agro- and silvopastoral productivity at edge of parks | • Maintain TNC mission | • Public-non-profit partnerships |

| Institution | Existing Policy Tools | Institutional and Social Constraints and Challenges | Potential Policy Tools | Type of Policy |
|---|---|---|---|---|
| **NGO / International / Other, continued** | | | | |
| Academy for Educational Development (AED) | • Administers USAID funding<br>• Conducts pilot project studies within sub basin communities | • Short term funding of pilot projects | • Follow through with goals to enhance rancher sub-watershed management structures | • Public-non-profit partnerships |
| Multilateral Lending Institutions for Canal Expansion | | | • As a contingency of funding, require that ACP administer additional environmental impact assessment fee per ship | • Taxes |

# WATER DEMAND

# Assessment of Existing Demand for Watershed Services in the Panama Canal Watershed

Mike Fotos
Fuphan Chou
Quint Newcomer

**SUMMARY.** This paper examines the existing demand for watershed services provided by reforestation in the Panama Canal Watershed. The

Mike Fotos is Visiting Assistant Professor of Public Policy at Trinity College, Hartford, CT 06106 USA. He was Guest Lecturer for the course Emerging Markets for Ecosystem Services in the Spring of 2005 at the Yale School of Forestry and Environmental Studies, New Haven, CT 06511 USA (E-mail: Michael.Fotos@trincoll.edu).

Fuphan Chou earned a Master of Environmental Management at the Yale School of Forestry and Environmental Studies and a Master of Business Administration at the Yale School of Management, New Haven, CT 06511 USA (E-mail: fuphan@gmail.com).

Quint Newcomer is Director of the University of Georgia's Campus in Costa Rica, San Luis de Monteverde, Costa Rica. Quint Newcomer was Teaching Fellow for the course Emerging Markets for Ecosystem Services during the Spring 2003 and Spring 2005 semesters at the Yale School of Forestry and Environmental Studies, New Haven, CT 06511 USA (E-mail: quintn@uga.edu).

[Haworth co-indexing entry note]: "Assessment of Existing Demand for Watershed Services in the Panama Canal Watershed." Fotos, Mike, Fuphan Chou, and Quint Newcomer. Co-published simultaneously in *Journal of Sustainable Forestry* (Haworth Food & Agricultural Products Press, an imprint of The Haworth Press, Inc.) Vol. 25, No. 1/2, 2007, pp. 175-193; and: *Emerging Markets for Ecosystem Services: A Case Study of the Panama Canal Watershed* (ed: Bradford S. Gentry, Quint Newcomer, Shimon C. Anisfeld, and Michael A. Fotos, III) Haworth Food & Agricultural Products Press, an imprint of The Haworth Press, Inc., 2007, pp. 175-193. Single or multiple copies of this article are available for a fee from The Haworth Document Delivery Service [1-800-HAWORTH, 9:00 a.m. - 5:00 p.m. (EST). E-mail address: docdelivery@haworthpress.com].

Available online at http://jsf.haworthpress.com
© 2007 by The Haworth Press, Inc. All rights reserved.
doi:10.1300/J091v25n01_08

analysis assumes certain watershed services to be potentially marketable (i.e., that these services do indeed exist and are fungible), and focuses on ascertaining the potential demand for dry season flow regulation, nutrient regulation, and sediment filtration. The analysis examines actual and potential demand for these services from five known water consumers: the Panama Canal Authority, private shippers who use the Canal, hydroelectric producers, the Comisión Interinstitucional de la Cuenca Hidrográfica, and the National Aqueducts and Sewage Institution. We find that actual demand is much lower than the potential indicated by the value each consumer realizes from its water use. We attribute the difference to scientific uncertainty regarding the link between dry season flows and forest conversion and to institutional factors specific to each consumer. doi:10.1300/J091v25n01_08 *[Article copies available for a fee from The Haworth Document Delivery Service: 1-800-HAWORTH. E-mail address: <docdelivery@haworthpress.com> Website: <http://www.HaworthPress. com> © 2007 by The Haworth Press, Inc. All rights reserved.]*

**KEYWORDS.** Hydrological services, watershed services, ecosystem services, Panama Canal Watershed

## *INTRODUCTION*

The people of Panama rely on the fresh water that flows from their land for the generation of electricity, for domestic consumption, and for the operation of the eponymous Canal–that critical driver of global trade and the nation's economy. As have many others, we note the economic value of the ecosystem services provided by the Panama Canal Watershed (PCW), and have at times succumbed to the intuitively pleasing notion that where such value is realized, a certain willingness to pay must inevitably follow. We admit to feeling a little puzzled by the fact that the existing demand for watershed services–i.e., the legally feasible, institutionally articulated capacity to pay for land management practices that provide or enhance hydrological services provided by PCW lands–is in fact rather limited.

As with any puzzle in applied research, hand-wringing over the stubborn refusal of the subject to behave as we wish does not solve the problem. It is better to understand the problem by employing a theoretically-sound study design and research methodology. Our method of choice is the policy sciences approach (see Clark and Willard, 2000). The chosen approach requires a level of self-scrutiny on the part of the researcher/observer and directs attention to the historic trends and conditions that have influenced the object of analysis, be it the study subject or the observers themselves (Clark and Willard, 2000:10). Our researcher/observer bias reflects our North American university training (see Ostrom, 1989). Our academic heritage instilled in us a reflexive attachment to an analytic paradigm of resource allocation decisions that lead reliably toward Pareto optimal levels of investment in reforestation and habitat restoration. We note the bias because it is potentially misleading and, thus, a little inoculation serves both the reader and the authors.

The requisite self-scrutiny reminds us of Oliver Williamson's commentary on the study of economic and social development "from the bottom up." Comparisons between the performance of existing institutional arrangements and their feasible alternatives are more useful than comparisons between the subject case and some theoretical ideal that doesn't exist in nature (see Williamson, 2000). In simple language, researchers are wise to remember that people do things for a reason.

The history of Canal administration under the U.S. Canal Commission and in recent years under the Government of Panama (GOP) forms a record of collective decisions made and confirmed with respect to the institutional arrangements that determine markets for ecosystem services. We believe the various Canal-related measures passed by Panama's democratically elected legislature in the post-Noriega period form a record of reaffirmation that deserves considerable weight in our analysis of existing demand for watershed services. As reported on the official website of the Panama Canal Authority (ACP) (ACP, 2005a), key parts of that record include:

- Law 44 of August 1999 defines the legal boundaries of the Canal Watershed to include the traditional Chagres River watershed plus additional lands in the provinces of Cocle and Colón (putatively to support proposed Canal expansion);
- Title XIV of the Constitution of the Republic of Panama and the Panama Canal Authority Organic Law have assigned to ACP the responsibility for the administration, maintenance, use and conservation of the water resources of the Panama Canal Watershed. The law also requires that the Panama Canal Authority administer such water resources to ensure the supply of water to adjacent populated areas; and
- The Organic Law of the Panama Canal stipulates that an Inter-institutional Commission for the Canal Watershed (CICH) should

be established for the purpose of integrating the efforts, initiatives, and resources of the Canal Authority and other government agencies for watershed conservation and management.

The subsequent record of ACP and CICH strongly infer that GOP policy is based on an expectation that these agencies will be responsive to the needs of citizens and groups in the Watershed (ACP, 2005b). Our investigation does not detect any expectation in the law or administrative practice that indicates either ACP or CICH are charged with changing existing institutional arrangements with respect to payments to landowners for watershed services.

We arrive at this conclusion without judging the potential value of such services and prior to a determination of whether or not the major water users are able or willing to acquire them. We proceed with the recognition that existing institutional arrangements are likely to endure and furthermore, these arrangements presuppose certain relationships among the users and providers of watershed services. In short, ACP is imbued with an organizational outlook, informed by history and its legal mandate that inclines it to "make" rather than "buy" any necessary ecosystem services. It is this institutional factor that explains why the demand for watershed services within the PCW is so limited.

## OVERVIEW OF WATER USAGE
## IN THE PANAMA CANAL WATERSHED

Annual run-off, the potential "supply" of water, "produced" on the 295,000 hectares of land lying in the traditional Panama Canal Watershed is 4.4 billion cubic meters. This water flows toward both the Caribbean Sea and the Pacific Ocean to meet the needs of the Canal locks, hydroelectric power producers, urban centers, and other water users.

The Canal accounts for most of the water use in the PCW. Water is stored in Lake Alajuela and Lake Gatún for Canal operations. The water stored in Lake Alajuela drains into Lake Gatún, and produces electricity along the way. Lake Gatún feeds into locks on both the Caribbean and Pacific slopes within the Watershed. Water not needed for Canal operation flows into the Gatún Spillway where it is directed to Gatún Dam for electric generation (ACP, 2005b).

The Canal Watershed also provides about 95 percent of the drinking water for the inhabitants of the cities of Colón, Panama, San Miguelito and in the near future, Chorrera. As noted in Table 1, annual drinking

TABLE 1. Water Users, Consumption and Value in the Panama Canal Watershed (quantity estimates from Condit et al., 2001; value estimates from Aylward, 2002)

| Water Users in the PCW | | Annual Water Use (billion m³) | Percent of Annual Runoff | Implied Value (US$/m³) |
|---|---|---|---|---|
| Canal Locks | | 2.6 | 59.1% | 0.011 (ACP) 1.160 (Shippers) |
| Gatún Spillway | Gatún Dam Hydropower | 1.2 | 27.3% | 0.004 |
| | Gatún Spillway | 0.33 | 7.5% | n/a |
| Drinking Water | | 0.27 | 6.1% | 0.112 |
| Total | | 4.4 | 100% | 1.297 |

water consumption in these cities totals 270 million cubic meters. There are also a number of hydroelectric dams in the PCW, the two largest being Gatún Hydroelectric Dam and Madden Hydroelectric Dam. Both are operated by the Canal Authority, and produce electricity for Canal operations and for sale to the local grid.

## PANAMA CANAL AUTHORITY AS CANAL OPERATOR

The Panama Canal Authority operates and administers the Canal. In this capacity, its actions are designed to ensure that the "Canal may operate in a safe, continuous, efficient, and profitable manner" (ACP, 2005a).

The ACP is an agency of the GOP and the majority of its employees are Panamanians who are responsible to a Panamanian Board of Directors. The history of the Canal and the national history of Panama are inexorably linked. For decades, Panamanian politics revolved around efforts to assert sovereignty over the Canal. Former President Omar Torrijos is among Panama's most significant and respected historical figures because of his role in negotiating the treaties that obligated the U.S. to turn control of the Canal and the Canal Zone over to Panama (Falcoff, 1998).

Nevertheless, the legacy of North American involvement retains a considerable pull on Canal affairs. ACP has many long-time employees, including a significant number of "ex-pats," who were hired when the Canal was under U.S. control prior to 1999. Compensation is generous by Latin American standards. ACP holds a number of advantages over other Panamanian organizations and government agencies because of its legal and financial autonomy. From time to time, it has used its legal powers to evict or relocate Panamanians living in areas deemed essential to Canal operation. Readers familiar with the public water and power agencies in the U.S. that date their founding to the time of Canal construction–the so-called Progressive Era, corresponding roughly to the period from 1890 to 1930–will note common features in organizational history and outlook including governance by independent commission, a bureaucracy staffed by career employees selected on the basis of education or credentials (typically related to a field of engineering), and a generally hierarchical, project-oriented method for planning and conducting business (a common characteristic of organizations run by engineers). With ample justification, Panamanians take pride in the Canal and its operations. We also detect ambivalence among interview respondents with regard to the attitudes and actions of Canal officials. This ambivalence suggests that public outreach efforts by ACP are important for assuring continued public acceptance of ACP's watershed management mandate.

The legacy of U.S. control has a continuing financial impact on Canal operation. For many decades the Panama Canal Commission operated the Canal on a "break-even" basis in part to subsidize U.S. shippers (Falcoff, 1998). When the Canal passed to Panamanian control, it came as an eighty-plus year old asset with many worn and irreplaceable parts. Moreover, it came at a time when inter-modal (ship-to-rail) carriers and larger container ships were gaining market power in the global freight business (Falcoff, 1998). The Canal is profitable today, as required by law, earning the equivalent of US$380 million on nearly US$1 billion in revenue in its most recently completed fiscal year (ACP, 2004). Yet the shadow of the future looms large. Aging infrastructure and growing competition for transit services are likely to increase the pressure to continually upgrade or expand Canal operations.

### Overview of Canal Operations

The Panama Canal relies on locks to raise and lower ships as they cross the isthmus. The locks are gravity-fed and use only fresh water. For every ship that travels the length of the Canal, called a "transit," approximately 52,000,000 gallons of fresh water are spilled into the ocean (Condit et al., 2001).

The Canal collects passage tolls on transits. Tolls and payments for passage-related services typically account for more than 90 percent of annual gross revenue (ACP, 2005a).

The Canal currently operates just below capacity, at an average of 40 ships per day. It is projected to reach its full capacity of approximately 47 transits per day (or 17,000 per year) by the year 2012 (Brooks, 2004). The Canal can currently transport only ships of "Panamax" size or smaller because a beam-width of 32.2 meters is the largest the canal can accommodate. To handle "post-Panamax" ships, the canal would need to be both widened and deepened.

To adapt to the increasing use of larger, more economical ships in global cargo markets, and to maintain the Canal's status as a global shipping conduit, ACP has analyzed various alternatives to expand Canal capacity. We assume that these analyses have as an objective the construction of a third set of locks that is wider and deeper than the existing two-lock sets (PRS, 2004b). This would both increase the number of ships the Canal can transport, as well as accommodate the larger vessels now favored by global shippers. At the time this paper was written, a nationwide referendum was tentatively scheduled for November 2005. This referendum was required before the *Asamblea Legislativa* (Panama's national legislature) could approve the construction of the proposed new set of locks (Endara, personal communication, August 2005).

The addition of a third set of locks would substantially boost the Canal's water needs. To accommodate this eventuality, the Legislative Assembly passed Law 44 in 1999 which adds approximately 257,000 hectares in Colón and Cocle provinces to the "traditional" watershed area (295,000 ha.) in the Chagres, Ciri, and Boqueron river systems (Aylward, 2002). The expanded Watershed has a total surface area of 552,761 hectares located in the provinces of Panama, Colón, and Cocle (ACP, 2005b). According to the Canal Authority's official website, the "new Western Region, because of its large water potential, can supply the future needs of the population of Panama and the Canal" (ACP, 2005b).

ACP has reviewed several different alternatives for capturing and moving additional water into the Canal system. Those that involve flooding areas of land and displacing people are, not surprisingly, highly controversial (King, 2004) and have sparked protests even as recently as October 2004 (PRS, 2004b). Nevertheless, ACP has held a number of public outreach events in the Western Region to seek stakeholder input on ways to divert water from there to other parts of the Canal Watershed (ACP, 2005b). ACP has also looked into recycling seawater, as is done in some European ports (King, 2004). Pending further studies and design decisions, it is difficult to predict how Canal expansion will affect total water usage in the watershed (Heckadon, personal communication, March 2005).

## Demand for Flow Regulation:
## More Dry Season Flow, More Toll Revenue

ACP's transit revenues are at risk from changing water levels. For example during the 1997-1998 El Niño, low water levels resulting from drought conditions had a significant impact on the Canal's operations. That rainy season was marked by the least rainfall in the Panama Canal's (then) 83-year history. Rainfall in 1997 was 35 percent less than average, and the levels of Madden Lake and Gatún Lake were lower than optimal for Canal operation (Panama Canal Commission, 1997).

In the latter part of 1997, ACP implemented water-saving measures that included stopping the operations of Gatún hydroelectric plant and adjusting operation of the Canal itself. The implementation of these measures cost ACP US$10 million. Forgone revenue from the sale of electricity totaled between US$5 million and US$8 million. In March 1998, low water forced the Panama Canal to implement draft restrictions limiting the depth to which a ship's hull extended beneath the surface. Consequently, four percent fewer ships passed through the Canal during the second trimester of 1998 in relation to the previous year. Despite the costs associated with addressing El Niño, ACP still succeeded in achieving a 10.6 percent growth in income over the previous year, due partially to increased tolls in 1997 and 1998 (Donoso, 2000).

From 1912 to 2002, passage tolls were levied based on a flat rate-per-ton for all ships; the size of the ship did not affect the per ton rate. The flat rate toll structure somewhat mitigated the financial impact of El Niño. However, as of 2002 ACP has in place a new toll system that levies tolls-per-ton based on the total volume of the ship. A draft restriction now would mean greater foregone revenues on larger draft ships. In 2002, the largest ships, the Panamax ships, accounted for about a quarter of traffic and 60 percent of revenue (Aylward, 2002). It is possible that draft restrictions, if implemented under the new toll system would have a greater negative impact on toll receipts.

It is important to reiterate that demand for increased dry season flow is not the same thing as demand for dry season flow regulation *provided by reforestation*. Although an organization may benefit from increased dry season flow, its managers may not view reforestation as a viable means of providing this increased flow (Anderson, this volume; Aylward,

2002). A later section addresses attitudes toward reforestation and watershed services.

## Demand for Reduced Sedimentation: Lower Dredging Costs

One potential driver of demand for sedimentation reduction is the prospective benefit of reduced dredging costs. The idea is that by using reforestation to reduce soil erosion and subsequent sedimentation of the Canal, ACP would spend less on dredging. At present, demand for sediment filtration to decrease maintenance costs is not significant. Approximately 20 percent of all dredging costs are driven by maintenance; the remaining 80 percent is for channel improvements (Salerno, personal communication, July 2003). The proportion of the maintenance dredging attributed to sedimentation varies by site; nevertheless, dredging due to sedimentation accounts for a minority of ACP's total dredging costs. We have not dismissed outright the potential demand for reforestation to reduce dredging costs. Rather, our analysis suggests that demand is likely to be limited to particularly sensitive locations or to projects where sediment reduction is one among several factors, perhaps including public outreach or nutrient regulation, that tip the benefit/cost calculus in favor of planting trees.

ACP currently employs strategies for reducing sedimentation. In some areas, ACP plants grasses and trees to reduce erosion, which is in itself a form of ecosystem service where ACP is both supplier and beneficiary. In addition to plantings, ACP also terraces hillsides and uses erosion control blankets made of coconut and polypropylene along the Canal banks. It also considers removal of all soil as a form of erosion control (Salerno, personal communication, July 2003).

## Demand for Nutrient Regulation: Lower Dredging Costs

Although most of the dredging in the Canal is for inorganic matter, the bulk of the dredging in Lake Gatún is for organic material. This is due to the high nutrient levels found in the water of Lake Gatún. There is the possibility that the change in nutrient levels in the water caused by reforestation would decrease the amount of organic material in the Lake in such a way as to decrease dredging costs (Anisfeld, personal communication, March 2005).

## ACP's Willingness to Pay for Ecosystem Services

Composing a detailed analysis of the environmental activities of an organization as large and varied as the Canal Authority is beyond the scope of this paper. We do know that previous proposals to create a reforestation fund using a dedicated portion of ACP tolls have not been embraced by the GOP or the Canal Authority. We are not surprised by this and offer possible reasons below.

As noted by a Panamanian reviewer who read an earlier draft of this paper, ACP is one of the few institutions in Panama that complies with ISO standards for the environment. ACP belongs to the World Business Council on Sustainable Development. And ACP has participated in a number of United Nations-sponsored conferences on sustainable development. From personal knowledge, the authors of this paper would characterize ACP's relationship with The Nature Conservancy, the Smithsonian Tropical Research Institute, and other environmental organizations as positive and, on notable occasions, supportive. We would describe ACP as an organization that is very interested in the environmental factors that determine sustainable water yields in the PCW.

Without water, there is no Canal. According to one estimate, ACP receives a benefit to net income (on a weighted average basis) of US$0.011 from each cubic meter of water it uses (Aylward, 2002). Those "pennies from heaven" add up fast when the use is 9.0 million cubic meters per day! The marginal net proceeds from additional dry season flows are presumably much greater than the average. In cases where reforestation yields water services that have economic value to ACP, we assume ACP would be willing to pay.

ACP is required by law to operate the Canal in a safe, continuous, efficient, and profitable manner. In addition to operating the Canal, it also manages the Canal Watershed as a whole for its own purposes and to provide water for public use. According to Article 84 of the Law of July 1, 1988, "the administration, use, maintenance, and conservation of the water resources of the hydrographic watershed of the Panama Canal will be the responsibility of the Panama Canal Authority, in coordination with the National Authority for the Environment." We presume that when investments in ecosystems services are legally and technically feasible and have a net positive return to Canal operations, the ACP is an organization that can be persuaded to make them.

We conclude this section with a note on an organization that may able to provide that persuasion. The Comisión Interinstitucional de la Cuenca Hidrográfica (CICH) was formed by the Legislative Assembly to bring together and coordinate the many interests who have a stake in PCW management. ACP chairs the CICH. Its other members include the Ministry of Government and Justice, the Ministry of Agricultural Development, the Ministry of Housing, the National Environmental Authority, the Interoceanic Region Authority, the NATURA Foundation, and Caritas Arquidiocesana (ACP, 2005a). As we note above, one task facing an in-· dependent and powerful actor such as ACP is the task of maintaining the democratic legitimacy of its mandate. We accept at face value claims that civil society organizations want a voice in management of the PCW; that Panama's elected officials would seek to grant them a voice subject to limits; and that whether with equanimity or ambivalence, Canal Authority officials would find value in having well-ordered means of consultation with key stakeholders.

CICH brings together and coordinates many of the various interests and organizations in the PCW. All environmental activity in the PCW must be carried out with the consensus of the organizations represented in CICH (Vallarino, personal communication March 2004). In 2003, the Fondo para la Conservación y Recuperación de la Cuenca Hidrográfica del Canal de Panamá was created. This Fund, whose purpose is to carry out the environmental objectives of CICH's constituents, is financed by a US$20 million loan from the Inter-American Development Bank (IDB) and by a US$10 million contribution from ACP (Vallarino, personal communication, March 2004).

## CICH Attitudes Towards Payment for Ecosystem Services

Members of CICH apparently hold mixed views on the impact of reforestation of the PCW on water services. A CICH executive told us that some members of the Commission believe there is a link between decreased water flow and deforestation while they and others believe, without contradiction, that reforestation does have an impact on water quality, and that erosion is among the more deleterious effects of deforestation (Vallarino, personal communication, March 2005). Seemingly in response to these views, ACP has begun small-scale reforestation projects to prevent erosion on land directly bordering the Canal. This activity is a far cry from paying land managers to do such work throughout broad reaches of the PCW.

We suspect that the alternative view linking reforestation to reduced or unchanged low season flow is the view that is more nearly consistent with ACP's actions so far. Its directors and managers have ample reason to doubt any claim that widespread reforestation of the PCW would benefit Canal operations. As reported to the World Bank, massive reforestation as called for in Law 21 would have an uncertain effect on water flows (Aylward, 2002). Under the most pessimistic scenario, full restoration of the PCW's original forest cover would cost the Panamanian economy

US$632,000,000 *mostly due to reduced Canal transits* (Aylward, 2002 emphasis added). Aylward also notes that the moderate implementation scenario under Law 21 would probably be more equitable and cost efficient than either the no action or the full recovery scenarios. We are therefore inclined to conclude that while ACP is unlikely to support payments to forest managers for ecosystem services to meet its own needs, the possibility exists that CICH, acting on behalf of its members, would be willing to pay for a moderate level of reforestation using the Conservation and Recuperation Fund as the source of those payments.

ACP's responsibility to sustainably manage the water resources of the PCW creates a large prospective demand for activities such as reforestation that enhance those resources. The consultative process formalized by CICH and the existence of the Conservation and Recuperation Fund provide the means to finance some reforestation. Although the Fund has an explicitly environmental function, we expect that CICH members (and the GOP) would approve financing only for environmental projects that have real returns in the form of improved water quantity and quality. ACP's apparent reluctance to finance massive reforestation to improve water quantity and quality is understandable given the scientific and economic uncertainty recorded by Aylward and others. The Conservation and Recuperation Fund exists to benefit all stakeholders in the Watershed, so its investment criteria may allow consideration of a broader range of projects.

One further condition should be noted with respect to CICH support for reforestation projects. To date, its attention has been focused primarily on the new Western Region of the PCW, presumably in anticipation of future Canal expansion (Heckadon, personal communication, March 13, 2004). We expect to find beneficial reforestation projects with greater frequency in the areas of the traditional Watershed that are in nearer proximity to Canal facilities and as a consequence we also expect that gaining CICH support for reforestation services will require lobbying its members to pay more attention to that area.

## *CARGO OWNERS, CARRIERS, AND THEIR INSURERS*

Cargo owners and their carriers share an interest in dry season flows due to the risk and costs of delayed shipments or higher freight rates. Among all the possible sources of demand, global shipping generates the highest implied value of water flow, US$1.16 per cubic meter (Aylward, 2002). Based on annual flows of 2.6 billion cubic meters, the

PCW generates economic rents worth over US$3.0 billion annually (see Table 1).

Investment banker John Forgach has proposed privately issued "forest bonds" to pay for reforestation of the Watershed. Buyers of those bonds would receive savings in the form of lower insurance premiums on cargo shipped via the Panama Canal (The Economist, 2005). Unless required by insurers or regulators with transnational authority, the purchase of forest bonds would be voluntary and thus would be subject to a free rider problem. Investments made by one shipper would benefit all and therefore none would be willing to buy into the program. Pending further development of this innovative instrument, we are unable to predict the level of demand for reforestation that forest bonds might generate. If the central scientific question can be answered favorably and with some degree of confidence, we suspect that the financial and market problems are surmountable simply because the implied value of water to global shipping is so great.

## HYDROELECTRIC PLANT OPERATORS

In the PCW, the two main hydroelectric plants, Gatún Hydroelectric Dam and Madden Hydroelectric Dam, are run by ACP. Gatún Dam impounds Gatún Lake. Some water from Gatún Lake flows through the Gatún spillway. Most of the water flowing through the Gatún spillway is used to generate electricity at the Gatún Dam. Madden Dam was built primarily to regulate Gatún Lake levels, an especially important function during the dry season. In the most recent fiscal year, ACP reported revenues of equivalent to US$35 million from the sale of electricity (ACP, 2004).

### Demand for Flow Regulation: Increased Production

Water flows through the Gatún spillway and spins the turbines only when the lake holds sufficient water to operate the locks. During the wet season (May-December), water in excess of that needed for canal and hydroelectric plant operation simply runs into the ocean. During the dry season (January-April), the hydroelectric plant operates only after the locks' needs are met. An extreme example of dry season, low flow problems is once again the 1997-1998 El Niño, during which Gatún Dam was temporarily closed to save water for Canal operation.

It may be useful to examine Costa Rica as an example of what might be possible in Panama. In Costa Rica, the hydroelectric producers (HEPs) have been one of the large contributors for water services through the National Forestry Financing Fund (FONAFIFO), the agency established within the umbrella of the Environment Ministry to administer payments for the environmental services program (Pagiola, 2002). Funding from the HEPs is justified by the belief that reduced sediment loads associated with forested watersheds help extend the project life of hydroelectric plants, and the recognition of dry-season benefits from flow regulation offered by intact forests (Pagiola, 2002).

### *Demand for Nutrient Regulation–Decreased Maintenance Costs*

Nutrients also play a role in a hydroelectric plant's productivity. For example, there is a link between anoxia, or the absence of oxygen, in the lakes that feed the hydroelectric plants and deforestation that might concern the HEPs. Under anoxic conditions, certain minerals such as ammonia, iron, manganese and hydrogen sulfide increase to levels that can cause physical damage to hydroelectric power facilities (Malack, 2001), such as some "pitting" of the blades (Anisfeld, personal communication, March 2005). Such a link between deforestation and higher generator maintenance costs make HEPs a possible source of demand for reforestation.

### *HEPs' Attitudes Towards Payment for Ecosystem Services*

The views of ACP and other hydroelectric producers in the Watershed with regard to reforestation and watershed services are unclear. The estimated value of water for hydroelectric is a penny or less per cubic meter, the lowest among the three uses of water assessed (Aylward, 2002). Nevertheless, this is an area that merits further investigation to assess the value of reforestation with respect to water chemistry and project lifespan.

## *INSTITUTO DE ACUEDUCTOS Y ALCANTARILLADOS NACIONALES (IDAAN)*

IDAAN is the public water utility that serves over half of the people in Panama. IDAAN manages a number of water purification plants, including Chilibre (daily capacity 123 million gallons), which draws from Lake Alajuela and supplies water to Panama City, and Sabanitas (daily capacity 80 million gallons), which is located near the Caribbean, and supplies the city of Colón. IDAAN also purchases purified water from· ACP, provided by the Miraflores plant (daily capacity 47 million gallons) near Panama City. Demand is growing rapidly and IDAAN is presently trying to fund a US$224 million, five year investment program (U.S. Commercial Service, 2005).

According to U.S. and Canadian government sources, IDAAN is inefficiently operated and financially drained by the uncompensated use of its primary product, treated water. Annual revenues (in 2002) were approximately US$80 million (Industry Canada, 2005). Estimated water losses during that period amounted to half of all water treated (Industry Canada, 2005). Of the lost water, roughly 40 percent is lost due to leaks or other technical causes and the remainder to users who have spliced into the system without bothering to register their usage (U.S. Commercial Service, 2005). Past efforts to raise tariffs or enforce service contracts have met with violent resistance that has dried up political support for rationalizing the public utility sector, including water and sewerage (PRS, 2004a).

## *Demand for Drinking Water Quantity Expected to Grow Rapidly*

Population in Panama is expected to double in the next 30 years. The extraction of water from the Madden and Gatún Lakes for drinking, commercial and industrial use will also grow due to the anticipated population growth of cities bordering the PCW: Panama, Colón, Arraiján, La Chorrera, and the eastern part of Panama City, including Chepo (Niesten and Reid, 2001). Despite a US$48.8 million project to expand the Chilibre treatment works, capacity is not expected to keep up with the demand from Panama's rapidly growing urban centers (U.S. Commercial Service, 2005).

## *Demand for Water Quality: Decreased Filtration Costs*

The raw water that IDAAN receives to treat is relatively clean, both from pathogens and turbidity. The water flowing to the Miraflores plant is relatively dirty because it is from the Canal. The plant is operated by ACP, which sells the purified water to IDAAN at a fixed price. Dry season turbidity has driven up bottled water sales in parts of IDAAN's service area (U.S. Commercial Service, 2005). We suspect, without being able to confirm, that the turbidity is related to Canal dredging but we do not know if it is dredging related to low flows or vegetation blooms. Nevertheless, the evidence strongly infers that IDAAN is not particularly sensitive to revenue losses and thus we anticipate little demand from that sector for reforestation services to improve the quality of raw water inputs

## IDAAN's Capacity to Pay for Reforestation and Water Services

We believe that as a technical matter, professional engineers at IDAAN (or any other public water utility for that matter) would take a positive view of PCW reforestation. Such views are moot in this instance. As a matter of law, IDAAN does not have legal jurisdiction over the sources of the water it uses; ACP does. Investments in infrastructure to meet rapidly increasing demand and worsening problems with sewage collection and treatment promise to absorb IDAAN's funding capacity for the foreseeable future. Moreover, operational inefficiency and political constraints on revenue collection make IDAAN an un-promising prospective customer for ecosystem services

## CONCLUSION

We examine five potential sources of demand for watershed services provided by reforestation and find that four of the five have some economic incentive for investing in them (see Table 2). However, the fact remains that no organization is willing to pay significant amounts for these services within the Panama Canal Watershed. The primary scientific challenge is making the link between increased reforestation and increased dry season flows, particularly as they might benefit planned Canal expansion. If this link can be made, the ability to pay for these services that already exists should be amenable to conversion into a broader willingness to do so.

We also identify a number of institutional factors that limit the demand for water-related ecosystem services. First and foremost, ACP operates under a grant of legal authority that assures its capacity to "make" rather than "buy" the water-related services it needs. It has exercised this authority by adding 257,000 acres to the Watershed area under its jurisdiction, an act approved by an elected government. Other potential buyers of watershed services are restrained by a variety of institutional factors, including consensus-based decision making (CICH)

TABLE 2. Potential Sources of Demand for Water-Related Services

| | ACP–Canal | CICH–Watershed Stakeholders | Voluntary Forest Bonds | Private Hydro-electric Producers | IDAAN |
|---|---|---|---|---|---|
| **Incentive to regulate flow** | Yes; low water reduces transit revenue, requires water conservation measures. | Maybe; links between forests and flows are uncertain | Yes; shippers bear high cost for alternative modes of transport. | Yes; low water levels limit electricity sales in dry season. | No; drinking water takes precedence over other uses. |
| **Incentive to decrease sedimentation** | Limited; link between deforestation and sediment loads is location sensitive. | Yes; for social and habitat benefits of higher water quality. | Yes; to avoid draft restrictions. | Probably; but more investigation is required. | Probably no; sedimentation is not a cost driver; revenue effects do not drive decisions. |
| **Incentive to change nutrient regime** | Maybe; reduced organic matter in Lake Gatun may reduce dredging costs. | Yes; for social and habitat benefits of higher water quality. | No. | Maybe; anoxia may damage equipment. | No; not a contributor to present treatment costs. |
| **Possesses financial resources** | Yes; but has other priorities such as Canal expansion. | Yes; from the Conservation and Recuperation Fund. | Yes. | Yes. | No. |
| **Possesses political ability/will** | Maybe; legal, financial, and technical capacity is great; political will is probably low. | Maybe; requires reviewing projects with stakeholders. | Unknown; bond purchases would be voluntary and subject to free rider problem. | Unknown. | No; only the ACP has the jurisdiction to protect the watershed. |
| **Organizational priorities/ politics** | Probably low; because of the watershed capacity of the new Western Region. | Unknown; focus of activity is on Western Region. | Unknown; would depend on reduced insurance premiums. | Unknown; would depend on likely impact on profits. | No; top priority is adding network infrastructure to meet growing demand. |

191

and overcoming the problem of free riders (private shippers). Nonetheless, the economic value of the water flowing from the PCW is so great that we recommend continued investigation of the links between flows and forest cover. We also recommend the promotion of opportunities to link land managers in the PCW with the organizations that depend on those flows economically.

## REFERENCES

Anderson, K. 2007. Existing Supply of Watershed Services in the Panama Canal Watershed. *Journal of Sustainable Forestry* 25(1/2):121-145.

Autoridad del Canal de Panamá (ACP). 2004. Report and Financial Statements (translation of financial statements originally issued in Spanish, 26 November).

Autoridad del Canal de Panamá (ACP). 2005a. General Information. Retrieved April, 2005 from http://www.pancanal.com/.

Autoridad del Canal de Panamá (ACP). 2005b. Watershed Information. Retrieved 10 August, 2005 from http://www.pancanal.com/eng/cuenca/la-cuenca.html.

Aylward, B. 2002. Strategic Framework: Program for the Sustainable Management of the Rural Areas in the Panama Canal Watershed. Ministry of Agricultural and Livestock Development with the cooperation of the World Bank, and technical assistance from the Investment Centre of FAO. Panama.

Brooks, M. 2004. The Proposed Expansion of the Panama Canal. Retrieved February, 2005 from http://www.alternatives.ca/article1516.html.

Clark, T.W. and A.R. Willard. 2000. Learning About Natural Resources Policy and Management. Pp. 3-31 in: T.W. Clark, A.R. Willard, and C. Cromley. 2000. Foundations of Natural Resources Management. Yale University Press, New Haven, CT.

Condit, R., W.D. Robinson, R. Ibanez, S. Aguilar, and A. Sanjur. 2001. The Status of the Panama Canal Watershed and Its Biodiversity at the Beginning of the 21st Century. *BioScience* 51(5):389-398.

Donoso, M. 2000. Panama Canal Case Study: Impacts and Responses to the 1997-98 El Niño Event. Retrieved April, 2005 from http://www.esig.ucar.edu/un/panama_ canal.html.

The Economist. 2005. Environmental Economics: Are You Being Served? *The Economist* 375(8423):76-78.

Falcoff, M. 1998. Panama's Canal: What Happens When the United States Gives a Small Country What It Wants? The AEI Press, Washington, DC.

Industry Canada. 2005. Panama Country Commercial Guide FY 2004: Leading Sectors. Retrieved 26 September, 2005 from http://strategis.ic.gc.ca/epic/internet/ inimr-ri.nsf/en/gr119820e.html.

King, N., Jr. 2004. Panama Canal at Crossroads; Waterway Must Add Locks, at a Cost of Billions, or Lose Importance as Trade Route. *Wall Street Journal.* January 7, B1.

Malack, J.M. (ed.). 2001. Planning and Management of Lakes and Reservoirs: An Integrated Approach to Eutrophication. The International Environmental Technology

Centre of the UNEP. Retrieved 20 June 2005 from http://www.unep.or.jp/ietc/Publications/TechPublications/TechPub-12/1-4.asp.

Niesten, E. and J. Reid. 2001. Economic Consideration on the Panama Canal Watershed Expansion. Hardner & Gullison Associates, LLC and Conservation Strategy Fund. Retrieved April, 2005 from http://www.conservation-strategy.org/Reports/panama_canal_fullreport_eng.pdf.

Ostrom, V. 1989. The Intellectual Crisis in American Public Administration, 2nd ed. The University of Alabama Press, Tuscaloosa, AL.

Pagiola, S. 2002. Paying for Water Services in Central America: Learning from Costa Rica. Pp.37-61 in: S. Pagiola, J. Bishop and N. Landell-Mills (eds.). 2002. Selling Forest Environmental Services. Earthscan Publications Limited, London.

Panama Canal Commission, Office of Public Affairs. 1997. Panama Canal Announces Impending Draft Restrictions Due to El Niño. Panama. December 17.

Political Risk Services (PRS). 2004a. Panama Country Forecast, 1 March. The PRS Group.

Political Risk Services (PRS). 2004b. Panama Country Forecast, 1 December. The PRS Group.

U.S. Commercial Service. 2005. United States Department of Commerce Official Website. Retrieved 26 September, 2005 from http://www.buyusainfo.net/docs/x_9509761.pdf.

Williamson, O. 2000. Economic Institutions and Development: A View from the Bottom. Pp. 92-118 in: M. Olson and S. Kähkönen (eds.). 2000. A Not-So-Dismal Science: A Broader View of Economies and Societies. Oxford University Press, New York.

doi:10.1300/J091v25n01_08

# Policy Alternatives to Improve Demand for Water-Related Ecosystem Services in the Panama Canal Watershed

Mike Fotos

Quint Newcomer

Radha Kuppalli

**SUMMARY.** The Panama Canal plays a prominent role in Panama's economy. The functioning of the Canal is dependent on the Canal Watershed (PCW), which provides over two billion gallons of fresh water on a daily basis. Furthermore, the PCW supplies potable water for the major urban centers of the country, including Panama City and Colón.

Mike Fotos is Visiting Assistant Professor of Public Policy at Trinity College, Hartford, CT 06106 USA. He was Guest Lecturer for the course Emerging Markets for Ecosystem Services (Spring semester 2005) at the Yale School of Forestry and Environmental Studies, New Haven, CT 06511 USA.

Quint Newcomer is Director of the University of Georgia's Campus in Costa Rica, San Luis de Monteverde, Costa Rica. Quint Newcomer was Teaching Fellow for the course Emerging Markets for Ecosystem Services during the Spring 2003 and Spring 2005 semesters at the Yale School of Forestry and Environmental Studies, New Haven, CT 06511 USA (E-mail: quintn@uga.edu).

Radha Kuppalli is Manager of Business Development and North American Programs, New Forests Pty Limited. She earned her Master of Environmental Management at the Yale School of Forestry and Environmental Studies and MBA at the Yale School of Management, New Haven, CT 06511 USA.

Address correspondence to: Radha Kuppalli (E-mail: rkuppalli@gmail.com).

[Haworth co-indexing entry note]: "Policy Alternatives to Improve Demand for Water-Related Ecosystem Services in the Panama Canal Watershed." Fotos, Mike, Quint Newcomer, and Radha Kuppalli. Co-published simultaneously in *Journal of Sustainable Forestry* (Haworth Food & Agricultural Products Press, an imprint of The Haworth Press, Inc.) Vol. 25, No. 1/2, 2007, pp. 195-216; and: *Emerging Markets for Ecosystem Services: A Case Study of the Panama Canal Watershed* (ed: Bradford S. Gentry, Quint Newcomer, Shimon C. Anisfeld, and Michael A. Fotos, III) Haworth Food & Agricultural Products Press, an imprint of The Haworth Press, Inc., 2007, pp. 195-216. Single or multiple copies of this article are available for a fee from The Haworth Document Delivery Service [1-800-HAWORTH, 9:00 a.m. - 5:00 p.m. (EST). E-mail address: docdelivery@haworthpress.com].

Available online at http://jsf.haworthpress.com
© 2007 by The Haworth Press, Inc. All rights reserved.
doi:10.1300/J091v25n01_09

*195*

While demand for fresh water is high, by all accounts the provision of water supply is taken for granted in Panama. Although the deforestation of the PCW affects both water quality and quantity, there is little institutional will or social pressure to address these concerns. The result is an absence of formal demand for watershed services, either through direct regulation of land use in the PCW or indirectly through financial inducements offered by the government or water users to land managers. We conclude that the most effective policy alternatives to stimulate demand for such services will complement or address politically salient concerns of the Government of Panama, such as job creation, expanding forestry sector exports, and Canal profitability. Additional information-based campaigns might focus on a long-term goal of raising public awareness of the value of hydrological services and the importance of water conservation. doi:10.1300/J091v25n01_09 *[Article copies available for a fee from The Haworth Document Delivery Service: 1-800-HAWORTH. E-mail address: <docdelivery@haworthpress.com> Website: <http:// www.HaworthPress. com> © 2007 by The Haworth Press, Inc. All rights reserved.]*

**KEYWORDS.** Ecosystem services, hydrological services, Panama Canal Watershed, water policy

## INTRODUCTION

The effects of forest cover and management on the hydrological cycle are covered in the analyses of existing water supply and policy alternatives to improve water supply (see Lichtenfels, this volume; Anderson, this volume). Our analysis assumes that increased forest cover reduces sedimentation and improves water quality. We acknowledge the scientific uncertainty attending the link between forest cover and improved dry season water flows. Building on that assumption, we present a suite of policy alternatives that could help increase demand–the legally feasible and financially adequate capacity to pay for land management practices that provide or enhance hydrological services–for reforestation of the Panama Canal Watershed (PCW). These alternatives have been selected by applying an analytic framework grounded in a socio-political analysis of the PCW.

Part 1 offers a brief assessment of the current state of demand for hydrological services in the PCW. Part 2 describes several types of policy options generally used by governments to manage or solve environmental problems that may also increase market demand for hydrological ecosystem services in the PCW. Part 3 presents an institutional analysis of the Panamanian public sector and a social analysis of relevant participants in the PCW. Part 4 presents several potentially feasible policy alternatives suggested by the analysis, and Part 5 concludes the chapter with a brief description of areas for further research.

## CURRENT DEMAND FOR HYDROLOGICAL ECOSYSTEM SERVICES IN THE PANAMA CANAL WATERSHED

The current state of demand for hydrological ecosystem services in the PCW is analyzed in detail in the chapter by Fotos, Chou, and Newcomer (this volume). Their analysis examines the demand from the Panama Canal Authority (ACP), the Institute for National Water Supply and Sewerage Systems (IDAAN), hydroelectric power producers in the PCW, and global shippers who use the Canal. Fotos et al. identify the ACP as the primary potential source of demand for and provision of hydrological ecosystem services. Improved forest management and reforestation in selected areas of the PCW could improve canal economics by decreasing dredging costs and enhancing Canal operation during the dry season. Reforestation may also provide good public relations for the ACP, especially if such programs can be linked to benefits recognized by member organizations of the Interinstitutional Commission for the Canal Watershed (CICH) or other PCW stakeholders (e.g., farmers, cattle ranchers, and the forestry sector). However, it appears that ACP has not publicly "demanded" reforestation because (1) the link between reforestation and improved dry season flows is unclear, and (2) ACP's apparent belief that the new Western Region of the PCW will supply enough water for future Canal expansion. The recommended policy alternatives outlined in this chapter are intended to improve demand for hydrological ecosystem services in the PCW. They are primarily informed by the findings and analyses of the other water-related chapters of this volume and by our own socio-political analysis of Panama, which focuses on a narrower set of PCW-related issues.

## ENVIRONMENTAL POLICY OPTIONS

Governments may choose from a suite of policy options to increase demand for hydrological forest ecosystem services. These policy options could be applied directly or indirectly to increase reforestation.

Table 1 provides an extensive list of policy options based on a generally applicable framework for evaluating regulatory policy (Gentry, 2005; Gunningham and Sinclair, 1998). The efficacy of any given policy tool depends a great deal on the context of the problem and the implementation capacity of the responsible authority. Moreover, the aim of our policy recommendations is a market-enhancing outcome, analytically a

TABLE 1. Examples of Environmental Policy Options (adapted from Gentry, 2005)

| Policy Type | Description | Example |
| --- | --- | --- |
| Information | Government requires entity to disclose information regarding its environmental impact | Require drinking water supply companies to disclose information about origin and quality of water and efforts to protect water supply |
| Liability Rules | Government makes entity liable for environmental damage and must provide remuneration for damages | Have a government enforcement body that prosecutes violations of liability rules |
| Command and Control | Government requires and enforces environmental standards; government can impose management or technology standards to achieve requirements | Require water utility to practice certain forest management guidelines to achieve water quality standards if it owns property in the watershed |
| Taxes and Emissions Charges | Government imposes emissions charge on every unit of pollution generated or on each unit of production leading to pollution

Government imposes tax for usage of ecosystem service | Require water polluters to pay tax per unit of pollution

Require shipping companies to pay environmental user fee for canal passage |
| Subsidies | Government provides tax breaks for desirable activities | Provide tax breaks to hydropower companies and farmers who pay for investments in upstream forestland management |
| Property Rights | Government assigns property rights over right to pollute; rights may be tradable | Allow for trading of water quality credit trading within assigned watersheds |
| Public Investment | Government contributes public funds to increase demand for ecosystem services | Buy forest ecosystem services (or related products) from sellers in the market |
| Joint Ventures | Government actively participates in payments/markets for ecosystem services by partnering with non-profit and for-profit entities | Enter into JV with land owner to start reforestation operations

Provide non-profit entity with funding to develop payments for forest ecosystem services |

different goal from the conventional justification of regulatory policy–
to correct market failure (Weimer and Vining, 1992). We began this·
project with the presumption that stimulating demand for ecological
services requires a less conventional approach to policy design. Indeed, our recommendations tend to avoid direct regulation in favor of
measures that influence behavior by providing information or altering
incentives.

We employ a number of metrics to assess each policy option for its
suitability to local context and implementation capacity. They include:
(1) environmental effectiveness; (2) equity and the promotion of environmental and social justice; (3) cost effectiveness; (4) demand on government capacity; (5) adaptability or feasibility in relation to the political
and cultural context; and (6) promotion of capacity building. All of
these metrics are important and, when feasible, we incorporate them in
the evaluation of policy recommendations. Due to data constraints and
the exploratory nature of the research conducted for this analysis, the
policy recommendations are evaluated from a qualitative rather than
quantitative perspective. Furthermore, cost effectiveness, demand on
government capacity, and adaptability/feasibility (political and cultural) are given greater weight in our evaluation of policy options because of the desirability of avoiding competition with policy areas that
occupy higher positions of political and funding priority such as job creation, poverty reduction, and the provision of basic services such as
public water supply, sewage treatment, electricity, etc. Resources are
limited, particularly for environmental policies that may not be viewed
as "essential." In this sense Panama is similar to the rest of the world.
Policy options deemed cost effective and workable–and potential contributors to job creation or government revenues–have a greater chance
of being adopted and enforced.

## SOCIO-POLITICAL ANALYSIS
## OF THE PANAMA CANAL WATERSHED

This section provides the analytic framework of our policy recommendations. The framework uses two levels of analysis: (1) an institutional analysis of the public sector in Panama; and (2) an analysis of
social groups' interests in the Panama Canal Watershed. The data collection methodology is described below and is followed by the framework.

## Data Sources

Data for this analysis were gathered from published sources and interviews conducted in Panama. Key individuals were interviewed in Panama between March 7 and March 11, 2005. These individuals were identified by the Smithsonian Tropical Research Institute's staff, and include current and former national environment ministry officials, current ACP scientists and officials, and current staff of local and international non-governmental organizations (NGOs), such as the Panamanian Center for Social Study and Action (CEASPA), the Smithsonian Tropical Research Institute, The Nature Conservancy, and the Academy for Educational Development.

## *Institutional Analysis of the Public Sector in Panama*

We assume that the success of policies to increase demand for water-related forest ecosystem services will depend on the administrative quality and capacity of the public agencies that administer them. Table 2

TABLE 2. Questions to Ask for Analysis of Panamanian Public Sector (adapted from Gentry, 2005)

---

**Public Sector Management and Institutions**

- How effectively does the government bureaucracy in Panama design and implement public policy? Are there some strong or weak areas of public administration (e.g., environmental policy or forest policy)?
- Is private economic activity in Panama protected by well-defined property rights, an effective legal system, and rule-based governance?
- What is the quality of fiscal management? Are revenues and expenditures consistent with the approved budget?
- What is the quality of the mechanism for government revenue collection and allocation?
- How transparent and accountable are government procedures and employees? What is the degree of corruption in the public sector?

**Structural Policies**

- How "free market" are policies affecting the goods and labor markets?
- What, if any, is the existing environmental policy framework in Panama?

**Economic Management**

- How stable and/or effective is the macroeconomic situation in Panama? Is there large public debt?
- Is there sustained political commitment and public support for government economic policies?

**Social Inclusion and Equity**

- Do public policy objectives in Panama strive to include poverty reduction, equity, and education?
- Who participates in public policy making, and how do they participate (e.g., are there open forums for public debate, public demonstrations, etc.)?

---

contains a list of questions that guide our analysis of Panama's public sector. The questions are separated into four groups: (1) public sector management and institutions; (2) structural policies; (3) economic management; and (4) social inclusion and equity. Answers to these questions provide a general impression of how environmental policies fit into Panama's public policy regime and form the basis for our qualitative assessments of the effectiveness, capacity, and adaptability/feasibility of the recommended policy options.

Our investigation of the questions listed in Table 2 reveals the following about Panama's public sector.

## Public Sector Management and Institutions

- *Quality of design and implementation of public policy.* The quality of public administration varies significantly across agencies and among presidential administrations. It is probably too early in the new presidential term to rate the quality of public policy and public administration under the current President, Martin Torrijos. Mirei Endara, former Administrator of the National Environmental Authority (ANAM), observed (personal communication, 7 March 2005) that Panama is still very "immature" in its institutions. Furthermore, Panamanian institutions and their leaders, including important sub-executive positions, are subject to high turnover rates when political control passes to a new administration. The result is variability and inconsistency over time in policy objectives, design, and implementation of environmental policy.
- *Quality of financial management.* President Torrijos has made fiscal reform a key platform of his administration. This reform package is aimed at reducing the non-financial, public sector operating deficit to below 5 percent of GDP, which is still above the 2 percent mandated by law (EIU, 2005). President Torrijos presently enjoys widespread public support. The strength of that support after the effects of fiscal austerity are felt by the public and the public employee unions remains an open question.
- *Revenue collection and allocation.* As noted by Fotos et al., elsewhere in this volume, ACP nets approximately US$350 million and contributes over US$ 100 million to the Panamanian treasury on annual revenues of US$1 billion. On the other hand, IDAAN "loses" half the water it treats to leaks and unauthorized hook ups. It is also faces rapidly growing demand and a number of infrastructure problems that will require hundreds of millions of dollars in

new capital investment over the next several years. Funding for these improvements is likely to be problematic due to a number of factors including the fiscal austerity measures noted above and Panama's tradition of popular opposition to rationalizing the public utility sector (Fotos, Chou and Newcomer, this volume).

- *Transparency and corruption.* The Panamanian public sector suffers from an image of corruption and non-transparency as a consequence of the many political scandals that have occurred throughout the country's post-independence history. This perception continues to impair business and investment (EIU, 2005; PRS Group, 2004a).

### Structural Policies

- *Management of private economic activity/structural policies.* Traditionally, Panama has been open to investment and does not distinguish between foreign and domestic businesses. Panamanian law forbids anti-competitive and monopolistic behavior. Property rights are well-protected. Both domestic and foreign entities have found government bureaucratic obstacles in doing business (PRS Group, 2004a). According to research by the World Bank's Doing Business unit (World Bank, 2004), Panama performs better than the region on most indicators related to ease of doing business and performs just under the OECD countries on average. Some key indicators are summarized in Tables 3-5, below (World Bank, 2004).
- *Environmental policy framework.* The military regime under Noriega created the first natural resources authority in Panama in the late 1980s, which was primarily focused on the creation of national parks. Today, environmental policy in Panama is conducted through ANAM, which was created in 1997. ANAM is concerned with issues such as air and water pollution, land use change and management, and forestry (Endara, personal communication, 7 March 2005). The Government of Panama passed a General Environmental Law in 1998 (GOP, 1998). It is intended to be a forward looking instrument that gives policy makers flexibility in how they regulate new developments (Endara, personal communication, 7 March 2005). "The law established controls and regulations regarding the use of natural resources and set forth measures to protect the environment. As a result, industrial establishment, municipalities, hospitals, hotels, etc. will have to implement a number of measures in order to comply with regulations aimed at protecting the environment, [such as] wastewater treatment procedures" (PRS Group, 2004a:7).

TABLE 3. Ease of Starting a Business in Panama (adapted from World Bank, 2004)

| Indicator | Panama | Regional Average | OECD Average |
|---|---|---|---|
| Number of procedures | 7 | 11 | 6 |
| Time (days) | 19 | 70 | 25 |
| Cost (% of income per capita) | 25.1 | 60.4 | 8.0 |
| Min. capital (% of income per capita) | 0.0 | 28.9 | 44.1 |

TABLE 4. Protecting Investors through Disclosure of Information and Financial Information (scale of 0 to 7, with 7 being highest level of disclosure) (adapted from World Bank, 2004).

| Indicator | Panama | Regional Average | OECD Average |
|---|---|---|---|
| Disclosure Index | 1 | 2.3 | 5.6 |

TABLE 5. Ease of Enforcing Contracts (adapted from World Bank, 2004)

| Indicator | Panama | Regional Average | OECD Average |
|---|---|---|---|
| Number of procedures | 45 | 35 | 19 |
| Time (days) | 355 | 462 | 229 |
| Cost (% of debt) | 37.0 | 23.3 | 10.8 |

## Economic Management

- *Stability of macroeconomic situation.* Panama's country risk rating is "C." GDP growth is expected to average a respectable 3.6 percent in 2005-06. The economy has slowed recently due to government austerity measures, closure of public works projects, and economic slow down in the US and China. Overall, Panama's macroeconomic situation is positive (EIU, 2005; PRS Group, 2004b).

## Social Inclusion and Equity

- *Policy making for poverty reduction, equity, and education.* We have not formed a strong impression of whether these goals permeate all policy making decisions. Several interview respondents indicated that policies that improve the standard of living of Panamanian people and provide employment are priorities of the Torrijos administration (Heckadon, personal communication, 7 March 2005; Endara, personal communication, 7 March 2005; Vallarino, personal communication, 8 March 2005; Guardia, personal communication, 11 March 2005). These statements are consistent with the PRD party's history of welcoming international trade and financing while simultaneously pursuing populist economic policies that include heavy spending on public works projects such as public health clinics and schools (Falcoff, 1998; Ropp, 2000; Zimbalist and Weeks, 1991).

- *Public participation through voting and democratic representation in government.* Panama holds a national plebiscite every five years to elect a president who may serve a single five-year term (Library of Congress, 1987). Martin Torrijos, the son of the late strong man and PRD founder Omar Torrijos, was elected to his present term in 2004 (PRS Group, 2004b). Presidential politics tend to be highly personal and the winner usually dominates the other branches of government (Library of Congress, 1987; Falcoff, 1998; PRS Group, 2004b). The legislative branch is made up of a single house with 78 members (Library of Congress, 1987). The PRD holds a simple majority of 42 seats and thus is able to govern without joining a coalition of minority parties. In the past, legislative and presidential terms ran concurrently. Under a new arrangement advanced by the Torrijos administration the legislative assembly will be reduced to 67 members elected at more frequent intervals (PRS Group, 2004b). The judicial branch is the weakest of the three branches and the Torrijos administration has taken steps to bring it under even tighter political control (PRS Group, 2004b). The ACP is run by an independent commission whose members tend to be political insiders hand-picked by the president (Falcoff, 1998).

## *Social Analysis of Actors in the PCW*

The second level of analysis involves the entities interested in policy outcomes involving the PCW. Policy recommendations should be based upon a better understanding of the interests of these entities. Important questions to ask include: How would different policy recommendations affect these actors' behavior in a social, economic, or political manner? Would this behavior increase their demand for hydrological forest ecosystem services? The analysis focuses on the perspectives, values, situation, and strategies–defined below–of select entities (see Clark, 2002 for a detailed description of the policy process and framework for analysis). The analysis is summarized in Tables 6-9 below.

- *Participants.* This analysis is narrowly-focused, and looks only at ACP, IDAAN, the Ministry of Health (MINSA), ANAM, and Panamanian citizens. These groups have been chosen because: (1) they currently have the most potential demand for ecosystem services, and/or (2) because policy changes could increase their need or ability to demand ecosystem services. A more inclusive analysis would examine hydroelectric power producers in the PCW and global shippers and their insurers (see Fotos, Chou and Newcomer, this volume).
- *Perspectives.* How does each participant currently think about water quality and water quantity with respect to the PCW, and specifically, the relationship between forest systems and hydrological services? Would the participant consider making payments for forest ecosystem services? If there is interest, what kind of policies would increase the participants' demand for hydrological ecosystem services? What level of confidence or trust does each participant have in relation to other participants in the PCW?
- *Values.* According to the policy sciences framework individuals and institutions seek to obtain and accumulate certain "value assets" (Clark, 2002). The framework notes eight categories of value: power, wealth, well-being, enlightenment, skill, affection, respect, and rectitude (Clark, 2002). In studying the social context, questions include: What are the primary values that motivate each participant? How might policy recommendations strengthen or weaken the participant's position in relation to their ability to obtain more of and/or maintain certain levels of those values?
- *Situation.* What major challenges do the participants currently face (or expect to face in the future)? What kind of internal or external threats and/or opportunities do the participants have? What are their strengths in terms of existing or potential market position for hydrological services?
- *Strategies.* How do the participants traditionally go about achieving their objectives (e.g., coercive vs. persuasive, cooperative/participatory vs. independently-acting, etc.)?
- *Impact of policy.* How might policies to increase demand for ecosystem services change the situation or meet the value demands of each participant? What might be the benefits and/or losses for the different participants under the different policy options? What options are most likely to satisfy common interests? Which ones might create inequities among participants?

TABLE 6. Social Mapping of the Panama Canal Authority (ACP)

| | |
|---|---|
| **Perspectives** | The official ACP line is that reforestation is very important for maintenance of water quality (not quantity) in the PCW (Vallarino, personal communication, 8 March 2005; Warren, personal communication, 11 March 2005). However, it is unclear whether the ACP views large-scale reforestation in the PCW as important for Canal operations and/or public reforestation and whether the organization would voluntarily engage in payments for ecosystem services. However, the ACP is examining the environmental and social impact of Canal operations and expansion. For example: |
| | Panama has received a $20 million loan for watershed management from the Inter-American Development Bank. The Panamanian government will provide $15 million in matching funds. The $35 million will fund projects that rehabilitate and expand the watershed and water quality and protect natural resources. The ACP is also establishing a $10 million investment fund to finance community projects and a sustainable development project for the watershed (Business News Americas, 2004). |
| | The ACP is studying the inhabitants, land, and wildlife in the Canal watershed to see how expansion plans will affect the people and the environment in the area. This is in part due to protests by poor people against Canal expansion (EFE News Service, 2004; PRS Group, 2004b). |
| **Values** | The ACP is motivated by power, wealth, skills, and respect. The Canal is still run much as it was when the U.S. controlled it because many of its present employees and engineers were recruited and trained by the Americans (Falcoff, 1998). For many Panamanians, the ACP is considered a "republic within a republic." It is very clear in its mission and purpose to be a First World institution (Endara, personal communication, 7 March 2005). It is required by law to maintain an operating profit. In addition to passing ships through the Canal, the ACP also has a constitutional mandate to protect the PCW and to provide drinking water within the PCW. These legal obligations with strong social implications drive the ACP to be a responsible entity (Vallarino, personal communication, 8 March 2005). |
| **Situations** | The ACP is considering building another set of locks to accommodate larger, post-Panamax container ships. This could cost upwards of $8 billion, which could burden Panama with a large amount of debt. The ACP is also considering the technical, economic, and environmental feasibility of increasing the size of the reservoir system (King, 2004; RiverDeep.net, 2000). |
| | The ACP is also considering an increase in tolls to fund its $5 billion expansion plan. The proposal would increase tolls for container ships by as much as 65%, which could mean an increase in revenues to the Panamanian government. This may enhance public perception of the expansion plan, which is good from the ACP's perspective because any increase in tolls would have to be approved by public referendum (The Shipping Times, 2004; Journal of Commerce, 2005). |
| | "In 2002, the Canal also eliminated a 1912 pricing system that charged all ships a flat per-ton rate and it began setting rates based on the type of ship and cargo" (Zamorano, 2004). However, increasing rates is not easy for the ACP because they must consult with their customers, and their customers have other shipping options. |

| Strategies | The ACP seems to use both legal and coercive strategies to achieve its objectives. The ACP values its constitutional mandate, and will act in a way that fulfills the letter of the law. The ACP can operate with a significant amount of autonomy because of its importance to the country's economy and standing in the world, its contribution to government revenues, and perhaps the implicit U.S. security guarantee of its operation. |
| --- | --- |
| Impact of Policies | Policies that would force ACP to engage in reforestation could increase operating expenses. Policies that create incentives (monetary, public relations, etc.) for ACP could improve the long-term situation of Canal operations from both an economic and social perspective. |

TABLE 7. Social Mapping of the National Aqueducts and Sewage Institute (IDAAN) and the Ministry of Health (MINSA)

| Perspectives | The objective of IDAAN is to provide clean drinking water to citizens. It must adhere to water quality and waste water standards established in Law 2 of 1998 (Pérez, personal communication, 13 April 2005). It has no control over the PCW which is legally under the domain of ACP. Therefore, there is no evidence that IDAAN is considering engaging in payments for ecosystem services or is interested in reforestation in the PCW. |
| --- | --- |
| Values | It is unclear but it appears that IDAAN is motivated by the well-being of citizens. It likely also seeks respect from the public and other government agencies as it is a financially troubled institution. Policy recommendations that improve drinking water quality and accessibility would improve the standing of IDAAN in the eyes of the people. |
| Situations | IDAAN is formally a part of the Ministry of Health and under its jurisdiction. |
|  | IDAAN is in charge of water works in all towns larger than 1,500 residents and serves 400,000 customers. IDAAN submitted an $83.6 million budget to the congressional budget committee for operations and investment in 2005. One of the main objectives of the utility will be to collect $60 million in late payments (Business News Americas, 2004). Due to the inability to collect water payments, IDAAN has a major deficit every year. IDAAN anticipates capital needs of $224 million over five years to meet anticipated growth and to correct urgent water quality and sewage problems (Fotos, Chou and Newcomer, this volume). |
|  | In towns smaller than 1,500, MINSA is responsible for organizing communities to manage and administer rural aqueducts. The major problem is the lack of local capacity to manage the aqueducts because of limited fee collection and low fixed tariffs ($2-5 per month). There are no water meters to measure use (and thus charge for consumption), and revenues do not cover costs of operation and maintenance. |
|  | In 1998, the government initiated a plan to privatize IDAAN, but there was major public protest (PRS Group, 2004a). The main concern was that rates would increase, but a loss of national sovereignty over water (seen as an "open-access" resource) was also a central focus of protests. It is unlikely there will be another move soon to privatize IDAAN. |

### TABLE 7 (continued)

| | |
|---|---|
| **Situations** (continued) | IDAAAN loses approximately 42 percent of its total potable water production–half of this is due to broken pipes, and the other half is stolen through spliced pipes. Consequently, there is pressure to produce more and more drinking water and to build more treatment facilities (instead of fixing the delivery infrastructure) (Guardia, personal communication, 11 March 2005). In addition to quantity issues, IDAAN is also facing an imminent water crisis from poor quality. An increasing amount of sewage is entering water sources. |
| **Strategies** | The Ministry of Health dictates national policy on water quality and waste water (Pérez, personal communication, 13 April 2005). |
| | By all accounts, IDAAN rarely uses coercive strategies to reduce water theft or to collect outstanding accounts. Panamanian appear willing to tolerate annual budget deficits so as to not provoke public unrest over higher fees for public utility services. |
| | MINSA regularly has educational campaigns for awareness of water quality in rural communities and closely monitors rural water quality to control diarrhea, vomiting and dehydration, especially in children (Pérez, personal communication, 13 April 2005). However, in Panama City there are no such campaigns. |
| | In terms of inter-institutional cooperation on water concerns in the Canal watershed, IDAAN coordinates with the ACP and other government institutions through the Interinstitutional Commission of the Canal Watershed (CICH) |
| **Impacts of Policies** | Policies to increase demand for ecosystem services could be beneficial to IDAAN if they help the agency to improve drinking water quality. Focusing on the health benefits to both rural and impoverished urban communities would likely be an effective approach to present new policy alternatives. |

### TABLE 8. Social Mapping of the National Environmental Authority (ANAM)

| | |
|---|---|
| **Perspectives** | Water quantity and quality and reforestation are very important to ANAM. ANAM has thought about instituting payments for ecosystem services for hydrological services, although currently there is no formal program. ANAM is currently engaged in international carbon markets (see Lauterbach, this volume; Grossman, this volume). |
| **Values** | ANAM is motivated by the well-being of citizens, and the charge of effective ecosystem management requires ANAM to steward Panama's wealth of natural resources. ANAM seeks to gain respect from the public and other government agencies, as it is a relatively powerless agency. Policy recommendations that involve ANAM and increase public awareness of ANAM's role in improving drinking water quality would likely improve the standing of ANAM in the eyes of the people. |
| **Situations** | Although "authority" is in its title, ANAM has little authority or sway in terms of influencing national policy regarding demand for hydrological services in the PCW. ANAM has limited financial resources and little political leverage. It is a young agency struggling to implement the country's nascent environmental law. |
| | Issues with illegal logging and poaching of prized wildlife (such as Harpy eagles and jaguar) from National Parks continue to be challenges for ANAM. |

| | |
|---|---|
| **Strategies** | As seen in programs working with small landholders within Chagres National Park, ANAM has made some attempts to establish cooperative management agreements for management of previously degraded Park lands. While some landholders within Chagres National Park willingly relocated to areas closer to Park boundaries, ANAM has been forced to confront other landholders who do not move willingly. |
| | ANAM is assigned the task of watershed protection. However, ANAM relies primarily on persuasion and partnership with more powerful institutions rather than on its own coercive abilities to influence national water policy. |
| **Impacts of Policies** | Policies to increase demand for ecosystem services could be beneficial to ANAM if they help the agency to improve environmental quality while providing employment or economic opportunities. Policies that improve services provided to small landholders in and around National Parks would benefit ANAM, although national policy has tended to provide only minimal support to such constituencies for fear of encouraging increased settlement in these areas. |

## TABLE 9. Social Mapping of Panamanian Citizens

| | |
|---|---|
| **Perspectives** | Overall, there is a sentiment among Panamanians that there is no water quantity problem. Water is a "gift from God" that is bountiful and should be available for free (or very cheaply) (Endara, personal communication, 7 March 2005). Water quality and access is an issue for many poor Panamanians within the PCW. |
| **Values** | At such a broad scale of analysis, it is impossible to pinpoint which value categories most motivate Panamanians in general. Generally, Panamanians would likely support policies that promote reforestation and payments for ecosystem services as long as these policies provide benefits such as health, employment, and economic opportunities. As noted below in "strategies," Panamanians exhibit power as a lobbying group, especially against rate increases for water. |
| **Situations** | The majority of Panama's 3 million people are concerned with basic needs such as job security, improved health care, housing, and education. Average annual income per capita is $3,990. The reported literacy rate is 91%; 56% of the population lives in urban areas; 24% of the workforce is classified as agricultural (PRS Group, 2004b). |
| **Strategies** | There seems to be a vibrant civil society in Panama, where large public protests are a common way to express public sentiment. Citizens groups have joined with the Catholic Church to fight Canal expansion, and citizens vociferously protested the IDAAN privatization proposal in 1998. |
| | As noted elsewhere in this analysis, many people routinely steal water, either by not paying their bills or by splicing into supply lines. |

TABLE 9 (continued)

| | |
|---|---|
| **Impacts of Policies** | Policies to increase demand for ecosystem services could be beneficial to people if they provide employment/economic opportunities and improve environmental quality. Effective policy would likely be accompanied by long-term educational campaigns that show the direct benefits related to improved water infrastructure, a functioning revenue collection system, and water conservation. It is not easy to change attitudes, and such programs take time to show demonstrable results. However, long-term policy impacts that shift public attitudes toward water could be critical for the long-term ability of the hydrological systems of the Canal watershed to meet increasing demand for fresh water. |

## *POLICY OPTIONS*

This section presents several policy alternatives that might help to increase the demand for hydrological ecosystem services in the PCW. Our recommendations reflect two key attributes of the Panamanian context. First, the PCW has been a focal point for scientific research and government regulation over the past 100 years. Consequently, some of the policy options may overlap with previous research or regulations. Second, the Panamanian context does not seem ripe for fundamental changes in Watershed policy. This is surprising given how important the PCW is to Panama. There are several roadblocks to policy change: the national government is strapped for cash and must deal with a number of pressing security, economic, and humanitarian problems; ACP is financially independent and enjoys a legal mandate to manage the Watershed directly, and therefore not surprisingly, it has been reluctant to embrace paying for watershed services; Panama does not have a strong indigenous environmental movement as evidenced by the weak structure of ANAM and the ineffective implementation of existing environmental laws; and, finally, forestry and reforestation are not among the foremost priorities of the national government or the private sector. As a consequence, we conclude that less costly and less coercive measures are more likely to be adopted and thus are more likely to have a positive effect on the problem. Therefore, the policy alternatives presented here emphasize information generation and the building of a forest conservation movement in Panama that is not dependent on North American NGOs or international aid donors. We also recommend more detailed research into the likely implementation scenarios of these alternatives in order to make better predictions of their impact on demand for hydrological services.

## Information Policy Tools

- *The Government of Panama could require that the Canal Authority and the financial institutions supporting Canal expansion assess the environmental impact of Canal expansion on water quality and quantity in the PCW, with special attention given to the problem of dry season flows. Critical components of such a report would be the assessment of the relationships among forest cover (both existing and as a result of planned reforestation), increased water demand, and the long-term impacts of Canal expansion on the ecological functions of the PCW.* This alternative is feasible because ACP and lending institutions are obligated to respond to such legal requirements and, depending on study results, the information provided could help reduce the scale, scope and subsequent social impacts of technical measures to extract water from the new Western Region of the PCW. One major issue to be resolved would concern who would conduct the impact assessment. Technical support committees of researchers have conducted such evaluations related to Law 46, which mandated reforestation of the Canal Watershed. Given that there are no public or private post-graduate research universities in Panama, an organization such as the Smithsonian Tropical Research Institute, which has substantial credibility in Panama, might be able to partner or work in conjunction with ACP to conduct this research.

- *The Government of Panama could require the Canal Authority to widely disseminate the results of the environmental impact assessment of Canal expansion, and also require ACP to seek input from a broad range of interested parties, including the general public. Again, such reports should focus on the role, if any, of reforestation in mitigating the negative impacts of Canal expansion on water quality and quantity (e.g., its availability during the dry season).* It would be important for an environmental assessment to address the extent of recommended reforestation, and clearly identify priority areas based on bio-geophysical conditions and the needs of landowners and communities within the PCW. Requiring that banks and other financial backers (e.g., World Bank, IADB) of Canal expansion to consider a wider range of views and subsequently to disseminate the environmental impact assessments more widely might increase the consideration given to the social costs and environmental risks associated with funding such a landscape-altering project. More participation and information will increase the legitimacy of any decision and assist the citizens of Panama in making informed decisions about Canal expansion and land management in the PCW. One question concerns who would be responsible for collecting and disseminating the information to diverse constituent groups and gathering feedback critical for decision-making. CICH already exists for the purpose of assuring that major PCW environmental measures reflect a consensus of stakeholder organizations. We therefore suggest that CICH would be well-situated to help organize information dissemination and gather feedback relevant to reforestation and Canal expansion.

- *ACP, MINSA, and ANAM could launch educational campaigns directed at the general public to promote water conservation.* Given the several reports we received regarding the public's general lack of awareness regarding the use of potable water (Heckadon, personal communication, 7 March 2005; Endara, personal communication, 7 March 2005), a campaign to heighten pubic awareness of Panama's water resources and the benefits of conserving potable water would be a long-term effort with few short-term results. However, such a campaign would mark a critical first step in a long term effort to change public attitudes and behavior with respect to water consumption and waste. Such informational campaigns could build the case for economically rational rate structures, improved metering to measure usage and reduce theft, and public acceptance of policies that enhance the market demand for hydrological services.

### Command and Control

- *If justified by the scientific research, the Government of Panama could require the ACP and financial backers of expansion to carry out appropriate reforestation programs as a condition of Canal expansion.* We expect that any measure requiring reforestation of the PCW will generate both scientific and political controversy. Implementation raises many questions concerning the political feasibility of mandatory forest planting and the administrative capacity of the government or ACP agents who would take responsibility for the program. Furthermore, there is a continuing scientific debate regarding the effects of reforestation on water flow (Smyle et al., 2005), and one can anticipate that this policy's opponents will be only too happy to point out this fact. It is for this reason that we propose inclusion of this question in the environmental impact assessment discussed above. On the other hand, reforestation might

be cost-effective for the ACP in the long term and proper management of restored forests would offer ecologically sustainable, long-
term economic benefit to landowners and workers.

## Taxes and Emissions Charges/Subsidies

- *The Government of Panama could earmark a portion of Canal
  revenues for Watershed improvement and restoration.* As an earmark on an existing revenue stream, an environmental passage fee
  would be relatively easy to implement but tough to approve. ACP
  would be responsible for collecting the revenue as it does at present.
  However, the allocation of these funds is likely to be politically
  contentious. The environmental impact studies and prioritized reforestation plans described above could serve as procedurally fair
  guides for how and where to spend the money. However, Canal
  revenues constitute a significant portion of government revenues.
  One can imagine those revenues have many powerful claimants already. Furthermore, ACP's capacity to raise tolls for transit services
  is limited by competition from other service providers notably the
  inter-modal (i.e., ship-to-rail) shippers and very large cargo ships
  (Falcoff, 1998).
- *The Panamanian Legislative Assembly could modify the tax code
  to provide suitable tax incentives for sustainable forestry practices, including reforestation with native tree species.* Law 24,
  which went into force in late 1992, included tax incentives for reforestation (GOP, 1992). As originally passed, the law contained a
  number of perverse incentives that cost the GOP revenue and encouraged the depletion of native forests. It has been partially re-
  pealed (Harrick, personal communication, 10 March 2005) and,
  we believe but have been unable to confirm, other parts have been
  substantially revised. Properly written, a modified version of Law
  24 could promote reforestation using native species and provide a
  stimulus for the forest products industry in Panama. Although the
  design of a lobbying campaign is beyond the scope of this paper,
  the combined ecological and economic benefits of such a bill
  would suggest that a coalition of government ministries, environmental NGOs, landowners, and forest industry representatives
  could feasibly be organized in support of this proposal.

## AREAS FOR FURTHER RESEARCH AND CONCLUSION

This project is necessarily limited in scope and thus a number of questions regarding potential sources of demand for hydrological services await further investigation.

- The Ministry of Health sets drinking water quality standards for ACP and IDAAN, and IDAAN is formally a part of MINSA. What is the MINSA position regarding the public health benefits provided by forested watersheds? What potential influence might MINSA have on the demand for hydrological ecosystem services? What legal or scientific leverage does MINSA have to influence the land management regimes supported by ACP and IDAAN?
- What are the potential contributions of hydroelectric power generators to the demand for hydrological ecosystem services? How does sedimentation from land use malpractice affect water quality and quantity at each of these operations? Would improved forest management and reforestation improve the economics of hydro power by reducing dredging costs and extending project life?
- Sewage contamination is the main source of water quality problems for IDAAN and would not be significantly reduced by reforestation. What strategies have the potential to engage IDAAN as a source of demand for hydrological ecosystem services? Are there any productive links between a campaign to collect late payments and reduce water theft and educating the public on the benefits of water conservation and the ecological services provided by intact forested watersheds?
- How might international awareness and influence be used to increase demand for hydrological services in the PCW? What roles can international NGOs, aid donors, and multinational businesses with a commercial interest in the canal play in such an effort? Would more pressure for reforestation jumpstart the demand for watershed services, or might it offend the Panamanian sense of sovereignty and thus be counterproductive? If the latter is more likely, how might one cultivate demand from within Panama using Panamanian institutions?
- Instead of turning to "all the usual suspects" for more aid money or more strings on existing aid, what might environmental NGOs do to create demand among shippers and insurers for so-called "forest bonds" to pay for PCW ecological services (see Fotos, Chou and Newcomer, this volume; The Economist, 2005)?

In conclusion, the demand for hydrological services within the Panama Canal Watershed is slight and many barriers limit the opportunities for increasing it. The policy problems are compounded by a difficult political environment for environmental goods generally and by the country's limited capacity for coordinating policy implementation among the several government agencies with responsibility for different parts of the environmental portfolio. While the Panama Canal itself constitutes a grand resource and a signal opportunity for creating a functional market in watershed services, anything having to do with the Canal requires engaging the Government of Panama at the highest levels. Moreover, even though Panama is a small country it is ethnically, economically, and institutionally diverse. As a consequence, politics and policy must be attuned to a complex set of relationships among a diverse group of individuals and organizations. Finally, history casts a long shadow over the attitudes and endowments of Panama's citizens. Perhaps the most effective course of action for further research and policy development is also the most democratic. We need more time in the field listening to the citizens of Panama as they reflect on the benefits and uses they wish to derive from the forests of the PCW.

## REFERENCES

Anderson, K. 2007. Existing Supply of Watershed Services in the Panama Canal Watershed. *Journal of Sustainable Forestry* 25(1/2):121-145.

Business News Americas. 2004. IDAAN Presents 2005 Budget to Congress. *Business News Americas*, November 2.

Clark, T. 2002. The Policy Process: A Practical Guide for Natural Resources Professionals. Yale University Press, New Haven, CT.

The Economist. 2005. Environmental Economics: Are You Being Served? *The Economist* 375(8423):76-78.

Economist Intelligence Unit (EIU). 2005. Country Report: Panama. Retrieved 22 March 2005 from http://www.eiu.com/report_dl.asp?issue_id=728214272&mode=pdf.

EFE News Service. 2004. Panama Conducts 'Inventory' to Help Preserve Canal Watershed. *EFE News Service*, September 18.

Falcoff, M. 1998. Panama's Canal: What Happens When the United States Gives a Small Country What It Wants? The AEI Press, Washington, DC.

Fotos, M., F. Chou, and Q. Newcomer. 2007. Assessment of Existing Demand for Watershed Services in the Panama Canal Watershed. *Journal of Sustainable Forestry* 25(1/2):175-193.

Gentry, B. (ed.). 2005. Emerging Markets for Ecosystem Services: Draft Framework for Analysis (January 9). Yale School of Forestry and Environmental Studies, New Haven, CT.

Government of Panama (GOP). 1998. Ley General del Ambiente. Retrieved 5 April 2005 from http://www.anam.gob.pa/pdf/leygralambiental.pdf.

Government of Panama (GOP). 1992. Legislative Assembly Law 24, November 23, 1992. Retrieved 6 April 2005 from http://www.panamadera.com/law_24.htm.

Grossman, J.M. 2007. Carbon in Terrestrial Systems: A Review of the Science with Specific Reference to Central American Ecotypes and Locations. *Journal of Sustainable Forestry* 25(1/2):17-41.

Gunningham, N. and D. Sinclair. 1998. Designing Environmental Policy. Pp. 375-453 in: N. Gunningham and P. Grabosky (eds.). 1998. Smart Regulation: Designing Environmental Policy. Oxford Press, New York, NY.

Journal of Commerce. 2005. Paying in Panama. *Journal of Commerce*, January 10.

King, N. Jr. 2004. Panama Canal at Crossroads. *Wall Street Journal*, January 7, B1.

Lauterbach, S. 2007. An Assessment of Existing Demand for Carbon Sequestration Services. *Journal of Sustainable Forestry* 25(1/2):75-98.

Library of Congress. 1987. Panama. Library of Congress Country Profiles. Retrieved 2 June 2005 from http:///www.trincoll.edu/library.

Lichtenfels, M. et al. 2007. Improving Markets for Ecosystem Services. *Journal of Sustainable Forestry* 25(3/4):337-364.

Political Risk Services (PRS Group). 2004a. Panama Country Forecast. The PRS Group. March 1.

Political Risk Services (PRS Group). 2004b. Panama Country Forecast. The PRS Group. December 1.

Riverdeep.net. 2000. Water Woes at the Panama Canal. Retrieved January 2005 from http://www.riverdeep.net/current/2000/12/120800_panama.jhtml.

Ropp, S.C. 2000. Panama: Militarism and Imposed Transition. Pp. 111-130 in: T.W. Walker and A.C. Armony (eds.). 2000. Repression, Resistance, and Democratic Transition in Central America. SR Books, Wilmington, DE.

The Shipping Times. 2004. Panama Considering Canal Toll Fee Increase. *The Shipping Times*, October 21.

Smyle, J., B. Stallard, S. Bruijnzeel, I. Calder, and H. Elsenbeer. 2005. Subject: "Economist article: Panama hydrologic services ('sponge effect')." E-mail correspondence 25 April-12 May 2005.

Weimer, D.L. and A.R. Vining. 1992. Policy Analysis: Concepts and Practice, 2nd edition. Prentice-Hall, Englewood Cliffs, NJ.

World Bank. 2004. Snapshot of Business Environment–Panama. Retrieved 4 April 2005 from http://rru.worldbank.org/DoingBusiness/ExploreEconomies/BusinessClimateSnapshot.aspx?economyid=149.

Zamorano, J. 2004. Five Years After Handover, Panama Canal Making Money, Looking to Expand. *Associated Press Newswires*, December 30.

Zimbalist, A. and J. Weeks. 1991. Panama at the Crossroads: Economic Development and Political Change in the Twentieth Century. University of California Press, Berkeley, Los Angeles, Oxford.

doi:10.1300/J091v25n01_09

# SECTION 3:
# BIODIVERSITY

# Can Bioprospecting Save Itself?
# At the Vanguard
# of Bioprospecting's Second Wave

## Patrick Burtis

**SUMMARY.** Bioprospecting has had a bumpy ride over the last twenty years. High expectations for bioprospecting peaked in 1991 when Costa Rica's INBio program reached a signature deal with Merck Pharmaceuticals. But hopes have waned as bioprospecting has yielded few promising compounds and little in the way of conservation benefits. This paper examines the potential for bioprospecting to contribute to conservation efforts, both broadly and within the specific context of Panama. Today, global markets for bioprospecting services stand at an estimated $60 million per year. A new model for bioprospecting, exemplified by Panama's ICBG project, may be emerging, one that takes a more business-oriented approach to finding drugs. By using ecological insights to guide sample collection, monetizing compounds earlier, and leveraging institutional clout, ICBG Panama may be increasing its odds of scientific success and contributing to conservation in non-monetary ways. I argue that in addition, ICBG Panama, its funders, and other

Patrick Burtis is a Kauffman Fellow and Cleantech Associate with Amadeus Capital Partners in London, and a Research Fellow at the Energy Futures Lab at Imperial College, London, UK. Patrick Burtis earned a Master of Environmental Management at the Yale School of Forestry and Environmental Studies, New Haven, CT 06511 USA (E-mail: pat@patburtis.com).

[Haworth co-indexing entry note]: "Can Bioprospecting Save Itself? At the Vanguard of Bioprospecting's Second Wave." Burtis, Patrick. Co-published simultaneously in *Journal of Sustainable Forestry* (Haworth Food & Agricultural Products Press, an imprint of The Haworth Press, Inc.) Vol. 25, No. 3/4, 2007, pp. 219-245; and: *Emerging Markets for Ecosystem Services: A Case Study of the Panama Canal Watershed* (ed: Bradford S. Gentry, Quint Newcomer, Shimon C. Anisfeld, and Michael A. Fotos, III) Haworth Food & Agricultural Products Press, an imprint of The Haworth Press, Inc., 2007, pp. 219-245. Single or multiple copies of this article are available for a fee from The Haworth Document Delivery Service [1-800-HAWORTH, 9:00 a.m. - 5:00 p.m. (EST). E-mail address: docdelivery@haworthpress.com].

Available online at http://jsf.haworthpress.com
© 2007 by The Haworth Press, Inc. All rights reserved.
doi:10.1300/J091v25n03_01

bioprospectors must increase the scale of their operations if they are to create sustainable entities in the Darwinian world of drug discovery. Finally, I make specific policy recommendations for improving the supply and demand of bioprospecting in Panama and globally. doi:10.1300/ J091v25n03_01 *[Article copies available for a fee from The Haworth Document Delivery Service: 1-800-HAWORTH. E-mail address: <docdelivery@ haworthpress.com> Website: <http://www.HaworthPress. com> © 2007 by The Haworth Press, Inc. All rights reserved.]*

**KEYWORDS.** Bioprospecting, biodiversity conservation, ecosystem services, Panama

## *INTRODUCTION*

Bioprospecting is the practice of mining natural genetic and biochemical resources, usually from tropical forests and other terrestrial or marine ecosystems, in the search for pharmaceutical, therapeutic, or agricultural products. In principle, funds derived from the successful commercialization of products are to be channeled back to pay for conservation of threatened ecosystems, to compensate indigenous peoples, nations, and related stakeholders for access rights, and in some cases, to reward indigenous peoples for their intellectual capital.

Although scientists have relied on and commercialized natural products for hundreds of years, and some of the most ubiquitous agricultural and pharmaceutical products derive from natural compounds (Clapp and Crook, 2002), the modern incarnation of bioprospecting, with its emphasis on environmental and social altruism, dates only to the mid 1980s (Pagiola et al., 2002). Since then, bioprospecting has had a bumpy ride, to say the least. Enthusiasm for bioprospecting arguably peaked in 1991, when Merck signed a 10-year, $1.3 million deal with Costa Rica's INBio (Instituto Nacional de Biodiversidad), a national consortium dedicated to collecting, cataloguing, and screening the biodiversity resources of Costa Rica.

Since then, it has been largely downhill for bioprospecting. Despite the fact that at least 88 modern pharmaceuticals can trace their origins to ethno-botanical uses (Clapp and Crook, 2002), and despite some mainstream successes such as Taxol (discovered through a National Cancer Institute bioprospecting program), modern bioprospecting ventures such as those described in this article have yielded little in the way of commercial results (Clapp and Crook, 2002).

INBio, perhaps the most famous of all bioprospecting projects (Castree, 2003), epitomizes bioprospecting's shortfalls. Despite more than fifteen years of prospecting, and execution of more than twenty agreements with major pharmaceutical companies, universities, and NGOs (Castree, 2003), I could find no evidence that INBio has yet delivered a compound to the market. Similarly, Shaman Pharmaceuticals, the only major privately-funded bioprospecting company, went out of business in 2001, heralding for many the end of the bioprospecting dream. As a result of this and several other factors, enthusiasm for bioprospecting among major pharmaceutical companies, governments, environmentalists, and social scientists appears to be at a low ebb (Landel-Mills and Porras, 2002; Castree, 2003; Dalton, 2004b).

In addition to finding few major commercial compounds, pharmaceutical bioprospecting has also failed to produce significant funds for conservation of wild spaces; the bulk of conservation results in bioprospecting have derived from the research process itself (Pagiola et al., 2002).

There are good reasons why so many bioprospecting programs have failed. For starters, finding novel, effective, and safe drugs is an incredibly difficult task. Most drug development projects fail, even those within "big pharma." Based on this author's experience, a pharmaceutical industry rule of thumb is that ninety-nine out of one hundred optimized leads will fail at some point between lead optimization and commercialization, often at enormous cost. Similarly, by some estimates, 80% of biotech startups fail in their first three years (Hunt, 2003). In one sense, then, given the small scale and number of bioprospecting projects, the fact that few have ever generated a commercial product is not surprising.

But that is letting bioprospecting–and the people who have promoted it–off the hook too easily. Biosprospecting's failures are not just the result of long odds. Succeeding in the pharmaceutical industry requires exceptional scientific *and* business acumen. The typical modern bioprospecting venture is the brainchild of environmentalists or ecologists, parties not well known for their business acumen or their expertise in drug development. The orthogonal motives driving these erstwhile drug developers often translate into management priorities that ignore or underestimate the brutal competitiveness of the pharmaceutical industry. As an example, I recount a comment made to me by a scientist deeply involved in an ongoing bioprospecting project. When asked how success was measured, this biologist replied: "By the number of papers we publish" (Anonymous, personal communication, March 2005).

While understandable on some level, this comment betrays a fundamental misunderstanding of–or perhaps capitulation to–the hard-nosed realities of managing a complex, results-oriented business for the long-term. In short, drug discovery is–like it or not–big business. And if bioprospectors want to succeed in generating funds to support their altruistic goals, I argue that they must learn to act as businesspeople–or at least manage their ventures in light of the proven rules and principles that govern modern pharmaceutical development.

The rest of this paper lays out a logic for a new model of bioprospecting ventures, a model that is being tried by several new programs, including one in Panama. Fundamental to this new bioprospecting logic are seven key principles, summarized in the conclusion of this document. Adhering to these principles would not only help bioprospectors find more marketable products, but also assist the environmental community in finally connecting the dots that, in theory, link bioprospecting to one of its elusive goals: funding large-scale conservation.

## THE ECONOMICS OF THE PHARMACEUTICALS INDUSTRY

Pharmaceuticals are a huge, global business. Estimates of industry revenues range from $330 billion to $550 billion dollars per year (Grifo et al., 1997; Gilbert et al., 2003), and industry-wide R&D expenditures now approach $50 billion per year (Gilbert and Rosenberg, 2004). The gold standard in the pharmaceutical business is a "blockbuster": a drug with $1 billion or more in annual revenues. As of 2004, 72 drugs met this standard (Bioportfolio.com, 2005). Some had much greater sales: Pfizer's anti-cholesterol drug Lipitor generated almost $11 billion in sales in 2003 (Pfizer, 2004). The industry's average gross margin is a remarkable 75% (Yahoo! Finance, 2005).

Given these tantalizing prizes, it is not surprising that environmentalists dream of siphoning a portion of these profits for their own aims. Even a small royalty on a successful drug can yield enormous returns: a 2% royalty (not uncommon in bioprospecting deals [Capson, personal communication, 11 March 2005]) on a $1 billion annual drug would net a bioprospector $20 million dollars per year, perhaps for as long as ten years. Two hundred million dollars can protect a lot of forest for a long time in a developing country.

But despite strong growth in the 1990s, all is not well in big pharma. Declines in R&D productivity, longer commercialization times, and pressure from health management organizations (HMOs) and governments to reduce prescription costs have led to an explosion in the average cost of new drugs, and threats to the big pharma business model. By one recent estimate, when all hidden costs are considered, it now costs a drug company $1.7 billion to bring a major drug to market. This has resulted in a steep decline in return on investment (ROI) for pharmaceutical investments, to a paltry 5 percent (Gilbert et al., 2003).

In addition, recent high-profile recalls of blockbuster drugs like Merck's Vioxx have prompted concerns that the US Food and Drug Adminstration (FDA) will adopt more stringent criteria for drug approval (Kellman, 2005). And a recent spate of pharmaceutical mergers is resulting in layoffs, consolidation of research activities, and a rethinking of the accepted industry approach, away from the blockbuster model and towards a more broadly diversified model that focuses on smaller, less costly drug projects (Gilbert et al., 2003).

These changes create both difficulties and opportunities for potential bioprospectors. On one hand, potentially declining R&D budgets and a more risk-averse approach could make it harder for bioprospectors to find funding for new projects. Industry consolidation potentially reduces the number of prospective partners for struggling bioprospectors (Clapp and Crook, 2002). And the emergence of new technologies, such as high throughput screening and genetic sequencing, allow drug developers to synthesize and screen tens of thousands of compounds per week, arguably lessening the value of naturally extracted samples.

On the other hand, a break from the traditional blockbuster business model may result in a willingness of big pharma to place more, smaller bets, including some on bioprospecting. And dramatic improvements in compound screening rates mean that drug companies need more compounds to keep their machines and scientists busy (Moran et al., 2001). Under this scenario, it is conceivable that technological enhancements to the productivity of drug development may result in a complementary, rather than substitutional, relationship between bioprospecting and automated drug development technologies (Pagiola et al., 2002).

Finally, despite all the technological advances, there is still no replacement for nature's ingenuity. Regardless of advances in technology, nature still produces compounds that man can neither imagine nor in some cases even understand (Clapp and Crook, 2002). Based on this property alone, bioprospecting has a unique and durable advantage over the lab.

Underlying these trends in the pharmaceutical industry is a drug development value chain that is still expensive and complex. Figure 1

FIGURE 1. Drug Discovery Value Chain and Costs (Including Cost of Failures) (adapted from Gilbert et al., 2003)

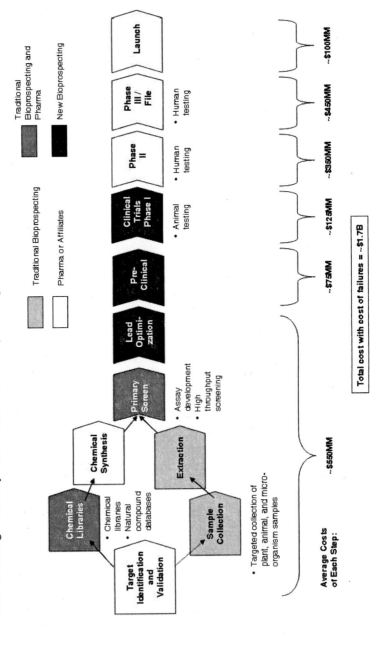

shows the typical steps in the drug development process, with average industry costs for each step, including failures.

Embedded in these costs at each step is the money spent to develop the many compounds that fail along the way for a variety of reasons. The later in the process a drug fails, the more expensive its failure. And indeed, more drug projects are failing now than in recent years. Studies from the early 1990s estimated that only 1 in 10,000-40,000 naturally-derived compounds ever made it to market (Principe, 1991; Reid et al., 1993; Clapp and Crook, 2002). There is reason to believe those odds have worsened. Gilbert et al. (2003) estimate that the cumulative success rate (defined by commercialization) for drugs entering preclinical trials has fallen from 14 percent for the period 1995-2000 to only 8 percent in 2000-2002.

Time is also an important factor. A rule of thumb in the pharmaceutical industry is the "$30 per second" rule. Thirty dollars is the approximate profit one forgoes for every second of delay in bringing a blockbuster drug to market. The reason for this is the finite life of pharmaceutical patents. Drug patents in the US are protected for twenty years (Herper, 2005). Yet to protect their interests, drug developers must patent compounds very early in a development process that can take ten or fifteen years (Thomas Eisner, paraphrased in Castree, 2003). Once the patent expires, revenues drop off rapidly as generic substitutes encroach on what was previously a monopolistic market (Hisey, 2004). If, by sourcing highly active lead compounds from bioprospectors, drug developers can shave, say, six months off the time between patenting and commercialization of a $1 billion drug, the increase in eventual profits would be in the hundreds of millions of dollars. There is some evidence that natural compounds *can* have faster time to market than traditional lab-generated compounds, particularly those that have been vetted in some form by indigenous peoples. Two of Shaman Pharmaceuticals' development candidates reached clinical trials in 16 and 24 months after lab testing, remarkably short by drug industry standards (Clapp and Crook, 2002).

I present these economics to highlight a major point, one that underlies the entire proposition of bioprospecting. Bioprospectors may never perform a significant portion of the drug development value chain, but because the financial stakes are so high, any improvement they can bring to the productivity of drug development for big pharma is extremely valuable. In aiming to help their partners, bioprospectors should focus on four primary levers: (1) finding novel compounds that cannot be created in the lab; (2) increasing the odds of success for those drugs entering the drug development value chain by identifying those with the most biological activity and effectiveness; (3) speeding up the time to market of those drugs; and (4) lowering the costs of drug development. If bioprospectors can do any of these things–and prove it–someone will pay them lots of money.

## EXISTING SUPPLY AND DEMAND OF BIOPROSPECTING

The market for bioprospecting services is hard to estimate; indeed, none of the literature I reviewed attempted to quantify the global supply of or demand for bioprospecting services actually performed. The difficulty in estimating this market arises from several factors: the small, non-commercial, and ephemeral nature of bioprospecting ventures; the often fuzzy line between bioprospecting and ecological research; and the secretive practices of the commercial pharmaceutical industry. Nonetheless, there are some clues as to the size of this market.

### Demand

One way to measure demand for bioprospecting is to examine the value of natural products in the pharmaceutical market. Two oft-quoted statistics are: 57 percent of the top 50 prescription drugs in 1993 contained active ingredients derived directly or synthetically from natural products (or from analogs thereof) (Grifo et al., 1997); and in 1997, 11 of 25 top-selling drugs derived from natural products (Newman and Laird, 1999).

These statistics surely overstate the value of bioprospecting to the pharmaceutical industry. A more skeptical examination finds that the value of plant, animal, and microbial products *directly* used in the manufacture of prescription pharmaceuticals totals less than $12 billion in annual sales (Ortega, 1998). As a portion of the total market, this represents roughly 2.1 to 3.6 percent of industry revenues, and that includes animal-derived products that are not considered in this analysis. Further, one must conclude that only a small portion of those products were the result of "bioprospecting" in its current incarnation, since so few bioprospecting projects can claim commercial successes.

Another measure of bioprospecting demand is the willingness of pharmaceutical companies to invest in such partnerships, with money, time, or other resources. By one count, 12 of the 15 most profitable pharmaceutical companies in the world in 1999 were engaged in bioprospecting in 1993 (Clapp and Crook, 2002; World Resources

Institute, 1993). Yet despite this historic activity, the pharmaceutical industry's present investments in bioprospecting are almost certainly small. Merck's famous investment in the INBio project, which is widely regarded as big by bioprospecting standards (Capson, personal communication, 11 March 2005), averaged only $130,000 per year in cash, plus some equipment and resources (Castree, 2003). Merck's annual R&D budget, by contrast, was $4 billion in 2004 (Merck, 2004).

In addition to demand from private corporations, bioprospecting also receives public funding from organizations such as the US National Institute of Health (NIH), the US National Science Foundation (NSF), the US Department of Agriculture (USDA), the National Cancer Institute (NCI), the World Health Organization (WHO), and the Inter-American Development Bank (IDB). Environmental NGOs such as Conservation International, the World Conservation Union (IUCN), the World Resources Institute (WRI), and the Bioresources Development and Conservation Programme are also active supporters of bioprospecting (Moran et al., 2001).

NIH, NSF, and USDA jointly support bioprospecting efforts in 14 countries through the International Cooperative Biodiversity Groups (ICBG) program, arguably the most prominent public funder of bioprospecting in the world. The total budget for the ICBG in 2001 was $4.0 million (John E. Fogarty International Center, 2005).

These demand estimates suggest that for pharmaceutical companies, bioprospecting is little more than a "check the box" activity–a two-bit lottery chip in the vast serendipitous game of drug discovery. We can also posit that the public relations value to pharmaceutical companies of being seen as funding conservation and capacity building in developing countries is worth more than the value of any compounds they hope to gain from those arrangements. (To be fair, pharma's continuing involvement in bioprospecting may also be a competitive hedge, a way of maintaining a bioprospecting partnering capability in the event that bioprospecting someday becomes an important competitive frontier.)

## *Supply*

How one measures the supply of bioprospecting depends on whether one considers the hypothetical market or the realized market. In hypothetical terms, it can certainly be said that there are more hectares of biodiverse forest and ocean in the world, and more active compounds, than the pharmaceutical industry is willing to pay to access.

I argue, however, that the supply of biodiversity is very different than the supply of bioprospecting services. Bioprospecting is not just walking around in the woods collecting leaves. To supply bioprospecting services, one must make considerable investments and clear significant entry hurdles. An entity must be willing to devote highly trained and qualified personnel to a project. Permission must be obtained from the host country, region, and/or park, and jurisdictional entities to access the prospecting site. Rules must be established for the assignment of intellectual property rights among prospectors, partners, governments, and local peoples. Suitable partners must be attracted, partnership agreements fashioned, and local politics and opposition managed.

In many cases, these entry hurdles have proven prohibitive. In the Philippines, bureaucratic access requirements have driven researchers to other countries (Reid et al., 1995; Clapp and Crook, 2002). And five years after Diversa Corp. signed a 1997 agreement with the US National Park Service to prospect for enzymes in Yellowstone National Park, Diversa pulled out after bureaucratic foot-dragging and a lawsuit by environmentalists prevented completion of a benefits-sharing agreement (Dalton, 2004c). (Some efforts have been made to reduce these transaction costs, with the goal of enhancing supply *and* demand for bioprospecting. INBio, for instance, is attempting to codify and stream-line transactional processes through its bioprospecting clearing-house [Clapp and Crook, 2002].)

The realized supply of bioprospecting services can perhaps be best estimated by quantifying the number of extant bioprospecting projects. My preliminary (and far from exhaustive) search for bioprospecting ventures active in the last decade identified 33 countries with bioprospecting activities.

By making several conservative assumptions–that I have under-counted participating countries by a factor of two; that there are, on average, 1.5 projects per country (for which there is no evidence); that all these projects are active; and that the average bioprospecting budget is equal to that of INBio's (again, unsupported, and probably overly generous)–we can construct an order-of-magnitude estimate of the global supply of bioprospecting services, as measured by operating expenses. Under these assumptions, there would be approximately 99 active bioprospecting programs globally. INBio's 2003 budget for bioprospecting was $608,958 (INBio, 2003). Using these estimates suggests that the realized global supply of bioprospecting services (as measured by funds expensed for bioprospecting activities) is approximately $60 million per year.

Despite the array of shaky assumptions in this estimate, one can surmise that bioprospecting is of only miniscule significance to the pharmaceutical industry, certainly financially, and probably scientifically. Nonetheless, the revenues represented by bioprospecting would constitute respectable sums in the environmental arena if a significant portion of that money were to flow to conservation efforts. But by and large, that has not happened.

## THE FAILURES OF BIOPROSPECTING ...
## AND OF ITS PROPONENTS

Critics make two valid claims against the concept of bioprospecting: that bioprospecting has not reliably generated commercial products, and that it has failed to deliver results in conservation. These failures are exemplified by bioprospecting's flagship project, INBio. Despite more than a decade of work in inventorying and monitoring thousands of species, identifying some novel, active compounds, and providing much-needed outreach and education on biodiversity, I could find no evidence that the venture has discovered a compound that eventually became a commercial drug. Indeed, INBio's public face conspicuously lacks a focus on commercial drug development. Nowhere in its mission statement, annual report, or strategic plan does INBio state that one of its goals is to discover or commercialize a drug. Instead, accomplishments are measured in the number of samples collected and screened, books published, students taught, and visitors to INBioparque, INBio's on-site biodiversity demonstration park (INBio, 2003).

This emphasis is reflected in INBio's budget, which explicitly allocates only 10% of its $6.0 million annual budget to bioprospecting (INBio, 2003). INBio's supporters would probably argue that, indeed, the main goal of INBio is *not* bioprospecting, and that the project should be measured along other parameters. This is a fair stance, but the fact that the most famous bioprospecting project in the world (Castree, 2003) has taken such pains to distance itself from drug discovery could justifiably lead the observer to question the basis for bioprospecting in the first place. To punctuate the point, Merck recently stopped funding INBio, citing a lack of marketable products after a decade of investment (Dalton, 2004b).

INBio has been somewhat more successful on other levels. Between 1991 and 1998, INBio steered approximately $1.2 million towards preservation of Costa Rican protected areas (Castree, 2003). While admirable and helpful, these funds are unlikely to make a significant dent in Costa Rica's environmental problems. Additionally, there is no mention of INBio funds distributed for direct conservation efforts in the 2003 annual report.

Perhaps INBio's greatest accomplishments are through its extensive outreach and teaching activities, and its world-class resources and databases for scientists and researchers. However, it is hard to see the direct link between these activities and large-scale conservation.

The intent of this analysis is not to castigate INBio. Rather, by highlighting the failures of a sophisticated, global experiment that is now into its second decade, I hope to highlight some opportunities for change that could help bioprospecting make significant, long-term contributions to the ultimate conservation goal: preserving biodiverse landscapes.

Bioprospecting's persistent difficulties stem, I believe, from four primary problems:

- *A mismatch in skill sets.* My strong hypothesis is that most bioprospecting ventures are founded by well-meaning environmentalists, ecologists, or biologists. Often, because of the small scale and remote locations for such ventures, those same people end up running what are essentially biotechnology companies. In the author's experience working with both scientists and businesspeople in a variety of fields, it is the rare individual who can jump seamlessly between both arenas, even with appropriate training. It is my unsupported opinion that this fundamental mismatch in skill sets is the single most important factor driving the long record of failures in bioprospecting. (Data to back up this hypothesis is very thin; it is a topic worthy of further investigation.)
- *Failure to fully internalize the economics of the drug discovery value chain.* The historical model employed for bioprospecting–that of collecting samples, and in some cases applying a primary screen for biological activity–sets bioprospecting up for failure in two ways. First, by merely passing on to a pharmaceutical partner the raw materials of genetic diversity, bioprospecting ventures do little to improve the odds of success for their partners. Second, this model guarantees that even if a prospected compound reaches the market, the royalties flowing to the bioprospecting entity will be small. By doing more for pharmaceutical companies, bioprospectors could not only increase their own odds of success, but have a legitimate platform from which to negotiate higher royalty rates in the future.

- *Failure to achieve a minimum efficient scale.* Most bio-prospecting projects are of a size well below minimum efficient scale for the biotech industry, and thus unable to weather the long droughts and frequent failures intrinsic to drug discovery. Large biotech companies like Affymax and Novartis typically keep thirty to forty potential products in their pipeline at any time to ensure that they always have products coming to market (Rachlin, 2002). This scale is unrealistic for most bioprospecting ventures, which are chronically under-funded. But increasing the size of bioprospecting ventures would do a great deal to increase the odds of success of individual institutions, and help them better weather individual project failures.
- *A lack of clarity on who the "customer" is, and a failure to focus on results.* My interviews and literature searches suggest that owing to the daunting odds of drug discovery, conservation-minded bioprospectors may, over time, implicitly or explicitly reorganize their ventures around other goals, such as capacity building and outreach, rather than viewing themselves first and foremost as the starting pointing in a long and complex drug-discovery value chain.

I maintain that it is this combination of factors, not capitalist greed or north-south colonialism, that has led to the scientific, financial, and conservation failures of most bioprospecting projects. Without a clear accounting of the difficulties that lie ahead, rational hedging plans to address those difficulties, and an insistent focus on the end results, bioprospecting will always be a house of cards–a perpetual race to find the next funder.

Given the historical failure of bioprospecting to yield commercial products, one criticism that *cannot* rationally be leveled at bioprospectors is that they have not funneled enough money into conservation programs. This is a classic case of putting the cart before the horse. Most current bioprospecting agreements examined for this study (particularly those of INBio) include provisions for royalty payments to local institutions. The problem is not one of legality or mal-intent, but of ineffectiveness. It is remarkable that so many critics rail against bioprospecting ventures for not delivering conservation funds without seeming the least bit concerned that most bioprospecting ventures have failed to generate any meaningful revenues from drug discovery. The reason these ventures have not contributed money to conservation efforts is because they don't have any. If environmentalists and scientists are serious about using bioprospecting to finance conservation, they must first solve the fundamental problem of how to make bioprospecting a productive venture. Doing so will require embracing a more capitalistic business model for bioprospecting, one that focuses less on publishing, outreach, and short-term justice issues, and more on short-term results, productivity, and hard-nosed portfolio management. This capitalistic approach rankles many environmentalists. But while there are no guarantees that bioprospecting will work (even with more business-minded managers at the helm), it is almost certain that bioprospecting *won't* work without a radically altered business model. Fifteen years of accumulated experience have shown as much.

What follows is an examination of the ICBG project in Panama (ICBG-P). Though ICBG-P shares some of the same flaws as traditional bioprospecting projects, it also exhibits several important characteristics that could make it an interesting model for a new breed of bioprospectors. Though not necessarily a definitive case, the degree to which ICBG-P succeeds or fails may well presage the ability of bioprospecting–broadly speaking–to address its recurring problems and finally become a meaningful force for conservation.

## THE INTERNATIONAL COOPERATIVE BIODIVERSITY GROUP PROJECT IN PANAMA

Panama, a small country at the southern end of the Mesoamerican isthmus, contains some of the highest plant diversity in the world (Barthlott et al., 1996). In an effort to capitalize on this, the Panamanian ICBG project was founded in 1992. It is administered by the Smithsonian Tropical Research Institute (STRI), and counts among its partners Novartis Pharmaceuticals, NIH (the main funder), Panama's Environment Authority (ANAM, from whom ICBG-P receives access to protected areas), the University of Panama, and the Institute of Advanced Scientific Research and High Technology Services (INDICASAT). In March of 2005, I visited the headquarters of ICBG-P in Panama City, and met with its founders, Dr. Phyllis Coley and Dr. Thomas Kursar, as well as Dr. Todd Capson, the ICBG-P Coordinator. The description that follows is based on those meetings and, where noted, published literature.

ICBG-P claims an annual budget of roughly $500,000 (Coley et al., 2005), six laboratories, ten senior scientists, and a staff of 60 (Dalton, 2004a). After some initial setbacks, ICBG-P has reorganized operations around finding drugs active against three cancer cell lines (breast, lung, and central nervous system); HIV; and three tropical diseases: malaria, leishmaniasis (a parasite), and Chagas' disease (Trypasonoma). ICBG-P scientists and staff collect leaf samples from protected lands throughout· Panama, including Chagres National Park, Coiba Island, and Barro Colorado Island, among others, and screen them against five bioassays (Coley et al., 2005). To date, ICBG-P has patented five alkoloids extracted from young leaves which have shown novel activity against leishmaniasis (Coley, personal communication, 6 September 2005). In the event of successful commercialization, ICBG-P would receive a small royalty, the proceeds from which would be split between STRI (50%), Fundación Natura (a Panamanian conservation NGO–30%), and Fondo Vida Silvestre, a conservation fund run by ANAM (20%) (Capson, personal communication, 11 March 2005).

Several aspects of ICBG-P distinguish it from typical bioprospecting ventures.

*Using Ecological Insight to Direct Bioprospecting.* ICBG-P employs ecological insight in the hopes of raising the odds of finding commercializable compounds. It does this in two ways: by focusing on young leaves, which tend to have higher concentrations of active compounds useful in herbivory defense than mature leaves (Crankshaw and Langenheim, 1981; Langenheim et al., 1986; Kursar et al., 1999; Coley et al., 2005); and by focusing on shade-tolerant plants, which tend to exhibit higher chemical activity than species adapted to high-light conditions (Coley et al., 2005). The hope is that in the search for unique, novel compounds, a focus on young and shade-tolerant leaves will provide the advantage that can allow ICBG-P to succeed where other bioprospectors have failed.

*Moving Up the Value Chain and Finding New Ways to Monetize Bioprospecting.* Rather than focus only on collecting samples, ICBG-P has made significant investments in extraction and screening capabilities, essentially moving parts of the drug discovery value chain to Panama. It has been estimated that up to one third of the pharmaceutical industry's $50 billion R&D activities could be performed in developing countries (Coley et al., 2005). ICBG-P, says Dr. Capson, is equipped to collect and extract compounds, screen them in bioassays, and conduct animal testing, placing ICBG-P further along the drug discovery chain than traditional bioprospecting programs. The aim is to sell lead compounds that will fetch far higher prices than raw plant samples, extracts, or screened compounds (Capson, personal communication, 11 March 2005).

In pursuing this strategy, ICBG-P has built significant local scientific capacity. Panama is a country of only three million people with no PhD programs and little scientific infrastructure. To date, ICBG-P has established bioassays for six disease and two agricultural targets, equipped a bioassay lab and a chemistry lab with equipment, employed more than 75 assistants, and provided opportunities to 14 volunteers (Coley et al., 2005). One of those bioassays, a fluorescence assay for antimalarial agents, has been patented and is now being used by researchers in Africa (Dalton, 2004b).

*Adopting a Flexible Approach.* Feeling increasing pressure to discover novel compounds, in a recent departure from the original mission of ICBG-P, Capson, Coley, Kursar and company have decided to leverage another asset unique to Panama: the Gulf of Chiriqui. This Gulf, with much warmer water than the adjacent Gulf of Panama, contains the highest number of endemic marine species on the Mesoamerican coast (Capson, personal communication, 11 March 2005). The relationship between fish and soft coral species presents a useful parallel to plant/insect herbivory. This makes many coral species ideal candidates for bioprospecting. Indeed, ICBG-P's marine prospecting has already yielded a novel compound that exhibits significant activity against malaria (Capson, personal communication, 11 March 2005).

*Leveraging Institutional Clout.* In an attempt to offset the long odds and long time-frames associated with royalty payments, ICBG-P personnel have used their scientific status to affect positive environmental results through non-financial means. ICBG-P personnel, along with other Panamanian advocates, personally met with both the former president of Panama and her cabinet, and by Capson and Coley's accounts, were instrumental in convincing them not to allow development of Coiba National Park. In this process, says Capson, the recently discovered coral-based anti-malarial compound played a key role. By appealing to what he calls Panama's "global patrimony," and illustrating the potential importance of a compound discovered in threatened Panamanian waters, ICBG-P personnel and other advocates were able to draw a direct link between Panamanian biodiversity, the health and security of Panamanian citizens, and bioprospecting. Capson is convinced that the involvement of STRI and ICBG-P was critical to the successful deflection of what most agree would have been extremely harmful development (Capson, personal communication, 11 March 2005). Indeed, in July 2005, Coiba National Park was named a World Heritage Site.

ICBG-P has also used the Panamanian press to their advantage. The coral discovery, and the ICBG-P program in general, have received frequent and positive press in Panama. Capson states that the bright red coral from which the anti-malarial compound was isolated has become something of a symbol of Panamanian environmentalism and national pride. More than once, says Capson, pictures of the coral have appeared on the front page of Panama City's newspaper in articles about pending developments in protected areas (Capson, personal communication, 11 March 2005).

The ICBG-P example and others illustrate some of the ancillary benefits of bioprospecting programs (Pagiola et al., 2002). While the ultimate goal of ICBG-P is still to generate tens of millions of dollars in royalties to pay for conservation, in the interim, ingenuity and initiative, coupled with the status allocated to what Capson calls "rich gringos," can sometimes create unusual opportunities to achieve conservation aims.

## UNCERTAINTIES ABOUT ICBG-P

ICBG-P is not without its flaws, and has earned some of the same criticism levied at other bioprospecting ventures: after twelve years of looking, ICBG-P has yet to produce a marketable drug (Dalton, 2004b). It is unclear whether this is the result of a fatal flaw in the strategy of bioprospecting or in the ineffectiveness of ICBG-P. However, the fact that ICBG-P has recently identified and patented several highly active compounds against diseases that affect billions of people worldwide, and has developed and patented a cost-effective novel bioassay, supports the hope that ICBG-P may yet defy expectations.

Lack of operating scale may constitute a crucial flaw in ICBG-P's strategy. With a budget of only $500,000 and 10 scientists (many of whom are presumably splitting time with other projects), ICBG-P is a fraction of the size of most commercial biotechnology companies. As mentioned, the long odds of the drug development chain suggest that it takes between 10,000 and 40,000 compound samples, and perhaps as many as 70,000, to bring one new drug to market (Principe, 1991; Reid et al., 1993; Gilbert et al., 2003). After more than a decade, ICBG-P has collected samples from 1,500 species (Coley, 2005). This suggests that no matter how well ICBG-P executes its mission, it will have only a small chance of finding a commercializable drug.

Additionally, ICBG-P appears to suffer to some degree from the philosophical disconnect that has plagued many other bioprospecting projects. While Dr. Capson appears focused on producing measurable results that pharmaceutical companies (or other funders) will ultimately pay for, Drs. Coley and Kursar seem less convinced of the ability of ICBG-P to reliably produce marketable drugs. While still hopeful that the project will someday generate significant royalty payments, Coley and Kursar make the case that the primary long-term value of ICBG-P derives from local capacity building, education, outreach, and policy influence. Referring to drug discovery as "basically a lottery," they articulate their most important near-term goals as finding additional research funds, maximizing the number of students they can take on and help gain access to world-class universities, and publishing their results (Coley and Kursar, personal communication, 8 March 2005). In short, says Coley, given the long odds of drug discovery, "the benefits are the process of drug discovery" (Coley, personal communication, 6 September 2005). While both perspectives are defensible, these sharp differences in philosophy raise a red flag to this observer about the long-term cohesiveness of ICBG-P's mission.

Finally, it remains to be seen whether ICBG-P's focus on collecting young leaf samples rather than mature ones, and on extracting compounds while the leaves are still young, inhibits the productivity and raises the costs of bioprospecting. I have no data by which to analyze the sample-collecting productivity of different bioprospecting ventures, but it would be worth investigating whether the trade-offs in terms of increased compound activity justify any added expense.

## BIOPROSPECTING OBSERVATIONS

This examination of the pharmaceutical industry, the bioprospecting industry, and of INBio and ICBG-P points out important differences between traditional models of bioprospecting and those that are now being employed by ICBG-P. In this section, I propose seven principles that could help bioprospecting projects be more successful. Not all of these recommendations will be feasible for every bioprospecting venture, and some projects may already employ these tactics. But this list may nonetheless provide a useful reference for contemplating various bioprospecting strategies.

First, bioprospectors would benefit by thinking of themselves as sophisticated businesses–essentially as tiny subsidiaries of big pharma–rather than as vehicles for basic research or scientific capacity building. This implies focusing more on producing measurable results that matter to their key customers (big pharma and biotech, and to some extent, life sciences NGOs), and less on publishing papers. Under such a model, bioprospectors would conduct more of the activities that pharma and biotech companies currently perform. (In business parlance, they would· "move up the value chain.") By doing so, bioprospectors could raise the odds of success for their partners and themselves.

Second, bioprospectors and their patrons might consider investing more in building homegrown scientific capacity to conduct their work. Because pharmaceutical companies are now less enamored of bioprospecting, they are less likely to provide the scientific and infrastructure resources needed to do the work. Without homegrown capacity, bioprospectors will find it impossible to change the odds of success in any meaningful way.

Third, wherever possible, bioprospectors need to increase the scale of their ventures. Given the very low odds of success in the pharmaceutical industry, it is unrealistic to expect that ventures with budgets of less than $1 million per year, and only a few drug programs running concurrently, will consistently find effective, novel compounds.

Fourth, bioprospectors would benefit from "monetizing" their work earlier. Rather than focusing on drug royalties, which can take decades to develop and are highly uncertain, bioprospectors may be able to realize short-term revenues by organizing their business models around the sale of lead compounds or other pre-commercial compounds. Monetizing other assets created in the drug development chain (such as novel bioassays, workflow methodologies, and equipment design, as ICBG-P has started to do) could also provide additional funding.

Fifth, bioprospectors, like private startups, would benefit from being more creative and flexible in their strategies. In the case of ICBG-P, this has meant branching out into marine prospecting when terrestrial plant prospecting was not yielding the desired results.

Sixth, bioprospectors in developing countries should consider leveraging one asset they have in abundance: cheap labor. Western pharmaceutical companies carry tremendous overhead and pay high salaries. As a result, many labor intensive activities of the drug discovery value chain are being outsourced to developing countries. Labs in China, for instance, now routinely synthesize compounds for western pharmaceutical companies at a fraction of the historical cost (Baxter, personal communication, November 2002). Providing these labor-intensive services would not only help developing bioprospectors build internal capacity, they would provide immediate revenue streams that could support ongoing research and be funneled back into conservation measures.

Finally, given the low odds and uncertain financial rewards of drug development, bioprospectors might consider using other levers to affect conservation and promote their altruistic goals. Influence, scientific persuasiveness, and public relations have all been effectively used in Panama to promote conservation.

## POLICY OPTIONS TO IMPROVE BIOPROSPECTING SUPPLY AND DEMAND IN PANAMA

To a large extent, ICBG-P will determine its own success or failure. I could identify only one major policy impediment preventing ICBG-P from carrying out its work in an effective, cost efficient way (described below, under *Access to Resources*), and no major impediments in marketing its products and services to potential customers. This is a testament to the managers and scientists at ICBG-P, STRI, and ICBG-P's various partners, including the government of Panama (GOP).

Nonetheless, there are policy steps that could help improve the market for bioprospecting in Panama. Assuming that the currently benevolent relationships enabling ICBG-P's existence (such as ICBG-P's residency at STRI, the Smithsonian's patronage of STRI, and ICBG-P's agreement with Novartis) are not in peril, we can turn our attention to the three policy institutions that most directly impact ICBG-P: the executive branch and assembly of the Panamanian government; ANAM; and the NIH, which through the ICBG program provides the bulk of ICBG-P's funding. To a lesser degree, ICBG-P is also potentially or occasionally impacted by the global Convention on Biodiversity (CBD); informal sociopolitical networks that contribute to corruption and inefficiencies within Panama; and private biotech and pharmaceutical companies.

For the sake of policy analysis, let us array the challenges facing bioprospectors in another way: by outlining the key requirements for the successful operation of ICBG-P's projects. These requirements are: access to resources (funding, human capital, and infrastructure); continued access to bioprospecting sites; a stable and equitable business environment (including reliable intellectual property laws); and demand for bioprospecting services, both within Panama and globally. Combining these dimensions with the array of institutional players outlined above suggests that multiple policy-makers could impact each of these fronts.

## Access to Resources

In my opinion, the single biggest impediment to success for ICBG-P is a lack of appropriate scale. As described above, ICBG-P is significantly below the traditional minimum efficient scale for the drug discovery industry. One possible remedy would be for NIH to reconsider its funding strategy. Rather than fund 5 or 6 ICBG projects annually at budgets of $500,000-$600,000, NIH could either provide more funds to fewer projects, or find a way to greatly increase their grant budget and fund ICBG projects at more appropriate scales. This is not just a problem with the ICBG program: my literature search supports the notion that most bioprospecting ventures operate on a similar scale. (A notable exception was Shaman Pharmaceuticals (Artuso, 2002).) A consolidation of projects–each funded more fully–and the development of broader portfolios, could increase the success rate of individual bioprospecting ventures.

Pharma and biotech partners may also want to address this fundamental flaw of scale in the current bioprospecting model. Placing larger bets on fewer bioprospecting projects, rather than sprinkling money around to a passel of sub-scale projects, would likely increase the odds of success for bioprospecting partnerships.

A seemingly logical reaction to ICBG-P's scale problem would be a recommendation that the Panamanian government fund a ICBG-P scale-up. However, ICBG-P has intentionally limited their dependence on the Panamanian government to avoid political co-opting and bureaucratic inefficiencies (Coley et al., 2005), so it is probably unlikely that ICBG-P management would approve of this recommendation.

Another resource in short supply in Panama is scientists. Because Panama has no domestic Ph.D. programs, ICBG-P must either import trained scientists, train locals in-country, or export students to international universities in the hope they will return after receiving their degrees. This is undoubtedly a problem in other developing countries as well. The Panamanian government could help rectify this by boosting science funding to the University of Panama, helping to establish one or more Ph.D. programs, or providing additional scholarship money for Panamanians to study overseas. Increased funding of science and education would serve broader Panamanian social goals as well.

Finally, ICBG-P has at times been constrained by a lack of modern scientific equipment (Coley and Kursar, personal communication, 8 March 2005). It appears this has been exacerbated by a cronyistic arrangement whereby any medical or laboratory equipment imported into

Panama must pass through a single distributor who has the power to charge usurious prices, and does (Coley and Kursar, personal communication, 8 March 2005). This hints at a broader problem of corruption in Panama. The government should consider liberalizing the relevant import laws (at the very least, eliminating patronage deals) that sustain this arrangement. More broadly, the GOP should consider ways to eradicate corruption throughout Panama, an admittedly monumental task that would create significant social benefits.

Finally, as INBio has done in Costa Rica, ICBG-P might be able to cheaply obtain used or obsolete research equipment from pharmaceutical or biotech companies or US national research facilities.

### Continued Access to Bioprospecting Sites

ANAM is the gatekeeper through which ICBG-P must pass to access bioprospecting sites in Panama. In interviews, Capson, Coley, and Kursar reported no difficulties in obtaining access to sites. However, as illustrated by the Coiba example, many of these sites are under imminent development pressure. The GOP and ANAM would aid both ICBG-P and Panama generally by ensuring the long-term protection of these sites. (To some extent, this would accomplish the ends through the means–after all, one of the goals of ICBG-P is to preserve these sites.) The GOP and ANAM could also consider giving special weight to those areas designated by ICBG-P as being particularly valuable. (It is worth noting that this might create conflicts with other conservation-minded parties in Panama that promote different agendas.)

### Business Environment

Based on my conversations with Capson, Coley, Kursar, and others, I have no reason to believe that Panama presents undo impediments to those in the "business" of bioprospecting. Panama is known as a business-friendly country by Latin American standards. Continued efforts by the GOP to promote a business-friendly environment would likely benefit (or at least not impede) bioprospecting efforts in the country.

Looking globally, the ratification of the Convention on Biodiversity has made bioprospecting more difficult in some countries (Nature, 2004; Pagiola et al., 2002). However, the CBD does not currently appear to be an impediment to ICBG-P or its partners in conducting business in Panama. However, as CBD decision-makers consider updates to the treaty, they should bear in mind the potential of current and future

CBD rules to impede well-intentioned bioprospecting arrangements around the globe.

## Demand

Three policy steps could help improve demand for bioprospecting in Panama. First, the codification and standardization of bioprospecting agreements, rules, and regulations would help lower transaction costs for both providers and buyers of bioprospecting services. INBio has done an admirable job of this, and Todd Capson indicated that ICBG-P staff are working to create templates from existing partner agreements to facilitate easier negotiations in the future. The benefits of codification are telling: it took Thomas Kursar nearly two years to negotiate ICBG-P's first agreement with Monsanto, yet it took only six weeks to complete a deal with Novartis, partly due to experience from the first deal, and partly due to the presence of existing contracts and documents (Capson, personal communication, 11 March 2005; Coley, personal communication, 6 September 2005).

Second, the GOP could conceivably help ICBG-P attract additional partners by aiding commercial outreach efforts. However, given ICBG-P's desire to remain independent from the GOP, it is unclear whether ICBG-P would prefer this approach.

Finally, and in summation, the biggest step these institutions could take to boost demand for bioprospecting would be to help ICBG-P achieve its first major drug success. This may sound self-evident, but bioprospecting managers and their proponents suffer severely from a lack of focus on demonstrable results (Castree, 2003). Castree points out that even critics of bioprospecting rarely evaluate projects on any rigorous criteria that would expose their scientific failings. Bringing one major compound to market could help validate the concept of bioprospecting, and potentially open the floodgates to a new wave of bioprospecting funding and interest.

## CONCLUSION

The principles laid out in this paper are largely untested in the bioprospecting arena. But many of them have been repeatedly validated by private biotechnology companies and pharmaceutical startups: focusing on results that matter to your customer, getting to minimum efficient scale, monetizing compounds earlier in the process, and being flexible and creative in portfolio management. The question is whether bioprospecting ventures, with their uneven skill set, unusual motives, and remote locales, can internalize these principles in time. It may well turn out that drug development and design is too complex a task for the dilettante, and that ultimately, these activities belong solely in the purview of those who are already experts at them–pharmaceutical and biotechnology companies.

We will soon have the answer to this question, and it may be definitive. Bioprospecting has already had one heyday, then a bust, and now lies at a critical juncture. A new model for bioprospecting, exemplified in part by the Panamanian ICBG project, represents a crucial second wave in attempts to link the mining of natural genetic stocks to the conservation of those stocks. A new spate of failures could spell the end of bioprospecting as a conservation tool. But success would validate bioprospecting as an innovative model for saving some of the world's great biological treasures. If so, it could open the doors to a new tide of bioprospecting interest and funding.

## *ACKNOWLEDGMENT*

This paper arose from an attempt to investigate the potential for payments from "biodiversity services" to contribute to conservation efforts in Panama. In examining this question, we considered two types of sites: Chagres National Park, a relatively undisturbed park of 129,000 hectares roughly 40 kilometers from Panama City; and reforestation projects within the Panama Canal Watershed, as typified by PRORENA (The Native Species Reforestation Project). While by no means representing the full spectrum of conservation challenges in Panama, these two examples arguably express the bounds of that spectrum: on one hand, a large tract of primary and secondary tropical forest that is highly rich in species and under continuing development pressure; and on the other, a heavily manipulated landscape plagued by invasive species (notably paja blanca [*Saccharum* spp.]), a frequent fire regime, and bearing limited economic value to local stakeholders. These two sites present challenges to the conservationist that are common in Panama and many other developing countries: uncertain land tenure, weak and overlapping national institutions, a lack of national and local funding, poverty-related development pressures, and a pastiche of largely uncoordinated and often conflicting (though well-intentioned) non-governmental organizations (NGOs) eager to play a role.

The biodiversity team examined a host of possible biodiversity products and services before deciding on four to investigate in more detail: eco-tourism (see Schloegel, this volume), land acquisition (see Wallander, this volume), certified non-timber forest products (NTFPs) (see Miyata, this volume), and bioprospecting. Although bioprospecting can refer to agricultural, pharmaceutical, and other therapeutic products such as cosmetics and dietary supplements, this paper considers only pharmaceutical bioprospecting, as that is the focus of the Panamanian program examined here.

## REFERENCES

Artuso, A. 2002. Bioprospecting, Benefit Sharing, and Biotechnological Capacity Building. *World Development* 30(8):1355-1368.

Barthlott, W., W. Lauer, and A. Placke. 1996. Global Distribution of Species Diversity in Vascular Plants: Towards a World Map of Phytodiversity. *Erdkunde* 50:317-327.

Bioportfolio.com. 2005. Blockbusters. Retrieved March 6, 2005 from http://www. bioportfolio.com/cgi-bin/acatalog/Blockbuster_sample_pages.pdf.

Brown, R. 1998. The Natural Way in Cosmetics and Skin Care. *Chemical Market Reporter* 254(2):8.

Castree, N. 2003. Bioprospecting: From Theory to Practice (and Back Again). *Trans Inst Br Geogr* NS 28:35-55.

Clapp, R.A. and C. Crook. 2002. Drowning in the Magic Well: Shaman Pharmaceuticals and the Elusive Value of Traditional Knowledge. *Journal of Environment and Development* 11(1):79-102.

Coley, P.D., T.A. Kursar, T.L. Capson, M.V. Heller, R. Aizprua, M. Correa, M. Gupta, P.N. Solis, E. Ortega-Barría, L.I. Romero, B. Gómez, M. Ramos, D. Cubilla-Rios, D. Quiroz, L. Emmen, W. Gerwick, and K. McPhail. 2005. Bioprospecting for Local Benefit: Linking Drug Discovery with Economic Development and Conservation in Panama. PowerPoint presentation, presented March 8, 2005, Balboa, Panama.

Crankshaw, D.R. and J.H. Langenheim. 1981. Variations in Terpenes and Phenolics Through Leaf Development in Hymenaea and Its Possible Significance to Herbivory. *Biochem Syst Ecol* 9:115-24.

Dalton, R. 2004a. Bermuda Gets Tough Over Resource Collecting. *Nature* 429:600.

Dalton, R. 2004b. Bioprospects Less Than Golden. *Nature* 429:598-600.

Dalton, R. 2004c. National Park Plan Delayed. *Nature* 427:576.

Gilbert, J. and P. Rosenberg. 2004. There's No Such Thing as a Free Drug. *The Wall Street Journal Europe*. April 19.

Gilbert, J., P. Henske, and A. Singh. 2003. Rebuilding Big Pharma's Business Model. *In Vivo–The Business and Medicine Report* 21(10):73-83.

Grifo, F., D. Newman, A.S. Fairfield, B. Bhattacharya, and J.T. Grupenhoff. 1997. The Origins of Prescription Drugs. Pp. 159-197 in: F. Grifo, and J. Rosenthal (eds.). 1997. Biodiversity Prospecting. World Resources Institute, Washington, DC.

Herper, M. 2005. Are Drug Patents Too Short? *Forbes.com*. Retrieved March 9, 2005 from http://www.forbes.com/sciencesandmedicine/2005/03/09/cx_mh_0309plavix. html.

Hisey, T. 2004. The Big Squeeze. Pharmaceutical Executive (Pharmex.com). Retrieved April 4, 2005 from http://www.pharmexec.com/pharmexec/article/articleDetail. jsp?id=129292&pageID=1.

Hunt, H.D. 2003. Bio-Tex. *Tierra Grande* 10(1) Retrieved April 4, 2005 from http://recenter.tamu.edu/tgrande/vol10-1/1599.html.

Instituto Nacional de Biodiversidad (INBio). 2003. Memoria INBio Annual Report 2003. Instituto Nacional de Biodiversidad, Santo Domingo, Heredia, Costa Rica.

John E. Fogarty International Center for Advanced Study in the Health Sciences. 2005. International Cooperative Biodiversity Groups (ICBG). Retrieved April 5, 2005 from http://www.fic.nih.gov/programs/icbg.html.

Kellman, L. 2005. FDA Seeks Specific Vioxx Power. Associated Press. Retrieved April 4, 2005 from http://www.cbsnews.com/stories/2005/03/01/health/main677435.shtml.

Kursar, T.A., T.L. Capson, P.D. Coley, D.G. Corley, M.B. Gupta, L.A. Harrison, E. Ortega-Barría, and D.M. Windsor. 1999. Ecologically Guided Bioprospecting in Panama. *Pharmaceutical Biology* 37(supl.):114-126.

Landell-Mills, N. and I.T. Porras. 2002. Silver Bullet or Fool's Gold? A Global Review of Markets for Forest Ecosystem Services and Their Impacts on.the Poor. International Institute for Environmental Development, London.

Langenheim, J.H., C.A. Macedo, M.K. Ross, and W.H. Strubblebine. 1986. Leaf Development in the Tropical Leguminous Tree Copaifera in Relation to Microlepidopteran Herbivory. *Biochem Syst Ecol* 14:51-59.

Merck & Co, Inc. (Merck). 2004. Annual Report 2004. Merck Public Affairs, Whitehouse Station.

Miyata, Y. 2007. Markets for Biodiversity: Certified Forest Products in Panama. *Journal of Sustainable Forestry* 25(3/4):281-307.

Moran, K., S.R. King, and T.J. Carlson. 2001. Bioprospecting: Lessons and Prospects. *Annual Review of Anthropology* 30:505-526.

Nature. 2004. Boosting Bioprospects. *Nature* 429:585.

Newman, D.J., and S.A. Laird. 1999. The Influence of Natural Products on 1997 Pharmaceutical Sales Figures. Pp. 333-335 in: K. ten Kate, and S.A. Laird (eds.). The Commercial Use of Biodiversity: Access to Genetic Resources and Benefit-Sharing. Commission of the European Communities and Earthscan Publicatons, Ltd., London.

Ortega, T. 1998. Natural Products Hold Their Own in Drug Discovery. *Chemical Market Reporter* 254(2):10.

Pagiola, S., J. Bishop, and N. Landell-Mills (eds.). 2002. Selling Forest Environmental Services: Market-Based Incentives for Conservation and Development. Earthscan Publications Limited, London.

Pfizer Inc. 2004. Pfizer Inc 2004 Financial Report. Retrieved April 5, 2005 from http://www.pfizer.com/annualreport/2004/financial/p2004fin01.htm.

Principe, P.P. 1991. Valuing the Biodiversity of Medicinal Plants. Pp 79-125 in: O. Akerle, V. Heywood, and H. Synge (eds.). 1991. The Conservation of Medicinal Plants. Cambridge University Press, Cambridge, UK.

Rachlin, E.N. 2002. Defying the Odds. *Venturemag.org*. Retrieved April 5, 2005 from http://www.venturemag.org/vol1/issue1/depts/defyingodds.html.

Reid, W.V., S.A. Laird, R. Gamez, A. Sittenfeld, D.H. Janzen, M.Gollin, and C. Juma, 1993. A New Lease on Life. Pp. 1-52 in: W.V. Reid, S.A. Laird, C.A. Meyer, R. Gamez, A. Sittenfeld, D.H. Janzen, K. ten Kate, and S.A. Laird (eds.) 1999. The Commercial Use of Biodiversity: Access to Genetic Resources and Benefit-Sharing. Earthscan Publications Ltd., London.

Schloegel, C. 2007. Sustainable Tourism: Sustaining Biodiversity? *Journal of Sustainable Forestry* 25(3/4):247-264.

Wallander, S. 2007. The Dynamics of Conservation Financing: A Window into the Panamanian Market for Biodiversity Existence Value. *Journal of Sustainable Forestry* 25(3/4):265-280.

Yahoo! Finance. 2005. Industry: Major Drugs. Retrieved April 5, 2005 from http://finance.yahoo.com/q/in?s=MRK.

doi:10.1300/J091v25n03_01

# Sustainable Tourism:
# Sustaining Biodiversity?

Catherine Schloegel

**SUMMARY.** New markets for ecosystem services have emerged in response to the failure of traditional biodiversity conservation mechanisms to effectively protect and conserve the processes that support ecosystem function and process (Landell-Mills and Porras, 2002; Pagiola et al., 2002). Sustainable tourism–one market tool that potentially supports biodiversity services–aims to balance the environmental, economic, and socio-cultural features of tourism development by maintaining environmental resources, the socio-cultural livelihoods of host communities, and providing stakeholder benefits (WTO, 2004). Proponents claim that sustainable tourism contributes toward maintaining biodiversity, while

Catherine Schloegel currently works as the community and research director at Ecomadera, a community-run conservation enterprise in Ecuador.

Catherine Schloegel earned a Master of Environmental Science at the Yale School of Forestry and Environmental Studies, New Haven, CT 06511 USA (E-mail: catherine.schloegel@aya.yale.edu).

The author thanks Professors Brad Gentry, Shimi Anisfeld and Teaching Fellow Quint Newcomer for designing this course. The author also thanks Mark Wishnie and Jose Manuel Pérez for making the Panama case study into reality and organizing the field visit. The author gives special thanks to Mirei Endara, Gina Castro, and Jessica Young for answering innumerable questions. Additionally, the author thanks the "biodiversity team"–Pat Burtis, Steve Wallander, and Yuko Miyata–for advice and support in the development of this chapter. Finally, the author thanks Anna Jetmore and Cesar Moran for sharing invaluable information regarding ecotourism.

[Haworth co-indexing entry note]: "Sustainable Tourism: Sustaining Biodiversity?" Schloegel, Catherine. Co-published simultaneously in *Journal of Sustainable Forestry* (Haworth Food & Agricultural Products Press, an imprint of The Haworth Press, Inc.) Vol. 25, No. 3/4, 2007, pp. 247-264; and: *Emerging Markets for Ecosystem Services: A Case Study of the Panama Canal Watershed* (ed: Bradford S. Gentry, Quint Newcomer, Shimon C. Anisfeld, and Michael A. Fotos, III) Haworth Food & Agricultural Products Press, an imprint of The Haworth Press, Inc., 2007, pp. 247-264. Single or multiple copies of this article are available for a fee from The Haworth Document Delivery Service [1-800-HAWORTH, 9:00 a.m. - 5:00 p.m. (EST). E-mail address: docdelivery@haworthpress.com].

Available online at http://jsf.haworthpress.com
© 2007 by The Haworth Press, Inc. All rights reserved.
doi:10.1300/J091v25n03_02

critics fear that marketing various components of biodiversity as distinct services (e.g., only protecting unique places for sustainable tourism, and only protecting extremely biodiverse places for bioprospecting), fails to protect the integrity of the functioning, and dynamic ecosystem (Landell-Mills and Porras, 2002). This chapter serves as one section of a four-part analysis of existing and emerging markets for biodiversity services using Panama as a case study. Based on projections of future sustainable tourism markets, this analysis presents policy options that could positively augment future sustainable tourism ventures. doi: 10.1300/J091v25n03_02 *[Article copies available for a fee from The Haworth Document Delivery Service: 1-800-HAWORTH. E-mail address: <docdelivery @haworthpress.com> Website: <http://www.HaworthPress.com> © 2007 by The Haworth Press, Inc. All rights reserved.*

**KEYWORDS.** Sustainable tourism, ecotourism, nature-based tourism, biodiversity, Panama Canal Watershed, ecosystem services

## INTRODUCTION

New markets for ecosystem services have emerged in response to the failure of traditional biodiversity conservation mechanisms to effectively protect and conserve the processes that support ecosystem function and process (Landell-Mills and Porras, 2002; Pagiola, Bishop et al., 2002). Proponents hope that beneficiaries of these emerging markets (primarily for carbon, water, and biodiversity) will reimburse service providers. Markets for biodiversity services significantly differ from those of carbon or water. Unlike carbon or water, that can be measured directly, biodiversity can be calculated using many different metrics, including species richness, species diversity, or species uniqueness. The use of different metrics suggests that a given place may be considered biodiverse by one standard but not another. In response, several distinct markets for biodiversity services have emerged, including: payment for biodiversity friendly products (e.g., eco-labeling of coffee, chocolate, vanilla, fruit, and timber); payment for access (e.g., sustainable tourism, bioprospecting, research/hunting/fishing permits); payment for biodiversity-conserving management (e.g., conservation easements, leases, and concessions); and tradable rights (e.g., biodiversity credits and/or biodiversity taxes) (Jenkins et al., 2004). Proponents hope that participation in markets for biodiversity friendly products, access, and management practices will contribute toward sustainable ecosystem management.

Using Panama as a case study, this chapter examines the potential for participation in a market for sustainable tourism ventures. In addition to discussions of market-based biodiversity preservation strategies (see Wallander, this volume), analyses of bioprospecting (see Burtis, this volume), and certified products/eco-labeling (see Miyata, this volume), this analysis of sustainable tourism provides landowners with options to capture market value for biodiversity conservation.

This chapter begins by defining pertinent terms and trends within sustainable tourism examining how sustainable tourism contributes toward biodiversity conservation, and the ways in which tourism infrastructure negatively affects biodiversity conservation efforts. The Panama Canal Watershed (PCW) is used as a case study to analyze existing and future markets for sustainable tourism. In final analysis, this chapter ends with a short list of policy alternatives and recommendations for future research.

## *SUSTAINABLE TOURISM?*

Given both its economic and geographic scope, tourism is arguably the world's largest industry (Honey, 2002; WTO, 2005b). By the late 1990s, the tourism industry reaped annual benefits of $5.3 trillion (Honey, 2002). More than just revenues gleaned from leading a guided tour, tourism revenues include plane tickets, car rentals, and accommodations. In addition, tourism has become the world's top employer, generating nearly 11 percent of all jobs (Honey, 2002). With expectations for future growth, the World Tourism Organization predicts that tourism will increase by 50 percent between 1990 and 2010 (Honey, 2002).

Tourism is any activity that carries a person to places outside his/her usual environment for recreation, business, or leisure (WTO, 2005a). As early as the 1980s, tourists cognizant of the industry's potential for ecological disruption and destruction began to demand ecologically conscious tourism options (Honey, 2002). As demand from this small segment grew, "nature," "adventure," "eco," and "sustainable" tourism options emerged. Most tourist ventures develop tours in response to market demand, mixing and matching activities as appropriate.

Recently, the World Tourism Organization, a United Nations (UN) agency, launched a sustainable tourism initiative advocating a new form of tourism that balances the environmental, economic, and socio-cultural features of tourism development by maintaining environmental resources, the socio-cultural livelihoods of host communities, and providing benefits to all stakeholders (WTO, 2004). Sustainable tourism connotes a mixture of nature, adventure, and ecotourism initiatives that strive to achieve the above-stated goals.

Nature, adventure, and ecotourism frequently overlap in practice, despite seemingly static definitions in academic literature. Nature tourism includes "travel to unspoiled places to experience and enjoy nature" (Honey, 2002:1). Adventure tourism usually includes participation in high-risk activities that require physical endurance (Honey, 2002). Ecotourism, hailed by many as responsible ecological tourism, is travel to natural areas that strives to be low impact, educate the traveler, and provide direct funds for conservation, as well as benefit the economic development and political empowerment of local communities. Finally, ecotourism aims to foster respect for local culture, human rights, and international labor agreements (Honey, 2002).

While many advocates hail sustainable tourism as a panacea for biodiversity conservation (Rainforest Alliance Sustainable Tourism Initiative, 2005; United Nations Environment Program Sustainable Tourism Program, 2002), others question this frustratingly amorphous buzzword, which signifies different practices in diverse locations. Proponents recognize sustainable tourism as one form of sustainable development (Honey, 2002). On the other hand, critics emphasize the ecological, social, and economic impacts of unregulated "sustainable" tourism. Many "eco" and "sustainable" tours do not adhere to guidelines promoting sustainable environmental, social, and economic benefits. Unregulated tourism can cause profit leakage to foreign investors, an increase in local prices, increased crime, pollution, landscape degradation, and the depletion of locals' natural resources, particularly water resources (Jetmore, 2004).

## THE POTENTIAL FOR SUSTAINABLE TOURISM IN PANAMA

At the confluence of two great continental plates, Panama acts as both a bridge and a barrier, serving as the southernmost range for North American species and the northernmost range for South American species (TNC, 2005). For its size, Panama is extremely biodiverse. While slightly smaller than South Carolina in total land mass (77,082 $km^2$), Panama hosts 900 resident and migratory bird species, and 218 known mammal species (WRI Earthtrends, 2004; TNC, 2005). Although ecologically diverse, Panama is economically poor. Per capita Gross National Income in 2003 was $4,250 (UNICEF, 2005), with over

7 percent of the population living on under $1 per day in the year 2000 (Globalis, n.d.).

Sustainable tourism provides one possible strategy for preserving biodiversity and promoting small-scale sustainable economic development. Some critics question how increased sustainable tourism income in areas of high biodiversity contributes toward biodiversity conservation. Two case studies in other regions of Latin America suggest that sustainable tourism revenues can act as an incentive for landowners to enact more rigorous measures to protect biodiversity. In Ecuador's Cuyabeno Reserve, communities dependent on tourism income (and with well-developed sustainable tourism infrastructure) have implemented stricter zoning around protected areas, including a community-supported hunting ban, than communities without such revenues (Wunder, 2000). In Costa Rica, the privately-owned Hacienda Barú National Wildlife Refuge has seen consistently increasing tourism revenues over the past decade following the conversion of cattle pastures to a sustainable tourism operation; during the same period, diversity of plant and animal species have also increased on this Refuge (Newcomer, personal communication, December 2005).

Panama's high degree of ecological threat and numerous endemic species make biodiversity conservation important. Threats to Panama's biodiversity include direct threats such as the expanding agricultural frontier, and logging. There are also institutional threats including the promotion of economic models of development that support deforestation (ANAM, 2004). Poverty, internal migration, and growing population also exert pressure on forested landscapes (ANAM, 2004). Evidence of these development pressures is reflected in the loss of natural forest cover (see Figure 1), which is particularly acute in Panama (WRI Earthtrends, 2004). Loss of natural forest cover also affects biodiversity loss, which in Panama span all taxonomic groups (see Figure 2).

International conservation organizations including Conservation International, World Wide Fund for Nature, and The Nature Conservancy have adopted science-based biodiversity ranking criterion (including "hotspots," and "ecoregions") to identify areas of global concern with both a high level of biodiversity and a high level of threat. Their ranking criteria have identified La Amistad International Biosphere Reserve (see CI, 2005) and five ecoregions (see World Wide Fund for Nature, 2005) as areas within Panama for immediate conservation. The work of these large environmental non-profits complements the work of organizations like the Native Species Reforestation Project (PRORENA) in Panama, which supports both small and large-scale native species

FIGURE 1. Percent Change in Forest Area by Type, 1990-2000 (adapted from Earthtrends, 2004)

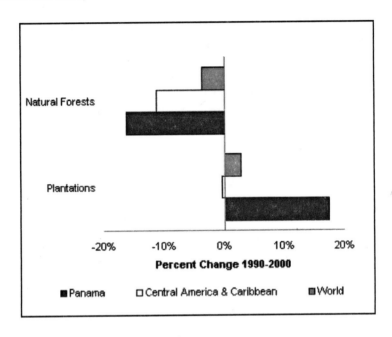

FIGURE 2. Threatened Species in Panama, 2002-2003 (adapted from Earthtrends, 2004)

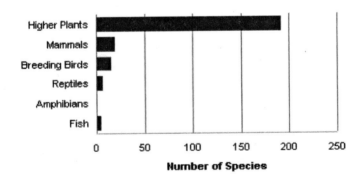

reforestation projects. PRORENA's mission is to reforest native species forests across degraded tropical landscapes, "demonstrating that large-scale ecological restoration in the tropics is technically feasible, socially attractive, and financially viable" (PRORENA, 2005).

## SUSTAINABLE TOURISM IN PANAMA–EXISTING SUPPLY

The Panamanian Institute of Tourism (IPAT) beckons tourists to experience Panama's "path less traveled" (IPAT, 2004). Influenced by neighboring Costa Rica's booming tourism industry, IPAT strives "for tourism to be the principal source of commerce for the country" (IPAT, 2004). With an equally, if not more ecologically diverse landscape, Panama's tourism infrastructure is not yet as developed as that of Costa Rica. As a catalog of existing supply, IPAT (2004) recognizes 52 tour operators in Panama who offer a variety of day trips and week-long adventures. Focusing on the PCW, a 2003 market survey of Panamanian tour operators identified the Panama Canal, Panama City, and Soberania National Park among the top 20 most frequently visited tourist destinations in Panama (Jiménez, 2003).

According to Gina Castro of the Academy for Educational Development (AED), Fundación Natura has made limited funding available to ecotourism projects through a designated Nature Fund (personal communication, 11 March 2005). Nevertheless, there is a growing awareness and emphasis on the development of sustainable tourism projects in Panama (Castro, personal communication, 11 March 2005). On a national level, support of sustainable tourism ventures is focused on projects in Bastimientos National Park and Coiba National Park (Castro, personal communication, 11 March 2005). To expand the scope of sustainable tourism projects in Panama, AED is promoting a new macro-level ecotourism project within the PCW (Castro, personal communication, 11 March 2005). According to Castro, the goals of the PCW project are: (1) to improve management within protected areas; (2) to find alternative economic development strategies for communities; and (3) to create conditions within the Panamanian National Environmental Authority (ANAM) to motivate private companies to invest in public conservation projects. AED aims to create a sustainable tourism cluster of activities directing tourists to the following sites in the PCW: Casco Viejo, Panama City; El Amador; Soberania National Park; the Panama Canal; and San Lorenzo and Achiote on the Caribbean side of the PCW.

None of the sites visited during the course-related field study were engaged in any form of tourism, sustainable or otherwise. Currently, there are no small-scale tourism projects at PRORENA research sites or within the smallholder communities visited inside Chagres National Park. However, several tours take visitors to Embera villages within Chagres National Park.

Considerations for future tourism development should address the following considerations: facility of access to the site, including proximity to transportation hubs; costs related to site and/or trail maintenance; publicity and marketing costs; partnerships with existing tourism companies; basic human infrastructure, including the cost of tour guides (preferably bi- or trilingual) and maintaining fee collectors; and construction/maintenance costs for physical infrastructure investments such as restrooms, dining facilities, and waste management.

## BURGEONING DEMAND FOR SUSTAINABLE TOURISM IN PANAMA?

The World Tourism Organization (WTO) estimates that between 1999 and 2000, tourism in Central America grew 9 percent, the largest growth in the Americas (Jiménez, 2003). According to the WTO 2003 statistics, Central America is the second fastest growing tourist destination in the world (Jiménez, 2003). Tourist growth in Panama has paralleled the general Central American trend. Over the past decade (1995-2004), overall tourist growth has increased 55 percent (IPAT, 2004). Arrivals at Tocumen International Airport in Panama City have shown a 125 percent increase (see Figure 3), but the most explosive growth is seen in the number of maritime visitors who arrive either in Panama City or Colón on cruise ships, showing a 557 percent increase over this same time period (IPAT, 2004).

Cruise ship tourists represent the most concentrated tourist market in Panama. In a 2004 interview with Jose Gandasegui from ANCON Expeditions of Panama, he estimated that 35 percent of tourists in Panama debark from the cruise ships and stay in the Panama Canal Watershed for up to eight hours on a shore pass visa (Moran, 2004). In one area, 3,000 tourists have debarked from cruise ships in a single day (Moran, 2004). Unlike other areas, Panama does not exhibit a high and low tourism season. In the years 2001 and 2002, tourism peaked in July, and was at its lowest in September-October and April-May (IPAT, 2004). For the

FIGURE 3. Annual Tourist Visits to Panama 1995-2004 (adapted from IPAT, 2004)

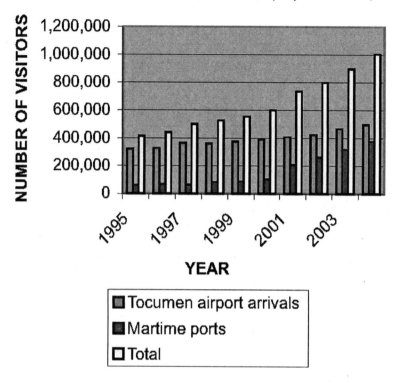

year 2002, Panama had an average of 35,496 visitors per month, with a low of 31,354 in September, and a high of 42,087 in July (IPAT, 2004).

Compared with neighboring Costa Rica, tourists in Panama spend significantly less time in the country. In Costa Rica the average tourist spends 10-11 days per visit (Madrigal, personal communication, 31 March 2005), while in Panama the average tourist in 2004 spent 2.2 days (IPAT, 2004). The average stay in Panama has remained constant (average 2.3 days, with a range from 2.1 to 2.5 days) over the past ten years (IPAT, 2004). Nonetheless, tourists in Panama spend nearly as much money in two days, $895.40 (Stanziola, personal communication, 8 April 2005), as Costa Rican tourists spend during 10-11 days, $934.23 (Madrigal, personal communication, 31 March 2005). Neither Panama nor Costa Rica had figures available regarding how much the average sustainable tourist spends per day. It is interesting to note that despite a massive increase in the total number of tourists visiting Panama over the past decade, the amount that they spend while in the country has not changed significantly over that period (IPAT, 2004). In an interview with ANCON Expeditions, Moran (2004) found that tourists in the PCW who choose to leave the cruise ship spend approximately US$50/person/tour.

Despite the explosive growth of tourism in Panama, it is difficult to identify existing demand for sustainable tourism opportunities given that no institution oversees or participates in monitoring or assisting such projects. Thus, a variety of proxies were used to approximate sustainable tourism demand within the PCW. ANCON Expeditions, a prominent tour agency in Panama, receives 8,000 tourists per year, including 1,000 birders; about 35 percent stay in the Canal Zone on a "shore pass" tourist visa and spend less than 8 hours on Panamanian soil as mentioned above (Moran, 2004). Many visitors fly directly to areas within the Darien region, Bastimientos National Park, or Coiba National Park to begin their tours (Moran, 2004). The Smithsonian Tropical Research Institute (STRI) annually receives 2,000 to 3,000 general visitors to their Barro Colorado Island facilities, located within the Panama Canal. These facilities are only open to the public three days a week, and local tour operators accommodate excess demand by offering trips to the back coves of the island (Angehr, 2005). Both ANCON and STRI serve as proxies for the sustainable tourism demand within the PCW and suggest that anywhere from 2,000-4,000 tourists annually visit Panama seeking sustainable tourism activities in the PCW.

## TOWARD THE CREATION OF FUTURE SUSTAINABLE TOURISM PROJECTS

Given that the majority of tourists visiting Panama arrive on cruise ships, one way to capture future sustainable tourism projects in the Panama Canal Watershed is to incorporate the burgeoning cruise ship market. Globally, cruise ships are a $12 billion per year industry, and continue to experience annual growth of 8 percent (Honey, 2002).

Sustainable tourism can occur along a variety of landscape gradients from pasture to forest, as well as along an infrastructure gradient of less intensive to more intensive. At the heart of all successful sustainable tourism projects is a unique product: experiencing a trip to a primary forest, bird/animal watching with a local guide, or visiting a beautiful spot. Successful tour development requires identifying the product at the initial stages of the planning process, and subsequently executing a formalized willingness to pay study prior to site development.

Three potential models for future PCW sustainable tourism initiatives are presented below (see Table 1). Each model was selected be-- cause of its applicability to the specific site conditions within the PCW with reference to the existing demand. While none of these models show overt links to biodiversity conservation, each program has multiple indirect links to broader biodiversity conservation goals.

TABLE 1. Summary of Proposed Sustainable Tourism Projects in the Panama Canal Watershed

| Scenario | Benefits | Challenges | Profitability |
|---|---|---|---|
| **Carbon Offset Tourism** | • Potentially large and unexplored cruise ship tourism market. | • There are high and low periods of tourist visitation.<br>• Willingness to pay for carbon offset tourism uncertain. | • Revenue is dependent upon the number of tourists who visit Panama. |
| **EarthWatch Scientific Research Tourism** | • Volunteers contribute monetarily as well as through "work" on site. | • Small market niche with high initial human infrastructure costs. | • Potential for profits based on quality of visitor experience. |
| **WWOOF Tourism** | • Well-established international volunteer program.<br>• Potential for volunteers to share new ideas with local farmers, and vice-versa. | • Uncertain revenue stream because of unpredictability of the number of volunteers and duration of their stay.<br>• Farmers must have adequate infrastructure (extra bed, food) to host an international volunteer, and homestay programs should have a local coordinator. | • Minimal profitability. International volunteers might provide labor to offset their costs and contribute toward a successful harvest. |
| **Other Nature-based Tourism** | • Established markets and established institutions.<br>• Potential for cooperation among NGOs, cruise lines, and tourism operators.<br>• Potential to receive donations for specific programs. | • Not all tour operators run ecologically-sensitive tours (requires training). | • Revenue is dependent upon the number of tourists who visit Panama.<br>• Likely the alternative with the greatest short-term potential to generate revenue for biodiversity conservation. |

- *Carbon Offset Tourism.* Invite cruise ship tourists to participate in a day-long trip to a native species reforestation plot within the PCW to plant a tree and offset their trip's carbon consumption. The focal point of the tour would be the opportunity to plant a tree seedling and learn about native species reforestation and biodiversity conservation efforts in Panama. Upon completion, tourists could receive a certificate with a description of the species of tree they planted and GPS coordinates of their tree. Perhaps a website could be developed to show reforestation plots over time, with specific characteristics of each tree (e.g., growth rates, diameter at breast height, carbon capture equivalent). Necessary infrastructure would include small buses for transportation from the ship to the site, trained and qualified guides able to provide bi- or trilingual interpretation, and site personnel to prepare and maintain planting areas and carry out on-going site research.
- *Scientific Tourism.* Modeled after EarthWatch, which charges anywhere from US $700 to $4,000 (excluding airfare) for 4-10 day volunteer work vacations throughout the world (Burtis, personal communication, January-April 2005), PRORENA might consider a similar volunteer work vacation package. This idea would require significant project planning and oversight, including a fully trained bilingual field staff in Panama, and a small coordinating/marketing/administrative staff in the United States. Possible projects for visiting volunteers might include a "jungle walk" to collect native seeds, helping PRORENA staff at the Gamboa nursery, a day planting seedlings, hand pollination of agroforestry products (e.g., vanilla), a day trip to Chagres National Park to assist CEASPA communities with activities including fence repair, planting improved pasture grasses, establishing organic gardens, reforesting around springs and river corridors, and building chicken coops, and a day with an educational tour of Barro Colorado Island.
- *Willing Workers on Organic Farms (WWOOF).* Small landholders with farms might consider participation in the WWOOF program. WWOOF aims to "enable people to learn first-hand about organic growing techniques, to enable town-dwellers to experience living and helping on a farm, to help farmers make organic production a viable alternative, and to improve communications within the organic movement" (WWOOF, 2005).
- *Other Nature-Based Tours.* Partnerships among existing operators, cruise lines and environmental NGOs to offer educational nature-based tours (e.g., sea kayaking around the islands, birding

tours, forest hikes, snorkeling/diving) and the opportunity to donate to biodiversity conservation projects offer perhaps the easiest programs to develop. There are already well-established markets for such tours and operators offering such services; currently there is little coordination among institutional actors.

## *Successful Implementation: Ideas for Consideration*

Implementation of a successful sustainable tourism project requires more than initial start-up funding and identification of tourist demand. Adequate training of all participating personnel, and creation of a yearly management plan will contribute toward building a successful enterprise. Implementing nationally recognized standards could help to strengthen Panama's tourism industry. To date, IPAT has not identified any tourist-to-guide ratios or promoted adoption of such standards. However, ANCON Expeditions of Panama, a sustainable tourism operator, has implemented internal ratios of 10:1 for birding tours, and 30:1 for retired farmer tours (Moran, 2004). Panamanian guides would also benefit from professional training programs. Outside of the ecological tourism degree offered to undergraduates at the University of Panama, there are no professional training programs currently available (Moran, 2004).

## POLICY ALTERNATIVES TO STIMULATE SUSTAINABLE TOURISM

Adopted June 14, 1994, Panama's Law 8 promotes tourism opportunities in Panama through the development of a "simple, swift and rational process for the development of tourist activities in the country" (Gray and Company, 2005: Article 1). This Law grants incentives to enterprises engaged in construction of new tourist infrastructure. Benefits include a tax exemption on all new tourist-related construction (Article 1), and a land tax exemption (Article 8.1.b) for projects whose costs are greater than $300,000 in metropolitan areas, or $50,000 in rural areas (Gray and Company, 2005). Article 12 extends similar benefits to all nightclubs, dance clubs, and restaurants for a period of three years.

Critics claim that Law 8 provides perverse incentives to develop high-end tourism infrastructure in ecologically sensitive areas (see Articles 4, 6.1, 6.2.) (Confidential sources, personal communications 7-11 March 2005). In 1998 lawmakers amended Law 8, adding Article 45, which allows the granting of the above-cited incentives through December 31, 2005 for areas not officially declared tourist development zones or zones of national interest. For areas of national interest and/or declared tourist development zones, Law 8 and its benefits are applicable through December 31, 2015.

One policy option is to require tourism developers to adhere to sustainability guidelines for site design and development. This option could be achieved by removing perverse incentives within Law 8 that encourage development, especially in ecologically sensitive areas (for example, tourism development within the islands of Bocas del Toro has killed much of the coral), and requiring that all developers submit management proposals to ANAM certifying that they abide by standards that consider social, environmental, and economic criteria (such as Forest Stewardship Council Principles and Criteria established for sustainable forest management). Benefits of adopting this policy option include an increased commitment to preserving existing biodiversity and minimizing future construction in ecologically sensitive areas. On the other hand, strict building guidelines could limit market entry opportunities for small operators with limited geographical ranges.

Gina Castro noted (personal communication, 11 March 2005) that Law 8 primarily serves landowners with a high level of capital to invest in projects, and discriminates against small holders who do not have at least US $50,000 for project investment. Following her suggestion, another policy option would be to allow small landowners to secure loans, and receive the same development incentives (e.g., no land taxes) for small-scale tourist investments. Benefits of this option include a more equitable distribution of benefits to all Panamanians interested in initiating sustainable tourism enterprises. Challenges associated with this policy option include risks associated with loaning money to small holders who may not encounter success with their project, and may have difficulty repaying the loans. Many small operators and landowners have a "build it and they will come" mentality, yet as stressed by Professor David Cromwell (personal communication, February 2005), successful entrepreneurship ventures are typically demand-driven. Furthermore, the administrative costs associated with supervising many small loans are greater than supervising a small number of larger loans.

Another policy option is to create a regional or national sustainable tourism certification program within Panama. Certification is a market-based strategy to establish an ethical standard for sustainable tourism practices. Martha Honey (2002:4) defines certification as "a process that assesses, audits, and gives written assurance that a facility, product,

process, or service meets specific standards . . . [and] awards a market-able logo to those that meet or exceed baseline criteria or standards."·
Certification is intended to give participating members a market advan-tage over non-participatory peers by lending an increased level of credi-bility and conferring the ability to charge higher prices (Honey, 2002).
Internationally, there has been rapid growth of ecotourism certification organizations whose certification standards verify that an agency's practices meet the heretofore agreed upon standards of the field (Tepelus and Cordoba, 2005; Rivera, 2004; Honey, 2002; for critique see Font and Harris, 2004).

Despite certification's popularity (see Rainforest Alliance Sus-tainable Tourism Program, 2005), entrepreneurs cite the long and costly certification process as the primary obstacle to program participation (Jetmore, 2004). The onus is particularly high for small enterprises (Jiménez, 2003). Furthermore, many question how much a green logo will increase business, given that internationally, only about 1 percent of consumers have knowledge of certification programs (Honey, 2002).

The example of the Certificate for Sustainable Tourism (CST) in Costa Rica provides an informative case study. Created in 1997, the CST, which is overseen by the Costa Rican Tourism Institute (ICT), manages and grants sustainable tourism certificates (Tepelus and Cordoba, 2005). Applicant businesses that wish to obtain the certifica-tion are evaluated by their performance on the following standards: physical-biological, infrastructure and services, external clients, and socio-economic development (Tepelus and Cordoba, 2005). While CST certification is free of cost, the cost to small tourism operators is often disproportionate; many state that they cannot afford to make the costly improvements to meet certification standards, while others cite the lengthy paperwork process as a significant imposition on their time (Jetmore, 2004). By 2004, nearly 6 years after its formal implementa-tion, the CST had only certified 5 percent of Costa Rica's hotels, many of these being larger hotels that are foreign owned (Jetmore, 2004). Low lev-els of participation within the Costa Rican sustainable tourism industry, and disproportionate participation by foreign-owned tourist operators, suggest that the CST has a big distance to cover in order to achieve its initial goals (Jetmore, 2004). Benefits of sustainable tourism certification include increased credibility, while challenges, as stated above, include low levels of participation, costly improvements that are out of the range of smallholders, and the requisite creation of a ministry or in-stitute to oversee. the certification program. Given these challenges, Jetmore suggests that the creation of small-scale, local certification programs that strive for 100 percent tourist provider participation and focus primarily on tourist education might be a successful alternative to nationally-based certification programs.

## CONCLUSION

Among some conservationists, sustainable tourism has become a popular market-based mechanism used to promote biodiversity conservation and economic development. Internationally, sustainable tourism initiatives carry mixed results. On one hand, projects like the ones in Ecuador and Costa Rica can confer positive benefits by contributing to local livelihoods and urging stricter conservation measures. On the other hand, poorly managed sustainable tourism initiatives are subject to profit leakage to foreign investors, and may be environmentally deleterious.

## SUGGESTIONS FOR FUTURE RESEARCH

- Investigate each of the 52 tour operators listed on the IPAT website to identify all operators by the types of tours that they offer (cultural, eco, adventure, nature, historical). Complete a secondary ranking with operators who currently offer a sustainable tourism option. Further, identify tourist operators who would be able to promote small-scale tourism projects in the future.
- Identify all existing tourism projects within the Panama Canal Watershed. Complete a market survey to determine levels of niche vacancy and saturation.
- Identify the amount of carbon emissions and wastes emitted by cruise ships during an average cruise. Use this information as a leverage point in negotiations with cruise lines to promote carbon-based tourism.
- Conduct a willingness-to-pay study for tourist services within the Panama Canal Watershed to identify how much tourists would be willing to pay for different tourism services, including: bird walks, canopy crane tours, nature hikes, and the above-referenced carbon-based tourism initiative.
- Conduct a study of these various tour types to estimate/evaluate their direct and indirect contributions to biodiversity conservation.
- Examine overhead and operational costs for implementing a work-based tourism program, similar to the EarthWatch model, within different PRORENA project sites.

- Conduct a policy analysis of local and regional certification systems. Complement this research with a feasibility study assessing implementation and participation in the heavily visited Panamanian provinces of Bocas del Toro and Panama.

## REFERENCES

Angehr, G. 2005. Contributions of Scientific Investigation to Ecotourism. Retrieved 20 April 2005 from https://www.denix.osd.mil/denix/Public/ES-Programs/Conservation/ Legacy/Panama/panamawrd6.html.

Autoridad Nacional del Ambiente (ANAM). 2003. Estadisticas Ambientales, 1995-2001. ANAM, Panama.

Autoridad Nacional del Ambiente (ANAM). 2004. Informe del Estado del Ambiente. ANAM, Panama.

Burtis, P. 2007. Can Bioprospecting Save Itself? At the Vanguard of Bioprospecting's Second Wave. *Journal of Sustainable Forestry* 25(3/4):219-245.

Conservation International (CI). 2005. Hotspots by Region. Mesoamerican Biological Corridor. Retrieved 19 February 2005 from http://www.biodiversityhotspots.org/xp/Hotspots/mesoamerica/.

Earthtrends. 2004. Earthtrends Country Profiles: Panama. World Resources Institute. Retrieved 25 March 2005 from http://earthtrends.wri.org/pdf_library/country_profiles/For_cou_591.pdf.

Font, X. and C. Harris. 2004. Rethinking Standards from Green to Sustainable. *Annals of Tourism Research* 31(4):986-1007.

Globalis. No Date. Globalis–Panama. Retrieved 24 June 2005 from http://globalis.gvu.unu.edu/indicator_detail.cfm?Country=PA&IndicatorID=50#row.

Gray and Company. 2005. Incentives legislation for the development of tourism in the Republic of Panama: Law 8. Translation to English. Retrieved 25 March 2005 from http://www.lawyers-abogados.net/en/Resources/Panama/Law-8_tourism_development_incentives.htm.

Honey, M. 2002. Ecotourism and Certification: Setting Standards in Practice. Island Press, Washington, DC.

Instituto Panameño de Turismo (IPAT). 2004. Datos Estadísticos de Turismo 2003-2004. Retrieved 5 May 2005 from http://www.ipat.gob.pa/estadisticas/.

Landell-Mills, N. and I.T. Porras. 2002. Silver Bullet or Fool's Gold: A Global Review of Markets for Forest Environmental Services and their Impacts on the Poor. International Institute for Environment and Development, London.

Jenkins, M., S. J. Scherr, and M. Inbar. 2004. Markets for Biodiversity Services. *Environment* 46(6):32-42.

Jetmore, A. 2004. Costa Rica's "Certification for Sustainable Tourism" (CST) Program: A Virtual Success or a Real Failure? Unpublished final paper. Yale University, New Haven, Connecticut.

Jiménez, S. 2003. Study of the Commercialization Chain and Market Opportunities for Eco and Sustainable Tourism. Sustainable Tourism Division of Rainforest Alliance for PROARCA/APM, San Jose, Costa Rica.

Miyata, Y. 2007. Markets for Biodiversity: Certified Forest Products in Panama. *Journal of Sustainable Forestry* 25(3/4):281-307.

Moran, C. 2004. "To: Panama Team; Re: Tourism; March 28." Unpublished memorandum. Yale University School of Forestry and Environmental Studies, New Haven, CT.

Native Species Reforestation Project (PRORENA). 2005. Home page. Retrieved 25 February 2005 from www.stri.org/english/research/facilities/terrestrial/gamboa/research_projects.php.

Pagiola, S., J. Bishop, and N. Landell-Mills. 2002. Selling Forest Environmental Services: Market-Based Mechanisms for Conservation and Development. Earthscan, London.

Rainforest Alliance Sustainable Tourism Program. 2005. Sustainable Tourism. Retrieved 18 May 2005 from http://www.rainforest-alliance.org/programs/tourism/index.html.

Rivera, J. 2004. Institutional Pressures and Voluntary Environmental Behavior in Developing Countries: Evidence from the Costa Rican Hotel Industry. *Society and Natural Resources* 17:779-797.

Tepelus, C.M. and R. Castro Cordoba. 2005. Recognition Schemes in Tourism–from "Eco" to "Sustainability"? *Journal of Cleaner Production* 13(2):135-140.

The Nature Conservancy (TNC). 2005. Panama Program. Retrieved 25 February 2005 from http://nature.org/wherewework/centralamerica/panama/index.html.

United Nations Children's Fund (UNICEF). 2005. At a Glance: Panama. Retrieved 24 June 2005 from http://www.unicef.org/infobycountry/panama_statistics.html.

United Nations Environment Program Sustainable Tourism Program. 2002. Sustainable Tourism. Retrieved 18 May 2005 from http://www.uneptie.org/pc/tourism/sust-tourism/home.htm.

Wallander, S. 2007. The Dynamics of Conservation Land Acquisition: A Window into the Panamanian Market for Biodiversity Existence Value. *Journal of Sustainable Forestry* 25(3/4):265-280.

Willing Workers on Organic Farms (WWOOF). 2005. World-Wide Opportunities on Organic Farm. Retrieved 25 March 2005 from http://www.wwoof.org/.

World Tourism Organization (WTO). 2005a. Concepts and Definitions. Retrieved 17 May 2005 from http://www.world-tourism.org/step/menu.html.

World Tourism Organization (WTO). 2005b. World Tourism Organization. Retrieved 24 March 2005 from http://www.world-tourism.org/.

World Wide Fund for Nature. 2005. Conservation Science–Global 200 Ecoregions. Retrieved 24 June 2005 from http://www.worldwildlife.org/science/ecoregions/g200.cfm.

Wunder, S. 2000. Ecotourism and Economic Incentives–An Empirical Approach. *Ecological Economics* 32:465-479.

doi:10.1300/J091v25n03_02

# The Dynamics of Conservation Financing: A Window into the Panamanian Market for Biodiversity Existence Value

Steven Wallander

**SUMMARY.** The central question for this paper is whether land managers in Panama might protect or restore forests on their lands in response to the market for the existence value of biodiversity. Conservation financing provided by non-Panamanian sources is used as a proxy for investigating the nature of the market for the existence value of biodiversity. Debt-for-nature swaps and environmental trust funds, such as the Global Environment Facility (GEF), provide examples of demand in this market. This paper examines trends and policies that could change the cost of supplying biodiversity protection and factors that could improve or undermine demand for the existence value of biodiversity. If ecological restoration receives as much support within the conservation community as protection of pristine areas has in the past, then demand in this market is likely to remain strong. The largest challenge for this market will be shifting to the provision of biodiversity conservation by private landowners rather than solely by the national government. doi:10.1300/J091v25n03_03 *[Article copies available for a fee from The Haworth Document Delivery Service: 1-800-HAWORTH. E-mail address: <docdelivery@haworthpress.com> Website: <http://www.HaworthPress.com> © 2007 by The Haworth Press, Inc. All rights reserved.]*

Steven Wallander is a PhD Candidate in Environmental Economics at the Yale School of Forestry and Environmental Studies, New Haven, CT 06511 USA (E-mail: Steven.Wallander@yale.edu).

[Haworth co-indexing entry note]: "The Dynamics of Conservation Financing: A Window into the Panamanian Market for Biodiversity Existence Value." Wallander, Steven. Co-published simultaneously in *Journal of Sustainable Forestry* (Haworth Food & Agricultural Products Press, an imprint of The Haworth Press, Inc.) Vol. 25, No. 3/4, 2007, pp. 265-280; and: *Emerging Markets for Ecosystem Services: A Case Study of the Panama Canal Watershed* (ed: Bradford S. Gentry, Quint Newcomer, Shimon C. Anisfeld, and Michael A. Fotos, III) Haworth Food & Agricultural Products Press, an imprint of The Haworth Press, Inc., 2007, pp. 265-280. Single or multiple copies of this article are available for a fee from The Haworth Document Delivery Service [1-800-HAWORTH, 9:00 a.m. - 5:00 p.m. (EST). E-mail address: docdelivery@haworthpress.com].

**KEYWORDS.** Biodiversity, existence value, Panama Canal Watershed, conservation land acquisition

## OVERVIEW

One of the most salient, most frequently invoked policy narratives of the conservation movement says that the biological diversity of our planet is highly threatened, rapidly diminishing, and must be saved. Ecological science clearly and convincingly demonstrates the losses of biodiversity. In Panama, the losses of biodiversity have been particularly striking and have spurred innovative conservation financing. A significant portion of Panamanian conservation financing has come from non-Panamanian sources–foreign governments, international NGOs (funded largely by individuals and foundations in industrialized nations), and multilateral funding agencies. Few of these 'financiers' will ever derive direct benefits from the Panamanian biodiversity protected with their funding. The central premise of this paper is that these forms of conservation financing constitute a market for the existence value of biodiversity. The central question for this paper is whether land managers in Panama might protect or restore forests on their lands in response to this market.

Vogel (1997:1) calls the existence value of biodiversity "the most immediate and largest value for the financing of habitats" but focuses his analysis on other biodiversity markets in which the trades are less idiosyncratic and more amenable to a case-study approach. Within the context of Panama, however, the amount of conservation financing arguably attributable to the existence value of biodiversity is too great to ignore. Given a number of identification and estimation difficulties, the lessons from a review of these transactions are limited to qualitative results. Nonetheless, there are encouraging trends concerning possible reductions in the costs of supplying this market. Indications as to whether demand in this market will remain strong are mixed. If the conservation community in Panama wishes to continue and even expand the role of the market for the existence value of biodiversity in Panama, significant demand-side research and policies will be needed.

## BARRIERS TO A QUANTITATIVE APPROACH

To the extent that conservation financing focuses on areas of high biodiversity and originates from parties with no potential for deriving any use value from the protected areas, it is one of the best proxies we have for the service of existence value. Krutilla (1967) developed the notion of existence value, along with several other types of non-use values, when he argued that environmental economics must encompass the fact that some people receive benefits from the conservation of natural resources that they will never use. Economists have positioned existence value and other non-use values within the total economic value framework (Pearce and Moran, 1994). Within this framework, biodiversity is thought to have relatively high existence values. For clarity, knowledge of the existence of (protected) biodiversity is an ecosystem service. Alternatively, biodiversity is a measurable attribute of ecological systems, an attribute that may or may not have significant existence value depending upon the circumstances. The following scenario, while unlikely to ever occur, motivates the premise that the existence value of biodiversity is a marketable ecosystem service.

Hypothetically, the more species-diverse an ecosystem or an area of land, the more of certain services it provides. Existence value is one such service. Intuitively, it seems reasonable to assume that given a choice between two otherwise identical natural areas, buyers in markets for the existence value of biodiversity will have a preference for financing the conservation of land with the greater biodiversity. It would be a conceptual mistake, however, to move from this scenario directly into an effort to estimate the price-per-acre or return-per-biodiversity based on the observed transactions in Panama. The limited number of transactions in this market and the lengthy negotiations involved in these transactions suggest that there is not a convenient unit with which the participants in these markets commodify biodiversity. Perhaps in another context, such as Costa Rica's payments for ecosystem services or a biodiversity credit program, such an approach would be valid.

In addition to the conceptual problem explained above, tracing conservation financing back to the core demand for existence value has its technical limitations. The primary problem is one of identification. Economic theory suggests that if the knowledge of the existence of biodiversity is a good, then existence value can be represented by a downward sloping demand curve. On this curve, as less biodiversity is available, the marginal existence value for biodiversity increases. Ideally, we would like identify transactions for the existence value of biodiversity so that we could identify points along this curve. The funding mechanisms looked at in this paper–debt-for-nature, trust funds such as the Global Environment Facility (GEF), and technical support for smallholders–typically serve multiple policy goals and capture buyers' demands for a bundle of goods that include more than just the existence value of biodiversity. This implies that any calculation of existence value from these transactions would overestimate the market for existence value by also including, say, the value of hydrologic services for the Panama Canal or the value of improved livelihoods for the rural poor.

A second technical limitation to using these transactions to calculate the size of these markets is one of estimation. Samuelson (1954) pioneered the application of traditional economic methods to the evaluation of public services and public goods, those goods that are non-rival and non-exclusive. We follow Samuelson in applying economic theory to the existence value of biodiversity, which is an extremely pure public good. If the government of Panama protects Chagres National Park and I value the existence of the biodiversity in Chagres, there is no way that the government can exclude me from enjoying the knowledge that Chagres is protected. Additionally, my enjoyment in the knowledge that Chagres is protected in no way limits the enjoyment of someone else in the knowledge that Chagres is protected, the feature of a non-rival good. Due to these two features, the existence value for biodiversity has a large free rider problem. For example, I may have a high willingness to pay for biodiversity, but if someone else is paying to protect it, my incentive to actually pay for it is quite low. Nonetheless, the payment mechanisms explored in this paper are one of the only measures available to examine actual payments for existence value, most of which are moving from higher income industrialized nations to developing nations. While the size of these markets is an important question, a more critical question is whether demand will persist into the future and whether the cost of supplying these markets is prohibitive for landowners and land managers. The following analysis is aimed at the latter two questions.

## *EXISTING SUPPLY*

At the most basic level, biodiversity is simply a measure of the variety of species in a given area. Often that area is an ecosystem or a watershed, but occasionally it is a much smaller area. Whatever the area being measured, there are a number of ways of calculating biodiversity, from a simple tally of the number of different species to complex indices that take into account the number of individuals within each species (relative frequency) or the sample size (Stiling, 1992). The importance of biodiversity as a measure (and one of the large reasons that markets for biodiversity even exist) is the growing absolute scarcity of biodiversity. Habitat destruction, over-exploitation and invasive species are causing rapid rates of extinction throughout the world. These rates of extinction, which register as sharp drops in biodiversity, are significantly larger than historic rates of extinction, and arguably warrant concern (Wilson, 1992). Land acquisition for conservation purposes is one market that is generally driven directly by this loss of biodiversity. As discussed in the next section on existing demand, a number of conservation organizations use the concept of biodiversity to focus their efforts (Redford et al., 2003), the GEF includes biodiversity as one of its six focal areas (GEF, 2005a), and the enabling legislation for debt-for-nature swaps in the United States includes biodiversity conservation measures as eligible activities to receive financing (USAID, 2005).

When it comes to protecting biodiversity through markets, location and site history are critically important. Globally, there are a number of hotspots where extremely high levels of biodiversity coincide with high levels of extinction (Myers et al., 2000). Panama happens to be in one of these spots (Condit et al., 2001). The supply of land with high biodiversity in Panama has been greatly reduced in the past decades, primarily due to deforestation associated with clearing land for cattle ranching. Much of the remaining supply of lands with high biodiversity has been protected through the Panamanian national parks system, but significant gaps remain.

Within the Alto Chagres region, much of the biologically sensitive area has already been protected through a multilateral debt-for-nature swap, however, a number of threats remain, which creates a need for better protection of the buffer area surrounding that part of the park. There are a number of areas within Alto Chagres that face specific threats, such as incompatible housing, habitat conversion due to agricultural activities, and mineral extraction (Candanedo et al., 2003).

While most conservation financing efforts focus on sites with a history of minimal anthropogenic disturbance, sites with less than pristine histories can also participate in markets for ecosystem services. Reforestation efforts within Panama have the potential to increase biodiversity. One of the most important aspects of these reforestation programs is that they can take ecologically low-value sites and, to a great extent, restore biodiversity, although generally not to pre-disturbance levels. Given the history of land use in Panama, there is ample supply of degraded land for reforestation projects.

One of the most notable developments in the supply of biodiversity is the Smithsonian's Native Species Reforestation Program (PRORENA).

Currently, PRORENA is largely focused on a research agenda to determine the optimal use of native timber species in reforestation, agroforestry, and timber plantation projects. PRORENA's work is much more applicable to the market for the existence value of biodiversity that other reforestation efforts within Panama, which tend to involve plantations of teak, a non-native species, with only minimal inclusion of native species.

EcoForest is an example of a private timber corporation incorporating existence value of biodiversity into overall management costs. In its lease agreement with the Panamanian government, EcoForest has obtained the rights to manage approximately 7,000 hectares of land in the Panama Canal Watershed. About 4,000 hectares of previously degraded lands were planted with teak, while the remaining 3,000 hectares of existing forest are managed for biodiversity protection. In this case, the existence value of biodiversity is essentially financed by company shareholders and considered part of the cost of doing business within the Canal Watershed.

Whether a particular site is degraded or pristine, a land manager must consider four categories of costs involved in protecting biodiversity: (1) opportunity cost; (2) information costs; (3) transaction costs; and (4) management costs.

As a barrier to a much larger supply of conservation lands, the most significant of these is usually the opportunity cost. If the land has reasonably high value for farming, ranching, silviculture, or residential development, land owners are not likely to forego the returns on their investment simply for conservation. However, in many cases this is not the enormous barrier that it would seem. In some cases the uses mentioned above can be compatible with protection of the most sensitive and diverse habitats. There are also a growing number of land managers who have conservation motives in buying, owning and managing their land, which means that they are often willing to forego at least some of the opportunity cost involved in land conservation. Stakeholder surveys have shown that stewardship is a primary value motivating the dedication of private protected areas in Costa Rica (Langholz, 1999).

One of the largest obstacles to overcoming the opportunity cost barrier, is the large number of conservation targets, globally and within Panama. As noted earlier, high levels of biodiversity and a recent history of major losses of biodiversity have focused a great deal of international attention on the protection of biodiversity in Panama. Nonetheless, the supply of lands that are promising as conservation targets is still much lower than the funds available to purchase and protect those lands. This drives the market price down to the landowner's reserve prices, usually the going rate for the land given other potential uses (Landell-Mills and Porras,· 2002). In this case, there is no special incentive for the landowner to sell to a conservation organization, or to maintain biodiversity in the hopes of selling to a conservation-minded organization.

A more common tactic employed in the effort to protect biodiversity is the reduction in incentives that skew opportunity costs in favor of exploitive enterprise. For instance, Panamanian officials were able to convince private banks to halt lending for cattle ranching that would require clearing of forest within the Panama Canal Watershed. This reduction in the availability of capital is one of the primary factors behind the reduction in deforestation rates in Panama (Heckadon-Moreno, personal communication, 8 March 2005).

Supplying biodiversity can also hypothetically involve the enormous information costs involved in cataloguing species and calculating an accurate measure of biodiversity on a given property. I am not aware of cases where owners have actively collected information on the biodiversity on their own land solely with the intention of selling it to a conservation buyer. This is partially a reflection that very few of the markets for biodiversity services, including land acquisition, require highly detailed information about biodiversity on a given site. When these markets use such information at all, it appears to be based on research conducted by other parties, perhaps by the demand side actors or perhaps by a third party such as the scientific community.

Transaction costs pose a particular problem within Panama, where as much as one-third of the rural, agricultural lands are untitled. Eighty-four percent of these lands are owned by the non-poor (World Bank, 2001a). The World Bank has financed a 15-year, $50 million loan to support modernization of Panama's land registration and administration systems. A key goal of the project is to address poverty by providing legal land titles to smallholders who currently only have possessory rights over their lands. Formal land titles should provide access to credit for these farmers. It is also expected that modernization of Panama's land administration system will provide improved collection of real estate taxes (World Bank, 2001b). Since lack of land title is typically an obstacle to land acquisition, this should reduce the cost of land acquisition and increase the supply of land available for conservation.

Finally, there is the problem of management costs, which are highly correlated with the threats facing a property. Many of the transfers of funds to Panama from NGOs or multilateral funding institutions include significant sums for land management. From the perspective of land acquisition, high management costs are more of a demand-side problem. For those individuals and organizations paying for land acquisition as a method for protecting biodiversity, high management costs require a significant commitment of funds as protection for their investment.

## *EXISTING DEMAND*

As in all markets related to real estate, the demand for the existence value of biodiversity is largely determined by location and site history. A combination of high biodiversity and high threat typically produces the highest demand for protection, as exemplified by the thirty-four biodiversity hotspots targeted by Conservation International (Mittermeier et al., 2005). These metrics focus international conservation financing on Panama to a greater extent than, say, Canada. On a smaller scale, other aspects of biodiversity focus demand on particular sites. Concerns over the diversity of species can focus demand on a site that provides habitat for rare species. Concerns over the diversity of habitats can focus demand on an ecotype that is underrepresented among existing protected areas. Concerns over the persistence of biodiversity into the distant future can focus demand on ensuring the continuity of larger systems such as the Mesoamerican Biological Corridor (MBC). Based on these observations, I suggest the following two principles. First, the demand behind the conservation financing for a particular piece of land in the existence value market often has more basis in its proximity to these areas of concern–rare species, habitat diversity, and connectivity/continuity of habitats–than in any measure of the biodiversity on that particular piece of land. Second, the smaller the piece of land in question, the more location supersedes measures of biodiversity as the key driver of demand.

Economic theory suggests that biodiversity is a public good that will be underprovided in an unregulated market due to the problem of free riders. An alternative to government provision of such a good is to create regulation that imposes scarcity on the market, such as a cap-and-trade emissions program. Unlike markets for carbon, there is not an international agreement for biodiversity that forces recognition of biodiversity losses in a way that creates a viable market. The Convention on Biological Diversity (CBD) does create recognition of increasing scarcity, and places some political pressure on industrialized countries to fund biodiversity conservation in less-developed countries. The realization of this political pressure is the Global Environment Facility (GEF), a multilateral trust fund that serves as the current funding mechanism for the CBD. The CITES treaty, another international agreement, severely limits the trade of endangered species, which reduces the overexploitation threat to biodiversity. It is questionable whether CITES addresses the threat of land use changes and coincident habitat destruction. Neither of these treaties creates the sort of restrictions on land use that could foster a market in biodiversity offsets or credits similar to the market for wetland mitigation that exists in the United States.

The GEF is a funding instrument that drives many markets for biodiversity services. In 1991, the GEF began as a $1 billion pilot program of the World Bank. Since 1991, three replenishments totaling US$7.75 billion have been authorized. The top contributors to the fund are the United States, Japan, Germany, France, the United Kingdom, Italy, Canada, the Netherlands and Sweden. The most recent replenishment, in 2002, garnered funds from 18 countries (GEF, 2005b). The GEF focuses its grants on six areas of concern: biodiversity, climate change, international waters, land degradation, ozone depletion, and persistent organic pollutants. Panama has received grants from the fund in 1994 for biodiversity conservation in the Darien region, and in 1998 for the Atlantic slope of the Mesoamerican Biological Corridor. In total, Panama has received eleven grants from GEF totaling US$24.7 million, and been a partial beneficiary of another $78 million in grants that have gone to projects focused on the Latin American region (GEF, 2005a).

Another large funding source that arguably captures some of the market for existence value of biodiversity is the debt-for-nature swap. Originating in 1987 with a project in Bolivia, the debt-for-nature swap is a bilateral (or multilateral) agreement in which the country holding foreign debt agrees to forgive a portion of the debt services in exchange for an agreement from the debtor nation to improve funding of nature conservation within its borders. An important benefit of this for the debtor nation is that it converts debt into its national currency. Since the primary goal of these programs is debt relief, it is difficult to establish what portion of these programs truly represents a market for existence value. A measure of the demand for existence value is more feasible when a third party is involved, such as a conservation-oriented NGO, to fund a portion of the cost of debt relief and to guide the creation and management of a trust fund used to dispense the funds within the country. Two such swaps have already occurred within Panama.

In 2003, the United States contributed $5.6 million and the Nature Conservancy (TNC) contributed $1.16 million toward a debt-for-nature swap that provided for the protection of Chagres National Park. Panama agreed to protect Chagres, and to provide $5 million for a trust fund (through Fundación Natura) and $5 million towards an endowment for the operation of Chagres. A second swap in 2004 provided for conservation financing in Darien. The United States contributed $6.5 million while TNC contributed $1.3 million to the Darien deal, while Panama agreed to conservation payments of $11 million over twelve years (The Nature Conservancy, 2005).

Looking forward, a critical question is whether demand for debt-for-nature swaps will persist into the near future or whether diminishing marginal returns will reduce interest of NGOs and foreign governments in additional debt-swaps. Three components of the current situation favor future debt-for-nature swaps. First, the cost of debt relief has dropped since the 1990s, which was a period when other methods of debt relief were more affordable for debtor nations and thus more popular. Within Panama, the transaction costs for providing the Darien debt-for-nature swap were significantly lower than for the Chagres debt-for-nature swap (Hanily, personal communication, 9 March 2005). Additionally, Panama's high debt could fuel demand, at least on the part of Panama, to pursue future swaps. One of the most important unknowns on the demand side will be the US Congressional authorization of future funding of the Portman Bill, the principle funding mechanism for these swaps when the United States is a partner in the transaction.

In essence, both the GEF and debt-for-nature swaps constitute an export market in which individuals in industrialized nations translate the high values that they place on biodiversity into either donations to NGOs or political support for the backing of debt-for-nature funding and GEF contributions. There are signs that demand for the biodiversity protection is growing within Panama, although it is less clearly demand for the existence value of biodiversity. Coiba Island was recently set aside for protection, although the core value in that case was genetic resources for bioprospecting purposes (see Burtis, this volume). Private protected, areas or private reserves, have also received a great deal of attention within Panama. The first private reserve in Panama, Punta Patino, was created in 1991 and protects over 30,000 hectares (ANCON, 2005). The use of these preserves is often closely linked to ecotourism enterprises, and often has links to the incentives under the tourism law (Law 8) (see Schloegel, this volume). Another important driver of demand for biodiversity in Panama is the large movement of retirees to Panama and the demands that they bring for protected lands in close proximity to their homes (Markels, 2005). However, none of these situations are clear examples of markets for the existence value of biodiversity. The participants in these examples derive significant use value from their decisions to protect or fund the protection of biodiversity.

In addressing the question of whether the market for the existence value of biodiversity will persist into the future, these examples motivate the question of whether growing support for biodiversity conservation among Panamanian stakeholders will reinforce or supplant the demand for conservation financing from international sources. One plausible scenario is that non-Panamanian funds for conservation will diminish in the future in response to greater participation of Panamanian sources. Another plausible scenario is that non-Panamanian stakeholders have numerous, unaddressed conservation goals remaining, along with a desire to protect past investments in Panamanian conservation. Both of these factors could lead to continued and possibly increased spending in the market for the existence value of biodiversity.

If demand for biodiversity existence value continues into the future, it will need to move beyond a concern for the national parks of Panama, which would ideally become less reliant on non-Panamanian conservation financing. The demand for biodiversity existence value will need to embrace ecological restoration efforts, such as PRORENA, and conservation on private property, often in cooperation with the ongoing agricultural activities of smallholders. One of the most promising examples of such demand is the program to encourage native reforestation by smallholders within Chagres National Park. This program is operated by the Centro de Estudios y Acción Social Panameño (CEASPA). At a number of sites within Chagres, ranging from five to forty hectares, smallholders have cleared monocultures of invasive grasses and planted a wide variety of largely native crops and trees. Many of these farmers and ranchers have relocated from more sensitive and pristine areas within the parks. CEASPA has supported their efforts through educational workshops and trainings, mapping of soils and water sources, and provision of basic supplies (e.g., wire for chicken coops and small-diameter piping for irrigation). The ecological and social benefits of this program are substantial, although a bit controversial. If international organizations embrace programs like this on a larger scale, the demand for the existence value of biodiversity will find a future perch in Panama.

## *POLICY ALTERNATIVES TO IMPROVE SUPPLY*

Most of the transactions explored in this paper–the debt-for-nature swaps and the GEF trust fund–involve payments to Panamanian agencies or the creation of trust funds to serve the management of existing parks. Given the conservation needs of Panama during the past few decades, such transactions were necessary to protect a core supply of biodiversity within Panama. Looking to the future–to likely trends such as urban sprawl, more extensive land titling, greater interest in timber plantations, and the potential for ecological restoration–the market for the existence value of biodiversity will of necessity become more focused on private lands. Whether such a market will be viable, whether such a market will attract the interest of both suppliers (i.e., landowners and land managers) and buyers (i.e., foreign governments and international NGOs), will depend largely on how policy decisions affect the four categories of costs described above.

Opportunity costs are likely to become greater barriers to land conservation as property values rise and tax benefits continue to draw foreign investment into Panamanian real estate. One solution to this problem is the strategy of bundling existence value with other compatible ecosystem services (Landell-Mills and Porras, 2002). Another possible solution is to reduce the opportunity costs of biodiversity protection or restoration by reducing the incentives driving destructive land uses. The example of the restrictions placed on loans to cattle ranchers within the Panama Canal Watershed is an illustrative example of this strategy. In summary, policies likely to reduce the opportunity costs of providing or restoring biodiversity include:

- Ensuring that payments for the existence value of biodiversity go directly to landowners who forego destructive land uses or undertake restoration would be likely to increase the number of landowners willing to supply this market;
- Limiting incentives for cattle ranching, building of second homes, and large-scale tourism developments to regions with lower conservation priorities would be likely to decrease the opportunity costs of supplying the biodiversity existence value market in areas with higher conservation priorities; and
- Fostering a sense of stewardship through an ongoing education campaign should reduce opportunity costs, since this would increase the non-monetary benefits that landowners receive from decisions to conserve biodiversity.

Information costs for this market will change as the scale of the market changes. If the market moves to a focus on smaller landowners, information on site-specific biodiversity could become a large burden to third parties such as the Smithsonian Tropical Research Institute, a primary source for a great deal of the information available on Panamanian biodiversity. Perhaps, a more grassroots effort, such as the mapping of smallholder farms by CEASPA, could provide the necessary information for this market. As suggested earlier, location–namely proximity to larger targets of conservation financing–should be a greater driver of demand at the small scale than site-specific measures of biodiversity.

Continuing and expanding the land-titling program would likely lower the transaction costs of acquiring land for conservation. Of course, this will also lower the transaction costs of acquiring land for non-conservation purposes as well, so there will likely be some increase of threats to biodiversity under this program. Transaction costs can also be lowered as parties to these transactions increase their experience in these markets. The lower transaction costs for the Darien debt-for-nature swap are case-in-point.

Controlling or lowering management costs is a bit more challenging. Park management costs could increase as the threats related to development and sprawl along the pan-isthmus highway become larger problems. For example, within Chagres, management costs could go down if the efforts to reduce the numbers of smallholders and consolidate their activities are successful. Perhaps the most critical question for addressing the dynamic between the Park and the smallholders is how to capture the benefits that come from the increased efficiencies of smallholder farming and ranching. As improvements in techniques are disseminated through CEASPA's efforts, and farmers are able to subsist on fewer hectares, and ranchers are able to raise more cattle per hectare, it would seem that the ideal solution for protection of the Park is to utilize improved efficiency to, at a minimum, maintain the same number of smallholders on a small footprint. However, many of these efficiency gains have come through significant input on smallholders' (and CEASPA's) part within the domain of their possessory rights.

- If smallholders are able to make efficiency improvements that allow for continued operations on fewer acres, then reimbursing these smallholders for reductions in their operations could reduce the management costs involved in achieving these efficiency improvements.

While this scenario suggests that supply will improve by lowering management costs for smallholders, if these reimbursements come from the funds to manage Chagres, then the management costs for Chagres will rise. This complication suggests that management costs for provision of biodiversity existence value are an area needing additional research.

## POLICY ALTERNATIVES TO IMPROVE DEMAND

The market for the existence value of biodiversity is an important export "industry" for Panama. As with any other export industry, increased marketing efforts could be focused at increasing international awareness of the significance of Panamanian biodiversity. One component for doing this could be an increased effort to catalogue Panamanian biodiversity, which, as discussed in the previous section, would also address the information cost concerns on the supply side.

As more national parks and federal lands receive funds through the biodiversity existence value market, this market could well extend to the protection of biodiversity on private lands. However, some of the buyers in previous transactions in this market may be unwilling to pursue transactions with private landowners. Efforts to reassure these buyers that biodiversity conservation on private lands can be just as successful could spur demand in this market. One important component of this would be visible support, legislative and judicial, for the use of conservation easements.

Traditionally, demand in the market for biodiversity existence value has been focused on the preservation of undisturbed areas of high biodiversity. Demand in this market could increase to the extent that ecological restoration becomes an additional focus for this market. This could be accomplished through the mechanisms already used for conservation financing in Panama. Reforestation is an eligible activity for financing under the Portman Bill, which means that Panama could pursue additional debt-for-nature swaps to fund large-scale reforestation efforts.

## CONCLUSION

Based on observations of conservation financing in Panama, the market for the existence value of biodiversity is a viable market. Currently, the land managers most likely to supply these markets are the agencies protecting national parks. However, promising examples of small-holder reforestation and experimentation with native species reforestation suggest that this market could expand beyond federal lands. If ecological restoration receives as much support within the conservation community as protection of pristine areas has in the past, then demand in this market is likely to remain strong. The largest challenge for this market will be shifting to the provision of biodiversity conservation by private landowners rather than solely by the national government.

## REFERENCES

Asociación Nacional para la Conservación de la Naturaleza (ANCON). 2005. Asociación Nacional para la Conservación de la Naturaleza. Retrieved 2 April 2005 from http:www.ancon.org.

Burtis, P. 2007. Can Bioprospecting Save Itself? At the Vanguard of Bioprospecting's Second Wave. *Journal of Sustainable Forestry* 25(3/4):219-245.

Candanedo, I., E. Ponce, and L. Riquelme. 2003. Alto Chagres Conservation Area Plan. The Nature Conservancy (TNC) and Asociación Nacional para la Conservación de la Naturaleza (ANCON), Panama City, Panama.

Condit, R., W.D. Robinson, R. Ibanez, S. Aguilar, A. Sanjur, R. Martinez, R.F. Stallard, T. Garcia, G.R. Angehr, L. Petit, S.J. Wright, T.R. Robinson, and S. Heckadon. 2001. The Status of the Panama Canal Watershed and Its Biodiversity at the Beginning of the 21st Century. *BioScience* 51(5):389-398.

Global Environment Facility (GEF). 2005a. Focal Areas. Retrieved 20 June 2005 from http://thegef.org/Projects/Focal_Areas/focal_areas.html.

Global Environment Facility (GEF). 2005b. Replenishment. Retrieved 20 June 2005 from http://www.gefweb.org/Replenishment/replenishment.html.

Krutilla, J.V. 1967. Conservation Reconsidered. *American Economic Review.* 57:777-786.

Landell-Mills, N. and I. T. Porras. 2002. *Silver Bullet or Fool's Gold? A Global Review of Markets for Environmental Services and Their Impact on the Poor.* International Institute for Environment and Development, London.

Langholz, J. 1999. Conservation Cowboys: Privately-owned Parks and the Conservation of Biodiversity in Costa Rica. Ph.D. Dissertation. Cornell University, Ithaca, New York.

Markels, A. 2005. Beauty and Tax Breaks Lure Buyers to Panama. New York Times. Feb. 13.

Mittermeier, R.A., P.R. Gil, M. Hoffman, J. Pilgrim, T. Brooks, C.G. Mittermeier, J. Lamoreaux, and G.A.B. da Fonseca. 2005. Hotspots Revistited: Earth's Biologically Richest and Most Threatened Terrestrial Ecoregions. Conservation International.

Myers, N., R.A. Mittermeier, C.G. Mittermeier, G.A.B. da Fonseca, and J. Kent. 2000. Biodiversity Hotspots for Conservation Priorities. *Nature* 403(6772):853-858.

Pearce, D. and D. Moran. 1994. *The Economic Value of Biodiversity.* Earthscan, London.

Redford, K.H., P. Coppolillo, E.W. Sanderson, G.A.B. da Fonseca, E. Dinerstein, C. Groves, G. Mace, S. Magginis, R.A. Mittermeier, R. Noss, D. Olson, J.G. Robinson,

A. Vedder, and M. Wright. 2003. Mapping the Conservation Landscape. *Conservation Biology* 17(1):116-131.

Samuelson, P.A. 1954. The Pure Theory of Public Expenditure. *Review of Economics and Statistics* 36(4):387-389.

Schloegel, C. 2007. Sustainable Tourism: Sustaining Biodiversity? *Journal of Sustainable Forestry* 25(3/4):247-264.

Stiling, P.D. 1992. *Ecology: Theories and Applications.* Prentice Hall, Upper Saddle River, New Jersey.

The Nature Conservancy. 2005. U.S.-Panama Debt-for-Nature Swap. Retrieved 4 April 2005 from http://nature.org/success/panamadfn.html.

United States Agency for International Development (USAID). 2005. Eligible Activities under the Tropical Forest Conservation Act (TFCA). Retrieved 20 June 2005 from http://www.usaid.gov/our_work/environment/forestry/tfca_acts.html.

Vogel, J.H. 1997. The Successful Use of Economic Instruments to Foster Sustainable Use of Biodiversity: Six Case Studies from Latin America and the Caribbean. *Biopolicy* 2(5):1-8.

Wilson, E.O. 1992. *The Diversity of Life.* W. W. Norton, New York.

World Bank. 2001a. Panama-Land Administration Project: Report No. PID8082. The World Bank.

World Bank. 2001b. Panama: World Bank Supports Land Administration Reform. News Release No:2001/298/LAC.

doi:10.1300/J091v25n03_03

# Markets for Biodiversity:
# Certified Forest Products in Panama

Yuko Miyata

**SUMMARY.** Certification, or eco-labeling, is potentially a useful tool to stimulate the growth of ecosystem service markets. Certification guidelines, such as the Forest Stewardship Council's Principles and Criteria, offer landowners clearly defined approaches to biodiversity-friendly forest management while also emphasizing the profitability of sustainable forestry operations. In some cases for forest products, market access now requires products to carry certification labels. However, Panama's domestic demand for certified forest products is negligible. The combination of a lack of international market awareness of many of Panama's native tree species, a young plantation forestry industry, and virtually non-existent industrial wood processing capacity have kept Panama's forest products exports, including certified wood products, to a minimum. In summary, on both the supply and demand sides of the equation, a host of socio-cultural, institutional, and economic obstacles prevent landowners from pursuing certification programs for forest management

---

Yuko Miyata is an Environment, Health and Safety Specialist with GE Commercial Real Estate Finance.

Yuko Miyata earned a Master of Environmental Management at the Yale School of Forestry and Environmental Studies, New Haven, CT 06511 USA (E-mail: yuko. miyata@aya.yale.edu).

The author wishes to thank Hannah Stutzman and Patricia Ruby for assistance with editing.

[Haworth co-indexing entry note]: "Markets for Biodiversity: Certified Forest Products in Panama." Miyata, Yuko. Co-published simultaneously in *Journal of Sustainable Forestry* (Haworth Food & Agricultural Products Press, an imprint of The Haworth Press, Inc.) Vol. 25, No. 3/4, 2007, pp. 281-307; and: *Emerging Markets for Ecosystem Services: A Case Study of the Panama Canal Watershed* (ed: Bradford S. Gentry, Quint Newcomer, Shimon C. Anisfeld, and Michael A. Fotos, III) Haworth Food & Agricultural Products Press, an imprint of The Haworth Press, Inc., 2007, pp. 281-307. Single or multiple copies of this article are available for a fee from The Haworth Document Delivery Service [1-800-HAWORTH, 9:00 a.m. - 5:00 p.m. (EST). E-mail address: docdelivery@haworthpress.com].

Available online at http://jsf.haworthpress.com
© 2007 by The Haworth Press, Inc. All rights reserved.
doi:10.1300/J091v25n03_04

and production of non-timber forest products. As a result, national and international markets for certified Panamanian forest products remain virtually unexplored business opportunities. To develop markets for certified forest products from Panama, a host of policy alternatives might be considered, including informational campaigns and extension programs for local landowners, incentive packages to defray initial costs of certification, and investments in international marketing campaigns coupled with investments in developing local manufacturing capacity and infrastructure. doi:10.1300/J091v25n03_04 *[Article copies available for a fee from The Haworth Document Delivery Service: 1-800-HAWORTH. E-mail address: <docdelivery@haworthpress.com> Website: <http://www.HaworthPress. com> © 2007 by The Haworth Press, Inc. All rights reserved.]*

**KEYWORDS.** Certified forest products, Panama, biodiversity conservation, ecosystem service markets

## INTRODUCTION

Biodiversity services have a broad meaning that can include any services that involve elements of an ecosystem. Such biodiversity services may include material goods (such as timber, fish, fruits, medicines, rubber, and sources of bioenergy) and environmental services (such as generating and maintaining soils, converting solar energy into plant tissue, sustaining hydrological cycles, storing and cycling nutrients, controlling the gaseous mixture of the atmosphere, and regulating weather and climate) (Myers, 1996). Unlike many environmental services that typically have been under-valued (e.g., climate regulation, hydrological cycle regulation), wood products have long been valued for providing human necessities. On the other hand, unregulated logging without regard to impacts on natural ecosystems has led to degradation and destruction of forest ecosystems, with direct negative impacts on biodiversity. For example, the world's ancient forests are rapidly losing species richness, due in large part to both timber harvesting practices that hold little regard for maintaining the integrity of ecosystems, and also from clear-cutting for agriculture (Tickell, 2000). Managing forests for uses other than timber, such as watershed protection, therefore has become a critical issue (Fanzeres and Vogt, 2000).

International initiatives for forestry conservation in the 1980s, such as the Tropical Forestry Action Program (TFAP) and the International Tropical Timber Organization (ITTO), have fostered a growing international awareness of the need for forest conservation. In 1992, management, conservation, and sustainable development of forests were included on the Statement of Forest Principles at the Earth Summit Conference (the UNCED in Rio) (United Nations, 2004). Sustainable forest management leading to the production of biodiversity-friendly products has become recognized as a possible approach to conserve biodiversity in forests while also deriving economic returns from forest resources. With an increasing international awareness of forest disruption from logging, concerned consumers, especially in developed countries, have started to avoid buying tropical hardwoods (Fanzeres and Vogt, 2000). Some conservation NGOs have even led successful boycotts of retailers that sell tropical timber and/or non-certified timber products with the intent of decreasing consumer demand.

### Paper Structure

The following analysis reviews whether (and if so, how) landowners, especially those in Panama, might benefit from certification programs for sustainable forest management. The goal of this chapter is to contribute to market development for biodiversity-friendly products, particularly sustainable wood products in Panama. Towards this goal, I first clarify the premise of my assessment and discuss certification as a policy tool. Second, I analyze the existing markets from the perspective of both demand and supply. And third, I include a package of policy alternatives that might contribute to improving the market for sustainable wood products.

Field observations and interviews carried out in Panama from March 7-11, 2005 are cited throughout this paper, and serve to illuminate specific points of the analysis and provide a basis from which policy options are developed and considered for feasibility. These case studies in Panama rely heavily on site visits and interviews with small landholders within the Chagres National Park and plantation forestry projects in the Panama Canal Watershed.

## PREMISE OF ASSESSMENT

### Certification

Certification is considered to be a type of eco-labeling. As such, it is a tool for consumers to "identif[y] wood and wood products that come from well-managed sources anywhere in the world backed up by a label that would be clear, unambiguous and easily recognized" (Tickell,

2000:3-4). At the same time, certification provides product suppliers with a communication tool to relate the credibility of biodiversity-friendly forest management to their customers. Certification can take many forms, from international voluntary certification (e.g., Forest Stewardship Council [FSC]) to branding by a bilateral agreement (e.g., Starbucks shade-grown coffee). This paper considers all approaches that provide a certain degree of credibility to a product for its biodiversity-friendly production, without discriminating between the various types of programs, or whether or not they include the title "certification."

### *What Are "Biodiversity-friendly" Forest Products?*

Due to its nature of extracting products from natural environments, especially from forests, biodiversity-friendly production does not always promise maximum biodiversity conservation. For example, by extending or maintaining natural habitats, shade-grown coffee is often referred to as being a "biodiversity-friendly" forest product. However, critics suggest harvesting shade-grown coffee can also have negative impacts on the understory of tropical forests (Ashton, personal communication, 1 February 2005). Yet shade-grown coffee is still regarded as a useful tool for preventing complete deforestation, in comparison with developing a regular coffee plantation by clearcutting natural forest. As Heaton and Donovan (1996:55) noted: "[t]here is no single definition of sustainable forest management . . . Scientific data do not yet support a single consensus on the definition of biological sustainability, especially given regional variations in ecology; the same is true for socio-economic sustainability. Nonetheless, certification can differentiate many of the key elements of good and bad forest management, and can begin to give clarity to the path toward sustainability."

In this analysis, therefore, it is very important to clarify that designating biodiversity-friendly forest products, or certified products, is not a single complete method for accomplishing the ultimate goals of biodiversity conservation. Certified wood products are viewed here as one of several complementary options to create economic value for landowners by allowing them to utilize the natural environment coupled with a conscious effort to maintain high levels of biodiversity. Yet this potential is dependent on developed markets for such products and landowner access to these markets.

## Categories of Products

There are a number of forest products that can be produced in sustainable, biodiversity-friendly operations. Timber and non-timber forest products (NTFPs) are two distinct categories of forest products. For the sake of this paper, only forest certification and timber products are evaluated. A worthy topic for future research is the study of the potential market opportunities for NTFPs (e.g., shade-grown coffee, cacao, ginger, vanilla, etc.) and the linkages (both direct and indirect) of certification and sustainable harvest of NTFPs with biodiversity conservation.

An Indonesian teak plantation was the first tree plantation, certified by SmartWood in 1990 (Elliott and Donovan, 1996). Certified tree plantations are now found around the world. One example of sustainable tree plantations in Central America is Tropical American Tree Farms (TATF) in Costa Rica. In TATF's plantations, 60 percent of trees planted were native species, while the other 40 percent were planted with exotic species. With this approach, the company restored denuded, steep hillsides by planting native species, and thus contributed to watershed protection. In addition, the planted native species serve as corridors that join existing forest fragments (Heaton and Donovan, 1996). In Panama, the six plantation companies whose forest management has been certified according to the Forest Stewardship Council (FSC) Principles and Criteria are primarily comprised of exotic (or non-native) species (FSC, 2005).

## Certification as a Policy Tool

Certification was originally developed voluntarily by NGOs and the private sector to inform consumers of the credibility of their products. From a policy perspective, certification for forest products is used as "a 'soft policy tool' by NGOs and the private sector to reach environmental goals through the provision of market incentives" which complements the inefficiency of international initiatives, government policies, and individual boycotts in reducing deforestation and promoting sustainable forest management (Elliott and Donavan, 1996:4). Assuming there is an existing market for certified products, certification is expected to provide economic incentives for landowners and land managers to voluntarily pursue sustainable forest management. Schneider and Ingram (1990) suggest categories of policy tools based upon their target: authority, incentives, capacity building, symbolic and hortatory, and learning. As a policy tool, certification of biodiversity-friendly products largely falls into the category of incentive tools with some elements of a learning tool (Elliott, 1996).

Most certification programs are based on a set of standards or guidelines (see Ervin and Elliott (1996) for a review of the variety of scales for standards and guidelines). Sector-specific standards usually focus on consultations within a specific constituency or communities of interest, such as industry associations (e.g., American Forest and Paper Association's Sustainable Forestry Initiative guidelines), NGOs (e.g., Greenpeace's clearcut-free standards), or standard-writing bodies (e.g., the American Standards and Testing Materials) (Ervin and Elliott, 1996). Regional standards are often set by forest type (e.g., Canadian Forest Service guidelines for temperate and boreal forest management), by biophysical characteristics (e.g., the Amazon Pact Agreement for different mountain ranges or river basins), or by political boundaries (e.g., standards for Sweden) (Ervin and Elliott, 1996). The choice of scale of standards depends in part on the goals of certification. While certification based on internationally-recognized standards is more likely to establish widespread credibility, certification based on regional standards may contribute to brand establishment in the local market.

## *Industry Structure: Supply and Demand*

Both the supply and demand sides of the certified products market are analyzed in this paper. Figure 1 shows the industry structure of certified forest products with a value chain of products and participants for each layer. The shaded layers indicate which participants are included in the present analysis. By looking at the industry structure and including not only the primary supplier and end consumer but also supplier aggregators and retailers/customers, the analysis covers a broader scope of the market.

## *DATA ANALYSIS*

### *Demand Side*

In the analysis of existing market demand, the current market situation is evaluated from the following perspectives: (1) Who is demanding these products? (2) What drives their demand? (3) What is the size of existing demand? (4) At what scale does demand exist (international/

FIGURE 1. Industry Structure of Certified Forest Products

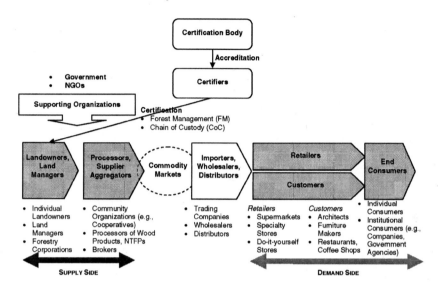

domestic, which segments of customers)? (5) How much growth in demand can we expect over a given timeframe? And, (6) are the price premiums and/or willingness-to-pay (WTP) enough to pay back costs? Given this assessment, the deficiencies in existing policies will be explored, and policy alternatives are proposed.

## Supply Side

In the analysis of existing market supply, the following five questions were asked: (1) What relevant products are currently produced in Panama? (2) Who are the existing suppliers? (3) What is happening in the area of forest certification? (4) What are existing or potential barriers that prevent suppliers from certifying forest management practices? And (5) what are existing institutional policies that support/discourage certification? Based on this analysis, the deficiencies of existing policies that do not currently cover the existing/potential issues are noted. Based on the assessment of existing market supply, policy alternatives for improving supply of certified products are proposed.

## ASSESSMENT OF EXISTING DEMAND

As defined earlier, there are several key participants who are likely to drive the demand for certified products. The first, and probably most important, is the end consumer who actually pays for certified forest products at the end of the value chain, and does not resell the products to others (except for possible second-hand use). Such end-consumers include the individual consumer, who buys the products for personal use, and institutional consumers such as a company, NGO, or government agency, which buy the products for institutional use. These consumers' willingness-to-pay (WTP) usually determines the final price of the products in the market.

What drives consumers' demand for certified forest products? A certain percentage of eco-consumers base their purchasing decision-making primarily on environmental values. Institutional consumers sometimes have environmental criteria formally incorporated in their purchasing policies. For example, many large companies in developed countries have green procurement policies, either to comply with legal requirements and/or as a part of their "green" PR or CSR (Corporate Social Responsibility) policies. In some cases, these policies include a higher WTP for these products. One of the reasons for such purchasing behavior may correspond to the value people place on the forests' environmental services (other than timber products). Specifying certified products is one way in which institutions can ensure that environmental standards are met in such green procurement policies.

The second participant is the retailer who sells the certified products to consumers. Retailers include do-it-yourself shops that sell certified wood products (e.g., HomeDepot, Lowe's, B&Q). Retailers increasingly respond to consumers' demand, and often play an important role in increasing consumers' recognition of a particular environment-friendly product. By targeting particular consumer segments, some stores use certified products as a marketing tool to differentiate their stores from others.

A third participant is the customer, who uses certified products to make their final products in manufacturing, assembling, or processing. Such customers include furniture manufacturers, architects, and paper producers. It is important to note the difference between the end consumer described before and the customer, because the customer might have different motivations for purchasing certified forest products than the consumer. The consumer pays the ultimate price for the products sold by the customer, but the decision to use certified wood products in manufacturing or construction is actually often determined by the customer.

Multiple factors drive the customer to demand certified products: (1) the desire to differentiate their final products; (2) the need to respond to the demand of eco-consumers; (3) the need to comply with their green/CSR policies or promotion of a certain public image. While the first two drivers correspond to consumers' awareness of certified forest products, the last is driven by internal corporate policy and reflect upon the level to which environmental concerns are embedded into corporate culture. In assessing the existing demand and considering policy alternatives, it is important to clearly define which participants are being targeted and how they might be affected by different policy choices.

Market share of certified forest products still remains a small percentage of the total market (1-5 percent) (Rubino et al., 2000). The main market for certified wood products is highly biased to countries in the developed world, especially in Western Europe and North America (Kanowski et al., 1999). Although the current market size of certified forest products remains limited, emerging global demand has been stimulated by increasing consumer awareness of the importance of forest protection and consumer recognition of certification as a tool to reflect standardized sustainable forest management. The main markets for certified forest products exist in developed countries, while markets in developing countries remain small to non-existent (although the Brazilian government recently initiated efforts to develop domestic demand for certified forest products). Within Panama, domestic demand for certified forest products is virtually absent (Eke, personal communication, March 2005).

Multiple studies on consumer's behavior or willingness-to-pay (WTP) toward certified sustainable forest products have been conducted in developed countries (Bigsby and Ozanne, 2002; Jensen et al., 2003; Ozanne and Vlosky, 1997; Veisten, 2002; Vlosky and Ozanne, 1997; Ozanne and Vlosky, 2003); however, whether the demand for certified forest products will generate sufficient price premiums to be attractive to suppliers remains uncertain. Sedjo and Swallow (2002:282) used economic analysis to arrive at the conclusion that certification is less likely to generate a price premium "if the demand for certified woods is small relative to overall demand, if the costs of certification are significant, and if the amount of new demand created by certification is modest" under a voluntary certification scheme. Given this fundamental information, the primary issues regarding the existing demand for certified forest products in Panama are described below.

## Social Factor 1: Lack of Awareness in Domestic Markets

In Panama, as in other tropical countries, consumers' awareness of the importance of biodiversity conservation and sustainable forest management is under-developed. As described earlier, Panamanians have been clearing forests for agriculture and cattle ranches for generations. Government policies have traditionally emphasized economic development, with little consideration for maintenance of natural habitats or accounting for natural resource depreciation (Harrick, personal communication, 10 March 2005; Solórzano et al., 1991). Many people interviewed over the course of fieldwork expressed that, in general, Panamanians have little recognition of forest certification programs. A recent study in a rural farming region of Costa Rica, for example, found that less than 20 percent of respondents had heard of FSC certification (Newcomer, personal communication, 22 April 2005). Based on interviews with multiple actors in the Panamanian forestry sector, it appears likely that a similar situation exists in neighboring Panama. In addition, although there were few chances to contact politicians or government officers in Panama, interviews with people involved in forest management generated enough insight to hypothesize that local policy-makers have not reached a consensus about policies to achieve sustainable forest management, or the promotion of certification as a tool for biodiversity conservation.

## Social Factor 2: Lack of Recognition of Panama in International Markets

In the international market for certified forest products, Panama is not widely recognized as a source of certified forest products. First, Panama has not established a unique brand-name for its rich diversity in wildlife and extensive forest diversity to the extent that its neighbor, Costa Rica, has done. Furthermore, forest products with the label "made in Panama" are not widely recognized in comparison to those made in Africa and Asia. This difference is in large part due to a very under-developed industrial wood processing sector in Panama, and the relatively young age of existing certified operations (Delvalle, personal communication, 10 March 2005).

## Institutional Factor: Lack of Institutions to Create Social Pressure

In addition, there are no Panamanian institutions or international NGOs working to create social pressure on customers and institutional end-consumers to purchase certified forest products. As previously noted, those participants are likely to have their own motivations, independent from individual consumers' WTP. For example, many European governments have standards to purchase only certified woods for government projects. In those countries, companies who wish to acquire government contracts face such institutional and social pressures to use certified products. Thus, purchasing certified forest products, especially certified wood products, is becoming standard for companies, which in turn gives more incentive for other companies to also procure certified products.

Such pressures do not currently exist, however, in Panama. There are currently no Rainforest Action Network-like campaigns targeted at local wood/forest products distributors. Nor are there any civil society groups lobbying Panamanian government agencies to adopt green purchasing policies.

It is recognized that Panama is a developing country with different political and economic situations than European countries. Thus, on one hand, the argument could be made that comparisons between these contexts in terms of government procurement policies and national environmental policy are not appropriate. However, it can also be argued that Panama has great opportunities to develop an integrated national environmental and economic policy strategy that both addresses biodiversity conservation and development of a sustainable forestry sector that is focused on capturing a portion of the growing international markets for certified timber products.

## Economic Factor: Uncertain WTP

As noted earlier, people's WTP for certified wood products remains uncertain. In Panama, there are no apparent local niche markets for such products. Futuro Forestal is apparently the only local company actively pursuing international niche markets for certified products. Because of the nature of the value of biodiversity as a public good, it is likely that stimulating people's WTP for certified wood products would be highly difficult.

## ASSESSMENT OF EXISTING SUPPLY

In Panama, forests account for 33,646 km$^2$, or 44.6 percent of total land area (75,517 km$^2$). Land in forest cover has been decreasing, from 69.4 percent in 1950, to 54 percent in 1970, to 48.5 percent in 1986 (Republic of Panama, 2005). Approximately 20 percent of total area was in pasture in 1996 (Kok and Veldkamp, 2001). There is an acknowledged lack of proper management and protection of natural forests, which negatively impacts key indicators of a healthy ecosystem (e.g., biodiversity, soil stability, water quality and quantity) (USAID, 2005).

On the other hand, there are growing reforestation efforts in Panama, including teak plantations, mainly because of incentives from the now-defunct Law 24. Beginning in the 1990s, private landowners, especially from the middle-class, took advantage of tax benefits and started to plant trees (mostly teak) (see Lichtenfeld, this volume; Grossman, this volume). In 1999, approximately 3,600 ha were reforested (nearly 2,400 ha in teak). Reforestation peaked in 2002, with 5,650 hectares reforested that year (which included 4,984 ha of teak), and then dropped back to about 3,600 ha total (2,218 ha in teak) in 2003 (Republic of Panama, 2005). In addition to serving as tax write-offs and/or tax-free investments, such projects were largely driven by an awareness of the un-tapped economic opportunities in timber production. Many such projects promised significant returns on investment from the trees within 15 to 20 years (Heckadon-Moreno, personal communication, 7 March 2005). However, only a few of these projects pursued certification, and environmental sustainability of forest management was not a requirement for receiving the tax incentive. Thus, Law 24 did little to stimulate the local supply of certified sustainable forest products.

In the commercial sector, six private plantation companies in Panama have been certified according to Forest Stewardship Council (FSC) Principles and Criteria (see Table 1). The first FSC certification in Panama was issued to Futuro Forestal in 1998 (FSC, 2005). The range of plantation size varies from 360 ha (Futuro Forestal) to 7,120 ha (EcoForest). Four of the six plantations are certified with monoculture teak plantations, while the other two are certified as multi-species plantations (FSC, 2005).

In addition to landowners and land managers that supply certified products, research institutes and local/international NGOs support landowners who may desire to implement sustainable forest management. One of these organizations is the Smithsonian Tropical Research Institute (STRI). Through STRI's Native Species Reforestation Program

TABLE 1. FSC-Certified Operations in Panama (FSC, 2005)

| Company | Certification | Certifier | Tenure | Forest Type | Area | Species |
|---|---|---|---|---|---|---|
| EcoForest (Panama), S.A. | Forest Management, Chain of Custody | SGS | Private | Plantation | 7,120 ha | Teak (*Tectona grandis*) |
| Futuro Forestal, S.A. | Forest Management, Chain of Custody | Smart Wood | Private | Plantation | 360 ha | Teak (*Tectona grandis*) Honduran Mahogany (*Swietenia macrophylla*) Nargusta (*Terminalia amazonia*) Rosita (*Hieronyma alchorneoides*) Pochote (*Bombacopsis quinata*) |
| Inversiones Agroforestales, S.A. (IASA) | Forest Management, Chain of Custody | SGS | Private | Plantation | 1,156 ha | Teak (*Tectona grandis*) |
| Nordic Management Group, S.A. | Forest Management, Chain of Custody | SGS | Private | Plantation | 551 ha | Teak (*Tectona grandis*) |
| Prime Forestry Panama, S.A. | Forest Management, Chain of Custody | Smart Wood | Private | Plantation | 2,481 ha | Teak (*Tectona grandis*) |
| Valleverde Desarrollo Forestal, S.A. | Forest Management, Chain of Custody | Smart Wood | Private | Plantation | 521 ha | Teak (*Tectona grandis*) Cedro espino (*Bombacopsis quinatum*) Laurel (*Cordia alliodora*) African mahogany (*Khaya senegalensis*) |

(PRORENA), a number of scientifically-driven reforestation projects are being carried out throughout Panama. PRORENA has been conducting research into optimal cultivation conditions for 70 native species in a nursery located in Gamboa. Of those native species, 40 percent are used as alternative timber woods, 30 percent are for social uses, and 30 percent are used in various types of reforestation programs (Diago, personal communication, 7 March 2005). In the reforestation sites, PRORENA is seeking ways to prevent the land from being invaded by paja blanca (*Saccharum spontaneum*), an aggressive, invasive cane species. Fast-growing tree species are of interest to PRORENA to both prevent the invasion of paja blanca and create economic value, while other slower-growing native tree species are of interest for long-term timber values and for the provision of various ecosystem services. Although there is no ongoing plan for certifying forest management/products from PRORENA sites, PRORENA's research and projects of native forest species provide other landowners with scientific data on seed germination techniques, optimal planting regimes, and growth rates, all of which are critical for evaluating the financial viability of reforestation efforts.

International NGOs also have been conducting projects in sustainable forest production in Panama. In association with USAID in Panama, the Academy for Educational Development (AED), a world wide non-profit human and social development organization, has been leading a GreenCOM project. AED has been working with farmers in Chagres National Park to develop a model for sustainable sub-watershed protection through reforestation. One of AED's main projects involves soil-friendly pineapple. This is the type of product that could help to launch Panama into international markets for certified NTFPs.

Despite the efforts of the above-mentioned organizations, the supply of certified forest products from Panama has remained small. The following is a review of the barriers that apparently prevent landowners from pursuing certification.

### Social Factor 1: Lack of Capacity

From a human perspective, lack of know-how of methods for sustainable forest management and the certification process are critical issues to be addressed. Capacity building and technical support are necessary to help land managers navigate toward new production regimes. While methods may differ depending on scale of production, both large and small landowners would benefit from increased familiarity with production processes and certification guidelines. In Panama, capacity has not been widely developed for sustainable forest management or for the requirements for forest certification.

## Social Factor 2: Disturbance by People's Traditional Values

People's values seem to cause a bottleneck for integrating certified products into local landowners' forest management plans. Several people interviewed noted that Panamanian people have historically appreciated the cattle ranch as a symbol of a stable life, regardless of whether raising cattle creates sufficient economic value for them (Endara, personal communication, 7 March 2005; Elton, personal communication, 11 March 2005). In reality, production from cattle ranches accounts for only 2 percent of Panama's total gross domestic product (Elton, personal communication, 11 March 2005). For many small rural landholders, cattle are an important part of subsistence living; four or five head of cattle can provide a "savings account" which can be drawn upon when cash is needed. However, traditional values and the social status associated with large-scale ranching encourage further deforestation.

On the other hand, the Panamanian government is starting to recognize the negative repercussions of unregulated cattle ranch expansion, and has started to protect more land within its National Park System. Additionally, the Panamanian National Bank and Chase Manhattan recently adopted a policy not to provide loans for the development of additional pasturelands within the Panama Canal Watershed (Heckadon-Moreno, personal communication, 7 March 2005). The impacts of the policy on farmers' behavior, farmer responses to the policy, and the social impacts of this policy shift merit further investigation. This example suggests an increasing awareness of the need for certain policies to change.

## Institutional Factor: Lack of Supply Aggregation

One of the major characteristics of small landholders within Chagres National Park is a lack of social networks among landowners, both among and within communities (Pizzaro, personal communication, March 2005; Elton, personal communication, 11 March 2005). Panama experienced significant population growth in the last century; the population of one-half million in 1920 increased to 3.5 million by 2000 (Heckadon-Moreno, personal communication, 7 March 2005). Part of population growth is due to immigration (including indigenous people from Colombia). This growth impacts both cities and rural areas, and has led to increased colonization of forested regions throughout Panama

(Heckadon-Moreno, personal communication, 7 March 2005). As colonization of the forests increased, the amount of forested areas declined, succumbing to the pressures of unregulated clear-cutting and burning for cattle ranches. According to Elton (personal communication, 11 March 2005), these relatively new settlers are rarely involved in community networks and do not have generations of kinship ties to the land they live on. Therefore, there is little shared identity regarding community, and virtually no effort to build community organizations. As explained below, such lack of supplier aggregation is a huge obstacle should small landholders desire to pursue certification.

While supplier aggregation might help to secure access to markets, the existing social fabric seen among the inholdings in Chagres does not support movement toward an aggregation process. The transaction costs for each landowner to enter new markets on their own will be prohibitively high. Although participatory programs have started to aggregate small landholders within Chagres, there is still concern that when their programs end, support networks will not hold up over the long-term (Pizarro, personal communication, 10 March 2005). Thus, the prospect for aggregated supply of produce, let alone group certification of these landholders, seems rather dim.

### Economic Factor 1: Economies of Scale

While certification may be a useful tool for larger companies seeking market access for export products, at the local level small landowners practicing sustainable forest management would not necessarily see any added benefit from certification. The overhead costs for certification assessment and implementation decrease per hectare as the scale of operations increases. To reduce the costs of certification for small landowners, aggregation can spread initial expenses for process change, equipment, nursery plants, legal documentation, and consultation services. In addition, these small landholders have virtually no access to the small local niche market or export markets for certified wood or wood products. Access to potential buyers is limited for small individual landowners, even when they are certified, because most purchasers will seek a guaranteed volume of supply.

Fabriciano, a farmer who has settled on lands inside the Chagres National Park, is one such example. In exchange for agreeing to participate in a resettlement program that involved a managed regeneration of degraded lands within the Park, Fabriciano received a USAID scholarship to attend a seminar on forest management and sustainable farming techniques at the University of Arizona. "Seven years ago, I was forced by the government to move from the center of the National Park where I lived for a long time. When I moved to the current place, the land was all covered by paja blanca. I cleared it and started to reforest plants which can contribute to maintaining the watershed to the river," don Fabriciano proudly recalled (personal communication, 9 March 2005). "I've been planting native trees instead of teak, because teak is not good tree to protect the watershed. It dries out the ground and makes it sterile." Fabriciano was also sponsored for a course in Nicaragua, where he learned how to grow organic coffee. Based on education and his own practice, he now produces organically-grown cacao, plantains, tree beans, achiote, and a variety of garden vegetables. His surplus produce is sold to nearby schools and at the local market.

In Fabriciano's case, certification would not add significant value to his product, nor increase his market access. Yet the benefits of ecosystem services provided to his productive activities as a result of reforestation around springs and waterways on the farm and adoption of organic farming techniques have a certain value that is being recognized. Furthermore, as a result of his experiences practicing biodiversity-friendly farm management, don Fabriciano is now hired by extension agents as a consultant for other local projects.

As mentioned, CEASPA supports small landholders such as don Fabriciano in their efforts to improve the sustainability of forest management and other productive activities on their farms. Currently, one of CEASPA's main programs is focused on developing participatory silvopastoral management systems with ranchers who have holdings in Chagres National Park. Again, this is not a program where certification would necessarily improve market access or brand recognition for their products; however improved management techniques–including windbreaks, shade trees, riverbank protection, and improved pasture grasses–help ranchers increase the carrying capacity of their farms while producing in a more environmentally-benign manner. Such programs also help to reduce further encroachment into the Park (Dixon Francois, personal communication, 9 March 2005).

Despite these successful participatory programs with landholders in the Chagres Park, CEASPA's programs are not likely to achieve sustainable land management at the scale which is supported by certification programs. Nevertheless, continued investment in programs that address the needs of small landholders, like those undertaken by CEASPA, are a valuable and much needed complement to capacity-building efforts that might encourage certification when working at a larger scale. There is also the long-run potential that if enough small landholders in an area adopt sustainable management techniques, some sort of bundling or group certification (even by local standards) might eventually make economic sense in terms of marketing aggregated production on the local market. Yet to reach this point, investment in education and extension programs are necessary first steps, and having access to such markets is critical.

### Economic Factor 2: High Initial Costs for Certification

Even for large operations, the high initial cost of certification is a significant obstacle to market entry (Eke, personal communication, March 2005; Delvalle, personal communication, 10 March 2005). The various costs associated with certification include costs for certification assessment, personnel costs associated with addition of management expertise, costs for operations changes needed to meet certification requirements, and worker training and equipment (see Maser and Smith (2001) for a detailed review of the certification process).

Many certifiers disclose their estimated fee for certification assessment for medium-to-large size of production; for instance, FSC-accredited SmartWood estimated $6,500 for 5,000 ha, up to more than $10,000 for multi-million ha operations (in 1994 dollars) (Heaton, 1994). According to Taggart (2000), the initial certification cost to a hypothetical small operation would be $2,720, with an annual audit cost of $785 per year for a 40 ha hardwood forest privately owned by a family in New England. Similarly, the initial certification cost for 405 ha of privately held forest in the Pacific Northwest region of the United States would be $11,660, with annual costs of $1,820 per year. These estimates, although based on cases in the US, offer a rough frame of reference for what certification of smaller operations might cost in Panama. These estimates give a sense of the relatively small costs for large operations compared to the expected revenue they can earn from the forest production.

The bulk of certification assessment costs are related to human resources. Certification is normally a four to six month process, excluding the time needed for operational improvements prior to certification. Forty to 60 person-days of labor are required to certify a forestry operation (Heaton and Donovan, 1996). Such intensive labor costs are usually not major problems for large suppliers, who are typically able to offset the increase in overhead costs by increased market access and sales. The problem is that overhead labor costs are relatively equal for all suppliers, regardless of the size of production. For example, EcoForest allocates a manager for initiating and managing the FSC certification process, for monitoring forest management operations, and for coordinating annual audits. For small suppliers, an increase of one full-time worker with a high-level of technical training would have a significant impact on profitability. There is no evidence of policies or programs which provide incentives (such as low-cost or volunteer consultation) for small landowners to pursue certification assessment in Panama.

Costs for changes to operations are likely to be the most problematic for suppliers pursuing certification. Costs for operations change vary depending on the conventional operations on each farm. For example, EcoForest incurred initial costs of between $200,000-300,000, primarily for process changes and training of its 300 workers, while the annual costs for auditing are relatively small (about $3,600) (Delvalle, personal communication, 10 March 2005). Although the initial costs also differ by the size of area to be certified, a large initial investment for companies can be a critical barrier to pursuing certification, especially for start-up companies in developing countries.

### *Economic Factor 3: Insufficient Financial Resources*

Ricardo Delvalle, General Manager at EcoForest, reflected that the hardest part in the certification process was for the company to source the capital needed for investment in process changes. "Funding or low rate loans for certification were hardly available in the country, which discourages land managers to try certification of their forest management," said Delvalle (personal communication, 10 March 2005), Since the high initial costs need to be paid upfront before the landowners can actually gain the revenue from products, sourcing funding for these initial costs is a critical issue to make certification more accessible to landowners, both large and small. However, as Delvalle noted, these sources are not readily available in Panama.

### *Economic Factor 4: Uncertainty of Price Premiums*

In addition to covering high costs for certification with insufficient finances, certified companies face difficulties in repaying the costs they initially paid for certification. Certified products can give suppliers two primary benefits: an access to the markets where certified products are desired and/or required, and, sometimes, a price premium. In fact, EcoForest receives a few contacts per week from buyers seeking FSC-certified wood. These contacts come from all over the world, and Delvalle (personal communication, 10 March 2005) attributes this to the FSC website, where EcoForest is listed. Delvalle took delight (personal communication, 10 March 2005), "Even though our company does not have our own website, people fax or call us after having seen our contact information on FSC's list of certified forest operations." This evidences growing buyers' interest in certified wood, and allows the company to be confident of future market access.

On the other hand, in the current market, the existence of a price premium for certified products remains uncertain (as described above). In the case of EcoForest, getting a price premium on their wood due to FSC certification is not their primary reason for pursuing certification. Indeed, the company does not expect to get much price premium, although the company does foresee a price increase for all wood as supply becomes increasingly scarce in the coming decades (Delvalle, personal communication, 10 March 2005). Despite the lack of price premiums in the current market, some expectations remain for price premiums on certified wood. For instance, plantation companies operated by the Investment Management Scheme in Australia offered their investors an expected price for their wood at much higher levels than the current market price. One such company, Gunns Plantation Ltd., issued in its prospectus an expected price for certified eucalyptus at 14 percent higher than the highest market price at that time (Edwards, 2003). Even adjusting for inflation and potential price increase, Gunns's expected ROI remains 10 percent (Edwards, 2003). However, given a review of market trends, it is not a wise business decision to base future earnings on price premiums. Overall, the uncertainty of the price premium, if any at all, requires landowners to assume additional risk on their investments in certification.

## POLICY ALTERNATIVES TO IMPROVE THE MARKET

Following is a presentation of alternative policy instruments that might be considered as tools for improving the future market for biodiversity services, both on the supply and demand sides. These options are intended to address areas where existing policies leave deficiencies for solving both existing and potential issues that prevent the expansion of markets for certified products. Here, "policy" is considered as a tool for inducing certain changes in the market with a clear target. In that context, policy need not necessarily be introduced by the government, and includes policies made and implemented by other organizations. The policy alternatives and their likely main constituents are described in Table 2 (demand side) and Table 3 (supply side).

TABLE 2. Summary of Existing Market Demand for Certified Products and Policy Alternatives to Improve Demand

| Factor | Issues Not Currently Addressed by Existing Policies | Policy Goal | Policy Alternatives and Possible Main Constituents |
|---|---|---|---|
| Social | • Lack of awareness in the domestic market<br>• Lack of Panamanians' awareness of the importance of sustainable forest management<br>• Lack of Panamanians' recognition of certification/ certified products<br>• Little consensus for developing certified products among policy makers | Learning (awareness development) | • National consumer education program (government, NGOs)<br>• Targeted educational programs about the importance of biodiversity, advantages of sustainable forest management, and certified products (schools, extension programs, educational media programs)<br>• Targeted information programs (e.g., publishing lists of certified products/ suppliers on the web), media campaigns |
| Social | Lack of recognition about Panama in the international market<br>• Lack of recognition of biodiversity richness of Panama in the international market<br>• Lack of recognition about wood from Panama in international markets | Panama-brand creation | • Enhance ecotourism and develop a campaign to raise the international recognition of rich biodiversity in Panama (IPAD, government)<br>• Pursue commercial diplomacy (government: President-level / Minister-level / politician-base) to promote Panamanian certified products and a biodiversity-rich image of Panama (like Costa Rica has done)<br>• Create local brand and develop a local certification program (local NGOs with international NGOs), e.g., "Chagres" brand, "Canal Watershed" brand |

TABLE 2 (continued)

| Factor | Issues Not Currently Addressed by Existing Policies | Policy Goal | Policy Alternatives and Possible Main Constituents |
|---|---|---|---|
| | | | • Organize inter-governmental initiative with other Latin American countries to gain competitive advantage in international markets (government, industry associations, chamber of commerce) |
| Institutional | • Lack of institutions to create social pressure/incentives for customers and institutional consumers | Build demand | • Establish government procurement policies that include environmental criteria (government) |
| | • Lack of policy to increase domestic consumers'/companies'/governments' purchase policies | | • Establish government-endorsed certification programs for bio-diversity friendly products (governments, NGOs, trade associations) |
| | • Lack of public pressure on consumers/ companies/ governments | | • Publicly recognize governments/ companies with leading environmental procurement programs |
| | • Lack of incentives for consumers/ companies/ government to purchase certified products | | |
| Economic | • Uncertain willingness to pay (WTP) • Uncertain WTP for certified products | Bundling with other values | • Develop packages of products delivering multiple values (supplier, industry associations) e.g., watershed protection, healthiness, taste, 'cool' image, other lifestyle images (e.g., bird-friendly bananas) |

TABLE 3. Policy Alternatives to Decrease the Costs and Risks Associated with Supplying Certified Products

| Factor | Issues Not Currently Addressed by Existing Policies | Policy Goal | Policy Alternatives and Possible Main Constituents |
|---|---|---|---|
| Social | • Lack of knowledge about sustainable forest management practices and certification assessment process (e.g., choice of certifications, advantages, requirements)<br>• Lack of human resources (local experts) to manage the certification process | Capacity building | • Provide educational opportunities for land managers about certification (local NGOs with funding by USAID, government, international NGOs)<br>• Provide technical support for certification process and operations change (local NGOs, e.g., PRORENA, TNC, with funding by USAID, government, international NGOs)<br>• Provide extension agent services and disseminate scientific information |
| Social | • Tradition of forest clearing for cattle ranching does not include silvopastoral management techniques<br>• Lack of awareness of "biodiversity-friendly" management regimes | Incentives | • Structure financial incentive schemes, including higher loan rates for cattle ranches and lower loan rates for certified production (banks), tax deductions (government), subsidies (government)<br>• Provide necessities for production, including equipment (government, local NGOs with funding by USAID, international NGOs) and nurseries to supply seeds/seedlings (PRORENA)<br>• Promote other benefits, such as total quality management, operational benefits, efficiency (local NGOs, industry associations) |

303

TABLE 3 (continued)

| Factor | Issues Not Currently Addressed by Existing Policies | Policy Goal | Policy Alternatives and Possible Main Constituents |
|---|---|---|---|
| Institutional | • Lack of existing aggregators makes the transaction costs high | Cooperative development | • Provide technical supports for building cooperatives (local government, local and international NGOs) |
| Economic | • High initial capital costs for operations change<br>• High initial capital costs for certification | Economic incentives | • Provide passive public investment (government), such as a government procurement policy or enhanced tax deductions for initial costs<br>• Develop joint ventures (government, private industry) |
| | • Difficulty in securing financial resources to cover high capital costs<br>• Long pay-back period for initial investment in certification | Sourcing | • Provide subsidies (government)<br>• Creative investment schemes (government, fund managers, industry associations) to defray initial costs of certification |
| | • Insufficient financial sources | | |
| | • Price premium is still uncertain for certified products | Risk mitigation | • Provide passive public investment (government) such as securing future procurement by government agencies<br>• Target export markets and domestic markets with higher prices (chamber of commerce, industry associations) |

## ISSUES FOR FURTHER INVESTIGATION

This analysis is intended to help landowners–in Panama and else-where–consider the benefits and drawbacks of certification. Policy alternatives have been provided based on the assessment of existing markets. This analysis aims to discover a broad range of obstacles and opportunities for developing certified forest products, and therefore avoids going into great depth on each issue. For example, the analysis has focused on evaluating the ability of landowners to pursue certification instead of evaluating the optimal suite of specific products that could fill niche market demand for specific certified products. Further investigation on those specific topics would be an appropriate and necessary next step to complement this analysis.

## REFERENCES

Bigsby, H. and L.K. Ozanne. 2002. The Purchase Decision: Consumers and Environmentally Certified Wood Products. *Forest Products Journal* 52(7/8):100-105.

Edwards, N.J. 2003. Plantation Promises Stretched to Breaking Point–What Happens When the Prospectus Assumptions Hit the Ground? Retrieved January 2004 from http://www.twff.com.au/pa.pdf.

Elliott, C. 1996. Certification as a Policy Instrument. Pp. 83-92 in: V.M. Viana, J. Ervin, R.Z. Donavan, C. Elliott, and H. Gholz (eds.). 1996. Certification of Forest Products: Issues and Perspectives. Island Press, Washington, DC.

Elliott, C. and R.Z. Donovan. 1996. Introduction. Pp. 1-10 in: V.M. Viana, J. Ervin, R.Z. Donavan, C. Elliott, and H. Gholz (eds.). 1996. Certification of Forest Products: Issues and Perspectives. Island Press, Washington, DC.

Ervin, J. and C. Elliott. 1996. The Development of Standards. Pp. 33-41 in: V.M. Viana, J. Ervin, R.Z. Donavan, C. Elliott, and H. Gholz (eds.). 1996. Certification of Forest Products: Issues and Perspectives. Island Press, Washington, DC.

Fanzeres, A. and K.A. Vogt. 2000. Origins of the Concept of Forest Certification. Pp.11-20 in:K.A. Vogt, B.C. Larson, J.C. Gordon, D.J. Vogt, and A. Fanzeres (eds.). 2000. Forest Certification: Roots, Issues, Challenges, and Benefits. CRC Press, New York, NY.

Forest Stewardship Council (FSC). 2005. Forest management certificate holders. Retrieved 1 April 2005 from http://www.fsc-info.org.

Grossman, J.M. 2007. Carbon in Terrestrial Systems: A Review of the Science with Specific Reference to Central American Ecotypes and Locations. *Journal of Sustainable Forestry* 25(1/2):17-41.

Heaton, K. 1994. Perspectives on Certification from the SmartWood Certification Program. Rainforest Alliance, Richmond, Vermont.

Heaton, K. and R.Z. Donovan. 1996. Forest Assessment. Pp. 54-67 in V.M. Viana, J. Ervin, R. Z. Donavan, C. Elliott, and H. Gholz (eds.). 1996. Certification of Forest Products: Issues and Perspectives. Island Press, Washington, DC.

Jensen, K., P.M. Jakus, B. English, J. Menard. 2003. Market Participation and Willingness to Pay for Environmentally Certified Products. *Forest Science* 49(4):632-641.

Kanowski, P., D. Sinclair, and B. Freeman. 1999. International Approaches to Forest Management Certification and Labeling of Forest Products: A Review. Report to Agriculture, Fisheries, and Forestry–Australia. Retrieved 16 January 2006 from http://www.dpie.gov.au/corporate_docs/publications/pdf/forestry/certification/cert_label_review.pdf.

Kok, K. and A. Veldkamp. 2001. Evaluating Impact of Spatial Scales on Land Use Pattern Analysis in Central America. *Agriculture, Ecosystems and Environment* 85:205-221.

Lichtenfeld, M. 2007. Improving the Supply of Carbon Sequestration Services in Panama. *Journal of Sustainable Forestry* 25(1/2):43-73.

Maser, C. and W. Smith. 2001. Forest Certification in Sustainable Development: Healing the Landscape. CRC Press, Boca Raton, FL.

Myers, N. 1996. Environmental Services of Biodiversity. *Proceedings of the National Academy of Sciences of the United States of America* 93(7):2764-2769.

Ozanne, L.K. and R.P. Vlosky. 1997. Willingness to Pay for Environmentally Certified Wood Products: A Consumer Perspective. *Forest Product Journal* 47(6):39-48.

Ozanne, L.K. and R.P. Vlosky. 2003. Certification from the U.S. Consumer Perspective: A Comparison from 1995 and 2000. *Forest Product Journal* 53(3):13-21.

Republic of Panama. 2005. Panamáen Cifras: Años 2000-2004. Contraloría General de la República, Dirección de Estadísticas y Censo. Retrieved 18 January 2006 from http://www.contraloria.gob.pa/dec and http://www.contraloria.gob.pa/dec/Publicaciones/17-02/cuadro3.pdf.

Rubino, M.C., D. Propper de Callejon, and T. Lent. 2000. Biodiversity and Business in Latin America. (Discussion paper.) Environmental Projects Unit, International Finance Corporation, Washington, DC.

Schneider, A. and H. Ingram. 1990. Behavioural assumptions of policy tools. *Journal of Politics* 52:510-529.

Sedjo, R.A. and S.K. Swallow. 2002. Voluntary Eco-Labaling and the Price Premium. *Land Economics* 78(2):272-284.

Solórzano, R., R. deCamino, R. Woodward, J. Tosi, V. Watson, A. Vázquez, C. Villalobos, J. Jiménez, R. Repetto, and W. Cruz. 1991. Accounts Overdue: Natural Resource Depreciation in Costa Rica. World Resources Institute, Washington, DC and Tropical Science Center, San Jos Costa Rica.

Taggart, J. 2000. Estimating Price Premiums Necessary to Pay for Forest Certification. Pp.277-285 in: K.A. Vogt, B.C. Larson, J.C. Gordon, D.J. Vogt, and A. Fanzeres (eds.). 2000. *Forest Certification: Roots, Issues, Challenges, and Benefits*. CRC Press, Boca Raton, FL.

Tickell, O. 2000. Certification: A Future for the World Forest. Retrieved 31 March 2005 from http://www.ssc-forestry.com/fc04/files/material/material/certwordwwf.pdf.

United Nations. 2004. Report of the United Nations Conference on Environment and Development. (A/CONF.151/26 (Vol. III)). Retrieved 16 January 2006 from http://www.un.org/documents/ga/conf151/aconf15126-3annex3.htm.

United States Agency for International Development (USAID). 2005. USAID Budget: Panama. Retrieved 16 January 2006 from http://www.usaid.gov/policy/budget/cbj2006/lac/pa.html.

Veisten, K. 2002. Potential Demand for Certified Wood Products in the United Kingdom and Norway. *Forest Science* 48(4):767-778.

Vlosky, R.P. and L.K. Ozanne. 1997. Forest Products Certification: The Business Customer Perspective. *Wood and Fiber Science* 29(2):195-208.

doi:10.1300/J091v25n03_04

# SECTION 4:
# INTEGRATED ASSESSMENTS

# Existing Markets for Ecosystem Services in the Panama Canal Watershed

Steven Wallander
Sandra Lauterbach
Krista Anderson
Fuphan Chou
Jesse Muir Grossman
Catherine Schloegel

Steven Wallander is a PhD candidate in Environmental Economics at the Yale School of Forestry and Environmental Studies, New Haven, CT 06511 USA (E-mail: Steven.Wallander@yale.edu).

Sandra Lauterbach graduated from the Yale School of Forestry and Environmental Studies (New Haven, CT 06511 USA) with a Masters in Environmental Management. Ms. Lauterbach is currently the Vice-President of The Compliance Incentive Network for Carbon Sequestration and Biomass Energy (CINCS) (E-mail: Sandra.Lauterbach@ aya.yale.edu).

Krista Anderson earned a Master of Environmental Management at the Yale School of Forestry and Environmental Studies, New Haven, CT 06511 USA. She is an Analyst with the U.S. Government Accountability Office in Boston, MA (E-mail: anderson_kb@yahoo.com).

Fuphan Chou earned a Master of Environmental Management at the Yale School of Forestry and Environmental Studies and a Master of Business Administration at the Yale School of Management, New Haven, CT 06511 USA (E-mail:fuphan@gmail.com).

Jesse Muir Grossman is the CEO and co-founder of Soltage, Inc., a solar renewable energy provider headquartered in Jersey City, NJ. Jesse Muir Grossman earned a Master of Environmental Management at the Yale School of Forestry and Environmental Studies, New Haven, CT 06511 USA (E-mail: jgrossman@soltage.com).

Catherine Schloegel currently works as the community and research director at Ecomadera, a community-run conservation enterprise in Ecuador. Catherine Schloegel earned a Master of Environmental Science at the Yale School of Forestry and Environmental Studies, New Haven, CT 06511 USA (E-mail: catherine.schloegel@aya.yale.edu).

[Haworth co-indexing entry note]: "Existing Markets for Ecosystem Services in the Panama Canal Watershed." Wallander, Steven et al. Co-published simultaneously in *Journal of Sustainable Forestry* (Haworth Food & Agricultural Products Press, an imprint of The Haworth Press, Inc.) Vol. 25, No. 3/4, 2007, pp. 311-336; and: *Emerging Markets for Ecosystem Services: A Case Study of the Panama Canal Watershed* (ed: Bradford S. Gentry, Quint Newcomer, Shimon C. Anisfeld and Michael A. Fotos, III) Haworth Food & Agricultural Products Press, an imprint of The Haworth Press, Inc., 2007, pp. 311-336. Single or multiple copies of this article are available for a fee from The Haworth Document Delivery Service [1-800-HAWORTH, 9:00 a.m. - 5:00 p.m. (EST). E-mail address: docdelivery@haworthpress.com].

Available online at http://jsf.haworthpress.com
© 2007 by The Haworth Press, Inc. All rights reserved.
doi:10.1300/J091v25n03_05

**SUMMARY.** Reforestation of degraded lands is occurring on a limited basis in portions of the Panama Canal Watershed (PCW). In theory, markets for ecosystem services could encourage more extensive reforestation and ensure that reforestation efforts provide more than just timber. The most relevant ecosystem markets for the PCW are carbon sequestration, watershed services, and four biodiversity markets–bioprospecting, certification of biodiversity friendly products, ecotourism, and existence value. This paper examines the possibility for a land owner or land manager to participate in two or more of these markets. Two land use scenarios–native forest plantation and small-holder agroforestry–emerge as likely candidates for participation in multiple ecosystem service markets. These scenarios are examined to determine whether the strength of incentives to provide a bundle of timber and ecosystem services is sufficient to encourage expansion of these land uses with the Panama Canal Watershed. doi:10.1300/J091v25n03_05 *[Article copies available for a fee from The Haworth Document Delivery Service: 1-800-HAWORTH. E-mail address: <docdelivery@haworthpress.com> Website: <http://www.HaworthPress.com> © 2007 by The Haworth Press, Inc. All rights reserved.*

**KEYWORDS.** Carbon sequestration, watershed services, biodiversity, Panama Canal Watershed, ecosystem services, reforestation, agroforestry.

## INTRODUCTION

At present, ecosystem services markets are of great interest to a variety of stakeholders for their promise to put market forces to work solving environmental problems. However, from the point of view of land owners and land managers in the Panama Canal Watershed (PCW), the provision of ecosystem services must make business sense, or else underprovision of these services will persist. In many cases, the income streams that might be received from providing an ecosystem service are not sufficient to justify a switch in land use (e.g., from cattle ranching to native species reforestation). However, by providing and selling more than one ecosystem service from the land, the ecosystem service management option can begin to look more favorable.

This paper begins with a summary of individual markets built upon previous studies of supply and demand for the following ecosystem services: carbon sequestration (Grossman, this volume; Lauterbach, this volume); dry season water yield regulation and water quality improvement (Anderson, this volume; Fotos, Chou, and Newcomer this volume); and biodiversity services. The biodiversity services evaluated include biodiversity-friendly products (Miyata, this volume), sustainable tourism (Schloegel, this volume), bioprospecting (Burtis, this volume), and existence value (Wallander, this volume).

Because the objective is to focus on the perspective of the landowner, four land management options that face a landowner in the PCW form the basis of our analysis: (1) teak plantations, (2) natural forests (i.e., undisturbed primary forests or secondary forests), (3) large-scale native species reforestation, and (4) small-scale agroforestry. We first assess the compatibility of different ecosystem services markets under these four land use scenarios. Two potential land use scenarios–natural forest plantations and agroforestry–show reasonable promise as providers of the mix of ecosystem services analyzed in this paper. We analyze the potential costs and revenues for these scenarios and offer conclusions.

## SUMMARY OF EXISTING MARKETS
## FOR ECOSYSTEM SERVICES IN THE PCW

### Carbon Sequestration Services

Formal and informal markets have recently emerged for the sale of carbon credits to address global warming through the mitigation of greenhouse gas (GHG) emissions. Coupled with national and regional regulations for reducing GHG emissions, these markets may provide strong financial incentives for mitigating carbon emissions through terrestrial carbon sequestration. An analysis of existing supply and demand of carbon sequestration services was conducted with specific reference to Latin America and Panama. The supply-side analysis (Grossman, this volume) demonstrated that the storage of carbon can be measured in a variety of land uses, including natural forests, native species plantations, teak plantations, and agroforestry plots. These different land uses were reviewed in light of inputs to production and maintenance, overall costs, carbon sequestered per unit area, and potential market access.

The Kyoto Protocol and the European Union emission trading scheme are the primary drivers of demand for carbon sequestration services. However, the demand-side analysis (Lauterbach, this volume) highlighted challenges to meeting the demand in the regulated markets. Among the challenges are: (1) relatively few approved afforestation and reforestation (A/R) Clean Development Mechanism (CDM) methodologies; (2) difficulty in meeting CDM specific criteria, such as additionality; and (3) the high transaction costs required for project design, approval and implementation. Voluntary or non-regulated markets play a significantly lesser role in driving carbon sequestration demand, and are smaller and extremely fragmented. Therefore, while carbon can be sequestered in a number of ways in Panama, meeting international demand may be difficult and expensive. Carbon sequestration might be marginally profitable for larger landholders due to economies of scale; however, providing carbon sequestration services may be prohibitively expensive for small landholders until the CDM A/R small-scale methodology is approved. Based on this, bundling revenue from other ecosystem services with carbon sequestration services for small landholders may be required to ensure profitability.

### Watershed Services

Watershed services potentially supplied by forest cover in the PCW consist of dry season water yield regulation and water quality improvement (Anderson, this volume). The Autoridad del Canal de Panamá (ACP), private shippers who use the Canal, hydroelectric producers, Comisión Interinstitucional de la Cuenca Hidrográfica (CICH), and the Instituto de Acueductos y Alcantarillados Nacionales (IDAAN) represent the potential buyers (Fotos, Newcomer and Kuppalli, this volume). Increased dry season water yields would be highly desirable for potential buyers in Panama. However, at present, the lack of scientific consensus limits the ability of land managers to claim provision of increased flows during the dry season (Anderson, this volume). Perhaps reflecting this state of knowledge, no buyer has clearly expressed a *willingness* to pay land managers for reforestation in the hopes that it will increase dry season water yields (Fotos, Chou and Newcomer, this volume). Thus, despite the significant future potential, there is currently no market for water yield regulation in the PCW. Water quality improvement services include reduced sedimentation, reduced pathogen levels, and increased dissolved oxygen levels (Anderson, this volume). However, IDAAN appears neither willing nor able to pay for watershed services because it lacks both the *legal mandate* and the *financial capacity* to pay for them. The ACP, on the other hand, has some *ability* to pay for reforestation to provide watershed services. Again, though, the ACP has not expressed a *willingness* to pay for reforestation to improve water quality seemingly because it has the legal authority to regulate land use in the watershed directly (Fotos, Newcomer and Kuppalli, this volume). Consequently, the market for water quality improvement services in the PCW is tenuous at best.

In addition to watershed-scale markets, a more local market may exist between adjacent or neighboring land managers, particularly among· smallholders in Chagres National Park. For example, one smallholder might compensate an upstream neighbor, perhaps in the form of donated labor, to reforest the area around the headwaters of the spring that serves as his water supply. Chagres smallholders indicated to the authors during a March 2005 research trip to Panama that planting trees increases the water available to them in their local springs. Thus, there is potential for informal, local transactions to improve water quality and flow regulation through small-scale reforestation efforts.

## *Biodiversity Services*

A growing body of literature claims that markets are emerging in which the beneficiaries of biodiversity services will reimburse the providers of these services (Landell-Mills and Porras, 2002; Pagiola et al., 2002). It is unrealistic to posit that there is a single, overarching market for biodiversity services; rather, there are many distinct markets. Some of these markets include: payment for biodiversity-friendly products; payment for access, including sustainable tourism, bioprospecting, and research/hunting/fishing permits; and payment for biodiversity-conserving management including conservation land easements, leases, concessions, and tradable rights including biodiversity credits and/or biodiversity taxes (Jenkins et al., 2004). This analysis focuses on the four biodiversity markets that are most relevant to Panama: certification of biodiversity-friendly products, sustainable tourism, bioprospecting, and existence value.

### *Biodiversity-Friendly Products*

Certification of biodiversity-friendly products (such as coffee, chocolate, vanilla, fruit, and timber) confers credibility through a readily recognizable brand name or label. Economic returns from certification provide incentives for landowners to pursue sustainable forest management. Although the standards from certification often involve numerous social goals and suffer from a lack of consensus on which methods best protect biodiversity, certification facilitates the process of identifying sustainable forestry management practices. Certification encourages improvements over existing forestry practices rather than adherence to only the most sustainable practices.

In Panama, the Forest Stewardship Council has certified six privately owned forest plantations, which vary in size from 360 ha to 1,720 ha (FSC, 2005). The Rainforest Alliance has initiated eco-labeling of bananas as well. Barriers to supplying certified products include lack of awareness, non-existent aggregators, high initial certification costs, and an uncertainty surrounding the price premium (Miyata, this volume). Demand for certified, biodiversity-friendly products occurs mainly in the Northern countries with ecologically conscious consumers. Demand-side barriers also include lack of awareness and absence of national demand.

## Sustainable Tourism

Sustainable tourism encourages sound natural resource management, seeks to maintain the functioning of social, economic, and ecological systems, and provides another economic incentive for landowners to pursue sustainable forest management. Sustainable tourism aims to attract eco-conscious consumers willing to pay a price premium, and it may include suitable eco, adventure, cultural, and nature tourism projects. Supply-side barriers to sustainable tourism include the need to identify a "unique" spot for tourism enterprises and difficulty in financing start-up costs. Demand-side barriers include the lack of recognition of Panama as a sustainable tourism destination, as well as the short duration (less than 2 days) of the average Panamanian tourist (IPAT, 2004). While annual tourist visitation in Panama has increased nearly 55% over the past decade, both the duration of the average visit (approximately 2 days) and the average amount spent per day (approximately $400/day), have remained fairly constant (IPAT, 2004). The cruise ship industry continues to be a major source of tourist visits, particularly within the PCW. The Panamanian Ministry of Tourism (IPAT) does not tally eco or sustainable tourism visits, but visitation numbers from PCW national parks suggest that a very small portion of Panamanian tourists currently seek sustainable tourism activities (Schloegel, this volume).

## Bioprospecting

The International Cooperative Biodiversity Groups (ICBG) program is the most prominent, and perhaps only, example of bioprospecting in Panama to date. While ICBG Panama is a notably well-run example of how to maximize the benefits of bioprospecting, it has obtained samples primarily from state lands and has focused on national-level transactions, especially knowledge and capacity transfers. ICBG Panama has also indirectly contributed to the preservation of pristine lands with high biodiversity. For the private land owner or land manager, however, there is nothing in the existing incarnation of bioprospecting in Panama to provide any incentive for the protection of biodiversity. There is no existing revenue stream in bioprospecting for the private landowner in Panama (Burtis, this volume).

*Existence Value*

In contrast to bioprospecting, existence value is one of the largest arenas in which payments are being made to protect biodiversity. The existence value of biodiversity drives payments from non-governmental organizations, governments, and individuals who support natural forest preservation and agroforestry for its positive impacts on biodiversity (Wallander, this volume). The political efforts to protect tropical biodiversity through regulatory and legal measures, such as the designation of national parks and world heritage sites, has resulted in a great deal of money transferred from northern, industrialized countries to tropical developing countries. These payments form the backbone of existence value for biodiversity services. Once again, however, most of the transactions occur at the national level and involve payments directly to the Panamanian government. Rather than capacity or knowledge transfers, most of these transactions involve large monetary payments.

It seems reasonable to assume that at least some of these payments could be made available as incentives to private land owners and land managers. In Panama, one could argue that the education and support provided by Centro de Estudios y Acción Social Panameño (CEASPA) to smallholders in Chagres National Park is an example of a payment for the existence value of biodiversity in at least two methods. On one hand, these payments help in the process of relocating smallholders away from sensitive areas within the park, a park management policy that involves a great deal of coercive regulatory action by other groups such as the National Environment Authority (ANAM). On the other hand, these payments support the creation of highly diverse organic farms on lands that were previously a monoculture of invasive grass.

## *ANALYSIS OF BUNDLING ECOSYSTEM SERVICES*

This analysis addresses the question: To what extent can ecosystem markets influence a landowner's management decisions? While up to this point we have been considering markets independently, managing for and selling more than one ecosystem service from the same parcel of land can enhance revenues. The constraint for this analysis is that the land must be managed in just one way to supply multiple services, a constraint that illustrates the potential opportunities and tradeoffs of bundling.

For our analysis of ecosystem services in the PCW, we focus on four types of forest-related activities in the region: (1) teak plantations; (2) large-scale native species plantations; (3) preservation of natural forest that might otherwise have been cut down; and (4) small-scale agroforestry, in which management targets woody perennials with agricultural crops and/or livestock.

Table 1 functions as a simplified screening matrix to demonstrate how the four land use types relate to the seven types of ecosystem services. Various exceptions and subtleties are inherent in such a basic summary; however, the table provides a useful first step for evaluating possible existing markets.

A market exists where there are both supply and demand for a given product that is derived from a given land management option. For example, there is a market for carbon sequestered by large-scale native species reforestation. There is not a market for increased dry season water yield because of the uncertainty in supply, but there may be one for improved water quality, where demand is somewhat unclear.

### *Managing Land to Sell Multiple Ecosystem Services: "Bundling" Services*

Managing one parcel of land to supply more than one ecosystem service represents an opportunity to increase the revenue streams flowing into one piece of land. At the same time, it raises a new set of issues. For one, there is an interaction effect between management techniques for different products. For example, managing a forest for maximum timber yield is different from managing a forest for maximum biomass and carbon sequestration. If the interaction between managing for timber or carbon is negative, the land manager must prioritize among different management goals.

A land manager has a choice as to how to bring the services to the market; the term "bundle" can mean one of two types of multi-service approaches. One is the merged bundle, whereby the group of environmental services are sold together to one buyer. Here, the key advantage is that of transactional simplicity, which results in lower transaction

TABLE 1. Existing Supply and Demand for Ecosystem Services in the Panama Canal Watershed Under Different Land Management Options

| Land Management Option | Carbon Sequestration | | | | Improved Water Quality | | Dry Season Water Yield | | Bioprospecting | | Sustainable Tourism | | Biodiversity Friendly Products | | Existence Value | |
| | Regulated | | Voluntary | | | | | | | | | | | | | |
| | S | D | S | D | S | D | S | D | S | D | S | D | S | D | S | D |
|---|---|---|---|---|---|---|---|---|---|---|---|---|---|---|---|---|
| **Teak plantation** | Y | Y | Y | M | M | M | M | – | – | – | – | – | – | – | – | – |
| **Large-scale native species reforestation** | Y | Y | Y | Y | Y | M | M | – | M | M | Y | M | Y | Y | Y | M |
| **Natural forest preservation** | Y | – | Y | Y | Y | M | M | – | Y | Y | Y | Y | Y | Y | Y | Y |
| **Small-scale agroforestry** | Y | Y | Y | Y | Y | M | M | – | M | M | Y | Y | Y | Y | Y | M |

S = Supply; D = Demand; Y = Yes there is supply (or demand); – = No supply (or demand); M = Might be opportunities for supply (or demand) "Demand" incorporates three components: (1) need for the service; (2) willingness to pay for reforestation to provide the service; and (3) ability to pay. If any one of the three components is lacking, there is no existing demand.

319

costs and the need to find only one buyer for one transaction involving all the goods.

The second approach to selling more than one ecosystem service is the shopping basket, whereby the services supplied by one parcel can be sold separately to different buyers. The shopping basket approach tends to be just slightly more common in the marketplace (Landell-Mills and Porras, 2002). The shopping basket approach can be more useful to landowners trying to maximize returns. The additional cash the land manager can earn from several sources can help make an ecosystem services management plan more profitable than alternatives such as agriculture or ranching (Landell-Mills and Porras, 2002). However, the shopping basket approach has higher transaction costs associated with identifying and structuring transactions with several different buyers.

## *Choosing the Basket of Services*

As shown in the matrix presented above in Table 1, a three-way screening–land management technique, feasibility of supply, and existence of demand–indicates that the markets shown in Table 2 may be viable. A market exists where there are both supply and demand for a given product supplied by a given land management option.

Our identification of potential bundling scenarios eliminates teak plantations and natural forests from further consideration. In the case of teak plantations, the only well-defined market that currently exists is the regulated market for carbon sequestration, and this market is uncertain given that as of January 2006 only one CDM A/R methodology had been approved. In addition, these non-native species are relatively water-intensive (Herrera Duran, 2001), may increase erosion (Calder, 2001), and provide minimal habitat for biodiversity due to the lack of understory vegetation. Consequently, teak plantations are not well matched with ecosystem services other than carbon sequestration, particularly if reducing negative externalities is at least part of the goal in developing markets for ecosystem services. Natural forests have greater potential than teak plantations for participation in markets for other ecosystem services. However as of early 2006, deferred deforestation and forest management were not eligible for CDM credits under Kyoto. Furthermore, this paper is focused on *reforestation* activities, rather than forest *preservation*, so natural forests are not given additional consideration here as a potential land use for ecosystem service bundling scenarios.

TABLE 2. Existing Markets for Ecosystem Services in the Panama Canal Watershed

| | Carbon Sequestration | | Improved Water Quality | Biopros-pecting | Sustainable Tourism | Biodiversity Friendly Products | Existence Value |
|---|---|---|---|---|---|---|---|
| | Regulated Market | Voluntary Market | | | | | |
| **Teak plantation** | Yes | Maybe | Maybe | No | No | No | No |
| **Large-scale native species reforestation** | No | Yes | Maybe | Yes | Yes | Yes | Yes |
| **Natural forest preservation** | Yes | Yes | Maybe | Maybe | Maybe | Maybe | Maybe |
| **Small-scale agroforestry** | Yes | Yes | Maybe | Maybe | Yes | Yes | Maybe |

Large-scale reforestation with native species and small-scale agro-forestry thus form the basis for two scenarios in which landowners may manage their land to provide multiple ecosystem services. Each of these scenarios is briefly described below and then analyzed in the next section of this analysis.

## Scenario 1: Large-Scale Native Species Reforestation

Large-scale native species plantations can simultaneously provide carbon sequestration services in the regulated and/or voluntary carbon markets, biodiversity services in the form of sustainable tourism, and water quality improvement. As noted previously, a market for water quality improvement in the PCW *may* exist, but the extent of ACP's demand is currently unclear. However, we include this service in the bundling scenarios as a possibility, dependent on stronger demonstration of demand by ACP. Under this scenario, land managers could reforest a large area of land, such as 1,000 ha, as a native species plantation; sell carbon credits; and potentially receive payments for watershed services. We have excluded certified timber harvesting from this scenario due to the current lack of price premiums for certified timber. Some larger plantation that are able to take absorb the costs of certification might do so for purposes of market access or in anticipation of future premiums, but under existing market conditions certification of timber would not signify a significant change over the returns received from non-certified timber.

## Scenario 2: Small-Scale Agroforestry

Small-scale agroforestry projects can simultaneously provide carbon sequestration services in the regulated and/or voluntary carbon markets, biodiversity services in the form of sustainable tourism, biodiversity-friendly products (certified timber and NTFPs such as vanilla, ginger, and pepper), existence value, and water quality improvement. Under the small-scale agroforestry scenario, land managers could implement a wide variety of possible agroforestry practices (described further in the next section); sell carbon credits; produce a variety of biodiversity-friendly products for personal consumption and sale at local markets; and potentially receive payments for watershed services.

# ANALYSIS OF BUNDLING SCENARIOS

## Scenario 1: Large-Scale Native Species Reforestation

Native species plantations are planted and managed for the sale of wood products to local or international markets, and are designed and managed similarly to exotic plantations located in temperate and tropical regions. Inputs to production, planting dynamics, and monitoring regimes parallel established non-native silvicultural models (Montagnini and Nair, 2004). Advantages to reforesting with native species as opposed to the exotic plantation species include a number of positive externalities that are conferred upon local and regional landscapes. Benefits include positive or neutral changes to soil chemistry, the creation of fruiting sources and other habitat niches for local fauna, a diversified stream of revenue to the local landowners in the form of non-timber forest products including as fruit and nuts, and an enhanced public image derived from social responsibility of local species use (Piotto et al., 2004; Montagnini and Mendelsohn, 1997).

Issues hindering the wide-scale embrace of native forestry practices include the uncertainty in both the internal growth rates of native species as well as the state of the international markets that exist for the sale of wood from native species. To address these points, provenance trials have been established in Panama, Costa Rica, and Nicaragua to generate primary data on individual species growth rates, rotation dynamics, site suitability, and related variables. Although obtained from young stands, data exists on a number of Central American trees that can be used to model the growth rates of potential native timber undertakings (Montagnini and Porras, 1998; Shepherd and Montagnini, 2001; Piotto et al., 2004; PRORENA, 2004; Montero and Montagnini, 2005).

Reforestation projects with goals of carbon sequestration have recently been examined for profitability under markets based on the Kyoto Protocol. Projects in Panama, such as EcoForest and FuturoForestal, are looking to incorporate the sale of carbon credits as an additional source of income on top of timber revenue. Reforestation projects are eligible to sell carbon credits under the CDM. To date, eighteen projects have been submitted for CDM Executive Board approval; only one has been approved, while nine have been rejected and eight remain under review. This has resulted in significant uncertainty in the market for A/R carbon credits.

Tourism in Panama has grown explosively over the last decade (IPAT, 2004). Demand for nature-based tourism in Panama, as measured by the number of official visits to Panamanian national parks, is harder to estimate. ANCON Expeditions, a prominent tour agency in Panama, receives 8,000 tourists per year, while the Smithsonian Tropical Resources Institute (STRI) annually receives 2,000 to 3,000 general visitors to their Barro Colorado Island facilities (Angehr, 2005). In contrast, maritime visits have increased 557% since 1995 (IPAT, 2004). Further, with nearly 378,000 maritime arrivals to the PCW in 2004, cruise ship tourists represent a burgeoning new market (IPAT, 2004).

In this scenario we use data from the above studies to examine the feasibility of bundling the profits accrued from native species timber plantations with those of carbon credit sales and sustainable tourism. We combine specific Central American case studies for data on costs and expected revenues from timber sales, carbon credit sales, and sustainable tourism to perform a rough benefit-cost analysis and a net present value (NPV) assessment of this scenario.

Present sales of native timber trees from Costa Rica yield an approximate value of $12,000 per hectare based on a fifteen-year rotation (Montagnini and Mendelsohn, 1997). Costs of establishing a native timber plantation are $6,500 per hectare, including the upfront costs of establishment as well as the incremental costs of management and monitoring (Herrera Duran, 2001).

Carbon accruals in a native species plantation are estimated to be 75 Mg C ha$^{-1}$ at the end of a fifteen-year rotation This could yield approximately $185 per hectare with sale on the regulated carbon market at a conservative value of $2.50 per ton $CO_2$ (Montagnini and Porras, 1998; Grossman, this volume; Lauterbach, this volume). Costs associated with preparing a project for access to regulated carbon markets are in the range of $40,000-$100,000 per project, with additional annual monitoring and audit costs of $5,000-$19,000 (Lauterbach, this volume). For non-regulated markets, initial costs are between $9,000-$15,000, with annual monitoring and audit costs of $4,000-$6,000 (Lauterbach, this volume).

Estimated revenues for sustainable tourism in this scenario are derived by examining the rates of tourist visitations in Panama, costs of infrastructure and marketing, and tourists' willingness to pay. Willingness to pay is derived from two prominent eco-tour agencies in Panama City (ANCON Expeditions and Eco Circuitos). With a potential to capture 2,000 visitors per year and each visitor paying $50, sustainable tourism in this bundled venture would yield a gross revenue of $100,000 per annum (Schloegel, this volume). Unconventional approaches, such as marketing to cruise ships, could capture a greater amount of the existing cruise tourism market, which could increase profitability to $200,000 (Schloegel, this volume).

It is important to note that the costs and revenues estimated for these ecosystem services are derived using the best sources available, yet all figures presented here are subject to assumptions and individual sources of error, which may self-propagate throughout this analysis. Using the above data, however, we can examine the approximate profitability of this venture and also observe how each individual ecosystem service contributes to the financial profile of the entire bundle.

Given a 1,000 hectare plot of land that provides three different ecosystem services, the net present value of revenue per hectare is $5,630, using a 14% discount rate (Table 3). As seen in Table 3, the sale of timber makes a disproportionate contribution to the overall financial profile of this venture. The relatively small contributions of both carbon credit sales and sustainable tourism revenues should be examined in light of the temporal aspects of these revenue streams. Timber businesses are characterized by large initial capital inputs with revenues realized only after a long delay (fifteen years in this scenario). The revenues of carbon sales and sustainable tourism, however, can be captured throughout the lifespan of the project, providing working capital during the years where the project would otherwise be operating with no annual revenue streams.

TABLE 3. Scenario 1 Analysis: Profits per Hectare (Net Present Value)

| Ecosystem Sales | Profit per Hectare (NPV) | Percentage of Profits |
|---|---|---|
| Native Timber[1] | $5,500 | 97% |
| Carbon Credits[2] | $55 | 1% |
| Sustainable Tourism[3] | $75 | 1% |
| Total | $5,630 | 100% |

This table examines an ecosystem service bundle on 1,000 ha.
The net present value of each revenue stream is calculated as well as the differential contribution of the different ecosystem service revenue streams to the overall profitability of the venture.
A discount rate of 14% is used for these calculations, with project life of 15 years.[4]
[1] (Montagnini and Mendelsohn, 1997; Hererra, 2001)
[2] (Montagnini and Porras, 1998)
[3] (Schloegel, this volume)
[4] (Lauterbach, this volume)

An important tradeoff in this scenario is the ability of landholders to manage their land to maximize certain services whose management goals conflict. For example, a land manager seeking to sell timber to wood markets will try to maximize the standing biomass in order to garner a high price at the marketplace. To achieve those ends, the forest will be managed to reduce extraneous biomass that detracts from the straight and tall growth of the trees. If a landholder was managing the forest only for sale of carbon credits, however, the goal would be to maximize the overall biomass, and therefore carbon, of the site. Following this logic, if managing a forest only for sustainable tourism, a land manager would change the management plan accordingly. In this scenario, however, a profit-maximizing land manager with a long time horizon would look to maximize the native timber growth.

### Scenario 2: Agroforestry

Agroforestry generally refers to the deliberate growth of woody perennials with an agricultural crop and/or animal husbandry component (Nair, 1989; Hauff, 1999). There are a number of different types of agroforestry systems, including windbreaks, alley cropping, riparian bugger strips, forest farming, and silvopasture (NRCS, 1998). Moreover, a variety of different tree species may be used in agroforestry systems. Agroforestry systems are often practiced on a small scale, with a functionally and temporally diverse stream of profits. The products of agroforestry are consumed primarily at the household level with occasional sale of surplus crops at local and regional markets. In addition to providing crops to landholders, agroforestry provides benefits including improved crop yields; carbon sequestration; diversification of crops and economies; enhancement of water and soil quality; reduction of soil erosion, flooding, and chemical use; and provision of habitat (NRCS, 1998; Hauff, 1999). Additional research would be required to determine how well the different types of agroforestry systems and species mixes may sequester carbon, as well as how they impact biodiversity and crop production.

Agroforestry has been analyzed in the Panama Canal Watershed in several areas, including Agua Buena and La Bonga in Chagres National Park (Hauff, 1999). These existing projects were developed with external support from the Asociación Nacional para la Conservación de la Naturaleza (ANCON) and other non-governmental organizations (Hauff, 1999). The planted crops included manioc, plantains, corn, papaya and tree beans (Hauff, 1999). In general, these projects had mixed success; while agroforestry may provide benefits, agroforestry in Panama faced a number of challenges, including access to markets and economic feasibility.

In this examination of possible strategies for bundling ecosystem services in Panama, we examine the potential for combining agroforestry with the sale of carbon credits, certified agricultural products, and existence value. The primary ecosystem market that will be analyzed in the context of agroforestry is carbon sequestration services. Several researchers have found that "virtually any type of agroforestry activity should produce carbon credits" via the inclusion of woody plants in crop production (Sampson, 2001). Carbon credits can potentially be sold to regulated and voluntary markets. Carbon sold from agroforestry operations based in Panama would be sold under the CDM Land Use, Land Use Change and Forestry projects (LULUCF) (Lauterbach, this volume). The CDM Executive Board (EB) has only approved one CDM LULUCF methodology which does not have a strong agroforestry component. In addition, the CDM EB has rejected other methodologies which were more focused on agroforestry (UNFCCC, 2005).

In terms of the non-regulated carbon market, agroforestry operations can sequester carbon for sale of credits in voluntary markets, which exist primarily in the United States and Australia. While the non-regulated market is fragmented and potentially small, one example of an agroforestry project that has yielded carbon credits in a non-regulated market is a project implemented in Guatemala by Applied Energy Services (AES). In the 1990s, AES invested over $2 million in an existing agroforestry project called CARE (Cooperative for Assistance and Relief Everywhere) (Moura-Costa, 2001; Lauterbach, this volume). While AES did not necessarily make this investment to reduce its emissions, this investment has been seen a voluntary carbon sequestration measure (Moura-Costa, 2001).

In addition to carbon sequestration services, there are two biodiversity markets in which a smallholder practicing agroforestry might gain additional revenue streams: (1) certification of biodiversity-friendly products; and (2) the existence value of biodiversity. With some controversy, advocates of agroforestry have suggested three hypotheses of how agroforestry protects biodiversity: (1) by reducing pressure to deforest pristine areas; (2) by providing valuable habitat to native species; and (3) by establishing corridors to link protected areas. Significant evidence supports all three hypotheses, but only under specific social and ecological conditions (Schroth et al., 2004). Importantly, none of these hypotheses suggests that agroforestry has greater biodiversity values than pristine natural areas. Rather, each hypothesis posits the favorability of agroforestry over an alternative landscape–deforested, agricultural, and/or fragmented forested.

There are challenges and benefits to bundling ecosystem services with agroforestry. As described above, there are many benefits of agroforestry systems, including carbon sequestration, preservation of biodiversity, and reduced soil erosion. While agroforestry can be profitable, researchers have identified several challenges faced by agroforestry operations in Panama. These challenges include inadequate market opportunities, difficulty in marketing crops, and poor transportation and road infrastructure (Fischer, 2002). Another difficulty identified is smallholders' lack of economic resources to make a transition from one form of agriculture to another (Fischer, 2002). Researchers have concluded that despite agroforestry's benefits, in rural areas, agroforestry may not be profitable or successful (Hauff, 1999).

In bundling carbon with agroforestry, the main challenge is whether carbon sequestration revenue can offset costs associated with measuring and auditing carbon for sale (Sampson, 2001). Whether carbon sequestration in agroforestry systems will be profitable depends on the price of carbon, the amount of carbon sequestered, market entry costs, and the costs associated with monitoring and validating carbon sequestration projects. Potential exists for farmers to harvest trees on an ongoing basis for domestic use. This may pose challenges to ensuring that carbon is sequestered for carbon credit sale. For small farms, these evaluation and monitoring costs may be significant (Fischer, 2002). Moreover, these projects will need to prove additionality, permanence, and lack of leakage (Sampson, 2001).

In terms of the potential for agricultural certification, there has been tremendous growth in certification in the last decade. However, certified goods comprise only a small percentage of the market for most goods. A more important function of certification is its function as a barrier to market entry. What these niche markets lack in price premiums, they might have in demand stability. For example, demand for certification often originates with multi-national corporations that are being pressured by environmental NGOs to improve the environmental sustainability of their supply chains. Since in these cases the demand does not originate from consumers willingness to pay a premium for sustainable products, the multi-nationals are not willing to pay a premium to their suppliers (Gouyon, 2003). However, many of these suppliers will agree to certification due to the assurance of having a reliable buyer at the end of every harvest cycle.

If these benefits are not realized, it appears that certification is currently a very unattractive option for smallholder agroforestry with limited benefits and very high transaction costs. Two possibilities exist to improve the market for certification through bundling. The first is to bundle certification of biodiversity-friendly products with carbon sequestration. To achieve significant scale, this would require pooling across smallholders and a market for some sort of gold standard of certification. The second possibility is to cover the costs of certification under the market for existence value, i.e., to get a non-governmental organization, multilateral lending institution, or trust fund to fund the costs of certification.

Existence value remains one of the strongest existing markets for biodiversity conservation. However, while there have been significant payments for existence values to tropical areas, relatively few of these payments have been made to agroforestry operations. Importantly, though, a number of important cases do exist of funding for support and education of smallholders practicing agroforestry in Panama. There are also examples of direct payments to smallholders for biodiversity protection in other tropical countries.

To analyze the feasibility of bundling agroforestry, carbon sequestration and biodiversity services, it is essential to review potential profitability. It is difficult to estimate agroforestry costs as they may vary significantly depending on the crops planted, number of hectares planted, agroforestry system adopted, access to markets, and transportation costs. Agroforestry can be less profitable than other agricultural systems (Gomez, 1995). In addition, agroforestry costs are generally higher than managing a native species plantation. Studies have estimated that tropical agroforestry costs can range from 3 to 4 times the costs of forest management and 1.1 times the costs of plantations (van Kooten, 2004). Studies have also indicated that agroforestry projects in Panama may have lower net present values (NPVs) and Internal Rate of Returns (IRRs) in comparison to other Central American countries due to lower prices for wood products (Current et al., 1995). Thus, agroforestry is often more expensive than other land use options.

Agroforestry will also sequester less carbon than other land use options, such as native species reforestation. Estimates suggest that agroforestry operations in Panama could sequester 40% of the carbon in native species plantations (Grossman, this volume). Based on a high-level analysis of carbon and agroforestry bundling, small-scale agroforestry may be marginally profitable. The biggest challenges to profitability are the transaction costs associated with obtaining approval for carbon sequestration methodologies in the regulated market, as well as measuring and monitoring carbon in the non-regulated and regulated markets. Assuming a plot size of 40 hectares, transaction costs for entering the regulated carbon market range from $39,000-$87,000 for an initial investment and $5,000-$9,000 in ongoing monitoring (Lauterbach, this volume). The costs of entering the non-regulated carbon market are significantly lower, ranging from $9,000-$15,000 for initial investment and $4,000-$6,000 for the non-regulated market (Lauterbach, this volume). However, the lower prices and smaller size of the non-regulated carbon sequestration market may limit revenue potential for agroforestry projects.

## ALTERNATIVES

In this analysis of two baskets of services, we have demonstrated that the bundling of environmental services with both native species plantations (see Table 4) and agroforestry (see Table 5) increases the overall profitability of these ventures. In a comparative sense, the scenario of planting native timber species expressed a qualitatively higher value than that of the agroforestry bundling scenario. Quantitatively, net present value calculation for the native species plantation scenario demonstrates that the sale of the timber is still the chief source of revenue while the additional revenue streams stemming from the inclusion of the environmental services of carbon credit sale and sustainable tourism add small but constant levels of additional revenue throughout the lifespan of the project. Revenue from other ecosystem services may be useful to increase the profitability of the overall operation. While agroforestry may provide environmental benefits, the economic benefits are less obvious and there are significant barriers to successfully implementing agroforestry on a wide scale.

### Alternative 1

Reforestation with plantations of native tree species is a highly viable land use alternative that would help to regenerate degraded land as well as provide a strong base from which to access markets for ecosystem services however limited they might be at this time. On the research front, continued controlled field testing and development of best practices management regimes with respect to native species reforestation decisions are of the highest priority. Gaps in research on native species

TABLE 4. Scenario 1: Native Species Plantation + Carbon Sequestration + Sustainable Tourism

| Scenario | Benefits | Challenges | Profitability |
|---|---|---|---|
| Native Species Plantation | • Native species confer positive externalities to environment and local communities.<br>• Promotes existence of genetic diversity in native tree populations. | • Wood markets for native species are less developed than for exotic species.<br>• Growth rates of native species are still being determined. | • Native species is not as profitable as exotic species given present state of knowledge.<br>• Native species reforestation is less costly and potentially more profitable than agroforestry. |
| Carbon | • Provides a revenue stream throughout the life of a project.<br>• Can provide revenue stream with no additional plantation costs.<br>• Currently, the CDM EB is reviewing reforestation methodologies for carbon credit sales. | • High initial transaction costs to enter regulated and non-regulated markets.<br>• Currently no CDM approved methodologies for reforestation.<br>• Small landholders may have difficulty in addressing transaction costs of monitoring and approval.<br>• Need to prove additionality, non-leakage and permanence. | • Regulated carbon markets have high transaction costs that would need to be offset.<br>• Non-regulated markets have lower transaction costs, but these costs still may be an impediment to entering the market. |
| Sustainable Tourism | • Potentially large and unexplored cruise ship tourism market.<br>• Small but significant revenue stream throughout the life of the project. | • Tourism is seasonal.<br>• Willingness to pay for carbon offset tourism uncertain. | • Revenue is dependent upon the number of tourists who visit Panama. |

growth rates, site-specific suitability, and individual species' responses to environmental variables need to be further addressed before investors and landowners will fully support the establishment of native species plantations. This priority is being addressed by research and academic institutions in Central America, but more support for these objectives is essential to stimulate a shift in current land management practices and improve the possibilities for market development and expansion.

TABLE 5. Scenario 2: Small-Scale Agroforestry + Carbon + Existence Value + Certification

| Scenario | Benefits | Challenges | Profitability |
|---|---|---|---|
| **Agro-forestry** | • Agroforestry provides environmental benefits versus monoculture plantations.<br>• In some contexts can provide minimal economic benefits.<br>• Agroforestry may bundle well with carbon and biodiversity services. | • Agroforestry challenges include: lack of market development in Panama and lack of access in rural areas.<br>• Transitioning from other forms of farming to agroforestry may result in high costs. | • Agroforestry is marginally profitable in Panama.<br>• Agroforestry is more expensive than other land use options, e.g., plantations.<br>• Revenue will be dependent on crops sold and market demand for crops. |
| **Carbon** | • Carbon CDM projects are being reviewed, which may enable carbon credit sale in regulated markets.<br>• Any agroforestry system can sequester carbon. | • High initial transaction costs to enter regulated and non-regulated markets.<br>• Currently no CDM approved methodologies for agroforestry.<br>• Small landholders may have difficulty in overcoming high transaction costs of monitoring and approval.<br>• Need to prove additionality, non-leakage and permanence. | • Regulated carbon markets have high transaction costs which would need to be offset.<br>• Non-regulated markets have lower transaction costs, but these costs still may be an impediment to entering the market. |
| **Certification** | • May help agroforesters in marketing a recognizable brand.<br>• Assists market access.<br>• Ensures environmental externalities are included in agricultural production. | • High certification and annual auditing costs. | • High certification costs not offset by market premiums.<br>• Possible benefit of more steady demand. |
| **Existence Value** | • Demonstrated demand from traditional sources of conservation financing. | • Market more focused on pristine areas<br>• Limited funds reaching small holders. | • Impossible to measure since payments not tied to measurable product or service. |

## Alternative 2

Sustainable tourism in the Panama Canal Watershed (PCW) has potential for financial profitability due to the access to cruise ships and to Panama City. A survey of current tourist activities along with a willingness-to-pay study for a suite of sustainable tourism opportunities in the PCW would help to improve the assessment of this potential and to guide investment toward these ends.

## Alternative 3

If addressing poverty and social justice concerns is deemed an important objective of the Panamanian government, a significant challenge to the development of markets for ecosystem services in the Panama Canal Watershed will be the inclusion of the small-scale landholders. Of the four land use scenarios analyzed, agroforestry represents an opportunity for small landholders to enter into the ecosystem services market. To make the agroforestry bundle option more attractive to small-scale landholders, more research is required on interactions between tree and agriculture species, optimum rotation lifespan, other information on planting dynamics, geographic access to markets, and other issues regarding getting ecosystem services and all of the other timber and non-timber products to their respective markets.

## Alternative 4

Given the high initial capital and transaction costs to participation in markets for ecosystem services, further applied research is needed to develop innovative mechanisms whereby small landholders can aggregate individual parcels of land and access these markets in a collective manner. Support of participatory extension programs, such as CEASPA, that carry out such applied research initiatives would be a productive means to these ends.

## REFERENCES

Anderson, K. 2007. Existing Supply of Watershed Services in the Panama Canal Watershed. *Journal of Sustainable Forestry* 25(1/2):121-145.
Angehr, G. 2005. Contributions of Scientific Investigation to Ecotourism. Retrieved 5 May 2005 from https://www.denix.osd.mil/denix/Public/ES-Programs/Conservation/Legacy/Panama/panamawrd6.html.

Burtis, P. 2007. Can Bioprospecting Save Itself? At the Vanguard of Bioprospecting's Second Wave. *Journal of Sustainable Forestry* 25(3/4):219-245.

Calder, I.R. 2001. Canopy Processes: Implications for Transpiration, Interception and Splash Induced Erosion, Ultimately for Forest Management and Water Resources. *Plant Ecology* 153(1-2):203-214.

Current, D., E. Lutz, and S.J. Scherr. 1995. Adoption of Agroforestry. Pp 1-27 in: D. Current, E. Lutz and S.J. Scherr (eds.). 1995. Costs, Benefits, and Farmer Adoption of Agroforestry: Project Experience in Central America and the Caribbean. World Bank Environment Paper No. 14. The World Bank, Washington, DC.

Fischer, A. and L. Vasseur. 2002. Smallholder Perceptions of Agroforestry Projects in Panama. *Agroforestry Systems* 54(2):103-111.

Forest Stewardship Council (FSC). 2005. FSC Permits Worldwide. Retrieved 5 May 2005 from http://www.fsc-info.org/english.htm.

Fotos, M., F. Chou, and Q. Newcomer. 2007. Assessment of Existing Demand for Watershed Services in the Panama Canal Watershed. *Journal of Sustainable Forestry* 25(1/2):175-193.

Fotos, M., Q. Newcomer, and R. Kuppalli. 2007. Policy Alternatives to Improve Demand for Water-Related Ecosystem Services in the Panama Canal Watershed. *Journal of Sustainable Forestry* 25(1/2):195-216.

Gomez, M. 1995. Economic and Institutional Analysis of Agroforestry Products in Panama. Pp. 146-162 in: D. Current, E. Lutz and S.J. Scherr (eds.). 1995. Costs, Benefits, and Farmer Adoption of Agroforestry: Project Experience in Central America and the Caribbean. World Bank Environment Paper No. 14. The World Bank, Washington, DC.

Gouyon, A. 2003. Eco-Certification as an Incentive to Conserve Biodiversity in Rubber Smallholder Agroforestry Systems: A Preliminary Study. Indonesia: World Agroforestry Centre.

Grossman, J.M. 2007. Carbon in Terrestrial Systems: A Review of the Science with Specific Reference to Central American Ecotypes and Locations. *Journal of Sustainable Forestry* 25(1/2):17-41.

Herrera Duran, J.L. 2001. Growth Provenance Analysis and Financial Profitability of *Tectona grandis* L.f. in the West Zone of the Panama Canal. Master's thesis, CATIE. Turrialba, Costa Rica.

Hauff, R.D. 1999. A Case Study Assessment of Agroforestry: The Panama Canal Watershed. *Journal of Sustainable Forestry* 8(3/4): 39-51.

Instituo Panamano de Turismo (IPAT). 2004. Datos Estadísticos de Turismo 2003-2004. Retrieved 5 May 2005 from http://www.ipat.gob.pa/estadisticas/.

Jenkins, M., S.J. Scherr, and M. Inbar. 2004. Markets for Biodiversity Services. *Environment* 46(6):32-42.

Landell-Mills, N. and I.T. Porras. 2002. Silver Bullet or Fools Gold: A Global Review of Markets for Forest Environmental Services and Their Impacts on the Poor. International Institute for Environment and Development, London.

Lauterbach, S. 2007. An Assessment of Existing Demand for Carbon Sequestration Services. *Journal of Sustainable Forestry* 25(1/2):75-98.

Miyata, Y. 2007. Markets for Biodiversity: Certified Forest Products in Panama. *Journal of Sustainable Forestry* 25(3/4):281-307.

Montagnini, F. and R.O. Mendelsohn. 1997. Managing Forest Fallows: Improving the Economics of Swidden Agriculture. *Ambio* 26(2):118-123.

Montagnini, F. and P.K.R. Nair. 2004. Carbon Sequestration: An Underexploited Environmental Benefit of Agroforestry Systems. *Agroforestry Systems* 61:281-295.

Montagnini, F. and C. Porras. 1998. Evaluating the Role of Plantations as Carbon Sinks: An Example of an Integrative Approach from the Humid Tropics. *Environmental Management* 22(3):459-470.

Montero, M. and F. Montagnini. 2005. Modelos alométricos para la estimación de biomasa de diez espicies forestales nativas en plantaciones en la region Atlántica de Costa Rica. *Recursos Naturales y Ambiente (Costa Rica)* 45:118-125.

Moura-Costa, P. 2001. Forestry and the Climate Convention: 10 Years of Evolution. Paper prepared for the World Bank book on New Market-Based Mechanisms for Forest Conservation, edited by IIED, published by Earthscan. Retrieved 5/5/2005 from http://www.ecosecurities.com/download/Moura-Costa_10_years_of_Climate_Convention_IIED_World_Bank.pdf.

Nair, P.K.R. 1989. Agroforestry Systems in the Tropics. Kluwer, Boston, MA.

Native Species Reforestation Program (PRORENA). 2004. Esayo de Selección de Especies–RPO 07 (2003) y PRO 13 (2004). Proyecto de Reforestación con Especies Nativas: 2. Panama.

Natural Resources Conservation Service (NRCS). 1998. Agroforestry. *News and Views* 11.

Pagiola, S. 2002. Paying for Water Services in Central America: Learning from Costa Rica. Pp. 37-61 in: S. Pagiola, J. Bishop, and N. Landell-Mills (eds.). 2002. Selling Forest Environmental Services: Market-Based Mechanisms for Conservation and Development. Earthscan, London.

Pagiola, S., J. Bishop, and N. Landell-Mills. 2002. Selling Forest Environmental Services: Market-Based Mechanisms for Conservation and Development. Earthscan, London.

Piotto, D., E. Viquez, F. Montagnini, and M. Kanninen. 2004. Pure and Mixed Forest Plantations with Native Species of the Dry Tropics of Costa Rica: A Comparison of Growth and Productivity. *Forest Ecology and Management* 190:359-372.

Sampson, N. R. 2001. Agroforestry as a Carbon Sink. Paper presented at the 7th Annual Biennial Conference on Agroforestry in North America, Regina Saskatchewan, Canada.

Schloegel, C. 2007. Sustainable Tourism: Sustaining Biodiversity? *Journal of Sustainable Forestry* 25(3/4):247-264.

Schroth, G, G.A.B. da Fonseca, C.A. Harvey, C. Gascon, H.L. Vasconcelos, and A.N. Izac. 2004. Agroforestry and Biodiversity Conservation in Tropical Landscapes. Island Press, Washington, DC.

Shepherd, D. and F. Montagnini. 2001. Above Ground Carbon Sequestration Potential in Mixed and Pure Tree Plantations in the Humid Tropics. *Journal of Tropical Forest Science* 13(3):450-459.

United Nations Framework Convention on Climate Change (UNFCCC). 2005. Afforestation and Reforestation CDM Project Activities. Retrieved 5 May 2005 from http://cdm.unfccc.int/methodologies/ARmethodologies/Projects/pac/pac_ar.html.

Van Kooten, G.C., A.J. Eagle, J. Manley, and T. Smolak. 2004. How Costly are Carbon Offsets? A Meta-Analysis of Carbon Forest Sinks. *Environmental Science and Policy* 7:239-251.

Wallander, S. 2007. The Dynamics of Conservation Financing: A Window into the Panamanian Market for Biodiversity Existence Value. *Journal of Sustainable Forestry* 25(3/4):265-280.

doi:10.1300/J091v25n03_05

# Improving Markets for Ecosystem Services

Michelle Lichtenfels          Radha Kuppalli
Patrick Burtis                Michael Lichtenfeld
Alexander Hovani              Yuko Miyata

Michelle Lichtenfels works for Portland Energy Conservation, Inc. (PECI), Portland, OR 97201 USA, where she administers energy efficiency programs for large California utilities. She recently worked as the Forest Carbon Policy Analyst at Environment Northeast, New Haven, CT 06510 USA, where she focused on energy and climate change policy solutions. Michelle Lichtenfels received her Master of Forestry from the Yale School of Forestry and Environmental Studies, New Haven, CT 06511 USA (E-mail: mlichtenfels@gmail.com).

Patrick Burtis is a Kauffman Fellow and Cleantech Associate with Amadeus Capital Partners in London, and a Research Fellow at the Energy Futures Lab at Imperial College, London, UK. Patrick Burtis earned a Master of Environmental Management at the Yale School of Forestry and Environmental Studies, New Haven, CT 06511 USA (E-mail: pat@patburtis.com).

Alexander Hovani earned a Master of Forestry at the Yale School of Forestry and Environmental Studies and a Master of Business Administration at the Yale School of Management, New Haven, CT 06511 USA.

Radha Kuppalli is Manager of Business Development and North American Programs. New Forests Pty Limited. She earned her Master of Environmental Management at the Yale School of Forestry and Environmental Studies and MBA at the Yale School of Management, New Haven, CT 06511 USA (E-mail: rkuppalli@gmail.com.)

Michael Lichtenfeld works in international cleantech private equity. He earned a Master of Environmental Management at the Yale School of Forestry and Environmental Studies and a Master of Business Administration at the Yale School of Management, New Haven, CT 06511 USA (E-mail: skigreen@hotmail.com).

Yuko Miyata is an Environment, Health and Safety Specialist with GE Commercial Real Estate Finance. Yuko Miyata earned a Master of Environmental Management at the Yale School of Forestry and Environmental Studies, New Haven, CT 06511 USA (E-mail: yuko.miyata@aya.yale.edu).

Address correspondence to: Michelle Lichtenfels (E-mail: mlichtenfels@gmail.com).

[Haworth co-indexing entry note]: "Improving Markets for Ecosystem Services." Lichtenfels, Michelle et al. Co-published simultaneously in *Journal of Sustainable Forestry* (Haworth Food & Agricultural Products Press, an imprint of The Haworth Press, Inc.) Vol. 25, No. 3/4, 2007, pp. 337-364; and: *Emerging Markets for Ecosystem Services: A Case Study of the Panama Canal Watershed* (ed: Bradford S. Gentry, Quint Newcomer, Shimon C. Anisfeld, and Michael A. Fotos, III) Haworth Food & Agricultural Products Press, an imprint of The Haworth Press, Inc., 2007, pp. 337-364. Single or multiple copies of this article are available for a fee from The Haworth Document Delivery Service [1-800-HAWORTH, 9:00 a.m. - 5:00 p.m. (EST). E-mail address: docdelivery@haworthpress.com].

Available online at http://jsf.haworthpress.com
© 2007 by The Haworth Press, Inc. All rights reserved.
doi:10.1300/J091v25n03_06

**SUMMARY.** Panama contains some of the most productive and diverse ecosystems in the world, and receives many benefits from the natural services provided by those ecosystems. Yet formal markets for ecosystem services in Panama are poorly developed. We assume that functioning markets for ecosystem services would partially counter development pressures on Panama's natural forests and ecosystems, and propose a suite of policy alternatives that could help develop such markets with the expectation that revenues would fund conservation and restoration efforts. These recommendations fall into five broad categories: (1) increase conservation of existing forests; (2) promote reforestation; (3) strengthen institutional capacity; (4) lower transaction costs; and (5) build the Panama brand for environmental services. A variety of fiscal, legal, organizational, and information-based approaches are recommended. In addition, we recommend convening a national Ecosystem Services Task-Force to organize diverse stakeholders and implement policy alternatives deemed most appropriate for advancing market development. We emphasize policy alternatives that are consonant with political and economic conditions in the country, that leverage outside funding, that recognize political feasibility, and that build upon existing legal and institutional frameworks. doi:10.1300/J091v25n03_06 *[Article copies available for a fee from The Haworth Document Delivery Service: 1-800-HAWORTH. E-mail address: <docdelivery@haworthpress.com> Website: <http://www.HaworthPress.com>*
© 2007 by The Haworth Press, Inc. All rights reserved.]*

**KEYWORDS.** Panama, ecosystem services markets, carbon sequestration, watershed services, biodiversity conservation, land use, land use conversion, reforestation policy

## INTRODUCTION

The world's forests and natural ecosystems provide a host of valuable environmental services: water purification and flow regulation, carbon sequestration, and biodiversity services such as pollination, storage of genetic material, and existence value, to name a few. Unfortunately, these services are rarely recognized in private markets for goods and services. Indeed, ecosystem services have more in common with public goods than private goods: as long as they are available, we take them for granted. When they're gone, we miss them.

Traditional public policies and land use regulations have not adequately protected or fully valued environmental resources, and have thus failed to capture the full financial value of these services to society

(Johnson et al., 2002). As the pressures of development and deforestation mount globally, the environmental community is increasingly turn-- ing to markets for ecosystem services as means to protect ecosystems and promote conservation. Demand for these services has the potential to significantly impact the decisions of landowners, land managers, and private investors by increasing the incentives for creation or maintenance of forest ecosystems (Hovani and Fotos, this volume).

Panama produces ecosystem services, and benefits from the services its forested ecosystems provide. As the bridge between two continents, and the divider of two great oceans, Panama contains some of the most biologically diverse landscapes in the world (WRI, 2004; TNC, 2005). Conservation International (CI) designated the Mesoamerican Corridor, which stretches from southern Mexico to the Panama Canal, as a global biodiversity hotspot (CI, 2005). Panama's forests attract world-class research institutions, bioprospectors, and tourists. The forests of the Chagres and Grande River watersheds deliver the 500 billion gallons of fresh water per year needed to operate the Panama Canal, by far the most important economic entity in Panama. Forest ecosystems throughout the country deliver clean water to hydroelectric dams that provide the majority of electricity for the country. The list of other services is long.

One might expect, then, that Panama as a country would have a well-developed appreciation for the value of these natural services. But in fact, formal markets for ecosystem services in Panama are almost non-existent (Wallander et al., this volume). In addition, Panama's landscapes, and particularly forests, are under increasing pressure from a variety of sources including population growth, agriculture, tourism, factors related to poverty and (ironically) under-development, and an expansion of land devoted to monoculture tree plantations (Heckadon, personal communication, 7 March 2005; see Schloegel, this volume).

The loss of natural forests is the result of both market and institutional failures. Because the value of ecological services provided by forests (e.g., clean and abundant water supply, carbon sequestration, and biodiversity utility) is rarely taken into account when considering land use options, the economics of land use practices tend to favor conversion of natural forests to uses with short-term benefits, such as un-managed timber extraction, or clearing for cash-crop agriculture or livestock grazing. Even where local and federal governments have taken steps to correct market failures, Panama's institutions frequently fall short in their efforts to enforce or promote the desired changes. For instance, although cattle grazing and farming are largely prohibited in

Chagres National Park, we witnessed widespread agricultural activity within the park, and the chronically under-funded National Environment Authority (ANAM) has been unable to control it (Endara, personal communication, 7 March 2005). Other chronic institutional problems include lack of trained individuals, lack of transparency, lack of technology, and poor coordination among institutions.

The lack of institutional capacity derives at least in part from a lack of funding. Although Panama has the second highest per capita income of all countries in Central America (CIA, 2005), like many Latin American countries, it has high debt levels and few viable industries, leaving little in the country's coffers for reinvestment in social institutions. The Canal improves economic conditions in the country, but only so much. While ecosystem services markets could generate income for the country in the long term (and hopefully attract foreign investment and revenue), establishing these markets will first require significant investment and the establishment of stronger Panamanian institutions. The breadth and depth of these large social problems place them beyond the scope of this analysis. However, policies that promote ecosystem services must account for these persistent challenges.

Finally, market formation is also impeded by a lack of information about ecosystem services, both within and beyond the country's borders. Panama has many small-scale landowners utilizing a limited range of land management strategies. While many current land uses are compatible with ecosystem services markets, better dissemination of information is needed to promote desired land conversions, and to encourage participation in markets for environmental services. Additionally, potential domestic buyers of ecosystem services need to better understand the value of these services if they are to conserve and eventually pay for them. And international consumers of Panama's ecosystem services (such as carbon sequestration, which provides global benefits) will need to be educated about Panama's potentially important role in global markets for ecosystem services.

## CAVEATS AND CONSIDERATIONS

In the pages that follow, we propose a broad suite of policy recommendations designed to foster efficient markets for ecosystem services. First, however, a number of caveats are in order.

First, we do not attempt to draw a detailed roadmap for creating specific ecosystem services markets in Panama. Neither do we recommend a command-and-control prescription that attempts to insert markets where there are none today, nor to alter land-holder behavior by fiat. The focus of this analysis is on *setting the stage* for the development of ecosystem services markets in Panama, rather than establishing those markets directly.

Second, we recognize that ANAM, the Panama Canal Authority (ACP), Comisión Interinstitucional de la Cuenca Hidrográfica (CICH), the Inter-American Development Bank (IDB), World Bank, USAID, Fundacion NATURA, Conservation International (CI), The Nature Conservancy (TNC), and many other institutions currently sponsor or direct initiatives that utilize or embrace many of the policies mentioned here. Our intent is to point out the beneficial properties of those initiatives where appropriate. Elsewhere, we may have overlooked the contributions of certain entities simply because we are not familiar enough with their initiatives to comment. Our oversights are unintentional, but for those that occur, we apologize in advance.

Third, in recognition of the political and financial realities of Panama, we favor policy options that do not require significant public funds, and (with a few exceptions) are not politically controversial. Where possible, we attempt to work within existing legislative precedents or other institutional arrangements sanctioned by the Government of Panama. For instance, we suggest reforms of existing laws (e.g., Law 8 and Law 24) rather than passage of entirely new ones. We suggest acceleration and expansion of some existing programs (such as the land titling program) rather than wholesale creation of new ones. And we point out several places where Panamanian policymakers could potentially make better use of the international and domestic NGOs already working in Panama.

Finally, any recommendations seeking to affect policy change in Panama must be made in light of the role and present circumstances of The Panama Canal Authority (ACP). More than just an economic entity, the ACP is among the most powerful and important institutions in Panama. Though it appears that functioning markets for ecosystem services could benefit Canal operations by protecting the forests in the watershed, the ACP has thus far declined to take a role in developing these markets. Additionally, Canal expansion was the subject of a national referendum planned for November 2005. Canal expansion arrangements will depend on negotiations among national and international actors in all environmental, social, and economic sectors. The outcome of this process will influence whether and how the policy alternatives outlined in this paper could be implemented. As a result, any policies implemented before the Canal expansion plans are complete should emphasize flexibility and broad applicability, rather than dependence on any one of the possible expansion alternatives. Moreover, the fact that Canal expansion will constitute a negotiated outcome makes it imperative that proponents of ecosystem markets interject these ideas into the bargaining mix.

## OVERVIEW OF RECOMMENDATIONS

### The Challenge: Reaching Land Holders and Influencing Land-Use Decision-Making

In designing policy alternatives to create ecosystem services markets and influence land-holder decisions, we started from a landowner's perspective. Land-use decisions in Panama are driven by a diverse set of factors that include government policies and incentive structures; urban growth and rural-to-urban migration patterns; local political, economic, social, and natural forces; international and local investment; and lately, the prospect of Canal expansion. Within Panama, a variety of land use options are available to landowners and smallholders, including agriculture, livestock pasture, agroforestry, silvopastoral systems, forest plantations (both native and non-native species), natural forest preservation, and urban uses. These land uses can result in divergent economic and ecological consequences at local, provincial, and global scales (see Anderson, this volume).

At heart, ecosystem services markets attempt to change the economic equation governing land use decisions by individual landholders. By making explicit the financial contribution of natural resources, and allowing landholders to benefit from those contributions, ecosystem services markets seek to encourage landowners to choose more environmentally benign land uses than would occur in the absence of those markets. In the best cases, "win-win" scenarios develop, where the landholder benefits directly and substantially from making ecologically sustainable choices. In most cases, however, ecosystem services will not be the primary economic factor in landholder decisions. Instead, ecosystem services will be one of several factors (along with regulation, information dissemination, and NGO intervention) that tip the scales away from traditional resource-depleting land uses in favor of more ecologically benign outcomes.

A critical aspect of our ecosystem services approach is the integration, or "bundling," of multiple services such as carbon sequestration, water purification, and sustainable timber products with traditional land uses such as agriculture, cattle ranching, or tree plantations. Bundled land-·use strategies seek to maximize income to the landholder *and* provide improved ecological outcomes. Because bundling arrangements are inherently complex (often involving multiple sites and numerous transactions) no policy prescription can anticipate every bundling permutation. Consequently, the role of the policy-maker is to encourage the development of flexible markets for these services, thus allowing landowners or land managers and their ecosystem services customers to make arrangements that work for all parties.

In the case of Panama, six desirable classes of land uses (or land use conversions) are proposed to increase the range of ecosystem services provided by privately-owned lands:

1. Conversion of open cattle pastures to silvopastoral systems;
2. Conversion of degraded cattle pastures to timber plantations;
3. Shifting from agriculture to agroforestry through partial reforestation;
4. Plantation management changes that include:

   a. Changing from non-native monoculture forest plantation management (primarily teak) to a native/non-native species mix;
   b. Extending timber harvest rotations; and
   c. Promoting uneven-aged stand management;

5. Establishing or widening riparian buffer reserves; and
6. Maintaining existing natural forests (choosing *not* to clear for agricultural or ranching purposes).

Land use conversions should meet two criteria. First, they should directly benefit the landholder, and second, they should create ecological benefits. For instance, partial reforestation of active range land (conversion to silvopastoral systems) can increase the carrying capacity of the land, allowing more cattle per hectare, improve the condition of the cattle on that land, and improve water quality and dry-season flows for downstream users.

Conversely, if direct financial benefits to landholders cannot be achieved, the desired land use must create tangible external benefits for which others are willing to compensate the farmer. For instance, widening riparian buffers by twenty meters on a small cattle ranch may not appreciably affect the rancher's economics, but it can have significant impact on downstream water quality, saving money in filtration, dredging, and public health costs. Compensating the rancher with some portion of the realized benefit (i.e., redistributing the savings from not having to build additional water treatment plants) would encourage adoption of sustainable land use decisions.

### Five Primary Policy Goals

In order to effect the changes described here, we have identified a suite of policy options that could be employed. These options aim to achieve five primary goals:

1. Increase conservation of existing forest ecosystem services;
2. Promote increased reforestation and afforestation;
3. Strengthen relevant institutional capacity;
4. Lower transaction costs; and
5. Build the Panama brand.

In essence, the first two goals are intended to *develop ecosystem services supply*–improve the infrastructure needed to supply ecosystem services by maintaining existing forests and growing new ones. Goals three and four aim to *establish efficient markets*. And goal five attempts to *increase demand* by disseminating information about Panama's ecosystem services to customers and suppliers.

The policy recommendations set forth in this paper derive from the individually authored papers written for the three classes of ecosystem services examined–carbon, water, and biodiversity. Common themes and individual recommendations have been summarized and combined under the five broad categories listed above. Recommendations are designed to be comprehensive, but also pragmatic; every feasible policy alternative must be politically and financially saleable in the country of Panama.

### DEVELOPING ECOSYSTEM SERVICES: RECOMMENDATIONS

### An Ecosystem Services Task Force

One over-arching recommendation may help to facilitate those that follow. Given the complexity and diversity of the alternatives presented below, we propose as a first step the creation of a national-level Ecosystem Services Task Force. This task force would champion the cause and attempt to build policy consensus within the Panamanian government and among key constituencies and non-governmental actors. As outsiders, we do not presume to know who should serve on this task force. However, there are many possible institutions that might appropriately serve on it. The newly-created department of Environmental Economics within the National Environment Authority (ANAM) is dedicated to the development of environmental services and would perhaps be a logical coordinator for this task force (Endara, 2005). Other task force participants might include ANAM, the Ministries of Health, Agriculture, Tourism and Finance, NGOs such as TNC, the Centro de Estudios y Acción Social Panameño (CEASPA), CI, and multilateral financing institutions such as the World Bank, IDB, and the Global Environment Facility. Other possible task force members might include potential ecosystem services buyers and providers such as ACP, CICH and its members, Canal users, Kyoto-regulated companies, hydroelectric producers, private landowners, and so on.

While we list many possible participants, we recognize that having too many members on the task force could compromise its effectiveness. As envisioned, this task force would be a nimble facilitator, able to pull people to the table, broker deals, and build consensus among the many constituents. This vision argues for fewer, rather than more task force members. As such, we defer to the interested parties to determine if (and how) such a task force might best serve the goal of establishing ecosystem services markets.

## *1.0 Conservation Policies*

To some extent, increased funding for conservation of natural forests in Panama can be considered an expansion of ecosystem services markets *prima facie*. However, natural forests also play an important role as the underlying "infrastructure" that provides many other ecosystem services, particularly biodiversity and watershed services. As such, improved forest conservation is both a platform for provision of an ecosystem service (e.g., monetizing existence value) and also a key factor of production in the provision of other ecosystem services.

1.1 *Develop a clear set of conservation priorities and goals that unify constituencies supporting forest conservation.* The first task of the Ecosystem Services Task Force could be to adopt and adapt the previously published *National Environmental Strategy, a Vision for 2020*, with the aim of promoting forest conservation and developing ecosystem services markets. The National Environmental Strategy incorporates other concerns including urban environmental issues, but the Task Force could help to effectively disseminate the document and use it to guide investments and initiatives toward agreed priorities (Endara, 2005).

1.2 *Increase dissemination of sustainable agricultural and livestock management practices.* This recommendation would help mitigate many environmental threats. As we observed in Chagres National Park, some of the development pressure on natural forests is the result of long-term degradation of lands already cleared for farming and cattle ranching. Possessed of few other options, the logical course of action for many farmers is to abandon their existing land once it has been degraded, and clear new forest. This results in serious erosion and water quality problems, and increases deforestation rates.

Rather than remove farmers from reserves such as Chagres (which would be politically, socially and logistically untenable) another tack seems appropriate. Innovative programs such as those administered by CEASPA provide information and promote exchanges among smallholders that help farmers increase the productivity of farm and ranching lands while minimizing environmental degradation. An expansion in informational services like those provided by CEASPA could help remove some incentives for smallholders to clear additional forest. Policies should include safeguards to assure that assistance to farmers does not lead to further encroachment into the forest.

1.3 *Aggressively leverage external funding sources.* This recommendation applies to many initiatives described in this paper. However, it is of particular importance for conservation because significant external funding sources already exist specifically for conservation purposes. The United States' Portman Bill funds large-scale conservation through instruments such as debt-for-nature swaps. (These funds constituted the bulk of the Chagres National Park debt-for-nature swap [Hanily, personal communication, 8 March 2005].) Other developed countries may have similar programs. Additionally, NGOs such as TNC and CI maintain funds for conservation efforts in high-priority locations. A concerted effort from within the Panamanian government (e.g., through the taskforce described above) to attract foreign funds could significantly increase moneys available for conservation efforts.

1.4 *Increase promotion of conservation easements, and consider creating a formal, legally enforceable easement mechanism.* Conservation easements create opportunities for innovative conservation arrangements while also providing benefits to land owners. Typically, a land owner agrees to sell certain property rights (e.g., development or resource extraction rights) to a qualified conservation buyer (such as TNC) who retires those rights and retains the right to enforce the terms of the easement.

A TNC review of Panamanian law concluded that conservation easements are legally feasible in Panama (Hanily, personal communication, 8 March 2005). Four Panamanian conservation easements–the first ever in Panama–were scheduled to be completed in March 2005 (Hanily, personal communication, 8 March 2005). It may well be, then, that an appropriate legal structure already exists for long-term, enforceable, and transferable conservation easements in Panama. However, even in countries such as the US where easements have a well-established basis in statutory law; challenges to easements are not uncommon (particularly upon transfer of the property or death of the original grantor). Therefore, it may be wise to establish a more formal and customized legal mechanism executing, enforcing, and endowing conservation easements. This would eliminate any ambiguity in current property rights laws, and reduce the risk that changes to property rights laws might inadvertently invalidate conservation easements.

1.5 *Expand, accelerate, and prioritize the land titling program in the Panama Canal Watershed (PCW)* (Endara, 2005). A prerequisite to employing conservation easements–and to many of the other recommendations in this paper–is the establishment of clear property rights and ownership. Land titling benefits smallholders by formalizing their deeds, allowing them to sell their land or various rights accruing thereto, obtain credit, and invest in their land for the long term. Obtaining clear title may also provide significant non-economic benefits to the owner and his or her community.

The World Bank has provided a $47.9 million loan to help Panama modernize its land-titling and registry systems, with particular focus on small farmers, tenant women, indigenous peoples, and owners of small plots in and around urban areas. The program aims to title 80,000 properties and demarcate 600,000 hectares of priority protected areas. The project also includes a land valuation system and improved land registration at the local level (World Bank, 2001). This recommendation requires working closely with responsible officials of the World Bank and appropriate entities within Panama including the Ministry of Agriculture, which is responsible for rural land titling (Endara, personal communication, 7 March 2005).

1.6  *Remove perverse development incentives from Panama Law 8.*
Law 8 promotes tourism in Panama through several measures: an
expedited permitting process for the development of tourist activities
and projects; establishment of significant tax incentives and benefits
for tourism promoters/operators (including a twenty year exemption
on land taxes and any duties, fees and taxes on any plant, property and
equipment primarily associated with tourism); a 10-year depreciation
schedule for all assets except land; establishment of a National Tourism Registry, and more (Republic of Panama, 1994; Gray & Co.,
2005).

Observers have noted that Law 8 does not distinguish between pristine and developed areas, nor does it require "sustainable development"
practices. Thus, the law may create perverse incentives leading to destruction of ecologically sensitive or unique areas (Schloegel, this volume). For example, Law 8 specifically rewards the construction of golf
courses and theme parks regardless of the ecological sensitivity of the
proposed development area (Schloegel, personal communication, 4 April
2005). To address this, policy-makers might consider amending Law 8
to provide tax incentives only for ecologically sustainable developments
(Schloegel, this volume).

*Benefits of improved conservation policies.* These alternatives seek
to improve Panamanian conservation efforts primarily by changing the
economics of existing land use practices in ways that reduce incentives
for smallholders, other landowners, and developers to convert or use
natural forests in unsustainable ways.

*Feasibility of improved conservation policies.* Two of the recommendations (1.4 and 1.6) require changes to existing laws and it is difficult to gauge the political feasibility, potential controversy, or economic
impact of these actions. Nevertheless, the recommended policies should
not entail overwhelming cost burdens. The recommended policy alternatives require limited government funding to implement, or they rely
on funding from other governments or NGOs.

## 2.0  *Reforestation Policies*

A concerted effort to stimulate reforestation projects in Panama can
help accelerate the development of ecosystem services markets by
boosting the supply of ecosystem services such as carbon sequestration,
watershed protection, and biodiversity services (Pagiola et al., 2002). In
theory, payments for these services (in the form of domestic and foreign

investment in reforestation projects) would flow to land managers who reforest their property.

The development of reforestation policy in Panama is difficult because many of the options proposed here may prove costly to implement. Therefore, innovative means of funding reforestation policies may be required. Such financing mechanisms are discussed below.

The Panamanian government has tried in the past to foster reforestation through Law 24 of 1992. Law 24 has been substantially revised and in parts reversed because of problems with its implementation. Those problems included perceived abuses by large plantations, high costs in the form of lost tax revenues, and the existence of perverse incentives to deforest land in order to gain eligibility for the economic subsidies offered for reforestation. Therefore, new policies for reforestation must be crafted to avoid perverse incentives, excessive cost to the government, or opportunities for abuse by favored classes of landowners. The following recommendations discuss possible fiscal and non-fiscal policies for fostering reforestation projects in Panama that explicitly provide ecosystem services, and innovative means of funding such policies.

2.1 *Fiscal incentives for reforestation.* Eligibility for fiscal and non-fiscal incentives from the Panamanian government to fund reforestation projects should be contingent upon demonstration that such projects will promote the provision of ecosystem services (in addition to or in lieu of timber production). A requirement for those seeking eligibility might be provision of a detailed project design document. Eligible projects might include those that use a variety of management regimes including timber plantations, agroforestry ventures, silvopastoral systems, and set-aside semi-permanent reforestation projects (in sensitive watershed areas, for example). Considering these aims, eligibility for fiscal support under the new reforestation policies might require that land managers:

- Utilize native tree and plant species from a list developed by government and research organizations;
- Explicitly incorporate the provision of at least one ecosystem service (e.g., carbon sequestration, biodiversity services, or watershed protection) in the project design document;
- Provide for riparian buffer zones and other set-aside no-cut areas;
- Establish the project on land deforested prior to 1992 (the year that Law 24 was originally implemented) to avoid fostering perverse incentives to deforest land and apply for fiscal support for reforestation; and

- Give priority to areas that connect patches of native forest or increase buffers around areas of high conservation value.

The government of Panama might consider establishing a sliding scale for policy benefits based on how management plans address specified goals of the Panamanian government, perhaps as they are expressed in the National Environmental Strategy. By using a sliding scale of incentives, the policy may avoid excessive costs, since many projects will not be eligible for full benefits, while sending strong signals to land managers about which kinds of projects are most valued by the Panamanian government.

Law 24 primarily benefited large landholders with an eye on attracting foreign investment. The government of Panama may also wish to consider measures that direct a specified amount of fiscal support to projects sponsored by smallholders. We do not propose that the government of Panama turn away from its initial objective. However, we do suggest that a new goal for reforestation policy might be to support lower-income domestic smallholder projects through measures that encourage cooperative or bundled projects.

Finally, it is important to note that the alternatives presented here are intended to offer temporary assistance to the ecosystem services market and to stimulate an increase in reforestation projects that provide ecosystem services. The Panamanian government cannot be expected to shoulder the financial burdens of an inchoate market forever. Therefore, new reforestation policies would likely be given a predetermined date of expiration in anticipation of a more mature market in the future.

Projects eligible for financial support might receive benefits through the following policies, some of which were originally introduced under Law 24 (see articles 5, 6, 9, 11).

- *Tax deduction for investments*: All or a portion of the investment in eligible reforestation projects would be deductible for income tax purposes;
- *Tax deduction for research*: All or a portion of investments in reforestation research would be deductible for income tax purposes;
- *Import tax exemption*: Property, supplies, and equipment necessary for eligible reforestation projects would be exempt from import duties such as might apply to motorized equipment, agricultural chemicals, research equipment, seeds, cuttings, etc.;
- *Low-interest loan program*: Banks and other lending organizations (public and private) might be encouraged to loan money to

reforestation projects at below market rates by offering them favorable tax treatment on the interest charged to such projects.

*Benefits of fiscal incentives for reforestation.* Policies that provide fiscal incentives for reforestation will benefit land managers in many ways. These policies can bring costs down by subsidizing investment in reforestation projects. They can foster foreign investment in such projects. They can increase research into reforestation, including scientific aspects of best management practices and economic aspects of fiscal policies. Finally, they can facilitate access to capital through more affordable lending rates.

*Feasibility of fiscal incentives for reforestation.* The feasibility of implementing such a suite of policies is mostly contingent upon financing. This issue is explored in some detail below. However, the political feasibility of the above policies is quite strong. Although the original Law 24 was abused and eventually changed, stipulations governing the provision of fiscal incentives such as those mentioned earlier in this section can help to ensure the integrity of the policies. Furthermore, similar policies have been successfully implemented in other Latin American countries, such as Colombia, Chile, and Costa Rica (Hope et al., 2002; UNEP, 1999; World Bank, 2003; FAO, 1997). An evaluation of the outcomes and effects of these policies in other countries would be useful in crafting future Panamanian policy.

2.2 *Non-fiscal incentives for reforestation.* In addition to the fiscal policies outlined above, several non-fiscal mechanisms can be implemented to support reforestation for the provision of ecosystem services. These mechanisms include:

- *Land titling*: As previously discussed, the government of Panama might consider expanding and accelerating its land titling program to enable land managers to access capital from lending organizations and other institutions for reforestation projects, and to protect their land from squatters and other infringements of property rights;
- *Pooling projects*: Also mentioned earlier in this paper, government agencies such as ANAM and industry organizations such as ANARAP can play an important role in pooling reforestation projects together to make them more attractive to investors or buyers of ecosystem services. Pooling projects of all sizes can raise their collective value to buyers of ecosystem services while minimizing risk to both buyer and supplier (Landell-Mills and Porras, 2002;

see also Hovani and Fotos, this volume; Lichtenfeld, this volume; Grossman, this volume; and Lauterbach, this volume);

- *Joint ventures*: The government of Panama might consider engaging in reforestation ventures with land managers and private investors. The government might facilitate projects by providing deforested public land for private reforestation enterprises (using long-term, low-cost lease agreements such as has been done with EcoForest), providing ownership or property rights protection, giving political endorsement or regulatory support to the projects, or offering protection of property from squatters.

*Benefits of non-fiscal incentives for reforestation.* The benefits to land managers from these mechanisms would likely vary with land use types. For example, pooling projects together may be helpful for silvo-pastoral ventures attempting to sell small quantities of carbon credits from trees planted on cattle ranches. On the other hand, for reasons of scale the government of Panama may enter into joint ventures to sell carbon credits solely with owners of large-scale timber plantations.

*Feasibility of non-fiscal incentives for reforestation.* The feasibility of implementing these policy instruments depends primarily on the institutional capacity of Panamanian authorities, ministries, and other governmental actors. The fact that cooperation and communication among government agencies in Panama remains fragmented, particularly with regards to environmental issues, indicates that the policies outlined above may prove difficult to implement (Harrick, personal communication, March 2005; Pérez, personal communication, March 2005). On the other hand, certain government agencies, such as ANAM, may be capable of taking a leading role or partnering with non-governmental organizations (such as ANARAP and CEASPA) that may possess complementary institutional features (Gutierrez-Espeleta, personal communication, March 2005; Elton, personal communication, March 2005).

2.3 *Financing reforestation policy.* Regardless of the political feasibility, Panama's capacity to take on additional financial obligations is limited. We therefore recommend consideration of innovative funding mechanisms such as the following.

- *Canal user fees*: The government of Panama might consider levying an "environmental fee" on users of the Panama Canal over and above present charges for Canal passage. The revenues from this fee for environmental services could be managed in trust and directed towards reforestation projects that provide ecosystem services including carbon sequestration, watershed protection, or biodiversity. We are under no illusions about the difficulty of persuading ACP officials and Panamanian elected officials that a portion of the income stream from the economic engine of the country should be diverted to forest conservation. Nevertheless, the Canal and its watershed generate enormous wealth for the country and for shipping companies. It strikes us that a national conversation about sustaining what are literally "streams of value" is both timely, given present planning for Canal expansion, and necessary, given the rapid growth of water demand nationally (see Fotos, Newcomer and Kuppalli, this volume; Fotos, Chou, and Newcomer, this volume).

- *Hydroelectric tax*: Hydroelectric power companies rely on the watershed for the provision of their most important resource, the free flow of water. A tax commensurate with the imputed value of watershed services might be levied on such companies (see Fotos, Chou and Newcomer, this volume). For example, hydroelectric companies in Colombia are required to give 2 percent of gross revenues to either the national environmental authority or to a reforestation project (FAO, 1997; CIFOR, 2000).
- *Other land use taxes*: Many kinds of land use in Panama could be taxed to pay for reforestation. For example, timber or mining operators could be charged a flat fee per hectare of land deforested or a percentage of the export market value of raw logs or minerals. This system has been implemented in Indonesia (UNEP, 1999; World Bank, 2003). In South Africa (Act 36, 1998), a system for measuring and taxing the reduction of water flows from various land uses has been established, charging land managers for the loss of water resources (Hope et al., 2002). That system is based on good science and determined by species per hectare lost.
- *Foreign investment incentive*: To attract foreign investment and to help fund reforestation policies or projects, foreign investors who invest or donate substantial funds to reforestation projects could become eligible for an immigration visa.
- *International support*: As noted above, an important source of funding for reforestation is the international lending community. The World Bank, IDB, and GEF have demonstrated an interest and capacity in financing environmental market development and reforestation efforts (World Bank, 2003; IDB, 2005; GEF, 1999). We suspect that as plans for canal expansion proceed opportunities

for enhanced reforestation financing from multilateral lending agencies or aid institutions will emerge.

*Benefits of reforestation financing measures.* The economic benefits of the proposed reforestation policies are substantial. They include increased exports of timber and non-timber forest products, increased employment in rural areas, and increased private investment–three of President Torrijos' top priorities.

*Feasibility of reforestation financing measures.* We do not discount the political difficulty of attracting additional public funding for reforestation in Panama. The fact that President Torrijos has recently introduced or increased taxes on a number of sectors indicates that leveraging funds through taxation is politically feasible in Panama (Jackson, 2005). As a stable, business-friendly democracy, Panama has great potential for attracting significant foreign investment from both public and private sources.

## *SELLING ECOSYSTEM SERVICES*

### *3.0   Capacity-Building*

The scientific, institutional, and economic bases for ecosystem services markets are complex. Services must be quantified, articulated, packaged, and sold, and each of these steps requires coordination among multiple actors and across multiple scales–individual, national, international. The creation of these markets relies on a high level of sophistication and coordination and a high level of implementation capacity. Capacity building on all levels is one of the key areas that will stimulate and make possible ecosystem services markets.

Capacity-building is carried out at three levels: individual (attitudes and behaviors), institutional (performance and adaptability), and systemic (enabling environment for environmental governance). A key aspect of capacity-building is strengthening the national institutions responsible for managing the natural environment and the implementation of environmental objectives and sustainable development (LaFontaine, 2000). Technical assistance is a sub-component of capacity-building, in which specific technical skills, knowledge and technology are transferred. Capacity-building involves much more than acquiring technical equipment, skills or knowledge. Ideally, through capacity-building, the beneficiary acquires the ability to make decisions and perform functions in an efficient, effective and viable way.

3.1 *Capacity-building for individuals.* The scarcity of Panamanians with the technical expertise to create, manage, and support ecosystem services markets is a significant obstacle to their formation and development.

3.1.1 *NGOs and multi-lateral agencies could partner to create training programs that address the technical capacity of suppliers.* Land managers themselves require additional expertise to be able to fulfill ecosystem services contracts. Taking carbon services as one example, the participating land manager must have a working knowledge of approved methods for measuring carbon stocks, the Kyoto Clean Development Mechanism (CDM) approval process, best management practices for carbon sequestration, and consumer demands regarding compliance certification.

3.1.2 *More money for training the researchers, scientists, and bureaucrats necessary to develop ecosystem services markets could help make Panama more self-sufficient.* While some of the leading scientists in the world work in Panama, very few of them are Panamanian, and even fewer work within the government. Part of the reason for this is the absence of high level programs at the University of Panama and insufficient funding for sending students abroad to acquire advanced training.

Ecosystem services markets require technical expertise to develop the detailed approaches to forestry, carbon sequestration measurement, watershed protection benefits, and bioprospecting, to name only a few areas. Building local knowledge will help move the country toward self-sufficiency in the professional expertise necessary for dealing with the complexities of these markets.

3.2 *Capacity-building for institutions.*

3.2.1 *Separating agency staffing from the political process to a greater extent would help create stability in staff quality and consistency in policy implementation.* Building the capacity of individual agencies is critical. Panamanian government institutions and their leaders, including important sub-executive positions, change with each political administration, posing significant challenges to the effort to build institutional capacity. ACP is the notable exception of a high-capacity institution within the government, benefiting both from an independent revenue stream and a constitutionally-guaranteed, semi-autonomous governance structure.

3.2.2 *Improve institutional transparency.* The quality of financial management, revenue collection and allocation (particularly within

IDAAN), and the transparency of the institutions in Panama are serious problems. The Panamanian public sector continues to suffer from images of corruption and non-transparency after decades of political scandal. This perception impairs the country's economic and environmental performance.

3.2.3 *Technology transfer.* Ecosystem services markets may require specialized equipment, technology, and knowledge systems that Panamanian institutions do not possess. This is particularly true with regard to building bioprospecting potential in the country (Coley and Kursar, personal communication March 2005), but may also apply to carbon sequestration and watershed protection.

3.3 *Coordination among organizations.*

3.3.1 *Integration of multiple government agencies is complicated and could be improved through lesson sharing with peer countries and through training by international agencies.*

3.3.2 *Elevating ANAM's status within the government might help generate more public support for ecosystem services markets.* Our objective would be to enable ANAM to work on an even level with more powerful and established Ministries such as Agriculture and Finance perhaps by giving ANAM a formal voice in Cabinet meetings and decisions.

3.3.3 *Within the Canal Watershed, strengthening the capacity of CICH would assure better integration of the work of the different agencies and institutions.* Governmental institutions in Panama have not cooperated effectively to solve environmental problems (Harrick, personal communication, March 2005; Pérez, personal communication, March 2005), limiting the capacity of each to accomplish its goals. Ecosystem services markets are influenced by the activities of the Ministries of Agriculture, Health, Finance, and the Environmental Authority, to name just a few. Coordination among them has proved challenging, and strengthening the capacity of CICH to coordinate the work of the ministries, ACP, NGOs and local and provincial agencies could have a significant positive impact.

3.4 *Systemic improvements.*

3.4.1 *More basic research on ecosystem services could help make the case in Panama and other countries that these are important markets to develop.* Access to information about the functioning of these services would encourage local adaptation. Useful information to discover or disseminate would include more locally-applicable answers to common hydrologic questions such as the connections between forest cover and seasonal flows, internationally-accepted methodologies for carbon measurement, and methods for assessing the compatibility of different types of agriculture or tourism with biodiversity preservation.

*Benefits of capacity building.* Markets rest on a foundation of public institutional capacity. The recommendations above are intended to strengthen the capacity of Panamanian institutions to help land owners and land managers better participate in markets for ecosystem services.

*Feasibility of capacity building.* Improving the management of individual institutions and coordination among many institutions is extremely difficult. These issues are complex and systemic, and will require significant time and financial expenditures; even then, success is not guaranteed.

## 4.0 Reducing Transaction Costs

The development of viable markets for ecosystem services depends heavily on the management of transaction costs. One author defines transaction costs as the "costs associated with setting up and participating in market exchange, excluding the actual payments made to suppliers for the commodity" (Landell-Mills et al., 2002:223).

Transaction costs have played a significant role in slowing the development of markets for ecosystem services in the Panama Canal Watershed. For example, the costs associated with supplying carbon sequestration services, such as measurement and verification, have been high enough to deter many potential suppliers in Panama, particularly those with small land holdings and limited access to capital (Lichtenfeld, this volume). In the case of biodiversity markets, the high costs of certification assessment and verification have prohibited the development of biodiversity-friendly non-timber forest products and environmentally sustainable tourism (Miyata, this volume; Schloegel, this volume). In certain locales, the entry hurdles for bioprospecting–obtaining permission from the host country, establishing rules for property rights, establishing contracts, and managing local politics–have stymied the development of this market (Burtis, this volume).

A suite of policy alternatives are described below that could reduce transaction costs in these markets and provide greater incentives for reforestation and conservation in the Panama Canal Watershed.

4.1 *Develop local land cooperatives.* These cooperatives, comprised of small landholders in the PCW, could reduce transaction costs by sharing information and pooling or bundling ecosystem services (Hovani and Fotos, this volume; Lichtenfeld, this volume; Lichtenfels, this volume; Miyata, this volume; Schloegel, this volume). These cooperatives could be focused at the watershed scale to provide functionality and site-specificity to projects (Lichtenfels, this volume). Landholders could share both market information and technical information about forest management regimes for ecosystem services Pooling and bundling ecosystem services would allow landholders to take advantage of economies of scale in implementing certain land management systems and paying for the costs of measurement and verification. For example, the fee to verify carbon sequestration or certify NTFPs could be reduced for each individual if landholders were able to pool their land for management and verification reasons. On the non-governmental front, CEASPA is already working with land holders to develop cohesive land management plans that become self-sustaining due to the shared benefits of co-operation.

4.2 *Develop standardized contracts, rules and other such templates.* In the initial development of these markets in Panama, contracts could be developed for individual services. For example, the Panama International Cooperative Biodiversity Group (ICBG-P) is codifying and standardizing bioprospecting agreements, rules, and regulations to reduce transaction costs for buyers and providers of access to bioprospecting and biological material (Burtis, this volume). In the greenhouse gas emission reduction market, ANAM could work to develop standardized forms for transactions in Panamanian carbon credits. Such standardization would be particularly helpful in transactions of carbon sequestration credits, where international policy is uncertain (Hovani and Fotos, this volume). Over time, one could imagine the creation of standardized contracts by ANAM for bundled services as well.

*Benefits of reducing transaction costs.* The policy recommendations above would provide benefits to small and large landholders in different ways. The formation of local land cooperatives would be particularly beneficial to small landholders. Individual smallholders generally do not have sufficient financial resources to engage in ecosystem services markets, or are too small to be viable participants in the market. Local land cooperatives would reduce individual management costs and provide access to new revenue sources and jobs that otherwise would be out of reach. Accompanied by land titling as noted in section 1.5 above, cooperatives would benefit small landholders by improving their access to capital markets and perhaps increasing their capacity to restore or convert their land to higher value uses. Finally, standardized contracts and rules would benefit both small and large landholders. Standardization reduces time and legal costs associated with contract negotiation.

Properly done, standardization can also increase the transparency of negotiations.

*Feasibility of reducing transaction costs.* These policy options have varying levels of feasibility and effectiveness. The formation of land cooperatives has a low to medium level feasibility. From a cultural standpoint, small landholders in the Panama Canal Watershed are typically recent immigrants who lack a community network or similar foundation of social capital upon which to build a cooperative. However, long-term engagement by outside entities such as CEASPA can help communities to foster self-sustaining associations which can play an important role in reducing transaction costs, minimizing risks to buyers and sellers, and thus increasing small landholders' participation in these markets.

Although difficult to predict, the development of standardized contracts and rules have a medium to high level of feasibility and would likely be quite effective if widely adopted. Entities involved in the development of these standardized contracts and rules have examples and experience from other parts of the world to draw on. Standardized terms could save valuable time and costly legal fees.

## INCREASING DEMAND

### Building the 'Panama' Brand

The policy alternatives discussed above are designed to build Panama's capacity to participate in ecosystem markets. Building the Panama brand aims to enhance the country's competitiveness internationally by constructing a good reputation and image around its products, services, and investments. Once acquired, such an image grants Panama the opportunity to differentiate its products and increase market share or pricing power relative to other countries.

Stimulating demand for Panamanian ecosystem services has two broad goals. The first is to build a reputation that establishes Panama as the best provider for ecosystem services, especially those centered on carbon, biodiversity, and water. Panama's possession of the Canal, its strategic location as a global crossroads (the point of passage between two oceans and the bridge between the North and South American continents), and its designation as a hotspot of biodiversity are all obvious advantages and likely central components of the Panama brand of ecosystem services.

The second goal is to promote Panama as a good place to do business and as an investment destination. Besides its rich natural resources, Panama has established a base of international capital investments centered on the Panama Canal (Hovani and Fotos, this volume). Panama is a safe place to invest, which makes the country a "gateway" to other Latin American countries for business.

Assuming that more could be done in these two respects, our recommendations are as follows:

5.1 *Retain a professional brand consulting group to develop a country-wide, comprehensive ecosystem services marketing plan.* A competent private consultant could act as an information channel and coordinator among stakeholders in government, banking, the media, the donor community, the sciences, the arts, and business to help shape a consistent strategy for communicating the country's identity and message on ecosystem services. Through the development of a comprehensive marketing plan, the government could communicate to its citizens and international actors a vision for land management, thereby helping to focus investment on ecosystem services markets.

5.2 *Raise the visibility of ecosystem service markets to international audiences.* Coordination of the message on ecosystem services with the Ministry of Tourism's communication efforts would help in this goal.

5.3 *Educate Panamanian citizens about ecosystem services.* In many cases the primary ecosystem services buyers reside outside of Panama, but in all cases, the provision of those services depends on decisions made by Panamanians. As is the case in any democracy, the nation's citizens must be engaged in protecting the nation's natural heritage or it will not be protected. Efforts should be made to educate citizens about the benefits that intact ecosystems provide, the threats to those ecosystems, and the value that can be realized by sustaining intact ecosystems.

5.4 *Attract additional international NGO investments.* Certification enables enterprises of varying scales to connect with existing market arrangements, thus reducing the costs and risks associated with socially-conscious business strategies. These marketing arrangements help address social and environmental problems simultaneously. Money and effort spent on strengthening them are also investments in the infrastructure of ecosystems services markets generally. Aligning the Panama brand with existing certification programs could pay dividends for Panamanian businesses as consumers throughout the world increasingly turn to certified sources for lumber, coffee, bananas, and other products.

*Benefits of building the Panama brand.* As the recognition of the Panama brand increases, land managers will benefit from:

- Obtaining better access to markets where the brand image or certification matters;
- Reducing transaction costs, thereby stimulating supply and demand;
- Improved production and management practices;
- Enhancing the quality of their services by meeting certification standards or marketing claims; and
- Increased investment in the sustainable use of the country's natural resources.

*Feasibility of building the Panama brand.* The feasibility of this policy is high. The cost, although significant, is small in relation to the potential benefits of image and brand in a consumer-driven global economy.

## CONCLUSION

The policy alternatives set forth in this paper are designed to help promote the development of ecosystem services markets in Panama. These policies, if implemented, could offer financial incentives for land managers to reduce undesirable land conversion while increasing the capacity of their land to produce desirable ecosystem services (notably watershed protection, carbon sequestration and biodiversity). The challenges of building the market for ecosystem services in Panama are substantial. Limited institutional and financial capacity is among the most daunting. The factors that limit economic development also limit a nation's capacity to practice effective conservation, market-based or otherwise. Rather than dwelling further on the challenges and limits, we conclude by noting the great potential and many benefits these markets might offer Panama. As a country situated strategically between two oceans and two continents, and as repository of great natural riches and a diverse and talented population, Panama is well-positioned to become one of the world's foremost providers of ecosystem services. We strongly recommend it do so for the benefits it offers the citizens of Panama and the world.

## AUTHORS NOTE

The authors gratefully acknowledge Professor Bradford Gentry, Professor Shimon Anisfeld, Professor Mark Ashton, and Teaching Fellow Quint Newcomer at the Yale

School of Forestry and Environmental Studies; Mark Wishnie and José Manuel Pérez from the Smithsonian Tropical Research Institute; and the many people in Panama who provided guidance and assistance with this research.

## REFERENCES

Anderson, K. 2007. Existing Supply of Watershed Services in the Panama Canal Watershed. *Journal of Sustainable Forestry* 25(1/2):121-145.

Burtis, P. 2007. Can Bioprospecting Save Itself? At the Vanguard of Bioprospecting's Second Wave. *Journal of Sustainable Forestry* 25(3/4):219-245.

Center for International Forestry Research (CIFOR). 2000. Columbia Takes the Lead in Payments for Environmental Services. Retrieved March 2005 from http://www.cifor.cgiar.org/docs/_ref/polex/english/2000/2000_05_13.htm.

Central Intelligence Agency (CIA). 2005. The World Factbook. Retrieved March 2005 from http://www.cia.gov/cia/publications/factbook/geos/pm.html.

Conservation International (CI). 2005. Biodiversity Hotspots: Mesoamerica. Retrieved 7 January 2006 from http://www.biodiversityhotspots.org/xp/Hotspots/mesoamerica/.

Endara, Mirei. 2005. E-mail correspondence, "re: Integrated Policy Alternatives." August 21.

Food and Agriculture Organization (FAO). 1997. Financing Community Forestry Activities. In: An International Review of Forestry and Forest Products. Retrieved March 2005 from http://www.fao.org/documents/show_cdr.asp?url_file=/docrep/w3247E/w3247e09.htm.

Fotos, M., F. Chou, and Q. Newcomer. 2007. Assessment of Existing Demand for Watershed Services in the Panama Canal Watershed. *Journal of Sustainable Forestry* 25(1/2):175-193.

Fotos, M., Q. Newcomer, and R. Kuppalli. 2007. Policy Alternatives to Improve Demand for Water-Related Ecosystem Services in the Panama Canal Watershed. *Journal of Sustainable Forestry* 25(1/2):195-216.

Global Environment Facility (GEF). 1999. Elements for a GEF Operational Program on Carbon Sequestration. GEF/C 13/14.

Gray & Co. 2005. Environmental Law. Panama City, Panama. Retrieved 22 February 2005 from http://www.lawyers-abogados.net/en/Services/panama-environmental_law.htm.

Grossman, J.M. 2007. Carbon in Terrestrial Systems: A Review of the Science with Specific Reference to Central American Ecotypes and Locations. *Journal of Sustainable Forestry* 25(1/2):17-41.

Hope, R., I.R. Calder, J.W. Gowing, N. Laurie, P.J. Dixon, C.A. Sullivan, N.A. Jackson, G. von Maltitz, J. Bosch, D. LeMaitre, P. Dye, T. Netshiluvhi, N. Hatibu, and G. Paterson. 2002. Saving the Trees and the Poor? Catchment Management and Poverty (CAMP) in Innovative Financing Mechanisms for Conservation and Sustainable Forest Management. European Tropical Forest Research Network (ETFRN). Retrieved March 2005 from http://www.etfrn.org/etfrn/newsletter/news35/nl35_oip7.html.

Hovani, A. and M. Fotos. 2007. Policy Alternatives to Increase the Demand for Forest-Based Carbon Sequestration. *Journal of Sustainable Forestry* 25(1/2):99-117.

Inter-American Development Bank (IADB). 2005. Responding to Climate Change in Latin America and the Caribbean. Retrieved March 2005 from http://www.iadb.org/NEWS/Display/WSView.cfm?WS_Num=ws02305&Language=English.

Jackson, E. 2005. Torrijos Gets His Tax Increase. *Panama News Online* 11(6), Feb 6-19. Retrieved March 2005 from http://www.thepanamanews.com/pn/v_11/isue_03/business_01.html.

Johnson, N., A. White, and D. Perrot-Maitrele. 2002. Developing Markets for Water Services from Forests: Issues and Lessons for Innovators. Retrieved March 2005 from http://www.katoombagroup.org/Katoomba/publications.htm.

LaFontaine, A. 2000. Capacity Development Initiative: Assessment of Capacity Development Efforts of Other Development Cooperation Agencies. GEF and UNDP Strategic Partnership, New York, NY.

Landell-Mills, N. and I. Porras. 2002. Silver Bullet or Fools' Gold? A Global Review of Markets for Forest Ecosystem Services and Their Impacts on the Poor. International Institute for Environment and Development, London.

Lauterbach, S. 2007. An Assessment of Existing Demand for Carbon Sequestration Services. *Journal of Sustainable Forestry* 25(1/2):75-98.

Lichtenfeld, M. 2007. Improving the Supply of Carbon Sequestration Services in Panama. *Journal of Sustainable Forestry* 25(1/2):43-73.

Lichtenfels, M. et al. 2007. Improving Markets for Ecosystem Services. *Journal of Sustainable Forestry* 25(3/4):337-364.

Miyata, Y. 2007. Markets for Biodiversity: Certified Forest Products in Panama. *Journal of Sustainable Forestry* 25(3/4):281-307.

Pagiola, S. 2002. Paying for Water Services in Central America: Learning from Costa Rica. Pp. 37-61 in: S. Pagiola, J. Bishop, and N. Landell-Mills (eds.). 2002. Selling Forest Environmental Services: Market-Based Mechanisms for Conservation and Development. Earthscan, London.

Pagiola, S., J. Bishop, and N. Landell-Mills (eds.). 2002. Selling Forest Environmental Services: Market-Based Mechanisms for Conservation and Development. Earthscan, London.

Republic of Panama. 1994. Incentives Legislation for the Development of Tourism in the Republic of Panama–Law 8. Partial translation courtesy of Gray & Co. Environmental lawyers. Panama City, Panama. Retrieved 22 February 2005 from http://www.lawyers-abogados.net/en/Services/panama-environmental_law.htm.

Schloegel, C. 2007. Sustainable Tourism: Sustaining Biodiversity? *Journal of Sustainable Forestry* 25(3/4):247-264.

The Nature Conservancy (TNC). 2005. Panama Program. Retrieved 25 February 2005 from http://nature.org/wherewework/centralamerica/panama/index.html.

United Nations Environment Program (UNEP) 1999. Global Environment Outlook (GEO) 2000. Retrieved March 2005 from http://www1.unep.org/geo-text/0184.htm.

Wallander, S., S. Lauterbach, K. Anderson, F. Chou, J. M. Grossman, and C. Schloegel. 2007. Existing Markets for Ecosystem Services in the Panama Canal Watershed. *Journal of Sustainable Forestry* 25(3/4):311-336.

World Bank. 2001. Panama: World Bank Supports Land Administration Reform. World Bank press release, February 16. Retrieved 24 February 2005 from http://www.worldbank.org.

World Bank. 2003. International Workshop on Reform of Forest Fiscal Systems: Case Studies. Washington, DC.

World Resources Institute. 2004. Earthtrends Country Profiles: Panama. Retrieved 25 March 2005 from http://earthtrends.wri.org/pdf_library/country_profiles/For_cou_591.pdf.

doi:10.1300/J091v25n03_06

# CONCLUSION

# Emerging Markets for Ecosystem Services: What Did We Learn?

Bradford S. Gentry

**SUMMARY.** Four main areas of learning were pursued during this exploration of the emerging markets for ecosystem services. First, the markets in Panama are dominated by the Panama Canal Authority and by timber revenues. Any strategy for expanding ecosystem services markets will have to reflect these realities. Second, while the scientific and business components of the framework we used to analyze these markets covered all the key points, more work needs to be done on the policy component. Articulating a simple, yet effective approach for developing policy recommendations to improve ecosystem services markets in context remains a key need. Third, valuable lessons were learned about ensuring that the students capture the maximum benefits from an international, clinically-based field trip. Finally, interdisciplinary teaching/ research benefits dramatically from both a focus on a single problem

Bradford S. Gentry is Senior Lecturer and Research Scholar on Sustainable Investments at the Yale School of Forestry and Environmental Studies, New Haven, CT 06511 USA (E-mail: Bradford.Gentry@yale.edu).

[Haworth co-indexing entry note]: "Emerging Markets for Ecosystem Services: What Did We Learn?" Gentry, Bradford S. Co-published simultaneously in *Journal of Sustainable Forestry* (Haworth Food & Agricultural Products Press, an imprint of The Haworth Press, Inc.) Vol. 25, No. 3/4, 2007, pp. 365-375; and: *Emerging Markets for Ecosystem Services: A Case Study of the Panama Canal Watershed* (ed: Bradford S. Gentry, Quint Newcomer, Shimon C. Anisfeld, and Michael A. Fotos, III) Haworth Food & Agricultural Products Press, an imprint of The Haworth Press, Inc., 2007, pp. 365-375. Single or multiple copies of this article are available for a fee from The Haworth Document Delivery Service [1-800-HAWORTH, 9:00 a.m. - 5:00 p.m. (EST). E-mail address: docdelivery@haworthpress.com].

Available online at http://jsf.haworthpress.com
© 2007 by The Haworth Press, Inc. All rights reserved.
doi:10.1300/J091v25n03_07

and recognition that the key challenge is turning complex scientific knowledge into accessible, good advice. doi:10.1300/J091v25n03_07 *[Article copies available for a fee from The Haworth Document Delivery Service: 1-800-HAWORTH. E-mail address: <docdelivery@haworthpress.com> Website: <http://www.HaworthPress.com> © 2007 by The Haworth Press, Inc. All rights reserved.]*

**KEYWORDS.** Integrated market analysis framework, integrated policy analysis framework, ecosystem services markets, interdisciplinary teaching, clinical learning seminar, PRORENA

## INTRODUCTION

The introductory chapter to this collection explained what we set out to do in this clinical, interdisciplinary exploration of the emerging markets for ecosystem services in Panama. The individual chapters on water, carbon and biodiversity described what we found in our assessments of these many and varied markets. The integrated chapters on the existing and possible future markets brought these different strands together to help inform the choices land managers have to make across alternative management and policy approaches.

The purpose of this chapter is to summarize what we, the teaching and research team, learned during this process. It covers four main questions–what did we learn about:

- The markets for ecosystem services in Panama?
- The framework we used to analyze the markets?
- Clinical learning involving an international field trip?
- Interdisciplinary teaching and research?

In addition to our major findings, thoughts on areas for future work are also provided.

## WHAT DID WE LEARN ABOUT THE MARKETS FOR ECOSYSTEM SERVICES IN PANAMA?

### Dominant Players

There are two dominant players in the markets for ecosystem services produced by Panamanian forests–timber and the Panama Canal Authority (ACP). All of the financial models that included timber harvesting were dominated by timber revenues–compared to those from selling biodiversity, carbon and water services (Wallander et al., this volume). All of the policy analyses were dominated by the jurisdic- tional reach and resources of ACP (Lichtenfels et al., this volume). Understanding more fully the opportunities and limits posed by these dominant players will be a critical part of any future efforts to expand the markets for ecosystem services in Panama. Except in areas where timber harvesting is not allowed, ecosystem services are probably best viewed as an incremental, additional revenue stream produced as an in- tegrated part of the timber growth and harvesting cycles. Likewise, finding ways to have efforts to expand markets for ecosystem services complement or add value to the Panamanian Government's efforts to expand the Panama Canal are probably the best routes to more supportive policy regimes (see Figure 1).

### Biodiversity–The Most Diverse Markets

The emerging markets for watershed protection and carbon seques- tration involve relatively well defined services–water quality and/or quantity, carbon storage–across relatively well-understood scales–water/ regional, carbon/international. By contrast, the markets for biodiversity services involve a wide variety of services–genetic resources, eco-tourism, agricultural productivity, habitat protection and many others–that are in demand across a wide range of scales–local, regional and international. As such, care needs to be taken to define clearly the "biodiversity" services/commodities that one is seeking to supply to what potential

FIGURE 1. Possible Typology for Prioritizing Action

Market Readiness of Institutions

| | | Low | High |
|---|---|---|---|
| Suitability of Land | High | *Focus on building institutions?* | *Focus on building demand?* |
| | Low | *Explore non- market tools?* | *Focus on niche marketing?* |

consumers. For example, one set of transactions that does not receive much attention is the "purchase" of habitat restoration services by international conservation organizations (such as The Nature Conservancy) by providing technical assistance and equipment to farmers and ranchers who benefit from improved agroforestry or silvopastoral systems (Miyata, this volume). At the other extreme, efforts to expand the sale of eco-tourism or bioprospecting services require very different efforts at linking local supply with international demand (Schloegel, this volume; Burtis, this volume).

### *Water–The Most Scientific Uncertainty*

Many people involved in the class assumed that the greatest opportunities for selling environmental services in Panama were in the water sector. The Canal uses huge amounts of freshwater and spends large amounts on dredging. Panama's cities are expanding, putting additional pressure on water quality, as well as quantity. Yet, the water analyses find fewer market opportunities in these areas than initially expected (Anderson, this volume; Fotos, Chou, and Newcomer, this volume; Fotos, Newcomer, and Kuppalli, this volume; Lichtenfels, this volume). There appear to be two major reasons for this. The first reason is the dominance of ACP as noted above. If ACP decided to invest in reforestation as a major part of its plans to expand the Canal, it would transform the market. ACP's apparent hesitancy in making a major move in this direction points to a second major reason why the water markets are not as robust as expected–continuing scientific uncertainty. While the links between forest cover and water quality are relatively well understood, the driving concern in the Canal watershed is water quantity. With respect to volume and flow concerns, there seems to be general agreement that during the wet season forested areas in Panama release less water more slowly than do deforested slopes. The most important question, however, is what happens in the dry season–do forests release more water than deforested areas at the times when the Canal needs it most? *The Economist's* April 2005 article taking the view that they do release more water (The Economist, 2005), led to a spirited debate among water scientists holding different views (Smyle et al., 2005). The general conclusion was that more paired watershed studies in moist tropical areas would add useful data to the somewhat murky picture that currently exists. Meanwhile, the plans to expand the Canal continue to move forward.

## *Carbon–The Need to Institutionalize*

Neither the international markets for forest-based carbon credits, nor the Panamanian institutions involved in producing, approving and promoting such credits, are well developed. As of September 2005, the CDM Executive Board had yet to approve a methodology for producing reforestation-based credits. The Panamanian Government appears to have taken a reactive approach, waiting for the private sector to drive the development of the local production and marketing base. Most private land managers involved in reforestation have either not focused at all on the international carbon markets (particularly small holders) or are watching and waiting before incurring the additional costs of verifying and certifying the credits generated by their operations. So, a major "chicken or egg" situation exists with the result being that little investment is being made by any party while they all wait for others to act. Two areas where some incremental, additional investments might be made to help move forward Panama's ability to benefit from the 2005 entry into force of the Kyoto Protocol are: (a) paying more attention to carbon credits as part of the country's export promotion activities; and (b) exploring ways to bundle credits from the improved agroforestry/ silvopastoral practices described above for sale in the international markets.

## *Building Market Institutions*

The need to institutionalize the supply of carbon credits to the international markets is just one example of a number of areas where institutional development was found to be a key element of efforts to expand the markets for ecosystem services in Panama (Wallander et al., this volume; see also Hovani and Fotos, this volume). Whether the aim is linking carbon, ecotourism or bioprospecting to export promotion activities or clarifying land title and building growers' organizations for smallholders, expanding the capacity of institutions that encourage investment while linking supply and demand is key. Obviously, deciding where to focus one's efforts will vary depending on the level of institutional development and the state of the local supply of services. One possible way for determining priorities for action is shown in the following matrix:

### *Expanding Supply Is the Usual Focus, but Meeting Demand Should Be*

Most of the proponents of efforts to expand the markets for environmental services are focused on the supply side–how can one encourage land managers to keep their forests intact and healthy? The problem is that all the encouragement in the world will not save many forests if additional revenue streams are not forthcoming. And users of ecosystem services will only pay if doing so is their best option for meeting their needs. If they can get the services for free, why pay? If it is not clear whether investing in the services will meet their needs, why pay? More attention needs to be paid to the demand side. Demand for forest carbon will grow as regulations cause emitters of greenhouse gasses to internalize the costs of their activities. Demand for reforestation to increase dry season flows will grow only if scientists provide more convincing data of both the links between reforestation and improved flows, as well as the ancillary benefits (water quality, local jobs, etc.). Shifting the focus from providing more supply to understanding and building demand is the key next step in expanding the markets for ecosystem services. This should include efforts to understand better the potential social benefits of reforestation activities.

### *Beware of the "Pet Rock" Effect*

The need to increase demand leads to the final point–make sure that the demand is built around real, demonstrable added value to buyers. Lots of people will buy something on a whim–like the pet rocks sold in the US in the 1980s–but only once. Over-promising on the opportunities to make money or receive value from the markets for ecosystem services will undermine the future of these markets. Environmentalists need to be as careful of puffery as they expect business salespeople to be. Ecosystem services have real and growing market value. Future expansion should be built on sound science and verifiable performance over time.

## *WHAT DID WE LEARN ABOUT THE FRAMEWORK WE USED TO ANALYZE THE MARKETS?*

As described in the introductory chapter to this volume, the course was built around an analytical framework that considered the scientific, business and policy aspects of a land owner's engagement with

ecosystem services (Anisfeld, this volume). The hypothesis inform-
ing the framework was that while the potential for providing or using
ecosystem services is ultimately site and context specific, there are
general principles and questions that can be used to help guide site
specific investigations.

This hypothesis seems to have worked reasonably well on the science
and business parts of the class. With one exception, the students were able
to link their investigations of the scientific aspects of providing ecosystem
services from reforestation in the Panama Canal Watershed to broader scientific and management knowledge in a logical manner. The exception
was for dry season flows as described above and for which more research
appears to be warranted in the context of the wet tropics. Similarly, on the
business side, the basic questions to be asked are relatively well defined
and some data on expected costs and revenues was available. As the markets continue to grow, so too should the available data. It is also worth
noting that the analysis was simplified by assuming that reforestation of
former agricultural land was the primary activity for which investment
was needed. More complicated analyses across different silvicultural
treatment options are required for determining the basket of services that
could be provided from managing existing forests.

The policy aspects, however, presented more difficulties. Much of
this was due to a lack of clarity in the analytical framework offered for
moving from the scientific and business analyses to the development
of locally effective policy options. Many different approaches exist
across the social sciences: anthropologists and sociologists can describe the social context in which rules are set and enforced; political
scientists can tell us why certain policies came into being and what
their impacts have been; economists and lawyers can tell us the
strengths and weaknesses of different policy tools in different contexts. While all of these approaches were offered to and informed the
students' work, one is left with the feeling that they were more con-
fused than helped by these different perspectives. Going forward, efforts will be made to articulate more clearly suggested methods for:
(1) understanding the social context; (2) identifying the actions that
could be taken to expand the markets for ecosystem services in that
context; (3) investigating the opportunities to build politically effective coalitions in support of those actions across the stakeholders; and
(4) suggesting policy options based on that analysis.

## *WHAT DID WE LEARN ABOUT CLINICAL LEARNING?*

The clinical learning aspects of the course, including the field trip to Panama, were a major success, but could be improved still further. On the positive side, engaging professional students in a "messy," "real world" problem with external partners is a tremendous addition to the normal classroom activities. Students were selected from a wide range of backgrounds and interests–from water chemistry, through silviculture and business, to social ecology. As such, the group resembled the multi-disciplinary teams that many organizations use to address multi-faceted issues like ecosystem services. We also included several students with Spanish language capacity and experience in the region to help with the local information collection.

Perhaps the most important component of the clinical aspects of the course, however, were the local partners–the PRORENA project (see http://research.yale.edu/prorena/), its local host (the Smithsonian Tropical Research Institute (STRI), see http://www.stri.org/), and their many friends and advisors (such as Mirei Endara, F&ES alumna and former head of the Panamanian Environmental Agency, who donated huge amounts of time and information throughout the field trip and in follow-up activities). The partnership aspects of these relationships were key. The PRORENA project is attempting to build from its traditional research on the biophysical aspects of reforestation with native species into broader efforts to make its findings known to land managers who are considering reforestation investments. The students' work was designed to be as useful as possible to PRORENA as it expands into these areas. From the class' side, two aspects of PRORENA's involvement were critical. First, it made the field trip possible–from organizing logistics, to arranging meetings, to providing access to library resources and working space. Second, and possibly even more importantly, it upped the ante for the students. Instead of just being a class project, their work became a professional assignment paid for by the support PRORENA provided.

At the same time, there were aspects of the clinical experience that could have been improved. During the field trip, we should have set aside time for daily debriefings across the different groups (water, carbon, biodiversity) to make sure that they were on track and making the best use of the time in-country. After the field trip, we should have taken a more systematic approach to using our time with the students to ensure that they had collected the necessary information or, if not, still had time to gather what they needed to complete their analyses. When considering future field trips, one should also think carefully about picking one site under one land manager's control as the focus of the analyses in order to simplify the work–although there are benefits to taking a regional view and no one site was an obvious candidate in this case.

## *WHAT DID WE LEARN ABOUT INTERDISCIPLINARY TEACHING AND RESEARCH?*

Working in multi-disciplinary teams does not come as easily to academic organizations as it does to those in the "real world"–and even there it is difficult. Different languages, different concepts, different analytical methods, different values and many other items all stand in the way of joint work, as well as make it an incredibly rich and rewarding experience.

Embracing the messiness and focusing on solving one problem offer a way to bound these differences and make them somewhat more manageable. Having one or two faculty members "own" the entire class and its products is the key ingredient. Many "multidisciplinary" courses are just that–a collection of speakers from multiple disciplines talking about what they know in a linear fashion. "Interdisciplinary" teaching requires that one or more of these disciplinary experts take responsibility for making sure that the class sessions and the students' work integrate the contributions from the different disciplines into the best advice possible. Picking local partners in which the lead faculty have a continuing interest–such as Yale and the PRORENA project–is one way to help ensure that this happens. Assembling multi-disciplinary teams of students is another important ingredient as they will continue to feed the different concepts into the students' work outside of the class sessions.

Another key tension to embrace is that between complexity and simplicity. Any good scientist will tell you what we do not know and that environmental systems are inherently complex, site specific entities. Any effective land manager or policy maker looks for simple principles for making and explaining their decisions. Finding ways to use the complexity of scientific analysis to inform the simple decision rules sought by many decision-makers is a huge challenge.

One way to start is by acknowledging the "cones of complexity" that underpin valuable professional advice (see Figure 2).

If the answers were known or easy to develop, no one would turn to professionals for advice. So, the goal of professional education should be to expose the students to the best, most complex scientific analyses available, while developing the judgment needed to fill in the blanks (in

FIGURE 2. Cones of Complexity–Linking Theory and Practice

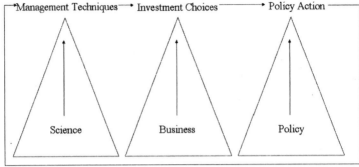

*Simplicity: Most Useful Advice*

*Complexity: Deepest Academic Inquiry*

the absence of complete information) and offer ways forward that are effective and relatively simple to explain. Integrated, clinical courses like this offer a tremendous opportunity to develop the skills needed to do so.

## REFERENCES

Anderson, K. 2007. Existing Supply of Watershed Services in the Panama Canal Watershed. *Journal of Sustainable Forestry* 25(1/2):121-145.

Anisfeld, S. 2007. Emerging Markets for Ecosystem Services: Setting the Context. *Journal of Sustainable Forestry* 25(1/2):1-14.

Burtis, P. 2007. Can Bioprospecting Save Itself? At the Vanguard of Bioprospecting's Second Wave. *Journal of Sustainable Forestry* 25(3/4):219-245.

The Economist. 2005. Environmental Economics: Are You Being Served? *The Economist* 375(8423):76-78.

Fotos, M., F. Chou, and Q. Newcomer. 2007. Assessment of Existing Demand for Watershed Services in Panama Canal Watershed. *Journal of Sustainable Forestry* 25(1/2):175-193.

Fotos, M., Q. Newcomer, and R. Kuppalli. 2007. Policy Alternatives to Improve Demand for Water-Related Ecosystem Services in the Panama Canal Watershed. *Journal of Sustainable Forestry* 25(1/2):195-216.

Hovani, A. and M. Fotos. 2007. Policy Alternatives to Increase the Demand for Forest-Based Carbon Sequestration. *Journal of Sustainable Forestry* 25(1/2):99-117.

Lichtenfels, M. 2007. Policy Alternatives for Improving Markets for Water Quality and Quantity in the Panama Canal Watershed. *Journal of Sustainable Forestry* 25(1/2):147-174.

Lichtenfels, M., P. Burtis, A. Hovani, R. Kuppalli, M. Lichtenfeld, and Y. Miyata. 2007. Improving Markets for Ecosystem Services. *Journal of Sustainable Forestry* 25(3/4):337-364.

Miyata, Y. 2007. Markets for Biodiversity: Certified Forest Products in Panama. *Journal of Sustainable Forestry* 25(3/4):281-307.

Schloegel, C. 2007. Sustainable Tourism: Sustaining Biodiversity? *Journal of Sustainable Forestry* 25(3/4):247-264.

Smyle, J., B. Stallard, S. Bruijnzeel, I. Calder, and H. Elsenbeer. 2005. Subject: "Economist article: Panama hydrologic services ('sponge effect')." E-mail correspondence 25 April-12 May 2005.

Wallander, S., S. Lauterbach, K. Anderson, F. Chou, J.M. Grossman, and C. Schloegel. 2007. Existing Markets for Ecosystem Services in the Panama Canal Watershed. *Journal of Sustainable Forestry* 25(3/4):311-336.

doi:10.1300/J091v25n03_07

# Index

Note: Page numbers followed by the letter "t" designate tables; numbers followed by the letter "f" designate figures.

Available online at http://jsf.haworthpress.com
© 2007 by The Haworth Press, Inc. All rights reserved.